The media's watching Vault!
Here's a sampling of our coverage.

"For those hoping to climb the ladder of success, [Vault's] insights are priceless."
– *Money magazine*

"The best place on the web to prepare for a job search."
– *Fortune*

"[Vault guides] make for excellent starting points for job hunters and should be purchased by academic libraries for their career sections [and] university career centers."
– *Library Journal*

"The granddaddy of worker sites."
– *U.S. News & World Report*

"A killer app."
– *The New York Times*

One of Forbes' 33 "Favorite Sites."
– *Forbes*

"To get the unvarnished scoop, check out Vault."
– *Smart Money Magazine*

"Vault has a wealth of information about major employers and job-searching strategies as well as comments from workers about their experiences at specific companies."
– *The Washington Post*

"Vault has become the go-to source for career preparation."
– *Crain's New York*

"Vault [provides] the skinny on working conditions at all kinds of companies from current and former employees."
– *USA Today*

*Manhattan*GMAT
the new standard

the world's largest GMAT-exclusive test preparation provider

Our Curriculum

ManhattanGMAT's exclusive curriculum was designed in accordance with our philosophy of test preparation, which centers on a balance between two competing emphases: test-taking strategies on the one hand, with in-depth content understanding on the other. The heart of the curriculum is the acclaimed ManhattanGMAT Strategy Guide Set, seven content-based books (five math and two verbal), and they are available through the ManhattanGMAT online store; they are also sold at Barnes & Noble and Amazon.com. The set, along with three other books and various online resources, is provided to all ManhattanGMAT program students.

Nine-Session Preparation Courses

Meet once per week in our popular group course, either in-person or live and online from your home or office.

Private Instruction

Work with one of our expert tutors (all of whom have scored 750+ on their official GMAT tests), who will design a customized program to suit your needs.

The Quest for 750 Workshop Series

Complete your preparation with emphasis on the most advanced content: data sufficiency, quantitative skills, and sentence correction.

Free GMAT Preview Classes

New to the GMAT? Learn GMAT test basics, principles of adaptive testing, and how to prepare at an online or in-person free GMAT workshop.

Questions?

Call Student Services at 800-576-4628 or send an email to studentservices@manhattangmat.com.

Get schedules and sign up at www.manhattangmat.com or 800-576-4628.

Boston:
140 Clarendon Street
Ground Floor
Boston, MA 02116
617-585-5665

Chicago:
222 West Ontario Street
Fourth Floor
Chicago, IL 60610
312-274-1591

New York:
138 West 25th Street
Ninth Floor
New York, NY 10001
212-721-7400

San Francisco:
870 Market Street
Sixth Floor
San Francisco, CA 94102
415-402-0218

Southern California:
at Pepperdine University in
Encino, Irvine, Long Beach,
Pasadena, West LA and
Westlake Village

Global:
Live instruction online in
our virtual classroom with
students from around the
world.

ManhattanGMAT corporate: 138 West 25th St, 7th floor New York, NY 10001 212-721-7400

THE VAULT
MBA CAREER BIBLE

THE VAULT
MBA CAREER BIBLE

VAULT EDITORS

For information about permission to reproduce selections from this book, contact Vault.com Inc.150 W. 22nd St. New York,
New York 10011-1772, (212) 366-4212.

Library of Congress CIP Data is available.

ISBN 1-58131-498-1

ISBN 13: 978-1-58131-498-4

Printed in the United States of America

Acknowledgments

We are also extremely grateful to Vault's entire staff for all their help in the editorial, production and marketing processes. Vault also would like to acknowledge the support of our investors, clients, employees, family and friends. Thank you!

Visit Vault at **www.vault.com** for insider company profiles, expert advice, career message boards, expert resume reviews, the Vault Job Board and more.

V/\ULT CAREER LIBRARY **vii**

Use the Internet's
MOST TARGETED
job search tools.

Vault Job Board

Target your search by industry, function, and experience level, and find the job openings that you want.

VaultMatch Resume Database

Vault takes match-making to the next level: post your resume and customize your search by industry, function, experience and more. We'll match job listings with your interests and criteria and e-mail them directly to your in-box.

VAULT
> the most trusted name in career information™

Table of Contents

Visit Vault at **www.vault.com** for insider company profiles, expert advice,
career message boards, expert resume reviews, the Vault Job Board and more.

VAULT CAREER LIBRARY   ix

INDUSTRY OVERVIEWS 45

Visit Vault at **www.vault.com** for insider company profiles, expert advice,
career message boards, expert resume reviews, the Vault Job Board and more.

VAULT CAREER LIBRARY   **xi**

Visit Vault at **www.vault.com** for insider company profiles, expert advice, career message boards, expert resume reviews, the Vault Job Board and more.

VAULT CAREER LIBRARY

xiii

Introduction

MBA Hiring Overview

So you've spent a few years in business school and (if you're like most B-school grads) a few years in the workforce before that. All of a sudden, you're back on the job market, with a new degree and newer skills, and you want to make sure that they pay off. Déjà vu?

Never fear, Vault is here! And the MBA hiring climate keeps getting better and better. According to a May 2007 article in *The Economist*, MBA graduates and programs have the best reputation among employers since the economic slump of 2002. That higher confidence means a higher rate of job offers—so candidates, get ready: touch up your resumes, press your suits and prepare to interview!

MBA hiring on the rise

MBA hiring began to strengthen in 2005 and continued to do so in 2006-2007, according to surveys focused on the hiring landscape for new business school graduates. In its annual 2007 Corporate Recruiters Survey, based on the responses of 1,382 recruiters representing 1,029 companies, the Graduate Management Admission Council (GMAC) found that companies planned to do more MBA hiring in 2007 than in 2006, as measured by planned on-campus recruiting, percentage of new hires expected to be new MBAs and other metrics. Recruiters surveyed expected to sign on 18 percent more MBA-holders in 2007 than in 2006, a larger increase than for any other type of hire.

"The heat is on for corporate recruiters," says Ronald Alsop of *The Wall Street Journal*. Competition for MBA graduates is so high that companies are increasing their recruiting efforts—visiting business schools earlier and more often. In the future, they're going to be looking at more candidates, too: the National Association of Colleges and Employers' (NACE) 2005 MBA Benchmark Survey notes that companies are visiting more business schools year after year.

From internships and recruiting to interviews

For many full-time business school students, on-campus recruiting and summer internships following the first year of are the most important methods of finding employment. According to GMAC's Global MBA Graduate Survey, which surveyed 5,641 graduating MBA students about their experience, 51 percent of MBA students surveyed received their job offers through internships or work projects.

But landing a great internship isn't the only way to get your foot in the door—far from it. On-campus recruiting is another fast track to employment and, as mentioned above, it is on the rise. Of the employers polled in GMAC's Corporate Recruiters Survey, 40 percent have formal recruiting programs. Even more encouraging, according to the Global MBA Graduate Survey, more MBA-holders—53 percent of the survey's respondents—were recruited while still in school.

And where recruiters go, interviews will follow—check with career services and fairs for dates. While companies usually make presentations and send representatives to business schools throughout the year, actual on-campus interviewing and recruiting tends to be structured on a predictable schedule. Investment banking and consulting firms, which hire large classes of both summer interns and full-time hires from business schools, tend to interview second-year students for full-time positions in October and November, and first-year students for summer internships in January and February. On-campus interviewing for Fortune 1000 companies traditionally happens later, with interviews in March and April for both full-time and internship hiring.

Visit Vault at **www.vault.com** for insider company profiles, expert advice, career message boards, expert resume reviews, the Vault Job Board and more.

VAULT CAREER LIBRARY   1

Shaking hands

In addition to a good hiring climate, MBA grads have the advantage of high starting salaries. For example, GMAC reported that 2007 salaries may start at an average base of $80,452, with 99 percent of employers adding other compensation and benefits. Though MBA starting salaries have stayed somewhat fixed in the past year, the numbers still soar above the salaries of other graduate school and undergraduate program graduates (by 27 and 76 percent, respectively). Signing bonuses are hefty, too: according to GMAC, two-thirds of 2006 job offers to MBA grads averaged a bonus of $17,603.

Taking stock

So is the degree worth it? You bet. According to former MBA CSC President Mindy Storrie, "Companies have stepped up recruiting at business schools and MBAs are getting more job offers." The current president of GMAC, David Wilson, agrees: "We have long referred to the MBA as a global currency—a degree that symbolizes value all over the world."

MBA grads concur. According to GMAC's 2007 MBA Alumni Perspectives Survey, 97 percent of MBA-holders say getting their degree was personally rewarding. Among alumni, 50 percent said that they were "extremely satisfied" or "very satisfied" with their current job position, and 64 percent have been promoted within five years of graduation. So go ahead, grads—get happy and get hired!

Good luck!

The Team at Vault

THE MBA
JOB SEARCH

Resumes

Ten Seconds

Studies show that regardless of how long you labor over your resume, most employers will spend 10 seconds looking at it. That's it.

Because of the masses of job searchers, most managers and human resource employees receive an enormous number of resumes. Faced with a pile of paper to wade through every morning, employers look for any deficiency possible to reduce the applicant pool to a manageable number. Thus, your resume must present your information quickly, clearly, and in a way that makes your experience relevant to the position in question. That means condensing your information down to its most powerful form.

So distill, distill, distill. Long, dense paragraphs make information hard to find and require too much effort from the over-worked reader. If that reader can't figure out how your experience applies to the available position, your resume is not doing its job.

Solve this problem by creating bulleted, indented, focused statements. Short, powerful lines show the reader, in a glance, exactly why they should keep reading.

Think about how to write up your experience in targeted, clear, bulleted, detail-rich prose. Here are some examples.

Before

Primary Duties: Computer repair and assembly, software troubleshooter, Internet installation and troubleshooting, games.

After

Primary Duties:

- Assembled and repaired Dell, Compaq, Gateway and other PC computers

- Analyzed and fixed software malfunctions for Windows applications

- Installed and debugged Internet systems for businesses such as Rydell's Sports, Apple Foods and Eric Cinemas

---

Before

Responsibilities included assisting with artist press releases, compiling tracking sheets based on information from reservationists and box office attendants, handling photo and press release mailings to media, assisting in radio copywriting and performing various other duties as assigned.

After

Experience includes:

- Wrote artist press releases that contributed to an increase in sales by 23%

- Compiled and maintained mailing list of 10,000—Cambridge Theater's largest-ever list

- Handled press release mailings to *Anchorage Daily News* and Fox Four Television

- Contributed to copywriting of promotion radio commercials for selected events

---

Visit Vault at **www.vault.com** for insider company profiles, expert advice, career message boards, expert resume reviews, the Vault Job Board and more.

VAULT CAREER LIBRARY   5

It's What You Did, Not What Your Name Tag Said

Resumes should scream ability, not claim responsibility. Employers should be visualizing you in the new position, not remembering you as "that account assistant from Chase." While some former employers can promote your resume by their mere presence, you don't want to be thought of as a cog from another machine. Instead, your resume should present you as an essential component of a company's success.

Think Broadly

Applicants applying for specific job openings must customize the resume for each position. Many job hunters, particularly those beginning their careers, apply to many different jobs.

A person interested in a career in publishing, for example, might apply for jobs as a writer, proofreader, editor, copywriter, grant proposal writer, fact-checker or research assistant. You may or may not have the experience necessary to apply for any of these jobs. But you may have more skills than you think.

When considering the skills that make you a valuable prospect, think broadly. Anyone who has worked a single day can point to several different skills, because even the most isolated, repetitive jobs offer a range of experience. Highway toll collection, for instance, is a repetitive job with limited variation, but even that career requires multiple job skills. Helping lost highway drivers read a map means "Offering customer service in a prompt, detail-oriented environment." Making change for riders translates as "Financial transactions in a high-pressure, fast-paced setting." But unless these toll-booth workers emphasize these skills to prospective employers, it'll be the highway life for them.

Selected History

A lot of things happen in everyone's day, but when someone asks, "How was your day?" you don't start with your first cough and your lost slippers. You edit. Resumes require that same type of disciplined, succinct editing. The better you are at controlling the information you create, the stronger the resume will be.

When editing your history to fit the resume format, ask yourself, "How does this particular information contribute towards my overall attractiveness to this employer?" If something doesn't help, drop it. Make more space to elaborate on the experiences most relevant to the job for which you are applying.

Similarly, if information lurks in your past that would harm your chances of getting the job, omit it. In resume writing, omitting is not lying. If some jobs make you overqualified for a position, eliminate those positions from your resume. If you're overeducated, don't mention the degree that makes you so. If you're significantly undereducated, there's no need to mention education at all. If the 10 jobs you've had in the last five years make you look like a real-life Walter Mitty, reduce your resume's references to the most relevant positions while making sure there are no gaps in the years of your employment.

Sample MBA Resume

EUGENE H. HUANG

5050 S. Lake Shore Dr., Apt. 1407
Chicago, IL 60615
(773) 555-1234
ehuang@uchicago.edu

EDUCATION

MIDWAY SCHOOL OF BUSINESS   Chicago, IL
Master of Business Administration – Finance and Strategic Management   June 2004

- Dean's Honor List
- Active member of Management Consulting, Corporate Management and Strategy, and High Tech Clubs

ANDERSEN COLLEGE   Boston, MA
Bachelor of Arts in Physics (Cum Laude)   June 1999
- Andersen College Scholarship for academic distinction; Dean's List all semesters
- Violinist in Andersen College Symphony
- Physics tutor for Bureau of Study Counsel; active participant in Habitat for Humanity
- Completed dissertation in the field of condensed matter theory

EXPERIENCE

SMART BROTHERS   New York, NY
Technology Project Manager – Investment Banking   June 2000 – July 2002

- Managed project teams to develop profit and loss systems for proprietary trading group
- Promoted to project leadership role in two years, well ahead of department average of four
- Developed an original mathematical algorithm for trading processing module, improving performance by 1,200%
- Led team of six analysts in firmwide project to re-engineer loan syndicate trading flows in firm's largest technology project of 1999. Recommendations established new firmwide standard for real-time trade processing
- Appointed lead developer of interest accrual team after just three months in department. Initiated and designed project to create customized, improved interest accrual and P&L applications for fixed-income controllers
- Selected to work on high-profile project to re-engineer corporate bond trading P&L system. Reduced overnight processing time from six hours to 20 minutes and improved desktop application speed by 350%
- Devoted 20 to 25 hours a month to instructing junior members of the team in interest accrual and trading

FINANCIAL TECHNOLOGY GROUP   New York, NY
Analyst   June 1999 – May 2000

- Developed cutting-edge analytic software for use by Wall Street traders
- Worked on a daily basis with clients to create and implement customized strategic software solution for equity traders. Helped create and deliver extensive training program for clients
- Initiated, created and documented new firmwide standard for software module development

OTHER

- Winner of Mastermaster.com stock trading competition in November 2000. Won first place out of over 1,600 entrants worldwide with one-month return of 43.3%
- Other interests include violin, soccer and the harmonica
- Recent travel to Yemen, Egypt and Venezuela

Visit Vault at **www.vault.com** for insider company profiles, expert advice,
career message boards, expert resume reviews, the Vault Job Board and more.

VAULT CAREER LIBRARY   7

Cover Letters

The Cover Letter Template

Your Name
Your Street Address, Apartment #
Your City, State Zip
Your Email Address
Your Home Phone Number
Your Fax Number

WONDERING WHAT GOES ON A COVER LETTER? HERE'S A STEP-BY-STEP GUIDE

Contact's Name
Contact's Title
Contact's Department
Contact's Name
Contact's Street Address, Suite #
Company City, State Zip
Company Phone Number
Company Fax Number

Date

Dear Ms./Mr. CONTACT,

The first paragraph tells why you're contacting the person, then either mentions your connection with that person or reveals where you read about the job. It also quickly states who you are. Next it wows them with your sincere, researched knowledge of their company. The goal: Demonstrating that you are a worthy applicant, and enticing them to read further.

The second and optional third paragraph tell more about yourself, particularly why you're an ideal match for the job by summarizing why you're what they're looking for. You may also clarify anything unclear on your resume.

The last paragraph is your goodbye: you thank the reader for his or her time. Include that you look forward to their reply or give them a time when you'll be getting in contact by phone.

Sincerely,

Sign Here

Visit Vault at **www.vault.com** for insider company profiles, expert advice, career message boards, expert resume reviews, the Vault Job Board and more.

VAULT CAREER LIBRARY 9

Date

Placement of the date, whether left justified, centered or aligned to the right, is up to your discretion, but take the time to write out the entry. If you choose to list the day, list it first, followed by the month, date and year, as follows: Tuesday, July 9, 2004. (Europeans commonly list the day before month, so writing a date only in numbers can be confusing. Does a letter written on 4/7/04 date from April 7th, or July 4th?)

Name and address

Your name and address on the cover letter should be the same as the one on your resume. Uniformity in this case applies not only to the address given, but the way the information is written. If you listed your street as Ave. instead of Avenue on your resume, do so on your cover letter, too.

Your header can be displayed centrally, just like the resume header—including your name in a larger and/or bolded font. But in most cases, the heading is either left justified or left justified and indented to the far right-hand side of the page.

If you choose to list your phone number, make sure that you don't list it somewhere else on the page.

Next comes the address of the person you are writing. In many circumstances, you'll have the complete information on the person you're trying to contact, in which case you should list it in this order:

• Name of contact

• Title of contact

• Company name

• Company address

• Phone number

• Fax number

However, in many cases, you have less than complete information to go on. This is particularly true when responding to an advertisement. If you have an address or phone or fax number but no company name, try a reverse directory, such as Superpages (www.superpages.com), which lets you trace a business by either its address or phone number.

When you're trying to get a name of a contact person, calling the company and asking the receptionist for the name of the recipient (normally, though not always, head of HR) may work. But usually, companies don't list this information because they don't want you calling at all. So if you call, be polite, be persistent, ask for a contact name, say thank you and hang up. Don't identify yourself. If you have questions, wait until the interview.

If you don't get all of the info, don't worry. There are several salutations to use to finesse the fact that you've got no idea who you're addressing. Some solutions are:

To whom it may concern: A bit frosty, but effective.

Dear Sir or Madam: Formal and fusty, but it works.

Sirs: Since the workforce is full of women, avoid this outdated greeting.

Omitting the salutation altogether: Effective, but may look too informal.

Good morning: A sensible approach that is gaining popularity.

Format

Unlike the resume, the cover letter offers the writer significant room for flexibility. Successful cover letters have come in various different forms, and sometimes cover letters that break rules achieve success by attracting attention. But most don't. Here are some basic guidelines on what information the body of a cover letter should deliver.

First paragraph

To be successful, this first paragraph should contain:

• A first line that tells the reader why you're contacting them, and how you came to know about the position. This statement should be quick, simple and catchy. Ultimately, what you're trying to create is a descriptive line by which people can categorize you. This means no transcendental speeches about "the real you" or long-winded treatises on your career and philosophy of life.

• Text indicating your respect for the firm's accomplishments, history, status, products or leaders.

• A last line that gives a very brief synopsis of who you are and why you want the position. The best way to do this, if you don't already have a more personal connection with the person you're contacting, is to lay it out like this:

I am a (your identifying characteristic)

+

I am a (your profession)

+

I have (your years of experience or education)

+

I have worked in (your area of expertise)

+

I am interested in (what position you're looking for)

And thus a killer first paragraph is born.

Middle paragraph(s)

The middle paragraph allows you to move beyond your initial declarative sentences, and into more expansive and revealing statements about who you are and what skills you bring to the job. This is another opportunity to explicitly summarize key facts of your job history. The middle paragraph also offers you the opportunity to mention any connection or prior experience that you may have with the company.

Tell the employer in this paragraph how, based on concrete references to your previous performances, you will perform in your desired position. This does not mean making general, unqualified statements about your greatness, such as "I'm going to be the best you've ever had" or my "My energetic multitasking will be the ultimate asset to your company."

Comments should be backed up by specific references. Try something along the lines of "My post-graduate degree in marketing, combined with my four years of retail bicycle sales would make me a strong addition to Gwinn Cycles' marketing team."

Or, "Meeting the demands of a full-time undergraduate education, a position as student government accountant, and a 20-hour-a-week internship with Davidson Management provided me with the multitasking experience needed to excel as a financial analyst at Whittier Finance."

Visit Vault at **www.vault.com** for insider company profiles, expert advice, career message boards, expert resume reviews, the Vault Job Board and more.

VAULT CAREER LIBRARY   11

Many advertisements ask you to name your salary requirements. Some avoid the problem altogether by ignoring this requirement, and this may be the safest route—any number you give might price you out of a job (before you have the chance to negotiate face-to-face at an interview). Alternatively, you might be pegged at a lower salary than you might otherwise have been offered. If you must give a salary requirement, be as general as possible. The safest bet is to offer as general a range as possible ("in the $30,000s"). Put the salary requirement at the end of the paragraph, not in your first sentence.

Some cover letter writers use another paragraph to describe their accomplishments. This makes sense if, for example, your experience lies in two distinct areas, or you need to explain something that is not evident on your resume, such as "I decided to leave law school to pursue an exciting venture capital opportunity" or "I plan to relocate to Wisconsin shortly." Do not get overly personal—"I dropped out of business school to care for my sick mother" is touching, but will not necessarily impress employers.

Final paragraph

The final paragraph is your fond farewell, your summation, a testament to your elegance and social grace. This should be the shortest paragraph of the letter. Here, tell your readers you're pleased they got so far down the page. Tell them you look forward to hearing from them. Tell them how you can be reached. Here's some sample sentences for your conclusion.

Thank you sentences:

Thank you for your time.

Thank you for reviewing my qualifications.

Thank you for your consideration.

Thank you for your review of my qualifications.

Way too much:

It would be more than an honor to meet with you.

A note of confidence in a callback:

I look forward to your reply.

I look forward to hearing from you.

I look forward to your response.

I look forward to your call.

Over the top:

Call me tomorrow, please.

MBA Summer Internship Cover Letter

February 1, 2008

Kimberly Sharpe, Recruiting Manager
Hexagonal Consulting
666 Avenue of the Americas
13th Floor
New York, NY 10010

Dear Ms. Sharpe,

I am a first-year MBA student at State Business School. I was extremely impressed with Hexagonal Consulting's approach to management consulting after attending the presentation given by your firm earlier this year. I also learned more about your firm by talking with William Field and several other summer interns. My discussions with them confirmed my interest in Hexagonal Consulting, and I am now writing to request an invitation to interview for a summer associate consulting position.

After graduating from Northern College with a degree in accounting, I worked as an associate in the finance department of AutoCo, a well-known automotive manufacturer. I gained solid analytical and problem-solving skills there. I was responsible for identifying and resolving financial reporting issues, as well as generating innovative methods to improve our processes. I also fine-tuned my communication and consensus building skills, as I often needed to present and market my work to middle and upper management. Finally, during my last year of employment, I took on a team leadership role, managing the daily work of five junior members of our team and taking an active role in our training for new hires.

I am excited by the strong potential fit I see with Hexagonal Consulting. I feel that the analytical, leadership and teamwork abilities gained through my employment and academic experience have provided me with the tools and skills necessary to perform well in a consulting career, and will allow me to make a significant contribution at your firm. I am particularly intrigued by the shareholder value focus of Hexagonal Consulting's methodology, since it fits well with my experience in finance.

I have enclosed my resume for your review. I welcome the opportunity to meet with you when you recruit at SBS for summer internships later this month, and I would greatly appreciate being included on your invitational list.

Thank you for your time and consideration. I look forward to hearing from you.

Sincerely,

Laura Haley
314 Broadway, Apt. 15
New York, NY 10007
lbethhaley@hotmail.com

Visit Vault at **www.vault.com** for insider company profiles, expert advice,
career message boards, expert resume reviews, the Vault Job Board and more.

VAULT CAREER LIBRARY   13

MBA Full-Time Cover Letter

Ms. Margaret Jones, Recruiting Manager
Mainstream Consulting Group
123 21st Street
Boston, Massachusetts 02145

November 19, 2008

Dear Ms. Jones:

It was a pleasure to meet you in person last week at the Mainstream Consulting invitational lunch on the Boston Business School campus. Having spoken with your colleagues at the event, I believe that Mainstream would be an exciting and challenging firm in which to build my career.

My background fits well with a position in strategy consulting. As a Midway University physics undergraduate, I developed an analytic, creative mind geared towards solving complex problems. I applied and enhanced my problem-solving skills as a technology project leader at Smart Brothers Investment Bank, where I focused on making business processes faster, more effective and more efficient. Creating these results for traders, financial analysts and senior management taught me how to effectively partner with clients throughout the various phases of business transformation. In addition, I gained valuable team leadership experience at Smart Brothers, guiding many project teams through the successful design and implementation of cutting-edge technology strategies.

As a telecommunications strategy intern at Global Consulting Associates this summer, I confirmed that strategy consulting is indeed the right career for me. Our project team helped a major telecommunications provider formulate a wireless data services strategy. I led the industry analysis and market opportunity assessment. This experience showed me that I am an effective contributor in a consulting environment, where industry knowledge, creative problem-solving skills, fact-based analysis and client focus are rewarded.

Mainstream appeals to me over other firms because of its focus on pure strategy projects, small firm atmosphere and accelerated career growth opportunities. Please consider me for your invitational campus interviews this fall. I am particularly interested in positions in the San Francisco and Chicago offices, and I have enclosed my resume for your review.

Thank you for your time, and I look forward to hearing from you soon.

Sincerely,

Michael A. Thomas
100 Wellany Way
Boston, MA 02111
michaelt3@bostonu.edu

MBA Interviews

Interviewing during on-campus MBA recruiting can be a harrowing process for several reasons. First, there is the sheer volume of interviewing: some students interview with a dozen or more companies within a few week period, all while maintaining a busy class schedule.

At each interview, students work to convince interviewers that they represent a good "fit" with the company. Part of being a good fit, of course, means that students have specific interest and knowledge of the companies with which they are interviewing. This crucial element of interview performance requires students to research the employers as thoroughly as possible in order to make their cases convincingly to many companies, a feat made more difficult by the large number of companies with which many students interview. To help students prepare for their interviews with specific companies, Vault publishes 50-page employer profiles of major MBA employers, as well as "snapshots" of thousands of other major employers online at www.vault.com.

Interviewers use a variety of techniques to test students. According to the Graduate Management Admission Council's (GMAC) Corporate Recruiters Survey survey of more than 1,000 MBA employers, behavior-based interviews (during which candidates describe specific examples of skills such as leading a team or managing a difficult employee) are used by 79 percent of recruiters, and are the most common technique used by MBA recruiters. More than half of the recruiters surveyed (53 percent) use "case" or situational interviews in which the interviewers describe a hypothetical or real business situation and ask the job seeker to work through a course of action out loud. And more than one-third (36 percent) use career question that measure position-specific knowledge (such as the ability to price a bond for a fixed-income finance position).

Case interviews and technical finance interviews can be particularly stress-inducing, as students cannot as easily predict questions and prepare answers for these types of interviews as they can for behavior-based interviews. (In fact, some interviewers, most notoriously in the investment banking industry, choose to deliberately make interviews stressful in order to assess how business school students respond to stressful situations.) To help students prepare for these types of interviews, we discuss case and finance interviews in detail in the next two sections.

Case Interviews

What is a case interview?

Simply put, a case interview is the analysis of a business question. Unlike most other interview questions, it is an interactive process. Your interviewer will present you with a business problem and ask you for your opinion. Your job is to ask the interviewer logical questions that will permit you to make a detailed recommendation. The majority of case interviewers don't have a specific answer that you, the candidate, are expected to give. What the interviewer is looking for is a thought process that is both analytical and creative (what consultants love to call "out-of-the-box" thinking). Specific knowledge of the industry covered by the case question is a bonus but not necessary. Business school students and candidates with significant business world experience receive case questions that require a deeper understanding of business models and processes.

The interview with a consulting company normally lasts about half an hour. Of this time, about five to 10 minutes is taken up with preliminary chat and behavioral questions and five minutes of you asking questions about the company. This leaves five to 15 minutes for your case interview question or questions. Make them count!

Why the case?

Your impressive resume may get you an interview with a consulting firm, but it won't get you the job. Consultants know that a resume, at its very best, is only a two-dimensional representation of a multifaceted, dynamic person.

Visit Vault at **www.vault.com** for insider company profiles, expert advice, career message boards, expert resume reviews, the Vault Job Board and more.

VAULT CAREER LIBRARY 15

And because consulting firms depend on employing those multi-faceted, dynamic people, the firms rely heavily on the case interview to screen candidates. The interview process is especially pertinent in the consulting industry, since consulting professionals spend the lion's share of their business day interacting with clients and colleagues and must themselves constantly interview client employees and executives.

Consultants must have a select set of personality and leadership traits in order to be successful. The consultant's work environment is extremely turbulent. There are nonstop co-worker changes, hostile client environments, countless political machinations, and near-perpetual travel. These factors mandate that an individual be cool under pressure, be influential without being condescending, be highly analytical, have the ability to understand the smallest aspects of a problem (while simultaneously seeing the big picture), and have the ability to maintain a balance between the personal and professional.

Consultants are often staffed in small groups in far-flung areas. As a result, the individual must be able to function, and function well, without many of the traditional workplace standards: a permanent working space, the ability to return home each night, easily accessed services such as administrative assistance, faxing and photocopying, and the camaraderie that develops among co-workers assigned to the same business unit.

All these factors necessitate a unique interview structure focused on assessing a candidate's ability to manage these particular circumstances with professionalism and excellence. The case interview has evolved as a method for evaluating these characteristics.

Types of case interviews

What case interviews are not designed to do is to explore educational, professional or experiential qualifications. If you've reached the case interview stage, take a deep breath—the consulting firm has already weighed your background, GPA and experience, and found you worthy of a deeper skill assessment. This means that the case interview is yours to lose. Triumph over your case interviews and chances are that a slot at the firm will open for you.

Case interviews vary widely, but in general they fall into three groups: business cases, guesstimates and brainteasers.

Business case

Case interviews vary somewhat in their format. The classic and most common type of case interview is the business case, in which you're presented with a business scenario and asked to analyze it and make recommendations. Most cases are presented in oral form, though some involve handouts or slides, and a few (like Monitor Company's) are entirely written. (In a written case, the interviewer will not contribute any other information besides what's on the handout.) Another variation on the case interview is the group case interview, where three to six candidates are grouped together and told to solve a case cooperatively. Consultants from the firm watch as silent observers. Though you should certainly be prepared for these variations on case interviews, you are most likely to come across the traditional, mano-a-mano case interview.

Guesstimates

Whether freestanding or as part of a case, learning how to make "back-of-the-envelope" calculations (rough, yet basically accurate) is an essential part of the case interview. As part of a guesstimate, you might be asked to estimate how many watermelons are sold in the United States each year, or what the market size for a new computer program that organizes your wardrobe might be. (For example, you might need to figure out the market size for the wardrobe software as a first step in determining how to enter the European market.) You will not be expected to get the exact number, but you should come close—hence the guesstimate. Non-business school students and others who appear to be weak quantitatively may get standalone guesstimates—guesstimates given independently of a case.

Brainteasers

Brainteasers are normally logic puzzles or riddles. They may be timed. Often, brainteasers are meant to test both analytic and "out-of-the-box" thinking, as well as grace under pressure.

Skills assessed in the case interview

Following your case interview, your consulting interviewer will complete a written evaluation form. The evaluation forms often include a list of qualities, traits and abilities, and ask the interviewer to assess the candidate against the list. Following is a list of these special traits that, according to consulting insiders, interviewers will be keeping an eye out for as you work through the case interview:

Leadership skills

You'll hear this from every consulting firm out there—they want leaders. Why, you might ask, would a consulting firm need a leader? After all, many beginning consultants are consigned to independent number-crunching and research. The fact is, however, that consultants are often called upon to work independently, shape projects with very little direction and direct others. You should demonstrate your leadership skills by taking charge of the case interview. Ask your questions confidently. Inquire whether the case interview relates to the interviewer's own experience. While your resume and previous leadership experience will probably most strongly convey your leadership ability, your demeanor in the case interview can help.

Analytical skills

The core competency of consulting is analysis—breaking down data, formulating it into a pattern that makes sense, and deriving a sensible conclusion or recommendation. You should display this skill through your efficient, on-target and accurate questions while wrestling your case to a solution.

Presentation skills

Presenting your analysis is an essential part of consulting. Once consultants have analyzed their case engagement and decided on the proper course of action, they must present their findings and recommendations to their case team and to their clients. Interviewers will be watching you closely to see if you stumble over words, use inadvisable fillers like "um" or "like" frequently, or appear jittery under close questioning. Remember: When you're speaking, slow down and smile. If asked a question that temporarily stumps you, take a deep breath and pause. It's always better to pause than babble. Ask the interviewer to restate information if necessary.

Energy

Even the most qualified and analytical hire won't be much good if she quits at 5 p.m. during a long and arduous engagement. Interviewers look for zest and energy—firm handshake, sincere and warm smile, bright eyes. Remember that consulting firms expect you to take a long flight and show up at work the next day alert, perky and ready to go. If you must, drink lots of coffee and use eyedrops—just be energized.

Attention to detail/organization

Consultants must be as painstaking as scientists in their attention to detail. And consultants who juggle two or more flights a week and engagements all over the world must be extremely organized. You can display this skill through a disciplined, logical approach to your case solution and by showing up for your interview prepared. You'll want to take notes, so bring a pad of paper and a pen. Interviewers notice when candidates must ask for these materials. You must arrive on time.

Visit Vault at **www.vault.com** for insider company profiles, expert advice, career message boards, expert resume reviews, the Vault Job Board and more.

VAULT CAREER LIBRARY 17

Quantitative skills

Those spreadsheets you'll be working with as a management consultant need numbers to fill them. Consulting interviews will inevitably test your grasp of numbers and your ability to manipulate them. Many interviewers will assess your quantitative skills by giving you a "guesstimate," either within the case question or separately.

Flexibility

Consultants may have to arrive at the office one day and be packed off to Winnipeg for six months the next. This kind of flexibility of schedule is mirrored in tests for mental flexibility. To test your grasp of a case interview, the interviewer may suddenly introduce a new piece of information ("OK, let's say the factories must be opened either in Canada or China") or flip the terms of the case interview ("What if this labor contract is not guaranteed, as I said earlier?") and then watch how quickly you're able to alter your thinking.

Maturity

Consultants must often work with executives and company officials decades older than they are. (This is why consultants are taught the right way to answer the question, "How old are you?") Eliminate giggling, fidgeting and references to awesome fraternity events you may have attended, even if the interviewer seems receptive.

Intelligence, a/k/a/ "mental horsepower"

Rather straightforward—consulting interviewers are looking for quickness of analysis and depth of insight. Don't be afraid to ask questions for fear of looking stupid—smart people learn by asking questions and assimilating new information. At the same time, asking your interviewer to repeat an elementary (or irrelevant) concept 20 times will not do you any favors.

What kind of case will I get?

While there's no way to tell for sure what case question you'll get, there are some things that can tip you off to the kind of case you'll receive.

For a business school student or graduate, the case question will probably be less open-ended and drive toward an actual solution. Your interviewer may posit something from her own experience—knowing what course of action the consultancy actually ended up recommending. This doesn't mean you have to make the same recommendation—but you'd better be able to back up your reasoning! Alternatively, one thing case interviewers love to do is look at your resume and give you a case question that relates to your past experience. "For example," says one consultant, "if you were on the advertising staff for the school newspaper, you might be given a question about investing in advertising agencies." For this reason, advise consultants, "it makes sense to follow up on your field in *The Wall Street Journal* because you may be asked about recent developments in it. If you know what's going on you'll be that much more impressive." Some guesstimates, like figuring out the total worldwide revenue of *Tarzan*, are broad enough so that most people can make a reasonable assumption of numbers.

Sample Case

You are advising a credit card company that wants to market a prepaid phone card to its customers. Is this a good idea?

Whoa! Better find out more about this prepaid phone card first before you even begin to think about recommending it.

You: What is the role of our company? Do we simply market the card or must we create them ourselves? Are we expected to provide the telephone services?

Interviewer: This card will be co-marketed with an outside phone company. We do not need to perform telecommunications functions.

You: What are our expenses connected with the card?

Interviewer: We must pay 15 cents for every minute we sell. We also have to pay $1 as a startup cost for the card and card systems.

You: What are our marketing expenses?

Interviewer: We normally use slips of paper that are attached to the backs of our credit card payment envelopes. We sometimes also send customers a direct mailing in a separate envelope. Or we can have telemarketers call selected customers.

You: What's the cost of each of these marketing techniques, and what is their response rate?

Interviewer: Telemarketers have a 2 percent response rate and cost $1 per call. Direct mailings cost us 41 cents per mailing and have a 0.50 percent rate of response. Our payment attachments have a 0.25 percent rate of response, but only cost us 5 cents each.

You: I'm going to assume we will sell one-hour phone cards. That will cost us $9 for the minutes and a dollar per card—so each card costs us $10.

Interviewer: OK, that sounds reasonable.

You: And what is our expected revenue on a one-hour phone card? What is the current market rate for a 60-minute phone card?

Interviewer: Assume it's 50 cents a minute.

You: So if we sell the cards for $30, we have a $20 profit, minus our expenditures on marketing.

Interviewer: What's our cost structure look like?

You: OK, let's figure this out. To sell 1,000 cards through telemarketing, we would need to contact 50,000 people. That would cost us $50,000. To use direct mail, we would have to contact 200,000 thousand people, which, at 40 cents per mailing, costs us $80,000. Since the envelope inserts aren't very reliable, we will need to contact 800,000 people using that method. But at 5 cents each, it costs only $20,000 to sell 1,000 cards.

We make $20 profit on each card. But even using the cheapest promotional vehicle, at $20 profit, we would only break even, because our profit on 1,000 cards would be $20,000. We shouldn't market this card, unless we can further cut our marketing costs or increase the price of the card. If we could slice the cost of the envelope attachments a penny or so, or sell the card for $35, or convince our co-marketer to reduce our costs, it might be worth selling.

Interviewer: What are some other issues you might want to consider? (Notice how the interviewer is nudging you to add to your analysis.)

You: We should also consider the competitive landscape for this business. Is the per-minute rate for calling card minutes expected to fall? If so, and our costs are held constant, we may lose money. Of course, we can learn more from marketing these cards. It could be that the people likely to buy these cards might be frequent travelers and could be targeted for other promotions

Sample Guesstimate

How many square feet of pizza are eaten in the United States each month?

Take your figure of 300 million people in America. How many people eat pizza? Let's say 200 million. Now let's say the average pizza-eating person eats pizza twice a month, and eats two slices at a time. That's four slices a month. If the average slice of pizza is perhaps six inches at the base and 10 inches long, then the slice is 30 square inches of pizza. So four

Visit Vault at **www.vault.com** for insider company profiles, expert advice, career message boards, expert resume reviews, the Vault Job Board and more.

VAULT CAREER LIBRARY   19

pizza slices would be 120 square inches. Therefore, there are a billion square feet of pizza eaten every month. To summarize:

- There are 300 million people in America.
- Perhaps 200 million eat pizza.
- The average slice of pizza is six inches at the base and 10 inches long = 30 square inches (height x half the base).
- The average American eats four slices of pizza a month.
- Four pieces x 30 square inches = 120 square inches (one square foot is 144 inches), so let's assume one square foot per person.
- Your total: 200 million square feet a month.

Finance Interviews

An overview of finance interviews

Investment banking positions and other finance positions are some of the more stressful and demanding positions on the planet, and this is reflected in the interview. In fact, insiders say that occasionally, an interviewer will yell at an applicant to see how he or she will react. Interviews normally go three or four rounds (sometimes as many as six or more rounds), and these rounds can have up to six interviews each, especially in the later rounds. Investment banking and finance interviews are also known for being deliberately stressful (as opposed to the attendant nervousness that goes with any interview). Some firms may ask you specific and detailed questions about your grades in college or business school, even if your school policy prohibits such questions. At other firms, interview rounds may be interspersed with seemingly casual and friendly dinners. Don't let down your guard! While these dinners are a good opportunity to meet your prospective co-workers, your seemingly genial hosts are scrutinizing you as well. (Hint: Don't drink too much.)

There are generally two parts to the finance hiring process: the fit part and the technical part. In asking technical questions, the interviewer wants to judge your analytical and technical skills. If you don't know the basic concepts of finance and accounting, your interviewers will believe (rightly) that you are either (1) not interested in the position, (2) not competent enough to handle the job. An important part of the interview is what is called "fit." As you go through recruiting in finance interviews, understand that you compete with yourself. Most firms are flexible enough to hire people that are a good fit.

The fit interview

They call it the O'Hare airport test, the Atlanta airport test, or the whatever-city-you-happen-to-be-applying-in airport test. They also call it the fit interview or the behavioral interview. It means: "Could you stand to be stranded in an airport for eight hours with this person?" Although bankers may have reputations for being aggressive individuals, don't act that way in your interview.

And while your performance in the fit interview partly depends—as the airport test suggests—on how well you gel with your interviewer, it also depends on your ability to portray yourself as a good fit as an investment banker, asset manager, etc. In other words, interviewers will try to figure out what your attitude towards work is like, how interested you are in a career in the industry, and how interested you are in the job for which you are applying.

I'm a hard worker

As a general rule, you should emphasize how hard you have worked in the past, giving evidence of your ability to take on a lot of work and pain. You don't have to make things up or pretend that there's nothing you'd want more than to work 100-hour weeks. In fact, interviewers are sure to see through such blatant lying. Says one I-banking interviewer, "If somebody acted too enthusiastic about the hours, that'd be weird." If you ask investment bankers and others in finance what they dislike most about their jobs, they will most likely talk about the long hours. Be honest about this unpleasant part of the job, and convince your interviewer that you can handle it well. For example, if you were in crew and had to wake up at 5 a.m. every morning in the freezing cold, by all means, talk about it. And if you put yourself through school by working two jobs, mention that, too.

Got safe hands?

As with all job interviews, those for finance positions will largely be about figuring out whether you can handle the responsibility required of the position. (In many cases with finance positions, that responsibility will mean making decisions with millions or billions of dollars at stake.)

An interviewer will try and figure out if you've got safe hands and won't be dropping the ball. "This is a critical I-banking concept," says one banker about safe hands. "The idea is: 'Can I give this person this analysis to do and feel comfortable that they will execute it promptly and correctly?' The people with safe hands are the ones who advance in the company. They are not necessarily the hardest workers but they are the most competent." Make sure you bring up examples of taking responsibility.

A mind to pick things apart

The world of finance is largely about number crunching and analytical ability. While this doesn't mean you have to be a world-class mathematician, it does mean that you have to have an analytic mind if you are to succeed. Explains one insider at a numbers-heavy Wall Street firm, "You can't be any old English major. You've got to have a really logical, mathematical head." Make sure you have examples of your problem-solving and analytic strengths.

T-E-A-M! Go team!

Teamwork is the buzzword of these days not just for the investment banking industry, but for every employer. Every finance position (except, perhaps, for research) requires that an employee work closely with others—whether this be in the form of investment banking deal teams, or finance officials working with marketers at a corporation. Interviewers will ask questions to make sure that you have experience, and have excelled, in team situations. Yeah, you can break out those glory days stories about the winning touchdown pass, but lots of other situations can also help describe your teamwork ability—previous work experience, volunteer activities, etc.

Preparing for finance interviews

When you review career options, don't discount the amount of time it takes to prepare for finance interviews. First of all, you should evaluate whether you actually want to be in investment banking, commercial banking, venture capital, etc. In short, you should know what you're getting into. Not only should you know this for your own sake (this is your future, after all), but your interviewers want to know that you understand the position and industry.

You should use the opportunity of nonevaluative settings (i.e., not an interview) to get answers to these questions. These are questions to which we strongly suggest you have answers before interviewing. Make a point to attend recruiting presentations by firms. Your informational interviews with alumni and (for those in business school) second-years are also good ways to get answers to some of your questions.

As for written materials, you can start with general business publications like *The Wall Street Journal*, *The Economist*, *BusinessWeek* and *The Financial Times*. From there, you can move on to trade publications that will give more industry-specific news and analysis. *American Banker*, *Institutional Investor*, *Investment Dealers' Digest* and *The Daily Deal* are some examples.

Your interaction with alumni can have direct results. The results can be good if you prepare properly before contacting them. You can also assure yourself a ding if you don't handle a meeting or phone conversation correctly.

Here are some questions about finance positions you should ask before you have your first interview:

Visit Vault at **www.vault.com** for insider company profiles, expert advice, career message boards, expert resume reviews, the Vault Job Board and more.

V∧ULT CAREER LIBRARY   21

- What is a typical day like?

- What are the hours in the industry really like? Are they 100 hours every week or every other week? Is it the same for every firm?

- How do people cope with the lifestyle issues in the industry?

- What kind of money do people make in the industry?

- What are the things I-bankers (or commercial bankers, venture capitalists, etc.) like about their jobs? What would they like to change?

- What is the future of the industry for the next few years? How will the industry change? How will the margins change? The return on equity?

- What is the career track in the industry? What skills are required at what stage?

- What is so exciting about this job?

- What is the culture of an I-banking firm as compared to a Fortune 500 company? Compared to a startup?

- What are the exit opportunities after 10 years in the industry? After two years?

Research individual firms

Once you've answered questions about the industry, you should begin to narrow your research to specific firms—both to know which firms to target, and to be knowledgeable for your interviews. Good sources for research are easily accessible publications like *The Wall Street Journal*, *BusinessWeek* and *Fortune*. If you have the resources (perhaps at a school library), you can also read through recent issues of trade publications like *Investment Dealers' Digest*.

Insiders at business school who have gone through the recruiting process suggest that you form research and interview practice teams. There is a lot of material to cover, and it is not possible to do it all by yourself. Form teams for researching industries and firms. Later, you can use the same teams to practice interviews. If you are in business school, your school will undoubtedly have such a club, or you may want to team up with other students who are looking into finance careers. Teams of four to six work quite well for this research process.

Practice your interviews

You should prepare answers to common questions given at finance interviews—whether they be fit questions, technical questions or brainteasers. While this may be easiest for technical questions and brainteasers (after all, we can help you to nail those questions with the right answers), it is also important to prepare for fit questions even if there are no right or wrong answers. We can steer you onto the right path with these questions, but you'll need to fill in the blanks. What's the hardest thing you've ever had to do? Can you give me an example of a time when you came up with a creative solution? You don't want to be cursing yourself after an interview, thinking about what you should have said, or examples you could have brought up.

One of the best ways to prepare answers to these questions is to use mock/practice interviews. You can practice by role-playing with your friends and classmates, or by taking advantage of interview training offered by your school. Many MBA career centers offer students the opportunity to perform mock interviews, which are normally videotaped. These practice sessions are conducted either by professional career counselors or by second-year students. The mock interviewees are given the videotape of their critique to watch at home (again and again). Students may choose what kind of interview they'd like to receive: finance, consulting, etc.

What mistakes are commonly unearthed by the videotaped interview? One business school career counselor says that he finds that "most MBAs don't have their story down. They can't elaborate why they came to business school, and why they want to work in the industry." The best candidates are able to describe their background and career history, and make a pitch about why they are interested in a firm, all in a minute or less, career counselors say. Another problem is that many students apparently "can't elaborate their strengths. They have them, but can't sell them. They are too modest." While there's no use demurring when explicating your good points, career center professionals warn that "there is also a danger of tooting your horn too much"—so make sure you're not making any claims for competency you can't back up with relevant experience.

To take full advantage of their mock interviews, career counselors say, students should take them as seriously as possible. Dress professionally "to get into the interviewing mindset." Afterwards, the interviewer will go over the session, assessing the candidate's strengths and weaknesses. It's a good idea to take notes on this feedback.

Mock interviewers also coach students on appropriate answers. "For example," explains one mock interviewer, "many candidates are asked to name their top three weaknesses. Answering with your actual weaknesses is not a good idea. So when I identify a student's weaker point—maybe they are weak on real teamwork experience—we strategize on an appropriate answer. It's better to say something like 'I wouldn't call them weaknesses, but there are three areas in which I still have room to grow,' and then choose three areas that are not deal-breakers."

Do interviewers thus end up hearing the same canned answers over and over again? "I do hear from some interviewers at certain schools—not mine!—that they do hear identical answers to certain questions," says one insider. "My advice to students is to always put answers into their own words."

Prepare questions

Finally, don't forget that finance interviewers often ask candidates whether they have any questions. Don't get caught looking like a job applicant who hasn't done research and is not curious about the opportunities. Read about the firms, read about the industries, and prepare some intelligent questions.

Sample Finance Interview Questions

What happens to each of the three primary financial statements when you change (a) gross margin; (b) capital expenditures; (c) other.

This problem tests your understanding of the interconnection between all three statements.

(a) If gross margin were to say, decrease, then your income statement would first be affected. You would pay lower taxes, but if nothing else changed, you would have lower net income. This would translate to the cash flow statement on the top line. If everything else remained the same, you would have less cash. Going to the balance sheet, you would not only have less cash, but to balance that effect, you would have lower shareholder's equity.

(b) If capital expenditure were to say, decrease, then first, the level of capital expenditures would decrease on the Statement of Cash Flows. This would increase the level of cash on the balance sheet, but decrease the level of property, plant and equipment, so total assets stay the same. On the income statement, the depreciation expense would be lower in subsequent years, so net income would be higher, which would increase cash and shareholder's equity in the future.

(c) Just be sure you understand the interplay between the three sheets. Remember that changing one sheet has ramifications on all the other statements both today and in the future.

How do you calculate the terminal value of a company?

The value of the terminal year cash flows (usually calculated for 10 years in the future) is calculated by calculating the present value of cash flows from the terminal year (in our case, Year 10) continuing forever with the following formula:

$$\text{TY FCF} = \frac{FCF_{10}\,(1 + g)}{(r_d - g)}$$

Visit Vault at **www.vault.com** for insider company profiles, expert advice, career message boards, expert resume reviews, the Vault Job Board and more.

V∧ULT CAREER LIBRARY   **23**

Here "g" is an assumed growth rate and r_d is the discount rate. Remember that you could also calculate the terminal value of a company by taking a multiple of terminal year cash flows, and discounting that back to the present to arrive at an answer. This alternative method might be used in some instances because it is less dependent on the assumed growth rate (g).

If you add a risky stock into a portfolio that is already risky, how is the overall portfolio risk affected?

a. It becomes riskier

b. It becomes less risky

c. Overall risk is unaffected

d. It depends on the stock

Answer: D. It depends on the stock. In modern portfolio theory, if you add a risky stock into a portfolio that is already risky, the resulting portfolio may be more or less risky than before.

A portfolio's overall risk is determined not just by the riskiness of its individual positions, but also by how those positions are correlated with each other. For example, a portfolio with two high-tech stocks might at first glance be considered risky, but if those two stocks tends to move in opposite directions, then the riskiness of the portfolio overall could be significantly lower. So the risk effect of adding a new stock to an existing portfolio depends on how that stock correlates with the other stocks in the portfolio.

When should a company issue stock rather than debt to fund its operations?

There are several reasons for a company to issue stock rather than debt. If the company believes its stock price is inflated it can raise money (on very good terms) by issuing stock. The second is when the projects for which the money is being raised may not generate predictable cash flows in the immediate future. A simple example of this is a startup company. The owners of startups generally will issue stock rather than take on debt because their ventures will probably not generate predictable cash flows, which is needed to make regular debt payments, and also so that the risk of the venture is diffused among the company's shareholders. A third reason for a company to raise money by selling equity is if it wants to change its debt-to-equity ratio. This ratio in part determines a company's bond rating. If a company's bond rating is poor because it is struggling with large debts, they may decide to issue equity to pay down the debt.

If inflation rates in the U.S. falls relative to the inflation rate in Russia, what will happen to the exchange rate between the dollar and the ruble?

The dollar will strengthen relative to the ruble.

This section was excerpted from the *Vault Guide to Finance Interviews* and the *Vault Guide to the Case Interview*. Get the inside scoop on consulting and finance interviews:

- **Vault Guides:** *Vault Guide to the Case Interview, Vault Case Interviews Practice Guide, Vault Guide to Finance Interviews, Vault Finance Interviews Practice Guide, Vault Guide to Advanced and Quantitative Finance Interviews*
- **Career Services:** One-on-One Finance Interview Prep, One-on-One Case Interview Prep
- **Vault Employee Surveys:** See what employees say about their interviews at top finance and consulting firms

Go to www.vault.com/finance
or
www.vault.com/consulting

or ask your bookstore or librarian for other Vault titles.

Visit Vault at **www.vault.com** for insider company profiles, expert advice, career message boards, expert resume reviews, the Vault Job Board and more.

VAULT CAREER LIBRARY   25

PLAY FOR MATTEL

At Mattel, play is our core competency. Unparalleled creativity, dynamic teamwork, respect of others, integrity and rewards for excellence are how we play. We welcome every race, gender, religion to come play for us.

Learn more about Mattel and our career opportunities at www.mattel.com/careers.

  ☆ American Girl

play to grow • play together • play with passion • play fair

MBA
DIVERSITY

ADI
Asian Diversity, Inc

2008 Asian Diversity
CAREER EXPO

May 2, 2008 New York
Madison Square Garden

Join one of the largest recruiting events for Asian Americans in the U.S.! Last year, our expo drew a record 101 exhibitors and over 4,000 job candidates. Here are just some of the highlights to expect at the career expo:

- Meet hundreds of qualified Asian American job seekers
- Recruit candidates interested in working in Asia
- Connect to working professionals in a wide range of industries
- Find bilingual and bicultural talent
- Recruit, market, and reach out to the Asian American community

www.adiversity.com

The Importance of Mentors

What makes the difference between a career that thrives and one that stalls? For many women and minorities, the narrow gap between failure and success is bridged by mentorships. Mentors are people who share their general business knowledge, as well as their knowledge of a specific company, with lucky mentees (someone who is mentored). Here is some advice on how to make these valuable relationships work for you.

Mentors can keep you with an employer

After several years at the prestigious consulting firm Booz Allen Hamilton, Cathy Mhatre had her first child. Mhatre credits her mentors at Booz Allen with keeping her at the firm. "I've now been at Booz Allen for six years, which is unusual for any consultant. One of the main reasons I am still here is because there were people who wanted to keep me here." Mhatre estimates that she has "four to six" mentors at the firm, and advises, "Because women mentors are scarce in general, find enlightened men."

Have many mentors for many reasons

Do you need help on balancing your family life and career without sacrificing your career viability? You could probably use some help from a mentor who's done just that at your company. Your work/life balance mentor, however, may not be the same person who can help you polish your presentation skills and confidence. If you seek someone who will be your advocate at performance and promotion reviews, look for someone at least two levels above you (or with four or more years of experience at the company).

Find out if your employer assigns you a mentor—then keep looking

Increasingly, employers assign mentors to incoming associates—a practice that has been common at law firms for some time and is spreading rapidly to other industries as well. Some consulting firms have entire mentor family trees—with a "founder" mentor, his or her mentees, their mentees, and so on. Make sure to take advantage of these mentors, who have specifically volunteered to serve as resources.

At the same time, the most valuable mentors are normally the ones that evolve from everyday working relationships. If someone appears willing to share their experience and skills with you and takes an interest in your career, it is likely that they would like to mentor you in some way.

Don't expect your mentor to share your background

While it's terrific to have mentors that share your ethnicity or gender, it's no sure thing. Some of the MBAs we spoke to indicate that the old "succeed and close the door behind you" ethos is still in existence. "When I was working," says Lanchi Venator, a NYU Stern MBA graduate, "it seemed that most successful women were not open to helping other women out. It was almost as if they were saying, 'I made it when it was tough on me. Why should I soften it for you?'"

Be careful of having only one mentor

One-on-one mentorship has its pitfalls. Corporate historians may recall the case of Mary Cunningham and William Agee at Bendix Corp. After rising rapidly through the ranks of Bendix, Cunningham, a 1979 graduate of Harvard Business School, was accused of sleeping with her mentor. Cunningham eventually left the firm. Even when the shadow of romance doesn't

Visit Vault at **www.vault.com** for insider company profiles, expert advice, career message boards, expert resume reviews, the Vault Job Board and more.

VAULT CAREER LIBRARY

29

Grow with Us!

Robert Half, the leader in specialized staffing services since 1948, invites you to learn more about exciting career opportunities as a member of our internal sales management team.

We are seeking Account Executives with accounting, finance, technology, legal, marketing or administrative backgrounds to work within one of our multiple lines of business. Our people are the core of our business. If you are interested in learning more about career opportunities in the United States and Canada, please forward your resume to **hqpemployment@rhi.com**.

enter a close mentorship, mentees with only one advisor run the risk of being seen as an appendage or sidekick, not a full professional. Whenever possible, seek mentorship from a wide variety of people.

Tips for mentees

It's not enough to find a good mentor—it's just as important to use them correctly. Here are a few tips to make the most of your mentor relationship.

- **Find mentors at all levels of the company.** The classic mentor is someone a few levels above you in an organization—close enough to your experience to guide you upwards in the ranks, experienced enough to have some pull. But you can also gain experience from mentors at your level and at other companies as well. Your business school professors are another invaluable set of potential mentors.

- **Don't approach someone and formally ask them to be your mentor.** This kind of artificiality is akin to handing your business card to someone and asking them to be your contact—it's too artificial to take root. If someone wants to be your mentor, they will indicate that fact through the interest they take in you.

- **Keep in touch with your mentors.** Mentorship is a relationship, and relationships are built from frequent, informal contact. This is important even when your mentor is assigned to you by your company. If you move on from a company, stay in touch with your mentor there.

- **Establish trust.** Everything you discuss with your mentor is between the two of you.

- **Have realistic expectations.** Your mentor is an advisor and advocate—not someone to do your career networking for you, or someone to cover your errors.

- **Find your own mentees.** Mentorship is a two-way street. As soon as possible, start finding people who are willing to learn from you. You never know when the mentee will become the mentor!

- **Don't pass up the opportunity to have a mentor.** Having a mentor can make a major difference in your career path and your self-confidence.

Vault Diversity Q&A: Pipasu Soni, Financial Analyst, Honeywell

Pipasu Soni is a 2003 graduate of the Johnson School of Management at Cornell University. A former engineer of Indian descent, he previously worked at Ingersoll-Rand before getting an MBA. He currently works in Minneapolis as a financial analyst with Honeywell's Automation and Control Solutions (ACS) division, an $8 billion division encompassing seven different strategic business units including environmental controls, fire solutions, security systems and more. He took time out to talk to Vault a bit about being a minority MBA and working at Honeywell.

Vault: How did you end up in your current position? Did you go to business school knowing you wanted to do finance?

Soni: Actually, I was initially interested in going into marketing, but after the very first semester, my focus shifted to finance. Previously I worked in new product development for Ingersoll-Rand. There's always some tension between the engineering and marketing side during new product introduction, and I was interested in exploring the marketing/product management aspect, to get more of a general management perspective.

But as an engineer, I enjoyed the technical side of finance and the role it played within an organization. When it came to recruiting, I really liked the Finance Pathways Program and the fact that the finance group at Honeywell is one of the keys to implementing the strategic vision of the organization.

Vault: Did you intern at Honeywell?

Visit Vault at **www.vault.com** for insider company profiles, expert advice, career message boards, expert resume reviews, the Vault Job Board and more.

VAULT CAREER LIBRARY   **31**

Soni: No actually, I interned with a consulting firm. I wanted to find out more about the consulting field, and decided it wasn't for me. I enjoyed being part of the day-to-day operations of an organization where I could influence the performance and visibly see the product. I knew Honeywell would be a great place to leverage my past experience with Ingersoll-Rand.

Vault: What sort of program were you hired into?

Soni: I was hired into Honeywell's Finance Pathways Program. It's one of their career development programs for MBA graduates. The program consists of two 18-month assignments across different Honeywell businesses. I'm in my first rotation, which ends this December. My current assignment consists of working in the corporate finance group supporting the annual operating plan, strategic plan, corporate initiatives, and other functional areas—Six Sigma and Technology. At the end of the assignment I'll move into an operational finance role at a business unit level.

Vault: Is there a formal mentorship program with the Pathways program?

Soni: No, not "formal." Mentoring takes several forms at Honeywell. All employees are encouraged to seek out mentors as well as offer to mentor others. My particular businesses assisted me in identifying a formal mentor at the beginning of my assignment. The main focus of my mentor is to provide a contact that can give me insight and advice as I move throughout my career.

In addition, you receive mentoring through working with managers on assignments. Also, your supervisor gives you regular feedback on performance and instructs you on training you should pursue.

Vault: Are there diversity organizations for you at Honeywell?

Soni: Yes, there's an Indian and Asian Association that meets on a regular basis. These groups usually meet once a month for a networking hour or a guest speaker presentation. Honeywell also has several other minority employee groups throughout the company, like the Hispanic Network and the Black Employees Network.

Vault: Did you get the feeling during recruiting that Honeywell targets minorities and women for diversity hiring purposes?

Soni: No, I don't think Honeywell specifically targets minorities, but focuses on recruiting individuals that are the right fit with the company. Honeywell defines diversity more as individual uniqueness. I don't think it's just gender, race and ethnic background, but also things such as educational and cultural background and work experience.

With that said, Honeywell's incoming Pathways class is a diverse group similar to what you would find in a typical MBA class.

Vault: What attracted you to Honeywell?

Soni: The things that attracted me the most were the people and the job assignments. For me, having a first assignment in financial planning and analysis at the corporate level allowed me to understand the strategic vision of the organization before moving into a business unit role.

Other things unique to Honeywell included the ability to work across several functions, mandatory green-belt training and certification for all incoming MBAs, and ability to switch roles—from finance to marketing if desired. I spoke with several Cornell alumni and other Pathway program members before joining and it seems that our perspective of Honeywell is very similar.

Vault: What aspects of your MBA education do you think have proved most helpful in your experience so far at Honeywell?

Soni: In my current assignment, finance, accounting and leadership classes have been the most helpful. The classes in accounting and finance have been invaluable in reviewing business unit results. The classes in leading, communicating and team building have been also valuable in day-to-day communication getting people to meet deadlines and goals.

You learn about metrics in business school and using metrics to drive performance, but you don't realize the significance until you actually use it. It's been a great experience, and I feel like I'm going to the next level in my ability to lead teams and drive results.

Visit Vault at **www.vault.com** for insider company profiles, expert advice, career message boards, expert resume reviews, the Vault Job Board and more.

VAULT CAREER LIBRARY 33

Vault Diversity Q&A: Ann Silverman, M&T Bank

A 2004 graduate of the Wharton School at the University of Pennsylvania, Ann Silverman was a project manager and exhibition developer at the Smithsonian Institution in New York prior to business school. She decided to get an MBA in order to have a greater impact on the community in which she lives and ended up choosing to join the executive associate program at M&T Bank in the Washington, D.C. metro area after graduation. She took time out to talk with Vault about her choice of regional banking and about being a woman professional in finance.

Vault: Going into business school, did you know that you wanted to go into finance and commercial banking?

Silverman: I knew that I wanted to go into finance, but I suppose coming from such a different background, I didn't know what individual buckets [in finance] there were. Once I got into business school and understood more, I knew that commercial banking in particular was what I wanted, and that I wanted a regional bank.

Vault: What in particular about regional banks and commercial banking appeals to you?

Silverman: At the Smithsonian, one of the things I loved most was the community impact of the job, but I felt that I wasn't going to have a real impact until I had a profession that hits people's wallets. When I looked at the landscape out there I thought, "Wow, commercial banking is really a wonderful area that contributes to the businesses in the community and the community at large."

Vault: Why did you choose M&T?

Silverman: Looking at all of the mergers and acquisitions activity that have gone on in the banking industry, I really wanted to find a place where I would have opportunities for business development and client interaction earlier rather than later and a smaller, regional bank seemed the best place to get this experience and the chance to contribute in meaningful ways. And M&T's mission emphasizes being really involved in the community, and I take that very seriously.

Vault: Can you describe the program that you were hired into? Is it a rotational program?

Silverman: M&T has what's called the executive associate program. It's not really a formal rotation program; you're hired into a functional position. I was hired into commercial lending as knew I wanted to be a lender. In my case, my title is relationship manager. "Executive associate" is more of a hiring title.

Vault: How long are you in the executive associate program?

Silverman: The first year is the more defined part of the program, though the bank does track us as executive associates throughout our career.

The first year has really been a mix of both project work, which gives you exposure to people throughout the bank, and learning the skills to being a lender, everything from the financial and industry analysis and the business development skills to integrating yourself into the community.

Vault: Are there training sessions for executive associates outside of on-the-job training?

Silverman: In the first year, we have seminars. Almost once a month, all the MBAs are brought together at the bank's headquarters in Buffalo. Each time, there's a lunch with one of the members of the executive committee, and bookending that in the morning and afternoon are presentations from departments throughout the bank. This way, you get a chance to meet the other EAs that you've been hired with and the managers and staff that work across the bank.

Vault: How many executive associates were there in your class?

Silverman: I believe there were 21 that were hired in my class.

Vault: Did you have any concerns about going into finance, which is notoriously male-dominated? And do you find, in comparing notes with your business school classmates, that commercial banking is any better than other areas of finance, such as investment banking or investment management?

Silverman: I would agree that finance is an area where women are underrepresented. I knew that that would be part of the world that I would enter regardless of where I went into finance. I don't feel that there's a difference between investment banking and commercial banking.

With the issue of representation of women in finance, it's only going to change as more of us come into the field. There are a lot of women who have certainly gone before me, and we need to keep that momentum. Taking my peer group at Wharton as an example, many of the women that I was friends with are going into finance, so there's continued progress.

Vault: How many women are there in your executive associate class at M&T?

Silverman: There were three of us. I know them quite well—we speak frequently and try to foster close relationships with each other.

One thing that was important to me about M&T is that it has a diversity council. It's a bank-wide initiative that's headed up by a gentleman on the senior committee of the bank. Particularly as the bank has grown in the last three years, it has made an effort to takes issues of diversity seriously, as evidenced by the formation of this group. The idea that you've really got to grow and nurture that, it doesn't happen overnight.

Vault: What types of companies and organizations are you working with as a lender?

Silverman: We service middle market companies, which are companies that have revenues above $10 million. The economy in D.C. is incredibly diverse. There are lots of life sciences and biotechnology companies, there are government related contractors, high technology companies. Just everything under the sun.

Vault: And how do you go about developing business with these organizations?

Silverman: One of the ways that we get a lot of business is through referrals. And one of the ways to do that is to make sure you're really well networked with accountants and lawyers in the region and others that work with businesses. People in the bank are very generous about making sure you get the external introductions you need. There are many business organizations in the county that have breakfasts, lunches, dinners, etc. Let's just say that my evenings are quite full.

Vault: Do you work with professional groups for women with respect to business development initiatives?

Silverman: Oh, yes. In the D.C. region, there's a group called Women in Bio, there's one called Women in Information Technology—there are a lot of those groups, and those are definitely resources I tap into.

Diversity Employer Directory

Bristol-Myers Squibb Co.

P.O. Box 4000
Princeton, NJ 08543-4000
Phone:609-252-4000
www.bms.com/career

  **Bristol-Myers Squibb**
Hope, Triumph and the Miracle of Medicine™

BMS offers opportunities for MBA students and graduates to join summer and full-time associate programs in the following areas: marketing, finance, information management, and technical operations.

Different perspectives make it possible. At Bristol-Myers Squibb, we're a diverse team of talented and creative people—each with a different perspective. We value each person's unique contributions and inspire each other to develop the innovative solutions that extend and enhance the lives of our patients around the world.

Flexibility makes it possible. At Bristol-Myers Squibb, our people find fulfillment in their work, extending and enhancing the lives of patients around the world. And they have fulfilling lives at home too. Bristol-Myers Squibb offers a flexible range of work/life programs that help our employees at each stage of their lives. We're proud to be ranked in the top 100 of *Working Mother* magazine's Best Companies for Working Mothers.

Opportunities make your growth possible. Ask yourself—how far do you want to go? At Bristol-Myers Squibb, we're determined to be the company where our employees can achieve their career goals. We offer a range of opportunities to help you get there. It's simple. Your growth helps us to better extend and enhance the lives of patients around the world.

Business schools Bristol-Myers Squibb recruits from: Columbia, Cornell, Dartmouth, Duke, NYU, U. Michigan, North Carolina, Thunderbird.

Credit Suisse

11 Madison Avenue
New York, NY 10010
www.credit-suisse.com/careers

 CREDIT SUISSE

Cultivating and fostering an inclusive workplace is a top priority and an integral part of Credit Suisse's business strategy. Credit Suisse's entrepreneurial spirit and innovation are enabled by our diverse backgrounds, experiences, expertise and ideas.

Our robust commitment to Diversity and Inclusion has brought significant external recognition across all our markets. We have received awards in numerous categories including:

• 100 Best Companies for Working Mothers
• Best Companies for Multi-cultural Women
• Setting New Standards in Diversity

Business schools Credit Suisse recruits from:
University of Chicago, Columbia University, Barnard College, Cornell University, Duke University, Georgetown University, Harvard University, Howard University, New York University, University of Pennsylvania, Princeton University, University of Michigan, Yale University, and many other top universities

Visit Vault at **www.vault.com** for insider company profiles, expert advice, career message boards, expert resume reviews, the Vault Job Board and more.

V∧ULT CAREER LIBRARY   37

Mattel, Inc.

333 Continental Boulevard
El Segundo, CA 90245
Phone: 310-252-3777
www.mattel.com

Recruiting E-mail:

MBAIntern@Mattel.com
UndergradIntern@Mattel.com

Mattel, Inc., (NYSE: MAT, www.mattel.com) is the worldwide leader in the design, manufacture and marketing of toys and family products, including Barbie®, the most popular fashion doll ever created. The Mattel family is comprised of such best-selling brands as Hot Wheels®, Matchbox®, American Girl® and Tyco® R/C, as well as Fisher-Price® brands (www.fisher-price.com), including Little People®, Rescue Heroes®, Power Wheels® and a wide array of entertainment-inspired toy lines. With worldwide headquarters in El Segundo, Calif., Mattel employs more than 25,000 people in 42 countries and sells products in more than 150 nations throughout the world. Mattel's vision is: the world's premier toy brands—today and tomorrow.

Osram Sylvania

100 Endicott Street
Danvers, MA 01923
Phone: (978) 977-1900
Leah Weinberg
Manager, Diversity Inclusion
www.sylvania.com/AboutUs/Diversity/
Recruiting E-mail: Diversity.recruiter@sylvania.com
www.sylvania.com/AboutUs/Careers

Osram Sylvania is honored to have received 2007 Best Diversity Company recognition. Affinity groups, a mentoring program, and strategic relationships with professional organizations and colleges all support Osram Sylvania's commitment to an inclusive environment where every talented individual can be proud to work.

Business schools Osram Sylvania recruits from: Bentley, GA Tech, Notre Dame, Ohio, Bryant, Penn State, UKY, UNH, Arizona State, Univ. of IL, Northeastern

MBA
ROTATIONAL
PROGRAMS

Visit Vault at **www.vault.com** for insider company profiles, expert advice, career message boards, expert resume reviews, the Vault Job Board and more.

VAULT CAREER LIBRARY 40

MBA Rotations

The internship after the first year of business school is a great opportunity for MBA students to experiment a bit and get a taste of a specific job or company. What if you're now in your second year and looking for your first position after business school, but still would like to try your hand at a variety of positions?

Some major employers provide rotational MBA hiring programs for new business school graduates that provide just this opportunity. MBAs who join rotational programs are hired into a specific function such as finance or marketing, but then can rotate through different specialties within the broader function (for example, treasury vs. risk management in finance). Rotations also allow for new MBA hires to gain experience with different business units at a large organization.

The following Vault Q&As will help give you a sense of how some of these rotational programs work.

Vault Q&A: Federico Sercovich, Citigroup

Upon graduating from the University of Maryland's Robert H. Smith School of Business in 2003, Federico Sercovich, joined Citigroup's rotational MBA Management Associate program with the company's North American credit card division. The program consists of two one-year rotations. Now finishing up his second rotation, he spoke with Vault about why he chose a rotational program and his experience with it.

Vault: Tell me a little bit about your pre-business school background.

Sercovich: I'm originally from Argentina. I spent four years doing marketing in Chile, in a variety of industries and functions within marketing. First I worked with the country's largest global advertising firm, BBDO, then at L'Oreal in brand management, then with B2B marketing for a smaller regional telecom.

Vault: Did you want to do a career change from marketing when you went to get your MBA?

Sercovich: Overall, the idea of doing the MBA was the opportunity to expand my skill set and move on to a more general management-oriented career path.

The management associate program at Citigroup allowed me—in a rather "safe environment"—to gain more experience in different business functions. While marketing is still my passion, I've expanded my skill base to achieve my long-term aspirations.

Vault: What do you mean by a "safe environment?"

Sercovich: You know it's a one-year term job, and so you get to learn a lot and to add value at the same time. However it's not something you will be doing for more than 12 months, it has a defined term, which allows you to go beyond your professional comfort zone

For example, during my current rotation which I'm finishing up this week, I'm in a CFO role supporting a new product function clearly outside my comfort zone. I was encouraged to take the risk and I've seen other people doing it and succeeding at it. The program gives you the opportunity to go ahead and do these kinds of things.

Vault: So tell me a little bit about the program and the rotations that you've done.

Sercovich: It's a two-year program, with two one-year rotations in different areas. My first rotation was in a marketing/strategy role in our merchant acquiring business. With that group, the customer is not the cardholder—unlike the rest of the North America Cards, it's merchants who want to take credit cards as payment instruments. During said rotation, I had the opportunity to leverage my B2B skills, and it provided me with a broad view of the payment landscape and the consumer's behavior at the point of sale.

Visit Vault at **www.vault.com** for insider company profiles, expert advice, career message boards, expert resume reviews, the Vault Job Board and more.

V∧ULT CAREER LIBRARY   **41**

Vault: Did you know that you were going to that type of position when you joined the management associates program?

Sercovich: I was actually first a summer associate during the summer between my first and second years of business school. I was in the e-business department, working with the strategic alliances team with various partners on different cross-sell initiatives.

At the end of the summer, at the end of my performance evaluation I was offered a position in the MA Program, which I happily accepted. The way it works—you know you have a job, but you initially don't know in which business you're going to be working. When it's closer to the point of joining, you start an interview process. You meet with different managers and network. I think it's pretty cool because you are completely in charge of your career choices—you get to decide for which opportunities you want to interview.

Vault: So what about your second rotation, your current role.

Sercovich: It's a CFO role in an area called cross-sell. I provide financial planning and analysis support for a new set of products under the umbrella of the alternate lending franchise. The products are unsecured personal loans.

These are new products, and this is a function I haven't been exposed to in my past. In this role, I do financial forecasting and profitability analyses, I have been solely in charge of the development of the 2006 financial plan for these products.

Vault: As a role outside of your "comfort zone" how have you found this experience?

Sercovich: Well, it's definitely stressful, but very exciting. The numbers I report roll up all the way to the CEO of Citi Cards and that's a big responsibility. The value I contribute to the business is clear and tangible.

Vault: So what are you drawing on to do your job, given that your background is in marketing?

Sercovich: It's part business school theory, part on-the-job training, and a lot of common sense. It's not rocket science—the math is fairly straightforward—but it was definitely a good challenge. I was able to put together from scratch the forecasting models for the business, which are now used every month.

Vault: Is there a formal mentorship program component to the program?

Sercovich: Last year, we joined the overall Citi Cards mentorship program, through which the MAs are paired up with a mentor who has been in the company for a while. But I think there is a huge component that is totally informal. As an MA, many doors are open, many times you can just call up a senior member of the organization and ask them for some time in their calendar. They are open to help you, and they give you wise career advice. It's sort of weird sometimes to be talking with these senior leaders who are dedicating part of their valuable time to giving career advice to a management associate.

Vault: So what will you be doing once you finish this rotation?

Sercovich: I have accepted a role in Citigroup International Cards, I will be working on strategic initiatives with different regions—global competitor analysis, different practices and products, taking a look at what's been successful in North America which could be rolled out elsewhere.

Vault Q&A: Rebecca Preston, Chevron

After graduating in 2001 with her MBA from the University of Michigan Business School, Rebecca Preston joined Chevron's finance MBA development program, one of several MBA hiring programs maintained by the company. After stints in London and Houston in a variety of roles, Preston returned to the company's corporate headquarters in California to oversee the program. She talked to us about the program, which has been around for close to 60 years.

Vault: How many MBAs does Chevron hire a year?

Preston: For the finance program, we just increased the target this year. Historically it's been six to eight and it's now eight to 10. The HR program does about four, the marketing program hires about four, supply and trading out of Houston hires about three, global gas is considering starting and MBA program, and procurement hires in the neighborhood of four. Every group has MBA summer interns. Finance has also increased its intern target, from six to eight; the other programs do between two and four.

Vault: How long has the finance MBA program been running?

Preston: The program started in 1946. We'll be 60 years old next year. The other programs are more recent.

Vault: I'd imagine that would mean that a lot of the company's leaders have come through the program.

Preston: Yes. The former chairman came through the program. The current vice chairman is off the program, our head of international upstream (exploration and production), vice president of government and public affairs, and our CFO are all program alumni. The finance heads for major strategic business units are off the program; the comptroller, the treasurer, they're all from the program.

Vault: Is there any crossover between the various MBA programs in terms of rotations?

Preston: Not in terms of rotations. Functionally the programs are quite different. However, we do some joint events. Typically these would be around general industry or company knowledge. For example, we bring in external instructors— last week we had a geophysics professor, Dr. Hines from University of Tulsa, lecture about topics from how the earth was formed and how oil was created through to drilling and production of resources. It's a very complex industry, so getting fluency outside of your discipline is important.

Vault: In what types of roles and locations are incoming MBA hires for the finance program placed?

Preston: I've got eight people coming in this year. Six are starting here in California, two are overseas...

Vault: You're already sending them overseas for their first positions?

Preston: These two are returning interns. If they've had an internship at HQ and so grounding with us, we're comfortable in sending them overseas right off the bat. One's in Aberdeen [Scotland] in the North Sea, and another's in Singapore with our treasury function. The international component is increasingly important.

Vault: How long is the program and how many rotations do employees do?

Preston: It's a two-year program. They do three or four rotations. Domestic rotations are typically six months long. Sometimes the international assignments will be longer, and someone may elect to do three rotations with a longer, more in-depth experience overseas. This is particularly true of people who have interned here. Other people might feel strongly they need to see four different areas while on the program.

We always try to maximize the diversity of experience with different business units, and different finance functions. I get contacted from Chevron businesses all over the world looking for the talent. Every month I send out an update that shows where everyone in the program is in the company, and what opportunities have come in.

Visit Vault at **www.vault.com** for insider company profiles, expert advice, career message boards, expert resume reviews, the Vault Job Board and more.

VAULT CAREER LIBRARY 43

We encourage people to do a rotation outside of the finance discipline, too, and we have had many people cross over in past years.

Vault: What sort of rotations would they do outside of finance?

Preston: Typically people cross over into two areas: planning and business development. The planning roles are corporate strategy roles within the business units—developing the business plan, the strategic plan for the organization, within overall corporate strategy. The business development roles might be supporting commercial teams looking for new opportunities. For example, you might be supporting a team that's negotiating for new opportunities in Russia.

Vault: With the program having been in place for so long, there must be a lot of alumni from the program.

Preston: Yes. There are about 150 alumni and we've got a very active alumni network for the program. As the program manager I maintain all that information. We have two to three events a year that pull in all the alumni. We do a "family picnic" every year. We have a summer cocktail, where people meet the interns and the new hires. This year, the CFO was there, the head of investor relations was there, and other senior people. And every year we do the holiday luncheon and that pulls in all the alumni as well. These are typically in the Bay Area.

About a quarter of the alumni are international now. There are alumni in Moscow, Kuwait, London, Singapore, Scotland, Barbados, Beijing, Bogotá, Angola, Venezuela…

Vault: Is there any resentment among other finance professionals toward what might be thought of as an elite group?

Preston: There's definitely the risk of it becoming sort of an elitist group, and if that were to happen, the program would lose much of its effectiveness. But that hasn't happened because we're highly selective in who we bring in. Our industry is enormously complex, so you have to be humble and learn from the experienced people around you. You also have to be very capable so that you can take these learnings and produce superior results in a short period of time (six months or less for the rotations). Fit is very important—we have a highly collaborative and cooperative culture at Chevron.

Bringing in people with strong teamwork orientation, combined with demonstrated performance, means that rather than resentment, there's a lot of respect for the program and its members. They're able to perform at a high level quickly so people are clamoring for program members to work on their teams.

There's brisk, brisk demand for program graduates once their 24 months on the program is over. A big part of my job is matching the right opportunity with a program member's individual interests and development goals. It's quite common to move every 18 months to three years after you're off the program, because you're building up a broad base of experience.

Vault: Do most of the people who join the program have energy industry experience?

Preston: Not necessarily. I'd say it's less than a quarter that have direct industry experience, although a lot of them have technical backgrounds, such as engineering or geosciences. A lot of people have finance backgrounds or economics backgrounds.

Vault: But when interviewing, you're trying to make sure they are interested in the industry.

Preston: That's very important. In the first round for full-time hires, I spend almost all of the time trying to understand fit and motivation—is energy something they're passionate about? Will they thrive in our culture or clash with it? I then use the second round to push on the technical skills. Can they do the job? We're looking for every hire to be a career hire. We have 90 percent retention over 10 years. Fit and motivation is what's going to sustain you over the long run.

Vault: Is there a formal mentoring program?

Preston: We do not do a formal mentor matching in the finance program, but some of the other programs do. Instead, our alumni are very receptive to program members. I facilitate connections and our members find diverse and successful mentoring relationships that way. For interns we do match them with a "buddy," someone who's currently on the program and can help them evaluate us as a full-time employer.

INDUSTRY
OVERVIEWS

Visit Vault at **www.vault.com** for insider company profiles, expert advice, career message boards, expert resume reviews, the Vault Job Board and more.

VAULT CAREER LIBRARY 46

Aerospace and Defense

Industry Overview

The Wright stuff

The aerospace industry consists of companies that produce aircraft, spaceships and the jets, engines and rockets that propel them. The defense industry produces a complementary group of goods, including satellites, ships and submarines, tanks and armored vehicles, and guns, bullets, explosives and other weapons. These industries are closely allied, with companies frequently participating in both spheres.

The aerospace industry makes most of its money by supplying individuals and commercial airlines with planes for business or pleasure. The commercial airline industry is notoriously cyclical, operating at the mercy of the business cycle; factors like the price of airline tickets and terrorism (or the threat thereof) can also affect the number of people who travel by air—and hence the rate at which airline companies purchase new planes.

The lucrative nature of defense contracts shouldn't be underestimated, either: the U.S. government is planning to spend a whopping $480 billion on defense in 2008—give or take the odd hundred million allotted for special items during the year. Since making fighter jets and cargo planes doesn't require wildly different skill sets, and defense contracts are a generally recession-proof form of revenue, nearly all many aerospace and defense companies have arms that handle both commercial and military production. Major manufacturers of engines for planes include Pratt & Whitney, a subsidiary of United Technologies, Westinghouse and GE, Rolls Royce and Daimler-Benz, which put the vroom in more than just cars.

Take it to the skies

The commercial aircraft market is dominated by archrivals Boeing and Airbus, who also have interests in defense contracts—Boeing derived nearly half its revenue from government contracts in 2006, while archrival Airbus is partly owned by EADS, the European Aeronautic Defense and Space Company. Smaller players, like Textron (which owns Cessna), Embraer and Bombardier also have interests in both commercial and military aircraft and technology. Other major defense contractors include contract leader Lockheed Martin; and ship- and submarine-builder Northrop Grumman, General Dynamics, Raytheon, BAE Systems and United Technologies.

Plane dealing

The biggest rivalry in the industry is between U.S.-based Boeing and European-owned Airbus. These companies are the two largest suppliers of large jets to airlines, and the summer of 2007 saw them battling it out with their newest offerings. Airbus hopes to tempt buyers from the airlines that ferry large numbers of people between major airports with its A380, a double-decker plane of Brobdingnagian proportions. It seats 500 passengers, give or take, but has been plagued by problems with its assembly and wiring, which delayed its release by two years, driving Airbus into the red—and its customers to Boeing's offerings, like the proven 747, which seats about 400. Boeing's newest offering, the 787 Dreamliner, is set to debut in July 2007. The plane has been designed to ferry comparatively smaller numbers of passengers—only about half as many as the A380—but its carbon-composite construction offers several advantages. The plane is lighter, and hence more fuel efficient; the construction also means that the plane requires less maintenance and isn't as prone to metal fatigue—a boon to airlines, whose margins have been falling as customers become more savvy about comparison-shopping for tickets. The composite structure also means several passenger-pleasing features, like larger windows and higher cabin pressure and humidity. As of a few days before its official launch, the plane is the fastest-selling commercial airliner yet.

Visit Vault at **www.vault.com** for insider company profiles, expert advice, career message boards, expert resume reviews, the Vault Job Board and more.

VAULT CAREER LIBRARY 47

A new player enters the game

Boeing and Airbus may face a third competitor, however. China is reveling in its newfound industrial might, and plans to launch its own aircraft manufacturer. Already AVIC, the China Aviation Industry Corporation I, has produced the ARJ-21, a short-haul plane tailored to the vagaries of air travel in China that can carry about 80 people; it is scheduled to enter service in 2009. The Chinese government is loath to see its rapidly growing market for air transport—which is expected to create a demand for 1,500 planes by 2010—farmed out to foreign companies, however, and AVIC has its sights set on producing large jets for the international market.

DE-fence!

Speaking of international relations, the defense portion of the industry has been affected by a wave of large mergers, as well as a shift in the way wars are fought. The industry inked 350 deals worth some $40 billion in 2006, and by the first half of 2007 had already announced 225 deals worth $33 billion. Aside from all that getting and spending, the defense industry is also coping with changes in the methods of warfare. Modern battles are unlikely to be fought on a traditional battlefield against a professional army fielded by a government, and to be more like the agonizing and protracted conflict going on in Iraq and Afghanistan. Of course, this means that enormous tanks are out—and smaller, faster and lighter equipment is in. Automation is also a growing trend. Machines, unlike humans, never need to sleep or eat, are always paying attention, and can be easily repaired or replaced in the event they are damaged. In 2007, Honeywell's MAV (micro air vehicle) was sent to Iraq in order to help troops identify and defuse bombs and other threats. The device, which is about the size of a breadbox, consists of a fan in a cylindrical housing (which provides lift) as well as a small payload of wireless cameras and other sensors. The MAV can hover inches above a suspected bomb, allowing it to be more closely examined, or climb to about 10,000 feet for surveillance of a larger area. Remotely operated sensors are also the latest trend in border surveillance. In 2007, Boeing set up its first 27-mile stretch of monitored border between the U.S. and Mexico. Aimed at preventing smuggling and illegal immigration, the border security consists of a series of towers outfitted with radar, cameras, loudspeakers and data links. The towers are tall enough to see over trees and other obstacles, and allow rangers to monitor the movements of people as far away as several miles.

Spatial relations

Then, of course, there's space, the final frontier, which is soon to become as crammed with tourists as Times Square the weekend before Christmas. After Richard Branson, owner of a number of Virgin properties, announced that he would be offering space tours via Virgin Galactic in 2004, EADS Astrium, the space wing of the European defense giant, announced in 2007 that it would be offering 1.5 minute stints in a weightless environment for €200,000. The space ship, which has yet to be built, would take off like an ordinary jet before lighting its rocket.

More prosaically, most effort in the space division of aerospace is devoted to the design, launching and maintenance of satellites for GPS devices, communications, weather prediction and research, television and radio. Specialized leaders in this field include Alcatel Space, Astrium, Orbital Sciences and Arianespace, a division of EADS. Government and military demand for satellite bandwidth is expected to quadruple in the next decade—and, as such, the two groups (which can't seem to launch satellites fast enough) have been attaching their tech to civilian birds. Other companies involved in the sector include Boeing, Northrop Grumman and Lockheed Martin. Major aerospace and defense companies continue to build space activities into their long-term investment plans, even though shooting for the stars won't turn cash flow positive in any time frame outside of a science fiction novel.

Working in the Industry

According to the AIA (Aerospace Industries Association), in 2006, 630 million people were employed in the aerospace industry, and only about half of those jobs were in manufacturing. According to the Bureau of Labor Statistics, the aerospace industry has a higher-than-average number of people with advanced degrees in subjects like mechanical and electrical engineering. In addition to engineers, defense industry employers are perennially seeking employees with security clearances. In order to obtain one, an employer (either a corporation or the government) must sponsor an employee, who must be a U.S. citizen and submit to a thorough investigation of his background.

Giving the kids their wings

Companies are trying to recruit the latest crop of young'uns, as a quarter of their workforce will be ready to retire in 2008. In order to woo their newest hires, major aerospace firms like Boeing and Lockheed Martin are getting all Web 2.0. Boeing lured in potential job seekers with the promise of a shot at winning an iPod, as well as sponsoring a Facebook group for former interns. Lockheed, on the other hand, allows potential job seekers to IM recruiters, while Rolls Royce's engine department instituted a fast-track management program that will promote new hires into management positions after a few years.

Roger, niner

So you've electronically networked your way into an interview. Now what? Insiders report that questions include behavioral questions—"Tell me about a time when you were working in a group and something when wrong. What went wrong? What was your role in the situation? What was the outcome?"—while some engineers report being given technical questions to test their expertise: "Have you ever had to resolve a complex technical challenge without all of the necessary information? If so, how did you find out what you needed to know?" Companies can give as little as one interview, or as many as three and these vary from an informal chat on the phone with a recruiter to a panel interview. Another common question relates to the interviewee's eligibility for security clearance, a necessary attribute when working in some defense sectors. Only U.S. citizens can be granted security clearances, and must submit to having their backgrounds thoroughly searched in order to obtain it.

Looking up

In the long term, both the aerospace and defense industries are poised to grow. Worldwide air travel is forecast to increase to nine billion passengers by 2025—twice the number that fly the skies today, and someone's got to build all those planes. Growth in this sector might be tempered by an economic downturn in the U.S. or Europe, which still account for the majority of airline customers, but it will be tempered by expansion in Asia.

In addition, the debacle in Afghanistan and Iraq, not to mention the increase in religious fanaticism in general, is highly likely to produce a bumper crop of terrorists, so the defense industry looks as if it's got its hands full for the time being. The U.S. defense budget is up about 60 percent over its 2001 levels, and politicians are unlikely to reduce it lest they appear to be neglecting domestic security.

Visit Vault at **www.vault.com** for insider company profiles, expert advice, career message boards, expert resume reviews, the Vault Job Board and more.

V/\ULT CAREER LIBRARY   **49**

Employer Directory

Airbus
1, Rond point Maurice Bellonte
31707 Blagnac Cedex
France
Phone: +33-5-61-93-33-33
Fax: +33-5-61-93-49-55
www.airbus.com

Honeywell International Inc.
101 Columbia Road
Morristown, NJ 07962
Phone: (973) 455-2000
Fax: (973) 455-4807
www.honeywell.com/careers

BAE Systems
6 Carlton Gardens
London, SW1Y 5AD
United Kingdom
Phone: +44-1252-373232
Fax: +44-1252-383000
www.baesystems.com

General Dynamics Corporation
2941 Fairview Park Drive, Suite 100
Falls Church, VA 22042-4513
Phone: (703) 876-3000
Fax: (703) 876-3125
www.gendyn.com

General Electric Company
3135 Easton Turnpike
Fairfield, CT 06828-0001
Phone: (203) 373-2211
Fax: (203) 373-3131
www.ge.com

L-3 Communications Holdings
600 3rd Avenue
New York, NY 10016
Phone: (212) 697-1111
Fax: (212) 867-5249
www.L-3Com.com

Lockheed Martin
6801 Rockledge Drive
Bethesda, MD 20817-1877
Phone: (301) 897-6000
Fax: (301) 897-6704
www.lockheedmartin.com

Northrop Grumman Corporation
1840 Century Park East
Los Angeles, CA 90067-2199
Phone: (310) 553-6262
Fax: (310) 553-2076
www.northgrum.com

Parker Hannifin Corporation
6035 Parkland Boulevard
Cleveland, OH 44124-4141
Phone: (216) 896-3000
Fax: (216) 896-4000
www.parker.com

Raytheon Company
870 Winter Street
Waltham, MA 02451-1449
Phone: (781) 522-3000
Fax: (781) 522-3001
www.raytheon.com

Textron Inc.
40 Westminster Street
Providence, RI 02903-2596
Phone: (401) 421-2800
Fax: (401) 421-2878
www.textron.com

United Technologies Corporation
One Financial Plaza
Hartford, CT 06103
Phone: (860) 728-7000
Fax: (860) 728-7979
www.utc.com

Agriculture

Industry Overview

Feed me

The agriculture industry's broad scope includes everyone from farmers and ranchers to scientists who devise new and better foods and the businesspeople who keep it all running. The various disciplines within the industry seek ways to more efficiently feed Earth's ever-growing population while improving profit margins for food-related businesses. Allied industries provide the infrastructure that makes this possible, including rail and road transportation, pesticides and fertilizers, and processors that transform raw products into comestibles.

Looking at the numbers, the agriculture industry is a massive undertaking. In 2007, more than 90 million acres of land—an area slightly larger than that of Germany—were devoted to planting corn, with wheat production taking up 60 million acres. To feed the protein-ravenous masses, more than 125,000 cattle and 378,000 hogs are slaughtered every day in the U.S. Agriculture's not just about edibles, though; rather it covers everything that is grown or raised for consumption. Cotton and wool are agricultural products, as are animal byproducts, ornamental plants, tobacco, lumber and the various fruits and grains used to produce alcohol. The industry, unsurprisingly, is huge, accounting for 1 percent of U.S. gross domestic product (GDP). That might seem like small potatoes, but 1 percent of the 2006 GDP—$13,246,000,000,000—is a hefty chunk of change.

The farmer's dilemma

Despite its significant contribution to the GDP, agriculture is very risky and often unprofitable. Profit margins, especially for crops such as soybeans, wheat and corn, are very low, so these plants are frequently grown on large, industrial farms, as tiny returns per acre make small-scale farming economically unfeasible. Fruits and vegetables offer higher returns on lower acreage, but the investment in plants, soil preparation and the necessary labor-intensive harvesting makes the likelihood of farmers breaking even in the first few years unlikely.

Farmers are also at the mercy of pests, plant diseases and weather, the king of all X-factors. While insecticides and pest- and disease-resistant strains of plants can mitigate these risks, they of course cannot be entirely controlled. Heat, drought, flooding, storms and other "acts of God" wreak havoc on yields and, in extreme circumstances, can even lead to famine. The weather doesn't even have to be especially dramatic to drive up prices: the per-bushel cost of 2006 corn went gone up 28 percent, a two-year high, due to a hot, dry spell in the Midwest in July of that year.

Further complicating matters is the fact that commodities such as corn, soybeans and wheat are subject to market forces. To wit: A good harvest suppresses the price of a commodity and lowers profits, while a poor one raises prices but causes shortages. This inverse relationship between productivity and profit has plagued agribusiness for decades. Government subsidies for corn, wheat, milk, cotton and a number of other farm products also affect the equation. Designed to hedge risks and lessen farmers' financial burden, these subsidies keep agricultural commodity prices artificially low in domestic markets and around the world.

All of the issues detailed above have forced the consolidation of farms and processing firms. Today, the real players in the industry are all big companies, such as Cargill, Archer Daniels Midland, Tyson, Perdue, Bunge and Pilgrim's Pride. ConAgra, at one time a major farming firm, is currently divesting its agricultural business to focus on branded and value-added packaged foods. Meanwhile, Bayer, Dow and DuPont all have a stake in biotech, fungicides and pesticides, each with its own crop sciences division. Monsanto, meanwhile, is a leader in the genetic engineering field.

Visit Vault at **www.vault.com** for insider company profiles, expert advice, career message boards, expert resume reviews, the Vault Job Board and more.

VAULT CAREER LIBRARY   51

Little. Yellow. Different.

When you think of corn, what initially comes to mind is probably something edible: creamy corn on the cob dripping with golden butter, crisp, salty corn chips or sweet sodas. It's unlikely that you would consider postage stamps, aspirin or imitation silk, but all of these goods are manufactured using corn byproducts. Archer Daniels Midland is one of the largest agricultural processors in the world, turning oilseeds (like soybeans), corn, wheat and nuts into food products like flour, sweeteners and emulsifiers, as well as plant-derived wood preservatives, industrial starches (which become everything from wallboard to glue) and ethanol. Bunge is the world's largest processor of oilseeds, turning them into such products as biofuels, livestock meal and mayonnaise, while Cargill is a highly diversified agricultural products processor, making such items as soy waxes, vitamins, pharmaceutical coatings, flavoring agents, dairy and meat products.

Fueling a greener future

Demand for biofuel has made the past few years a boom time for corn producers like Archer Daniels Midland. Ethanol—the alcohol-based fuel produced from fermenting corn, beets, wheat, or any other sugar-bearing feedstock—has quickly become the poster child for America's solution to gas shortages and the greenhouse effect. Mixed with gasoline to create E85 (85 percent ethanol, 15 percent gasoline), ethanol promises to replace America's reliance on foreign oil with a renewable, homegrown resource. The flurry of activity around the hot new fuel has caused corn prices to spike and corn production to swell—farmers planted 92.9 million acres of corn in 2007, a high not reached since 1944, when 95.5 million acres of corn were planted to supply depleted allies in Europe.

Another biofuel seeing growth is biodiesel, which can be produced from vegetable oils, animal fat and even leftover, artery-clogging grease used in restaurants. In its purest form, biodiesel releases 75 percent less carbon dioxide than petroleum diesel. Additionally, there's no conversion or new technology involved to scare off new consumers—as long as it runs on diesel, it'll run on biodiesel. The growing popularity of biodiesel has increased demand for soybeans (whose oil is commonly used for biodiesel), as production of the fuel tripled from 2004 to 2005 alone, reaching 75 million gallons a year.

Bean there, done that

Biodiesel aside, soybeans have taken a bit of a beating as of late, due to the sudden and resounding condemnation of trans fats in American foods. The process of hydrogenation that soybean oil undergoes to lengthen its shelf-life (and that of the products it's used in, including some brands of crackers, cookies and fish sticks) produces the much-loathed trans fats, which are believed to clog arteries and raise cholesterol levels when consumed in excess. Fast food restaurants and junk food manufacturers are cutting trans fats out of their products in response to growing consumer concern and outright bans—like New York's December 2006 decision to cut trans fats from its restaurants. Soybean farmers are being pressured to grow beans low in linolenic acid (a substance that causes soybean oil to go rancid), thereby eliminating the need for hydrogenation while keeping the soybean oil flavor intact. However, the conversion to low-linolenic soybeans isn't far enough along to replace the traditional, high-linolenic beans, although production of the coveted bean is expected to triple in 2008.

Not exactly American Pastoral

You're in for a shock if "agriculture" brings to mind amber waves of grain and fruited plains. Rather, agribusiness is as tech-focused and cutting-edge as every other industry these days. Steroids, hormones and antibiotics, for example, are routinely administered to U.S. meat and dairy animals. Steroids up the rate at which meat animals transform feed into muscle, while hormones, when administered through slow-release pellets implanted in the animal's ear, cause it to gain weight and, in cows, improve milk production. Hormones are also applied to fruits and vegetables. In order to ship fruit long distances, it must be picked before it is fully ripe to withstand the trip. Once it reaches its destination, it is treated with ethylene, the chemical which, in nature, causes fruits to ripen.

Antibiotics are given to animals to cure illnesses—a frequent occurrence when stock is kept in close conditions and fed an unnatural diet. Modern poultry flocks, for instance, are so large that sick animals frequently cannot be isolated, so producers treat all the birds that may have come into contact with the infected individual by adding antibiotics to their drinking water. Feed lot-fattened, corn-fed cattle must be given antibiotics, too, lest the distress caused their digestive tracts by eating corn kill them. Antibiotics are more widely used in subtherapeutic doses, or doses not large enough to cure an infection, a practice that encourages the proliferation of antibiotic-resistant bacteria (much as with a human who takes antibiotics at the first sign of every sniffle). Without competition, resistant bacteria can spread rapidly throughout a population and subsequently be transferred to people who eat raw or undercooked meat.

Begun, this clone war has

Beyond antibiotics and hormones, recent biotech advances have become major issues in the agriculture industry. While farmers have been selecting crops for higher yield, greater disease resistance, better flavor and other desirable qualities for the last 12,000-odd years, we are now able to manipulate individual genes in order to express specific traits. Genetic engineering has produced Golden Rice, designed to accumulate vitamin A—insufficient quantities of which can cause blindness and even death in children—in the edible portion of the grain, a boon for cultures in which rice is the staple crop and a varied diet unassured.

Researchers are looking into growing oral vaccines for hepatitis B and HIV in tomatoes, potatoes and even tobacco. Embedding drugs in plants promises a less expensive method than traditional vaccine production, which would make large-scale vaccination of the populations of poorer countries possible. Genetic tinkering has produced plants such as Monsanto's Roundup Ready corn, canola, soybeans and cotton, and Bayer CropScience's Liberty Link corn, which are, respectively, resistant to the proprietary herbicides Roundup and Liberty. Today, nearly all soy and half of the corn grown in the U.S. is genetically modified, as is 75 percent of cotton.

Scientists are also beginning to explore these methods for use on animals, seeking to increase egg and milk production, change fat content and speed maturity. Genetically modified varieties of catfish and tilapia, designed to grow faster, are already for sale in some countries, while bulls are being cloned in order to improve the breeding stock of cattle. Pet fish implanted with genes that produce luminescent proteins have been available for purchase since 2003.

However, such tinkering has spawned a number of advocacy groups that fear unforeseen consequences. Many groups argue that direct genetic manipulation could produce harmful side effects that simple hybridization and crossbreeding would not, while others warn that herbicide residue might remain in the tissues of resistant plant varieties, or that engineered genes might cross into wild plant populations. Environmental advocacy groups won a small victory in March 2007, when a federal judge halted the planting of Monsanto's Roundup Ready alfalfa, on the grounds that the plant had not undergone complete environmental impact testing before its 2005 release. The debate rages on, on a global scale: Mexico barred biotech companies from planting genetically-modified corn within its borders in October 2006. That same month, Japan increased its testing of rice imported from the U.S., sniffing out unapproved genetically modified rice in the 1.1 million tons of short- and medium-grain rice in its warehouses.

The organic green giant

Consumers, motivated by concerns about the above, as well as factory farming, animal cruelty and the health of the environment, are increasingly demanding organic, ethically-treated, free-range, and antibiotic- and hormone-free food products. And apparently they are willing to pay the premium price: according to the Organic Trade Association, Americans spent $17 billion on organic products in 2006, an increase of 22 percent over 2005. That year, organics accounted for 2.5 percent of all retail foods sold.

Many businesses are taking advantage of this surge in organic interest. The supermarket chain Whole Foods, started in 1980 and one of the more popular purveyors of organic produce, has the highest profit margin per square foot of any grocery store. At the other end of the spectrum, Wal-Mart began offering organic products in 2006. While such produce's widespread availability will certainly have tangible benefits for the environment and for customers, there are some drawbacks. Faced

Visit Vault at **www.vault.com** for insider company profiles, expert advice, career message boards, expert resume reviews, the Vault Job Board and more.

VAULT CAREER LIBRARY

53

with price competition, retailers will inevitably demand lower prices from organic farmers, which could put them out of business. In addition, though organic produce can be sourced from foreign countries—China, for instance—regulations stipulating what "organic" means are certain to differ from country to country, or could even be absent altogether.

You just can't get good help these days ...

Despite the increasing reliance on machinery to do the grunt work of the agriculture industry, there are still some jobs that require that human touch. Unskilled migrant and immigrant laborers have provided this necessary muscle power for relatively low pay for decades, often filling positions that more prosperous Americans don't want. However, as the sanctity of the nation's borders has come to the fore in this era of homeland security, the agriculture industry has struggled to find and keep cheap labor. In December 2006, immigration raids at Swift & Company's meat processing plants (Swift is the third-largest meatpacker in the nation, behind Cargill and Tyson Foods) netted more than 1,200 illegal immigrants—the replacement of which, coupled with lost production, cost the company $45 million. A solution to the problem remains elusive; an immigration bill that would give illegal immigrants a chance to obtain legal status was defeated in the Senate in June 2007, making meatpackers and farmers worry about increased raids and dwindling applicants.

Picking up the bill

Every so often Uncle Sam takes a look at the current policies aimed at aiding the agriculture industry in the form of the highly contentious Farm Bill. The 2007 incarnation will determine the direction of the agriculture industry for the next five years, taking under its aegis a broad range of ag-related issues including genetic modification of crops, organic farming, nutrition and farm subsidies. Government subsidies have a big impact on the American diet, since subsidized crops are less risky for farmers to produce, and thus cheaper for consumers to buy. The ubiquity of junk food—with ingredient lists that are heavily based on wheat, soybeans, corn and corn-derived sugars and fats—can be directly linked to the subsidies handed out to (you guess it) corn, wheat and soybean farmers. Secretary of Agriculture Mike Johanns introduced farm bill proposals in February 2007 that would end subsidies to large farming corporations and provide incentives to small farmers, in addition to $7.8 billion devoted to conservation of the environment. While it remains to be seen if Congress will turn Johanns's suggestions into law, the debate around the 2007 Farm Bill will no doubt focus on diversifying the American food supply through a careful analysis of the current subsidy system.

Another bone of contention in the pending farm bill has to do with the influx of imported food. According to *The New York Times*, the U.S. is importing $65 billion in food a year, or double the amount it imported 10 years ago. Consumer groups want that imported food to be labeled as such, arguing that Joe American has a right to know from whence came his beef. Opponents (namely, the meat lobby) say that the cost of such labeling would overburden the industry, and have successfully limited such labeling to seafood despite 2002 legislation requiring country-of-origin labeling on meat, produce and nuts. However, in light of recent scares regarding imported foods—including the massive pet food recall in March 2007 due to tainted wheat gluten from China, and the subsequent closing of 180 Chinese food plants in June after a nationwide inspection—those calling for enforced labeling of imported food are likely to find more sympathetic ears in Congress, analysts say.

From farmhand to finance

An enormous range of man- and womanpower is required to keep the culture of agriculture humming along. The agriculture industry is exceptionally diverse when you consider the number of different segments it encompasses. Operations include fish hatcheries, apple orchards, flower nurseries, slaughterhouses and more. Farm workers (who account for 90 percent of industry employees) require minimal training, but the Bureau of Labor Statistics (BLS) expects that more efficient machinery will reduce the number of such jobs in the future. However, small-scale farming, especially of the organic variety, is expected to grow. Managers, meanwhile, include farm and ranch owners, as well as those who operate ripening facilities or cold storage. Agricultural graders sort products, such as fruits and eggs, and inspectors evaluate the cleanliness of processing facilities. These professionals generally require both an agriculture degree and a background in the field.

The agriculture industry has plenty of opportunities for those who want to avoid getting their hands dirty, as well. Commodities merchants are needed to buy and sell grain, cocoa and other articles of commerce to ensure a consistent supply. Ecologists consult for the farming world as consumers and the government grew more concerned about the environmental impact of factory farming on the land and ecosystems. Agronomists (researchers in the many disciplines involving agriculture) start at the bachelor's degree level, and many have doctorates to perform "pure" research. Logistics experts get the stuff from where it is to where it's going, while veterinarians keep the livestock healthy (until it's time to kill it). Along with the usual jobs in HR, sales and IT, lawyers and MBAs are needed to keep good business practices and make sure everyone plays by the rules.

Although agriculture has been around since, oh, say, the dawn of modern man, the industry is constantly trolling for advanced technologies and the scientists who create them. Chemists come up with coloring and flavoring agents and new uses for agricultural byproducts. Agricultural scientists devise new food-processing methods, study soil and animal management, and frequently consult for the government or food processing companies. Bioengineers tweak genetic codes to create herbicide-resistant plants, Mexican jumping beans that can do the Lindy hop, or whatever other special function is required of an organism. Agricultural engineers design farm equipment for increased efficiency and reduced environmental impact. Depending on the career path they wish to pursue, these people generally have advanced degrees. The BLS reports that the agricultural scientist and engineer industries, specifically, are expected to grow by 14 percent between 2004 and 2014.

Vault Q&A: Darryl Barbee, Archer Daniels Midland

As a product manager in Archer Daniels Midland Company's (ADM) Specialty Food Ingredients division, Darryl Barbee is responsible for shepherding new products through the development process. From ADM's headquarters in Decatur, Ill., Barbee spoke with Vault about his position.

Vault: Tell me a little bit about your position at ADM.

Barbee: I primarily work on new business development, looking at the possibility of new products in my division to see what will be profitable for the company. I'll perform market research, as well as find the current market price domestically and internationally. I take a look at competition. Also, as it is important to keep open lines of communication with our customers, I will go out on sales calls to see what ADM products are working best for them or what could be changed.

Vault: Who are these customers?

Barbee: Our division's customers are typically major baking and beverage companies. ADM products go into food, animal feed, fuel and industrial products, so as a company we have customers in all of those markets.

Vault: As a product manager, what types of positions are your main customer contacts?

Barbee: I interact with research and development, as well as purchasing. I speak with R&D to find out what their likes and dislikes are about the products. With purchasing, I discuss the price of our products.

Vault: Is there a particular product set you work on?

Barbee: Yes. They're called acidulants, which covers citric acid and lactic acid. These are additives that go into food and industrial products.

Vault: Tell me a little bit about your background. Where did you earn your MBA?

Barbee: I received my MBA from Indiana Wesleyan in Indianapolis in May 2002.

Visit Vault at www.vault.com for insider company profiles, expert advice, career message boards, expert resume reviews, the Vault Job Board and more.

VAULT CAREER LIBRARY   55

Vault: Was it a full-time or part-time program?

Barbee: It was part-time. At the time, I was working for a different company as a financial analyst. Once I earned my MBA, I joined ADM as an assistant product manager for lecithin, a release agent you can find in cooking spray and chocolates, among other things.

Vault: How did you end up transitioning from your finance background into your current position? Were you looking for a change?

Barbee: Actually, when I was in graduate school, one of my professors asked me what I was currently doing. As I told him I was in finance, he told me I was in the wrong profession, and that I needed to get in sales. When I joined ADM, that was the direction that I wanted to pursue. As a product manager, I'm not only in sales, but also using my finance background, as I'm working a lot with numbers—P&L's, etc. It was a perfect fit.

Vault: So what is the project cycle like? How long does it take to launch a new product?

Barbee: It takes about 18 months to two years to get a new product out.

Vault: And how many would you release in a year?

Barbee: I'd say about one. Products can be tweaked many different times before they are released. I would say, if you get one product out a year, you're doing a good job. There are usually about eight to 10 products in the pipeline.

Vault: Does your involvement with a product end once the product is approved?

Barbee: No. From there a plant is built, and while the plant is being built, I interact with the plant to make sure everything is OK. I keep track of the timeline and make sure we're keeping up.

I'm also working with R&D. I'm passing along information I am gathering from the customers about the product. Our main goal is to use our resources to help meet the needs of today and tomorrow for our customers.

I get R&D, sales, marketing and regulatory affairs together. We all make sure we're on the same page. With marketing, I'll assist in developing a brand, logo and sales literature as needed. I'll also work with marketing to talk to the trade publications to let them know we're coming out with a new product.

Vault: What is the most recent product you launched?

Barbee: Calcium citrate. It's used in orange juice, and it's also used in tablets.

Vault: What sort of classes from business school do you find most helpful with what you're doing right now?

Barbee: I would probably say marketing and finance. Also, just being a leader in a group. My cost accounting skills definitely play a huge role in launching a new product. You're looking at estimating packaging costs, what type of packaging, how much do we need to start off with. You're doing this all without any preexisting data, so my MBA, maybe more than anything else, has given me the confidence to handle those challenges managing a new product as opposed to managing a product that's already on the market.

Vault: How do you find working for a large employer like ADM?

Barbee: ADM is a Fortune 50 company, so when I talk to people about working for ADM, they know I am working for a large, successful company. ADM tends to attract and hire the best people.

There are also benefits working at the headquarters of a large organization. There's a gym on site that's free to all employees, their spouses and dependents. At that wellness center, there is also a medical facility with an on-site doctor that employees can use.

Employer Directory

Archer Daniels Midland Company (ADM)
4666 Faries Parkway
P.O. Box 1470
Decatur, IL 62525
Phone: (217) 451-4906
www.admworld.com/naen/careers

Associated British Foods plc
Weston Centre, 10 Grosvenor Street
London, W1K 4QY
United Kingdom
Phone: +44-20-7399-6500
Fax: +44-20-7399-6580
www.abf.co.uk

Bunge Limited
2 Church Street
Hamilton, HM 11
Bermuda
Phone: (914) 684-3300
Fax: (914) 684-3295
www.bunge.com

Cargill
15407 McGinty Road West
Wayzata, MN 55391
Phone: (952) 742-7575
Fax: (952) 742-7393
www.cargill.com

ConAgra Foods, Inc.
1 ConAgra Drive
Omaha, NE 68102-5001
Phone: (402) 595-4000
Fax: (402) 595-4707
www.conagra.com

Corn Products International, Inc.
5 Westbrook Corporate Center
Westchester, IL 60154
Phone: (708) 551-2600
Toll Free: (800) 443-2746
Fax: (708) 551-2570
www.cornproducts.com

Perdue Farms Incorporated
31149 Old Ocean City Road
Salisbury, MD 21804
Phone: (410) 543-3000
Fax: (410) 543-3292
www.perdue.com

Pilgrim's Pride Corporation
4845 US Hwy. 271 North
Pittsburg, TX 75686-0093
Phone: (903) 855-1000
Fax: (903) 856-7505
www.pilgrimspride.com

Smithfield Foods, Inc.
200 Commerce Street
Smithfield, VA 23430
Phone: (757) 365-3000
Fax: (757) 365-3017
www.smithfieldfoods.com

Tate & Lyle PLC
Sugar Quay, Lower Thames Street
London, EC3R 6DQ
United Kingdom
Phone: +44-20-7626-6525
Fax: +44-20-7623-5213
www.tate-lyle.co.uk

Tyson Foods, Inc.
2210 W. Oaklawn Drive
Springdale, AR 72762-6999
Phone: (479) 290-4000
Fax: (479) 290-4061
www.tysonfoodsinc.com

Visit Vault at **www.vault.com** for insider company profiles, expert advice, career message boards, expert resume reviews, the Vault Job Board and more.

VAULT CAREER LIBRARY 57

Brand Management/Consumer Goods

Functional Overview

What is a marketer? The allure of brand management

Marketing encompasses a wide variety of meanings and activities. Some marketing positions are very close to sales, while others set overarching marketing strategy. What marketing positions have in common is the sense of ownership over the product or service, as well as the need to understand customer needs and desires and translate those needs into some kind of marketing communication, advertising campaign or sales effort. The manager of product or service marketing is called the brand manager—he or she is the ruler of that marketing universe.

Careers within the marketing/branding arena are high profile. The business world is now realizing that strong brands and solid marketing programs drive shareholder value, and that companies can no longer make fundamental strategy decisions without truly understanding how to market a product. Today's business challenges—the quest for company growth, industry consolidation and deregulation, economic webs and the emergency of new channels and technologies—make marketers even more valuable.

The titles of brand manager, product manager and, to a lesser extent, marketing manager are often used to describe the same function—some companies use one title, others use another. Marketing manager tends to be used in industries other than consumer packaged goods; product manager is often used in tech industries. "Brand management" implies more complete supervision of a product. The typical brand management framework gives a brand "group" or "team"—generally comprised of several assistant brand or assistant marketing managers and one supervising brand manager—responsibility for all matters relevant to their product or products. Whether this responsibility is in fact complete depends somewhat on the size of the company relative to the number of brands it has, the location of the brand group, and most importantly, on the company's attitude toward marketing.

How important is the individual brand manager?

Consider the company to determine the level of brand manager responsibility. The first factor: the size of the company relative to its number of brands. For a company with hundreds of different brands—Nabisco, for example—brand managers, or even assistant brand managers, may have a great deal of power over a specific brand. At companies with a few core products, brand managers will focus on narrower aspects of a brand. As one assistant brand manager at Coca-Cola comments: "They're not going to take an MBA and say, 'Okay, you're in charge of Sprite.'" Brand managers at such companies will instead be focused on marketing to a particular demographic or geographic group, or perhaps handling one aspect of the product's consumption (plastic bottles, cases of aluminum cans, and so forth).

International brand managers have historically held more sway than managers in the company's home market, but keep in mind that the daily tasks of international brand managers often lean more toward questions of operations, rather than questions of strategy or marketing. ("How much should we produce?" or "How is our distribution network affecting sales?" rather than "What do we want our brand identity to be?") International brand management is sometimes split into two positions. Global brand managers are more strategic, concentrating on issues such as protecting brand equity and developing product offerings that can be rolled out into subsidiaries. Local brand managers are more tactical. Local managers focus on executing global plans that are delivered to them, and tweak them for local consumers. Also know that with the increasing trend toward globalization and the truly global presence of certain brands, companies have sought to impose more centralization and tighter controls on the marketing of those brands from country to country. In the past, individual country

Visit Vault at www.vault.com for insider company profiles, expert advice, career message boards, expert resume reviews, the Vault Job Board and more.

VAULT CAREER LIBRARY 59

managers have had more discretion and leeway to make decisions about a brand's packaging, advertising, etc. Now, companies have established tighter guidelines on what can be done with regard to a brand around the world, with the goal of protecting and enhancing the value of the brand and ensuring a consistent product and message worldwide.

Finally, consumer goods companies place varying levels of importance on their brand or marketing departments. Some companies, such as the Ford Motor Company, are driven as much by financial analyses of production costs or operations considerations as by marketing. The level of emphasis on finance or operations matters at a firm will influence not only the independence and authority of marketing managers, but also potential marketing career paths. At some companies, marketing is the training ground for general management. At General Mills, marketing is considered so important that employees in other functions who show promise are plucked from their positions and put into the department.

Careers in Marketing

Taking charge of a brand involves tackling many diverse job functions—and different subspecialties. Decide where you'd like your main concentration to lie.

Brand management

In a typical brand management organizational structure, positions are developed around responsibility for a particular product rather than a specific functional expertise (e.g., you're an assistant brand manager for Cheerios). This structure enables you to be the "master of all trades," acquiring an expertise in areas such as manufacturing, sales, research and development, and communications. In brand management, the marketing function is responsible for key general management decisions such as long-term business strategy, pricing, product development direction and, in some cases, profit and loss responsibility. Brand management offers a terrific way to learn intensively about a particular product category (you could be a recognized expert on tampons!) and to manage the responsibility of running a business and influencing its performance.

The core of brand work is brand strategy. Brand managers must decide how to increase market share, which markets and demographic groups to target, and what types of advertising and special promotions to use. And at the very heart of brand strategy is identifying a product's "brand identity." Brand groups then figure out how to exploit brand strategy or, in some cases, how to change it. PepsiCo's Mountain Dew has built the drink's popularity among youth as a high-caffeine beverage into a "brand identity" of cutting-edge bravado that has boosted market share, while the Banana Republic chain underwent a transformation from an outdoor adventure store that sold actual Army-Navy surplus to an upscale, chic clothing store. In both cases, the brands have benefited from a shift in brand identity and, consequently, a shift in their market. Brand identity is normally created and confirmed through traditional print, radio and TV advertising. Advertising is usually produced by outside agencies, although brand insiders determine the emphasis and target of the advertising.

Some liken a brand manager to a hub at the center of a hub and spoke system, with the spokes going out to departments like finance, sales, manufacturing, R&D, etc. It is the job of the brand manager to influence the performance of those groups— over whom he or she has no direct authority—in order to optimize the performance of his or her brand or product line.

Direct marketing

Ever wonder who is responsible for making those coupons you receive in the mail? Or the Saab videotape you've received every two years since you bought your car in 1993? You can thank direct marketers. Direct marketers are masters in one-to-one marketing. Direct marketers assemble databases of individual consumers who fit within their target market, go after them with a personal approach, and manage the production process from strategy inception to out-the-door distribution.

Direct marketers have two main objectives: to stay in touch with their current consumer base and to try and generate more business by finding individuals who fit a target set of criteria but are not currently using their particular product. For instance, if you've ever checked out of the supermarket and got a coupon for Advil after buying a bottle of Tylenol, chances are a direct marketer is trying to convince you to switch brands by offering you a monetary incentive.

It's important to note that direct marketing isn't just through snail mail. It operates in multiple media such as the Web, telemarketing and in-store promotions. Direct marketers have a powerful new tool in their arsenal—the Internet. Marketers are able to track the online habits and behavior of customers. They can then serve up customized banner advertisements that are much more likely to be relevant to them. Many consumers have agreed to receive promotional offers on certain subjects—marketers can then send them targeted e-mail messages that allow for much easier access to purchase or action (a click on a link, for example) than a conventional mail direct marketing programs.

Affiliate/property marketing

If you're working with a major brand company like Nike, Disney, Pepsi, or L'Oreal, chances are you'll do a lot of cross-promotion, or "affiliate marketing." For instance, Nike has marketing relationships with the NBA, NFL, and a variety of individual athletes and athletic teams. Disney has a strong relationship with McDonalds; cute toys from the entertainment company's latest flick are often packaged with McDonalds Happy Meals upon the release of each new movie. L'Oreal works with celebrities like Heather Locklear and sponsors events such as the annual Academy Awards.

Marketers must manage the relationship between any two entities. If Disney wants to promote the cartoon du jour with McDonalds, or Pepsi wants to make sure that all Six Flags theme parks have a Pepsi Ride, then marketers ensure both parties are getting what they need out of the deal and staying true to their own brand image.

Price marketing/sales forecasting

Pricing is largely driven by market pressure. Most people, for example, won't pay more than $2.00 for a hamburger in a fast food restaurant. On the other hand, brand managers always have some pricing leeway that can greatly affect market share and profitability. An increase of a nickel in the price of a product sold by the millions can make huge differences in revenue—assuming the price rise doesn't cause equivalent millions less of the products to be sold. Brand managers need to figure out the optimal pricing strategy for their product, though it's not always a case of making the most money. Sometimes it makes more sense to win market share while taking lower profits. How do brand managers justify their prices? Through extensive research. Paper towels, for example, may be much more price-sensitive than a luxury item like engagement rings or foie gras.

Brand and marketing managers don't always have free reign over pricing. At some companies, such as those that sell largely through mail order, or those with complex pricing systems, pricing and promotional offers may be limited to what the operational sales system can handle. Explains one marketing manager at a long-distance phone company (an industry with notoriously tangled pricing plans): "It's very easy to offer something to the customer. It's very difficult to implement that in the computer system."

Another large part of the general management duties of brand managers is forecasting product sales. This means not only keeping track of sales trends of one's product, but anticipating responses to marketing campaigns and product launches or changes. The forecasts are used to determine production levels. Once a year, brand groups draw up budgets for their production, advertising and promotion costs, try to convince the finance folks that they absolutely need that amount, get less than they ask for, and then rework their budgets to fit the given budget. As one international brand manager at one of the world's biggest consumer goods companies puts it: "You don't determine the production and then get that budget; you get the budget, and then determine the production."

Visit Vault at **www.vault.com** for insider company profiles, expert advice, career message boards, expert resume reviews, the Vault Job Board and more.

V∆ULT CAREER LIBRARY   **61**

High-tech marketing

Not everyone markets applesauce for a living. Many people choose to enter the world of high-tech marketing because they want to work with products and technologies that reshape and improve the word around us. These marketers feel that they would rather change the way a person interacts with the world in a sophisticated way, rather than spend time understanding what hair color teenagers find most appealing. High-tech marketers spend much of their time understanding research and development issues and working on new product launches.

Technology companies like Intel, Dell and Microsoft have recognized the power of branding and are utilizing traditional marketing tactics more and more. Amazon's extensive marketing campaign in 1998 helped brand that company in the mind of consumers still new to e-commerce as the company to purchase books (and other products) online. Intel became perhaps the first semiconductor company readily identifiable to the public through its heavily branded "bunny people." Marketing in the high-tech world will continue to grow in importance over the next decade, as technology companies become more consumer-oriented (see Microsoft's X-Box). Marketing a service or software product versus a more tangible product is a bit different. It may be a bit more challenging to understand how consumers relate to the product. Inventory and distribution issues may be tracked differently.

Market research

If you are an analytical person who enjoys numbers and analysis, and enjoys tracking consumer behavior, then market research may be the field for you. A product is much more effective when a company understands the consumer it is targeting. That's where market researchers come in. Market researchers employ a variety of different qualitative and quantitative research techniques to understand consumers. Surveys, tracking systems, focus groups, satisfaction monitors, psychographic and demographic models, and trial/repurchase estimations are all methods researchers use to understand how consumers relate to their products. Researchers who find that consumers associate lemon scents with cleanliness, for example, may suggest that cleansers could drive up sales by adding a lemon aroma.

Marketing consulting

Although most well-known consulting firms are known for their expertise in general strategy, many consulting firms now hire industry or functional experts that focus on marketing issues. These firms need people with expertise in the areas of branding, market research, continuous relationship marketing, pricing strategy and business-to-business marketing—they tend to hire people with previous marketing experience and value consultants who have been successful marketing managers and have lived through the full range of business issues from the inside. McKinsey and Monitor are two general strategy firms that have begun to hire marketing specialists. Other boutique marketing consulting firms, such as Kurt Salmon, focus on certain product categories like beverages, health care and retail. Major ad agencies are also attempting to reinvent themselves as marketing partners focused on marketing strategy beyond simple advertising.

A Day in the Life: Assistant Brand Manager

You can often spot the assistant brand manager because they are the ones running around like a chicken with its head cut off. You must learn how to balance your time and prioritize. Here's a look at how your time might be spent:

Responsibilities	% of time per day
Meetings	30%
Analysis/data tracking	30%
Writing memos	30%
Answering management queries	30%
Interfacing with other departments	30%
Actually marketing	Optional

Although this is a humorous take on the day of an ABM (talk about giving 150 percent), there is some truth to it. Days and weeks will go by where you feel like you've just been pushing paper and trying to stay afloat. It is very easy to get comfortable maintaining the businesses rather than creating new opportunities. Although the role of an ABM is mostly one of maintenance, if you want to be a "star," you must shape your brand, not just maintain it.

A more realistic look at a day in the life of a brand manager

8:30 a.m.: Get into work. Listen to voicemails. Check e-mails. Print out calendar of today's events. Skim the markets section of *The Wall Street Journal* to find out what's happening "on the street." Go to the cafeteria and grab breakfast. (Of course, you're only eating products that your company produces or has some relationship with!)

9:00 a.m.: Meet with market research department to discuss specifics of your latest round of quantitative research. You are trying to understand why people are not repurchasing your product, but you don't feel that the data presented actually answers your questions. You decide that you'll need to design another round of research—but where's the money going to come from?

10:00 a.m.: Budget meeting to determine how you will be spending second quarter funds. Given the decision to spend more money on research, you might need to cancel an instant redeemable coupon or a local promotion in a poorly performing market.

10:30 a.m.: You head to the long-awaited product development meeting. Your team has recently discussed reformulating your product to take advantage of new technology. This new technology may raise your product's performance levels, but it will cost more to manufacture and will take some advertising effort (and more money) to explain the changes to the consumer. The group must decide whether these changes are strategically and financially justified. As always, very few people agree. You decide to summarize all the costs and benefits to the project and present the issues to your brand manager at the status meeting you have scheduled for the end of the day.

12:00 p.m.: A fancy lunch with a *People* magazine salesperson. For months the magazine has tried to convince you that your product should be advertised in *People*. During lunch, the represenative explains to you how the publication can effectively reach 18 percent of your target audience and how it can provide you with the extended reach you need to communicate with potential new users. You leave lunch with a fancy *People* backpack and a headache. Where can you find the money to add *People* to your media plan? Let's ask the media department (Note: While lunch with ad reps happens occasionally, the days of most brand managers are packed, without the time to spend schmoozing with ad reps. More often, brand managers, who are very focused on their jobs, grab lunch at a corporate cafeteria and take it back to their desks.)

1:30 p.m.: Media planning meeting. Because sales of your product have come in slightly under budget, you have been forced to give up 10 percent of your media budget. You now must meet with the media department to determine how to cut media

Visit Vault at **www.vault.com** for insider company profiles, expert advice, career message boards, expert resume reviews, the Vault Job Board and more.

V∧ULT CAREER LIBRARY   63

funds without sacrificing your goals (to reach 20 percent of your target group, and to have a continuous presence on TV). Maybe you can cut out two weeks of TV advertising in July when not many people are home anyway. But isn't that your product's peak purchase cycle? Decisions, decisions.

2:30 p.m.: Time to review changes to the latest advertising campaign. Your ad agency presented a new concept about three weeks ago that needed work. You and your brand manager made comments to the storyboard (a drawing that explains a commercial) and now you are anxious to see what the agency has produced. You review the changes with the agency via conference call and promise to present the new work to your brand manager at your status meeting later in the day.

3:15 p.m.: Keep the ad agency on the phone and bring in the in-house promotions department. This ad campaign will be introduced into a promotional campaign in the top-20 performing markets in the country. You want to make sure that before you get the promotions people working on a concept, they agree with the agency on the strategy going forward. The following 45 minutes is a creative brainstorming session that offers wonderful possibilities. You promise to type all ideas up and distribute them to the group later in the week.

4:00 p.m.: Strategy development with sales manager. Your category manager is insisting that all brands work to gain a better presence in supermarkets. You meet with the regional sales manager to understand what types of strategies might work to get better shelf space and more consistent in-store promotions. Once you hear his ideas, you start to price options and see if this is possible within your (reduced) current budget.

5:00 p.m.: Status meeting with brand manager. You present your proposal for increased research expending as well as the implications of the new product development issue. You also review the latest advertising changes and the changes to the media plan. You aggressively present your data and your opinion, and discuss these with your boss. The two of you decide on the next steps.

6:00 p.m.: End of the day. You spend an hour checking the 23 e-mail/voicemail messages you received during the day but failed to return. You go through your "inbox" to read any documents relevant to your product. You start to attack all of the work you have to do and promise that tomorrow you'll block out some time to make some progress.

Employer Directory

Campbell Soup

1 Campbell Place
Box 35D
Camden, NJ 08103
Recruiting Contact Phone: (856) 968-4362
careers.campbellsoupcompany.com

Campbell Soup Company is a global manufacturer and marketer of high quality soups, sauces, beverages, biscuits, confectionery and prepared food products. The company owns a portfolio of more than 20 market-leading businesses, each with more than $100 million in sales. They include Campbell's soups worldwide, Erasco soups in Germany, Liebig soups in France, Pepperidge Farm cookies and crackers, V8 vegetable juices, V8 Splash juice beverages, Pace Mexican sauces, Prego Italian sauces, Franco-American canned pastas and gravies, Swanson broths, Homepride sauces in the United Kingdom, Arnott's biscuits in Australia and Godiva chocolates worldwide.

At Campbell, we define diversity as the vast array of human differences and similarities, inclusive of everyone. In order to compete and succeed in a changing marketplace we must cultivate and embrace a diverse employee population that fuels our growth and enriches our global culture.

As part of our Campbell's Vision, "Together We Will Do Extraordinary Things in the Workplace and Marketplace," our commitment to building and strengthening teams has the greatest focus of our leadership. We must have diverse perspectives, talents and teams to meet this business challenge. You won't find a better place for your talent, ideas and experience than at Campbell Soup Company.

Business schools Campbell recruits from

University of Pennsylvania (Wharton School), University of Maryland (Robert H. Smith School), University of North Carolina (Kenan-Flagler School), Cornell University (Johnson School), University of Michigan (Ross School of Business), University of Virginia (The Darden School), Carnegie Mellon University (The Tepper School)

Procter & Gamble

1 P&G Plaza
Cincinnati, OH 45202
Phone: (888) 486-7691
E-mail: careers.im@pg.com
www.pg.com/Careers

Three billion times a day, P&G brands touch the lives of people around the world. Our company has one of the strongest portfolios of trusted, quality, including Pampers®, Tide®, Ariel®, Always®, Whisper®, Pantene®, Mach3®, Bounty®, Dawn®, Pringles®, Folgers®, Charmin®, Downy®, Lenor®, Iams®, Crest®, Oral-B®, Actonel®, Duracell®, Olay®, Head & Shoulders®, Wella, Gillette® and Braun. The P&G community consists of almost 140,000 employees working in almost 80 countries worldwide.

P&G embraces the principles of personal integrity, respect for the individual and doing what's right for the long term. We recognize our consumers, brands and employees as the pillars of our business.

Business schools Procter & Gamble recruits from

Various Schools throughout the United States.

Visit Vault at **www.vault.com** for insider company profiles, expert advice, career message boards, expert resume reviews, the Vault Job Board and more.

VAULT CAREER LIBRARY   65

Employer Directory, cont.

3M Company
3M Center
St. Paul, MN 55144
Phone: (651) 733-1110
Fax: (651) 733-9973
www.3m.com

adidas AG
Adi-Dassler-Straße 1
91074 Herzogenaurach
Germany
Phone: +49-9132-840
Fax: +49-9132-84-2241
www.adidas-group.com

Anheuser-Busch Companies, Inc.
1 Busch Place
St. Louis, MO 63118
Phone: (314) 577-2000
Fax: (314) 577-2900
www.anheuser-busch.com

Cadbury Schweppes plc
25 Berkeley Square
London, W1J 6HB
United Kingdom
Phone: +44-20-7409-1313
Fax: +44-20-7830-5200
www.cadburyschweppes.com

Callaway Golf Company
2180 Rutherford Road
Carlsbad, CA 92008
Phone: (760) 931-1771
Fax: (760) 930-5015
www.callawaygolf.com

Campbell Soup Company
1 Campbell Place
Camden, NJ 08103-1799
Phone: (856) 342-4800
Fax: (856) 342-3878
www.campbellsoup.com

The Clorox Company
1221 Broadway
Oakland, CA 94612-1888
Phone: (510) 271-7000
Fax: (510) 832-1463
www.thecloroxcompany.com

The Coca-Cola Company
1 Coca-Cola Plaza
Atlanta, GA 30313-2499
Phone: (404) 676-2121
Fax: (404) 676-6792
www.thecoca-colacompany.com

Coach, Inc.
516 West 34th Street
New York, NY 10001-1394
Phone: (212) 594-1850
Fax: (212) 594-1682
www.coach.com

Colgate-Palmolive Company
300 Park Avenue
New York, NY 10022
Phone: (212) 310-2000
Fax: (212) 310-2475
www.colgate.com

Columbia Sportswear Company
14375 NW Science Park Drive
Portland, OR 97229-5418
Phone: (503) 985-4000
Fax: (503) 985-5800
www.columbia.com

E. & J. Gallo Winery
600 Yosemite Boulevard
Modesto, CA 95354
Phone: (209) 341-3111
Fax: (209) 341-3569
www.gallo.com

Eastman Kodak Company
343 State Street
Rochester, NY 14650
Phone: (800) 698-3324
Fax: (585) 724-1089
www.kodak.com

The Estée Lauder Companies Incorporated
767 5th Avenue
New York, NY 10153-0023
Phone: (212) 572-4200
Fax: (212) 572-6633
www.elcompanies.com

Ethan Allen Interiors Incorporated
Ethan Allen Drive
Danbury, CT 06811
Phone: (203) 743-8000
Fax: (203) 743-8298
www.ethanallen.com

General Electric Company
3135 Easton Turnpike
Fairfield, CT 06828-0001
Phone: (203) 373-2211
Fax: (203) 373-3131
www.ge.com

General Mills, Inc.
1 General Mills Boulevard
Minneapolis, MN 55426
Phone: (763) 764-7600
Fax: (763) 764-7384
www.generalmills.com

H.J. Heinz Company
600 Grant Street
Pittsburgh, PA 15219
Phone: (412) 456-5700
Fax: (412) 456-6128
www.heinz.com

Employer Directory, cont.

Hasbro, Inc.
1027 Newport Avenue
Pawtucket, RI 02862
Phone: (401) 431-8697
Fax: (401) 431-8535
www.hasbro.com

The Hershey Company
100 Crystal A Drive
Hershey, PA 17033-0810
Phone: (717) 534-4200
Fax: (717) 534-6760
www.hersheys.com

J. Crew Group, Inc.
770 Broadway
New York, NY 10003
Phone: (212) 209-2500
Fax: (212) 209-2666
www.jcrew.com

Johnson & Johnson
1 Johnson & Johnson Plaza
New Brunswick, NJ 08933
Phone: (732) 524-0400
Fax: (732) 524-3300
www.jnj.com

Kellogg Company
1 Kellogg Square
Battle Creek, MI 49016
Phone: (269) 961-2000
Fax: (269) 961-2871
www.kelloggcompany.com

Kimberly-Clark Corporation
351 Phelps Drive
Irving, TX 75038
Phone: (972) 281-1200
Fax: (972) 281-1490
www.kimberly-clark.com

Kraft Foods Inc.
3 Lakes Drive
Northfield, IL 60093
Phone: (847) 646-2000
Fax: (847) 646-6005
www.kraft.com

L'Oréal SA
41 rue Martre
Clichy, 92117
France
Phone: +33-14-756-7000
Fax: +33-14-756-8002
www.loreal.com

L'Oréal USA
575 5th Avenue
New York, NY 10017
Phone: (212) 818-1500
Fax: (212) 984-4999
www.lorealusa.com

Levi Strauss & Co.
1155 Battery Street
San Francisco, CA 94111
Phone: (415) 501-6000
Fax: (415) 501-7112
www.levistrauss.com

Liz Claiborne, Inc.
1441 Broadway
New York, NY 10018
Phone: (212) 354-4900
Fax: (212) 626-3416
www.lizclaiborneinc.com

LVMH Moët Hennessy-Louis Vuitton SA
22 Avenue Montaigne
75008 Paris
France
Phone: +33-1-44-13-22-22
Fax: +33-1-44-13-21-19
www.lvmh.com

Matell, Inc.
333 Continental Boulevard
El Segundo, CA 90245-5012
Phone: (310) 252-2000
Fax: (310) 252-2179
www.mattel.com

McDonald's Corporation
1 Kroc Drive
Oak Brook, IL 60523
Phone: (630) 623-3000
Fax: (630) 623-5004
www.mcdonalds.com

Miller Brewing Company
3939 West Highland Boulevard
Milwaukee, WI 53201-2866
Phone: (414) 931-2000
Fax: (414) 931-3735
www.millerbrewing.com

Molson Coors Brewing Company
311 10th Street
Golden, CO 80401-0030
Phone: (303) 279-6565
Fax: (303) 277-5415
www.molsoncoors.com

Nestlé SA
Avenue Nestlé 55
Vevey, 1800
Switzerland
Phone: +41-21-924-2111
Fax: +41-21-924-4800
www.nestlé.com

NIKE Inc.
1 Bowerman Drive
Beaverton, OR 97005
Phone: (503) 671-6453
Fax: (503) 671-6300
www.nike.com

Nintendo Co., Ltd.
11-1 Kamitoba Hokotate-cho Minami-Ku
Kyoto 601-8501
Japan
Phone: +81-75-662-9600

Nintendo of America Incorporated
4820 150th Avenue NE
Redmond, WA 98052
Phone: (425) 882-2040
Fax: (425) 882-3585
www.nintendo.com

Visit Vault at **www.vault.com** for insider company profiles, expert advice, career message boards, expert resume reviews, the Vault Job Board and more.

VAULT CAREER LIBRARY   67

Employer Directory, cont.

Nokia Corporation
Keilalahdentie 2-4
P.O. Box 226
FIN-00045 Nokia Group
Finland
Phone: +358-7180-08000

Nokia Americas
6000 Connection Drive
Irving, TX 75039
Phone: (972) 894-5000
www.nokia.com

PepsiCo, Inc.
700 Anderson Hill Road
Purchase, NY 10577
Phone: (914) 253-2000
Fax: (914) 253-2070
www.pepsico.com

Polo Ralph Lauren Corporation
650 Madison Avenue
New York, NY 10022
Phone: (212) 318-7000
Fax: (212) 888-5780
www.polo.com

The Procter & Gamble Company
One Procter & Gamble Plaza
Cincinnati, OH 45202
Phone: (513) 983-1100
www.pg.com

Quiksilver, Inc.
15202 Graham Street
Huntington Beach, CA 92649
Phone: (714) 889-2200
Fax: (714) 889-3700
www.quiksilverinc.com

Reebok International Ltd.
1895 J.W. Foster Boulevard
Canton, MA 02021
Phone: (781) 401-5000
Fax: (781) 401-7402
www.reebok.com

Revlon, Inc.
237 Park Avenue
New York, NY 10017
Phone: (212) 527-4000
Fax: (212) 527-4995
www.revlon.com

Royal Philips Electronics, N.V.
Breitner Center, Amstelplein 2
1096 BC Amsterdam
The Netherlands
Phone: +31-20-597-7777
Fax: +31-20-597-7070
www.philips.com

S.C. Johnson & Son, Inc.
1525 Howe Street
Racine, WI 53403
Phone: (262) 260-2000
Fax: (262) 260-6004
www.scjohnson.com

Sony Corporation
6-7-35 Kitashinagawa
Shinagawa-ku
Tokyo 141-0001
Japan
Phone: +81-3-5448-2111
Fax: +81-3-5448-2244
www.sony.net

The Timberland Company
200 Domain Drive
Stratham, NH 03885
Phone: (603) 772-9500
Fax: (603) 773-1640
www.timberland.com

Unilever plc
Unilever House
PO Box 68 Blackfriars
London, EC4P 4BQ
United Kingdom
Phone: +44-20-7822-5252
www.unilever.com

Unilever USA
700 Sylvan Avenue
Englewood Cliffs, NJ 07632
Phone: (201) 894-7760
www.unileverusa.com

Whirlpool Corporation
2000 North M-63
Benton Harbor, MI 49022-2692
Phone: (269) 923-5000
Fax: (269) 923-5443
www.whirlpoolcorp.com

Wm. Wrigley Jr. Company
410 North Michigan Avenue
Chicago, IL 60611
Phone: (312) 644-2121
Fax: (312) 644-0015

Energy/Oil and Gas

What is the Energy Sector?

The energy sector produces, converts and distributes fuels to produce heat, light and propulsion. Oil, natural gas and coal are burned to make heat and electricity. Wind, flowing water and sunlight are converted into electricity. Oil is refined to propel cars, planes and industrial machines. And to achieve these things, the companies who are producing, transporting, converting and distributing these energy sources are supported by a variety of service firms, investors, equipment providers and government regulators.

There is a great divide in the energy sector between the oil and gas "side" and the electricity "side," each of which accounts for about half of the business jobs across the sector. "Oil and gas" refers to the exploration for and extraction and processing of oil and natural gas. In contrast, the electric power business revolves around converting fuel to electricity in power plants and distributing that electricity to consumers. The economics of the two fields, and the regulations that govern them, are quite distinct. Generally, people make their energy careers in one camp or the other, without too much crossover. Natural gas is one arena that bridges the oil and gas versus electricity divide—it is extracted from the earth together with oil, and is also a primary fuel for generating electricity.

When people refer to the "energy sector," they can actually mean any of the following: electric power, oil and gas, or both together. This guide takes a broad view of the industry, covering upstream (exploration), midstream (refining) and downstream (distribution and sales) oil and gas activities, electric power generation and transmission, equipment manufacturing, regulatory oversight, and lending to, investing in and advising companies involved in the sector.

Just how big is the industry that comprises all those diverse activities? Companies in the energy sector take in nearly $1 trillion in revenue annually, out of the $17 trillion earned by all U.S. businesses. Energy-related businesses employ about 2.5 million people, or 2 percent of the U.S. workforce—far more than banking, high tech or telecommunications. Energy companies as a whole employ a high percentage of production workers (the people who drive local utility repair trucks, laborers on oil rigs and gas station attendants), compared to other industries; of the 2.5 million energy jobs in the U.S., about 90 percent of them are blue-collar jobs or technical positions. But there are 250,000 energy-related business jobs out there: business analysts, finance associates, marketing managers, economic modelers and operations consultants, to name a few roles.

Energy sector positions capture about 2 percent of new MBA graduates, an amount roughly proportional to the industry's size. In contrast, the investment banking and investment management sectors together capture 40 percent of graduates, and consulting absorbs another 20 percent Even the significantly smaller high-tech industry takes on three times the number of new MBAs as does the energy sector. What this means for you as a job seeker is that the energy sector is not as dominated by people with graduate business degrees as some other popular arenas. There is plenty of opportunity for smart, well-trained college graduates to rise through the ranks without going back to school.

Sector	US employees in managerial, business or financial positions
Pharmaceuticals and biotechnology	50,000
Telecommunications	140,000
High technology	200,000
Banking and investment management	250,000
Energy	***250,000***
Consulting	500,000
Entire economy	11,500,000

Visit Vault at **www.vault.com** for insider company profiles, expert advice, career message boards, expert resume reviews, the Vault Job Board and more.

VAULT CAREER LIBRARY   69

Which Job Function?

In order to pursue a job in the energy sector, your first decision is what type of position you want—in other words, what functional role you want to play. Your function has a lot more impact on the nature of your job than does the type of company in which you work.

You can have a wide variety of business jobs in the energy sector:
• Asset development
• Corporate finance
• Quantitative analytics, risk management
• Trading, energy marketing
• Investment analysis
• Consulting
• Business development
• Banking
• Strategy and planning
• Economics and policy analysis

Different companies can have widely varying names by which they refer to these roles. For example, "marketing" in one company involves advertising and product promotion, whereas "marketing" in another can mean commodities trading. Similarly, "business development" can be more akin to sales in one company, or synonymous with strategic planning in another.

What Type of Company?

Job functions and company types intersect in numerous ways—for example, you can do corporate finance in a large oil company or with a small fuel cell manufacturer, or choose between asset development and trading within a given utility. Below, we have summarized the characteristics of each of the major energy sector employer types.

Oil companies

Oil companies engage in exploration and production of oil ("upstream" activities), oil transportation and refining ("midstream"), and petroleum product wholesale and retail distribution ("downstream"). The largest companies, known as the "majors," are vertically integrated, with business operations along the entire spectrum from exploration to gas stations. Smaller oil companies, known as "independents," are often exclusively involved in exploration and production. Upstream is considered the glamorous place to be, where all the big decisions are made. Upstream jobs also involve heavy international work, with many employees sent off to new postings around the world every three years or so. We should also note that E&P businesses are fairly similar in nature among oil companies and companies mining other natural resources like uranium or coal—moving among these types of firms during a career can be a logical path.

The majors are known for excellent rotational training programs, and a fair number of people take advantage of those programs and then jump over to independents for good salaries. Oil companies pay well in general, but jobs are not necessarily as stable as one might think. When oil prices drop, company operating profits are dramatically impacted, and layoffs are fairly common. American oil jobs are overwhelmingly concentrated in Houston. International hotspots include London, Calgary and the Middle East.

Some oil companies focus exclusively on midstream and downstream activities. They operate refineries to distill crude oil into its many commercially useful petroleum derivatives, like gasoline, jet fuel, solvents and asphalt. Refineries are, in theory, built to last 40 years, but some have been around for as long as 80 years. That means that new refineries are rarely built, and the refinery business is mostly about managing the razor-thin margins between purchased crude oil inputs and revenue from refined product outputs.

Oil services companies

Oil services companies provide a very wide range of outsourced operational support to oil companies, such as owning and renting out oil rigs, conducting seismic testing and transporting equipment. The fortunes of these companies follow the price of oil: when oil is expensive, oil companies drill a lot and make a lot of money, so business volume and revenue increase for their oil services contractors. Working for an oil services company probably means working in Texas or internationally, and can feel very much like working for an oil company, given the similarity in issues and activities.

Pipeline operators

Pipeline operators own and manage tens of thousands of miles of petroleum products and natural gas pipelines. Many of them also operate oil intake terminals, engage in commodities trading and energy marketing, and own natural gas storage facilities or petroleum refineries as well. Unlike the major oil companies, pipeline operation companies are not household names—nonetheless, the largest ones take in several billion dollars in annual revenue, comparable to the scale of a medium-sized oil company.

Utilities

Utilities are, by definition, located all over the country—everyone has to get their electricity and gas from somewhere, of course. However, as a result of massive consolidation among utility holding companies, the corporate offices for your local utility may not necessarily be that local. There are presently about 50 investor-owned utilities in the country, but industry insiders predict that in a few years mergers may leave us with as few as 10. The "graying" of the utility industry is a well-documented trend; 60 percent of current utility employees are expected to retire by 2015—meaning there's lots of opportunity today for young job seekers.

"Utility" is actually a loose term that we use to succinctly refer to gas utilities and all types of power generation companies: investor-owned utilities, government-owned utilities, municipal power companies, rural electric co-ops, and independent power producers (IPPs) or non utility generators (NUGs). Utilities differ greatly in terms of their lines of business: some have sold off most of their generation assets and are primarily distribution companies with power lines as their primary assets; others may own large amounts of regulated power plants, and may also own nonutility generators or individual independent power plants. As the electricity market fell apart starting in 2001, most IPPs sold off their assets piecemeal to large utility holding companies or financial institutions.

Transmission grid operators

Transmission grid operators, known as independent system operators (ISO) or regional transmission operators (RTO), provide a power generation dispatch function to a regional electricity market. They don't own the transmission lines, but coordinate how much power is generated when and where, such that supply and demand are equal at every moment. This is an extremely complex process, and necessitates the analytical skills of electrical engineers and other generally quantitative and analytical operations staff.

Visit Vault at **www.vault.com** for insider company profiles, expert advice, career message boards, expert resume reviews, the Vault Job Board and more.

VAULT CAREER LIBRARY   71

Equipment manufacturers

Equipment manufacturers make turbines, boilers, compressors, pollution control devices, well drilling and pipeline construction equipment, software control systems, pumps and industrial batteries. Many of them also provide engineering services and construction/installation of their equipment. The major gas turbine manufacturers, for example, also offer engineering, procurement and construction of entire power plants. Oil-related equipment makers are often characterized as "oil services" firms (above). The equipment manufacturers in the energy industry are not particularly concentrated in one geographic area, though of course many of the oil business-oriented ones have major offices in Texas.

Investment funds

Investment funds are a diverse bunch: mutual funds private equity funds and hedge funds. As a whole, the investment fund world is fairly concentrated in Boston, New York and San Francisco, but there are small funds dotted all over the country as well.

Mutual funds hire stock analysts primarily out of MBA programs to track, value and recommend stocks in a particular sector (e.g., energy, natural resources, consumer products) to the fund managers. However, there are a lot of other finance-related positions inside these massive firms where undergrads are sought after as well.

The number of hedge funds in the U.S. has been growing at a phenomenal rate in the past few years, but they are still notoriously difficult places to get jobs. Hedge funds often hire people out of investment banking analyst programs. They tend not to hire people out of the mutual fund world, given that their valuation approach is so different, their investing horizon is so much shorter, and their orientation many times is towards short-selling as well as buying stocks. While some hedge funds may focus exclusively on energy, most are generalist and opportunistic with respect to their target sectors.

Private equity funds invest money in private (i.e., not publicly traded) companies, often also obtaining operating influence through a seat on the portfolio company's board of directors. As a result, an analyst's work at a private equity fund is vastly different from that at a mutual fund or hedge fund. You are not following the stock market or incorporating market perception issues into your valuations and recommendations; instead, you are taking a hard look at specific operating issues, identifying concrete areas where the portfolio company can lower costs or enhance revenue. A few private equity firms specialize in energy investing, and many more do occasional deals in the energy space as part of a broader technology or manufacturing focus. Private equity firms hire just a few people straight out of college or MBA programs, and many others from the ranks of investment banking alumni.

Banks

Banks are primarily involved in lending money to companies, but they also have their own trading operations, private wealth management and investment analysis groups. Commercial and investment banks arrange for loans to energy companies, as well as syndicate loans (i.e., find other people to lend the money) for them. Investment banks manage IPOs and mergers and acquisitions (M&A) activities as well. The banking world is overwhelmingly centered in New York (and London), with some smaller branches in Chicago and San Francisco.

Consulting firms

Consulting firms offer rich opportunities for those interested in the energy industry. Consulting on business issues (rather than information technology or technical, scientific issues) is done at three types of firms: management consultancies, risk consulting and economic consulting shops. Consulting firms are often interested in hiring people with good functional skills rather than requiring specific industry expertise, and provide a broad exposure to energy sector business issues, as well as good training. Business consulting firm offices are located in most major cities, but much of the energy sector staff may be located in Houston, Washington, D.C., and New York.

Nonprofit groups

Nonprofit groups are tax-exempt corporations (pursuant to IRS code 501(c)3) engaged in issue advocacy or public interest research. Advocacy groups may focus on developing grassroots support for public policy changes, publicizing public interest issues or problems through direct actions, or working to influence politicians to enact or change legislation. Most of the energy-related advocacy groups focus on environmental topics, though some also cover corporate financial responsibility and investor protection issues. Think tanks are public policy research institutes, staffed mainly by PhDs who generate research and opinion papers to inform the public, policy-makers and media on current issues. Interestingly, the think tank is primarily a U.S. phenomenon, although the concept is slowly catching on in other countries. Some think tanks are independent and nonpartisan, whereas some take on an explicit advocacy role. Nonprofits are funded by individual donations and grants from foundations, and accordingly a substantial portion of their staffs are dedicated to fund raising. Most energy nonprofits are based in Washington, D.C., where they have access to the federal political process, but many of them have small regional offices or grassroots workers spread out across the country.

Government agencies

Government agencies at the federal and state levels regulate the energy markets and define public energy and environmental policy. Federal agencies are mostly located in Washington, D.C., and each state has staff in the state capital. Jobs can include policy analysis, research project management or management of subcontractors. The energy agencies tend to hire people with environmental or engineering backgrounds, and are lately following a policy of hiring people with general business and management education and experience.

Energy services firms

Energy services firms help companies (in any sector) reduce their energy costs. Working for an energy services firm is similar in many respects to consulting—except that you go much further down the path of implementation. Typically, an energy services firm first conducts an energy audit to understand where a company spends money on energy: electricity, heat and industrial processes. Then, the firm actually implements energy-saving measures "inside the fence" of the client company. This can involve investments and activities such as putting lightbulbs on motion sensors, upgrading the HVAC (heating, ventilation, air conditioning) system, negotiating better rates with the utility suppliers or developing a cogeneration power plant adjacent to the factory. Often, the energy services firm receives payment for these services in the form of a share in the net energy cost savings to the client. These firms are located across the country, with a few of the largest clustered in Boston.

Visit Vault at **www.vault.com** for insider company profiles, expert advice, career message boards, expert resume reviews, the Vault Job Board and more.

V∧ULT CAREER LIBRARY   **73**

Job Function	Possible Employer Types
Asset Development	Utility; Oil Company; Pipeline Operator; Energy Services Firm
Corporate Finance	Utility; Pipeline Operator; Oil Company; Equipment Manufacturer
Quantitative Analytics, Risk Management	Utility; Oil Company; Transmission Grid Operator; Pipeline Operator; Investment Fund; Bank
Trading, Energy Marketing	Utility; Oil Company; Pipeline Operator; Investment Fund; Bank
Investment Analysis	Investment Fund; Bank
Consulting	Consulting Firm; Oil Services Company
Business Development	Equipment Manufacturer; Utility; Oil Services Company; Pipeline Operator; Energy Services Firm
Banking	Bank
Strategy and Planning	Utility; Oil Company; Pipeline Operator; Oil Services Company; Equipment Manufacturer
Economic and Policy Analysis	Government Agency; Nonprofit Group; Consulting Firm

Who Gets Hired?

As in other technology-intensive sectors, the energy sector is populated by a disproportionate number of people with technical degrees (e.g., BS, MS, or PhD in engineering, hard sciences and math). Whether it's true or not, traditional energy company employers often feel that success in a job correlates to having a certain degree. This pickiness about your undergraduate major or master's degree field gets even stronger during economic downturns, when companies act more conservatively and have more bargaining power in terms of new hires.

In many energy jobs, the prevalence of people with technical pedigrees is somewhat a function of self-selection; individuals interested enough in the energy sector to make it their career were usually also interested enough in related topics to focus on them academically. On top of that, the prevalence of technical people is also self-reinforcing; in other words, engineers like to hire other engineers. There is also arguably an element of reality underpinning the preference for people with certain academic backgrounds—engineers communicate best with other engineers, and have proven in school that they can learn the ins and outs of a complex subject area.

This tendency is most characteristic of hiring preferences among oil companies, oil services firms, refineries, pipelines, grid operators, equipment manufacturers, energy services companies and utilities. These firms want to hire people who have their heads around how their technologies work—people who can master the jargon quickly, and who can fit into their culture. Even for their MBA hires, these companies often look for technical undergraduate degrees or pre-MBA work in energy or another technical field.

However, there are certainly many people with liberal arts backgrounds doing great work at these types of companies. A nontechnical degree does not in any way shut you out of any energy sector career path; it simply makes you slightly more unusual in the eyes of some interviewers. If you can craft a compelling story about why you are passionate about and deeply understand the energy world, your degree becomes far less relevant. In addition, if you are applying for a finance, economics or accounting job with a degree in those fields, you are also less subject to scrutiny about your knowledge of geology, electrical engineering or chemistry. Once you have a couple years of experience in the industry, that serves as a degree equivalent and you will have established your credibility.

Many of the service jobs in energy are interested in simply hiring smart people who demonstrate an ability to learn a new industry quickly. Energy consulting, banking and investing jobs often screen for nothing different than their counterparts in other industries. Similarly, the newer, alternative energy companies are often heavily filled with people who studied liberal arts, economics and government in college. These companies are progressive in terms of their business strategies, and usually this comes across in their approach to hiring as well. In addition, nonprofits typically first look for passion and commitment to advocacy work before they look for technical background.

Where you're coming from

Apart from academic background, traditional energy employers are also keenly interested in people who have a strong connection to the geographic region in which the company is located. These companies like to hire for the long term, so will often grill out-of-state candidates about why they would want to move to, for example, Houston or Atlanta. This can mean that, for a Houston oil company position, an MBA from Rice is a more attractive candidate than one from Wharton.

In fact, the energy sector offers particularly rich opportunities for students from second-tier undergraduate and graduate schools. Energy companies know that their industry is not typically considered as hot and glamorous as some other industries, and they can therefore often be skeptical about recruiting from name-brand undergraduate and graduate schools. The bottom line is that energy, as an industry, is simply less hung up on name-brand schools than some other industries, e.g., consulting, law and banking.

Moreover, during the past few years of our sluggish economy, many traditional energy companies tightened their recruiting budgets and reduced focus on first-tier schools—at the same time as service companies like consulting and banking firms reacted to a slow economy by canceling recruiting at second-tier schools and concentrating on only a limited set of top schools. Of course, those in the know are well aware that the energy sector is one of the most intellectually challenging, influential arenas in which to work! If you want to work in the sector, you can certainly seek out the energy employers, regardless of whether they visit your campus or target people from your alma mater.

In general, the best time to jump into the energy sector is right out of undergraduate or graduate (MA/MS, MBA or PhD) school. Like most employers, energy companies expect less in the way of industry experience from people who have just graduated, so it's a good time to get your foot in the door of a new field. Lateral hires of people a few years out of college or post-MBA are relatively rare, unless you have some specific industry background or functional experience a company needs. For example, a pipeline company might realistically hire someone with a couple years of general banking experience into a corporate finance role, but would be very unlikely to hire someone with a couple of years of, say, real estate experience into that same role—so if you had just graduated and never spent those couple of years in real estate, you'd have a better shot at the job.

This reluctance to hire laterally from other industries is far less common in the services sector (consulting, banking, investing, nonprofits). These employers are more interested in functional knowledge and pure brainpower, rather than a track record in one particular industry or another (though they have their own intransigence about hiring people laterally from other functional areas, i.e., it's awfully hard to get into consulting or banking if you don't do so your first year out of school). As a result, these jobs are an excellent way to get into the energy sector, and offer lots of options down the road—in other words, for example, it's relatively easy to go from an energy consulting role into a corporate job at other energy firms.

One caveat for those who move from one firm to another to position themselves for a future job: traditional energy employers like stability. If you have a lot of different jobs on your resume, you should make sure to have a good story to explain the necessity of your job-hopping, and why you are long-term play for the company (whether you truly are or not). This is true when interviewing with any firm, but large, traditional energy firms are certainly more sensitive to the issue.

Visit Vault at **www.vault.com** for insider company profiles, expert advice, career message boards, expert resume reviews, the Vault Job Board and more.

V\ULT CAREER LIBRARY   **75**

Employer Directory

Alliant Energy Corporation
4902 North Biltmore Lane
Madison, WI 53718
Phone: (608) 458-3311
Fax: (608) 458-4824
www.alliantenergy.com

American Electric Power Company, Inc.
1 Riverside Plaza
Columbus, OH 43215-2372
Phone: (614) 716-1000
Fax: (614) 716-1823
www.aep.com

Anadarko Petroleum Corporation
1201 Lake Robbins Drive
The Woodlands, TX 77380-1046
Phone: (832) 636-1000
Fax: (832) 636-8220
www.anadarko.com

Baker Hughes Incorporated
2929 Allen Parkway, Suite 2100
Houston, TX 77019-2118
Phone: (713) 439-8600
Fax: (713) 439-8699
www.bakerhughes.com

BP p.l.c.
1 St James's Square
London, SW1Y 4PD
United Kingdom
Phone: +44-20-7496-4000
Fax: +44-20-7496-4630
www.bp.com

Chevron Corp.
6001 Bollinger Canyon Road
San Ramon, CA 94583
Phone: (925) 842-1000
Fax: (925) 842-3530
www.chevrontexaco.com

ConocoPhillips Company
600 N. Dairy Ashford
Houston, TX 77079
Phone: (281) 293-1000
Fax: (281) 293-1440
www.conocophillips.com

Consolidated Edison, Inc.
4 Irving Place
New York, NY 10003
Phone: (212) 460-4600
Fax: (212) 982-7816
www.conedison.com

Duke Energy Corporation
526 S. Church Street
Charlotte, NC 28202
Phone: (704) 594-6200
Fax: (704) 382-3814
www.duke-energy.com

Eaton Corporation
Eaton Center
1111 Superior Avenue
Cleveland, OH 44114-2584
Phone: (216) 523-5000
Fax: (216) 523-4787
www.eaton.com

Edison International
2244 Walnut Grove Avenue
Rosemead, CA 91770
Phone: (626) 302-1212
Fax: (626) 302-2517
www.edison.com

Exelon Corporation
10 S. Dearborn Street, 37th Floor
Chicago, IL 60680-5379
Phone: (312) 394-7398
Fax: (312) 394-7945
www.exeloncorp.com

Exxon Mobil Corporation
5959 Las Colinas Boulevard
Irving, TX 75039-2298
Phone: (972) 444-1000
Fax: (972) 444-1350
www.exxonmobil.com

FirstEnergy Corp.
76 S. Main Street
Akron, OH 44308
Phone: (800) 646-0400
Fax: (330) 384-3875
www.firstenergycorp.com

GE Energy
4200 Wildwood Parkway
Atlanta, GA 30339
Phone: (678) 844-6000
Fax: (678) 844-6690
www.gepower.com

Halliburton
5 Houston Center
1401 McKinney, Suite 2400
Houston, TX 77020
Phone: (713) 759-2600
Fax: (713) 759-2635
www.halliburton.com

Hess Corporation
1185 Avenue of the Americas
New York, NY 10036
Phone: (212) 997-8500
Fax: (212) 536-8593
www.hess.com

Marathon Oil Corporation
5555 San Felipe Road
Houston, TX 77056
Phone: (713) 629-6600
Fax: (713) 296-2952
www.marathon.com

Employer Directory, cont.

Occidental Petroleum Corporation
10889 Wilshire Boulevard
Los Angeles, CA 90024
Phone: (310) 208-8800
Fax: (310) 443-6690
www.oxy.com

Pacific Gas and Electric Company
77 Beale Street
San Francisco, CA 94177
Phone: (415) 973-7000
Fax: (415) 267-7268
www.pge.com

Schlumberger Limited
5599 San Felipe, 17th Floor
Houston, TX 77056
Phone: (713) 513-2000
www.slb.com

Shell Oil Company
One Shell Plaza
910 Louisana Street
Houston, TX 77002
Phone: (713) 241-6161
Fax: (713) 241-4044
www.shellus.com

Sunoco, Inc.
1735 Market Street, Suite LL
Philadelphia, PA 19103-7583
Phone: (215) 977-3000
Toll Free: (800) 786-6261
Fax: (215) 977-3409
www.sunocoinc.com

Valero Energy Corporation
One Valero Place
San Antonio, TX 78249
Phone: (210) 345-2000
Toll Free: (800) 531-7911
Fax: (210) 345-2646
www.valero.com

The Williams Companies Inc.
One Williams Center
Tulsa, OK 74172
Phone: (918) 573-2000
Fax: (918) 573-6714
www.williams.com

Visit Vault at **www.vault.com** for insider company profiles, expert advice, career message boards, expert resume reviews, the Vault Job Board and more.

VAULT CAREER LIBRARY   77

Fashion

Fashion and the MBA

Like the entertainment industry, the fashion industry considers education to be less important than experience. So, if you want to go into the industry but don't have the previous experience, get a part-time job in sales or merchandising for an introduction to the industry. Unfortunately, most companies won't care much about your MBA unless it's a large corporation, such as Gap, Levi Strauss, Eddie Bauer, Limited or Nike. These companies tend to hire for finance, supply chain issues or CRM. Typically, you need a consulting, finance or marketing background to get a post-MBA job in the industry. Very few apparel companies have established programs to specifically hire MBAs. A few companies that do hire MBAs for the more creative positions include Cartier, LVMH, Federated and the Gap.

Hillary Shor recruits for the strategy and business development and consulting and assurance services groups of Gap, Inc. These groups are relatively small (about 20 to 30 people per group). Almost all candidates have an MBA, although many are not hired directly as MBA graduates. Shor says, "We actually look at what a candidate did prior to business school. The Strategy and Consulting groups look for candidates with consulting or industry experience (such as consumer products, goods or retail). Some of our candidates come from consulting firms such as A.T. Kearney and McKinsey."

The strategy and business development group at Gap identifies, develops and drives longer-term strategies and initiatives that will result in profitable growth (usually with a focus on new opportunities). "Strategy involves brand management, research, as well as planning," says Shor. Consulting and assurance services involves financial/operational analysis, process analysis and design and project management. Basically, this group acts as an internal consulting group for Gap. Team members may work with outside consultants and vendors.

Getting Hired

Build your resume correctly and you can get the interviews you need. In apparel, most of the job functions are very specific, such as design, merchandising, marketing, production and so on. Because many of the companies are small, there aren't very many traditional MBA "management" positions. Many of the people who work at these companies may have gone to trade schools or been in the industry for a long time. For example, the president of Gucci used to work as vice president at Richard Tyler. He was young when he left Richard Tyler for Gucci, but he had started working there when he was 18.

The Gap, Limited and Eddie Bauer all have internal consulting groups that traditionally hire MBAs. If you are interviewing for an internal consulting position, more than likely it will resemble a traditional consulting interview. You may be given a case study as part of the interview. (See the *Vault Guide to the Case Interview* for more information on this type of business interview.) Other jobs at fashion companies for MBA graduates may include planning, finance or strategy.

Pay and Perks

MBA jobs in the fashion industry will not pay well in comparison with other MBA graduate options. Salaries may hover around the $50,000 mark. There are two options here—you work to get the experience or to learn enough to start your own business. If you are thinking of the latter, gain experience that will help you manage your own business. For example, if you want to open your own jewelry store, get a job merchandising or selling jewelry. The best way to learn all sides of the business is to experience it yourself. The pay in the fashion industry is more negotiable than other industries. Most companies will not release this information and, because these jobs are not necessarily geared toward MBAs, the salaries are not standard.

Visit Vault at **www.vault.com** for insider company profiles, expert advice, career message boards, expert resume reviews, the Vault Job Board and more.

VAULT CAREER LIBRARY   79

Vault Profile: Judy Chang, Fashion MBA

Judy Chang graduated from the Anderson School at UCLA with a MBA in 2002. Her previous education included a BS and master's in industrial and operations engineering from the University of Michigan. After college, she worked as a program manager for DaimlerChrysler to coordinate the launch of a particular program in the automotive plants. Chang says, "I would work on program launches for each car model year and style (for specific windshield specifications). I came to Anderson knowing that I wanted to do something totally different." She also says, "If you really want to change careers, getting an MBA is essential. Without my MBA, I don't think I would have been able to switch careers successfully. Fashion companies would have looked at my resume and questioned my interest."

At the Anderson School, her emphasis was marketing, and it was the first time she began to seriously consider a fashion career. She had worked at Armani Exchange during college and enjoyed it—but didn't think that fashion would be a practical career choice. At Anderson, she joined the Fashion and Retail Association and began to do her research so that she could merge her interests and career goals. On campus, Macy's and Neutrogena came for interviews. Through the database, she found alumni and contacted them to speak about their experiences. Chang landed a summer internship in planning at Macy's West. She worked there for three months in the summer and is now there fulltime.

At Macy's West, Chang did two projects over the summer. (The department store Macy's is split into two regions and run completely separately. Macy's East is headquartered in NYC, while Macy's West is based in San Francisco.) To her surprise, Chang's operations experience was extremely relevant during the internship. Her first project was about handbag assortments. Her goal was to figure the optimum assortment level. She analyzed the number of styles bought for each cluster of stores, available table space for the handbags and discounted handbag sales versus regular stock. She used Macy's sales data as well as active visits to the Macy's floor to make her recommendations. Her second project was to standardize colors across a group of buyers. Each buyer used an individual color coding system. Macy's had no way of tracking sales by color or across categories. For example, although each buyer bought "red," each red item could be a completely different shade. Chang created a color tracking system that allowed the planners to analyze the sales by color and buyer. Macy's could now see which color sold during any a one-week period.

During her internship, Chang was excited to go to work every day (especially compared to her previous position). She found everyone to be supportive and very friendly. Macy's was a very different experience for her. Chang says, "At Macy's, it seemed like the workforce was 90 percent women and only 10 percent men. At DaimlerChrysler, I used to work with 90 percent men and 10 percent women. If there is something you really think will make you happy, you should do it—even in this difficult economy."

Employer Directory

Abercrombie & Fitch Co.
6301 Fitch Path
New Albany, OH 43054
Phone: (614) 283-6500
Fax: (614) 283-6710
www.abercrombie.com

Ann Taylor Stores Corporation
7 Times Square, 15th Floor
New York, NY 10036
Phone: (212) 541-3300
Fax: (212) 541-3379
www.anntaylor.com

The Body Shop International PLC
Watersmead
Littlehampton
West Sussex BN17 6LS
United Kingdom
Phone: +44-1-903-731-500
www.the-body-shop.com

Chanel S.A.
135, Avenue Charles de Gaulle
92521 Neuilly-sur-Seine Cedex
France
Phone: +33-1-46-43-40-00
www.chanel.com

Dolce & Gabbana SPA
Via Santa Cecilia, 7
20122 Milan
Italy
Phone: +39-02-77-42-71
www.dolcegabbana.it

Donna Karan International Inc.
550 Seventh Avenue
New York, NY 10018
Phone: (212) 789-1500
Fax: (212) 921-3526
www.donnakaran.com

Eddie Bauer, Inc.
15010 NE 36th Street
Redmond, WA 98052
Phone: (425) 755-6100
Fax: (425) 755-7696
www.eddiebauer.com

Estee Lauder Companies Inc.
767 Fifth Avenue
New York, NY 10153-0023
Phone: (212) 572-4200
Fax: (212) 572-6633
www.elcompanies.com

Gap Inc.
2 Folsom Street
San Francisco, CA 94105
Phone: (650) 952-4400
Fax: (415) 427-2553
www.gapinc.com

Guess?, Inc.
1444 S. Alameda Street
Los Angeles, CA 90021
Phone: (213) 765-3100
Phone: (213) 744-7838
www.guess.com

J. Crew Group Inc.
770 Broadway
New York, NY 10003
Phone: (212) 209-2500
Fax: (212) 209-2666
www.jcrew.com

Kenneth Cole Productions, Inc.
603 West 50th Street
New York, NY 10019
Phone: (212) 265-1500
Fax: (212) 830-7422
www.kennethcole.com

L'Oreal USA
575 5th Avenue
New York, NY 10017
Phone: (212) 818-1500
Fax: (212) 984-4999
www.lorealusa.com

Levi Strauss & Co.
1155 Battery Street
San Francisco, CA 94111
Phone: (415) 501-6000
Fax: (415) 501-7112
www.levistrauss.com

Limited Brands
3 Limited Parkway
Columbus, OH 43216
Phone: (614) 415-7000
Fax: (614) 415-7440
www.limited.com

Macy's, Inc.
7 West Seventh Street
Cincinnati, OH 45202
Phone: (513) 579-7000
Fax: (513) 579-7555
www.federated-fds.com

Nike, Inc.
One Bowerman Drive
Beaverton, OR 97005-6453
Phone: (503) 671-6453
Fax: (503) 671-6300
www.nikebiz.com

Nordstrom, Inc.
1617 Sixth Avenue
Seattle, WA 98101-1742
Phone: (206) 628-2111
Fax: (206) 628-1795
www.nordstrom.com

Visit Vault at **www.vault.com** for insider company profiles, expert advice,
career message boards, expert resume reviews, the Vault Job Board and more.

VAULT CAREER LIBRARY   81

Employer Directory, cont.

OshKosh b'Gosh, Inc.
112 Otter Avenue
Oshkosh, WI 54901
Phone: (920) 231-8800
Fax: (920) 231-8621
www.oshkoshbgosh.com

Pacific Sunwear of California, Inc.
3450 E. Miraloma Avenue
Anaheim, CA 92806-2101
Phone: (714) 414-4000
Fax: (714) 414-4251
www.pacsun.com

Polo Ralph Lauren Corporation
650 Madison Avenue
New York, NY 10022
Phone: (212) 318-7000
Fax: (212) 888-5780
www.polo.com

Reebok International Ltd.
1895 J. W. Foster Boulevard
Canton, MA 02021
Phone: (781) 401-5000
Fax: (781) 401-7402
www.reebok.com

Revlon, Inc.
237 Park Avenue
New York, NY 10017
Phone: (212) 527-4000
Fax: (212) 527-4995
www.revloninc.com

Tommy Hilfiger
25 West 39th Street, 14th Floor
New York, NY 10018
www.tommy.com

Financial Services and Insurance

Like a bazaar that offers something to satisfy every customer's potential needs, the financial services industry presents a little bit of everything to prospective clientele. But while the trade is a vast one, its subdivisions are specialized to meet individuals' fiscal needs. Although the evolution of the financial services business has been a long and storied one, its development and expansion continues well into this century.

Credit Card Services

Looming large

Issuing credit cards is one of the most common ways in which financial services firms provide credit to individuals. Via the credit card, firms provide individuals with the funds required to purchase goods and services, and in return, individuals repay the full balance at a later date, or make payments on an installment basis. Via the debit card, people avoid debt by withdrawing the purchase amount from their bank accounts and transferring it to the seller. Though you're most likely familiar with a how credit and debit cards work, you might not be aware of just how large the industry is today.

According to *The New York Times*-sponsored documentary *The Secret History of the Credit Card*, approximately 641 million credit cards are in circulation in the U.S. in 2006 and account for about $1.5 trillion in consumer spending. And worldwide, the number of credit cards in circulation hit 2.5 billion in 2006, with Visa leading the way with a 64 percent market share. The most popular card is the Visa credit, followed by MasterCard credit, then Visa debit, American Express credit, MasterCard debit and Discover credit.

Heavy metal

The credit card traces its roots back to 1914 when Western Union began doling out metal cards, called "metal money," which gave preferred customers interest-free, deferred-payment privileges. A decade later, General Petroleum Corporation issued the first metal money for gasoline and automotive services, and by the late 1930s, department stores, communication companies, travel and delivery companies had all began to introduce such cards. Then, companies issued the cards, processed the transactions and collected the debts from the customer. The popularity of these cards grew until the beginning of World War II, when "Regulation W" restricted the use of cards, stalling their growth.

After the war, though, cards were back on track. Modes of travel were more advanced and more accessible, and more people were beginning to buy expensive modern conveniences such as kitchen appliances and washing machines. As a result, the credit card boomed in popularity, as consumers could pay for these things on credit that otherwise they couldn't afford to buy with cash.

Charge-It

In 1951, New York's Franklin National Bank created a credit system called Charge-It, which was very similar to the modern credit card. Charge-It allowed consumers to make purchases at local retail establishments, with the retailer obtaining authorization from the bank and then closing the sale. At a later date, the bank would reimburse the retailer and then collect the debt from the consumer. Acting upon the success of Franklin's Charge-It, other banks soon began introducing similar cards. Banks found that cardholders liked the convenience and credit line that cards offered, and retailers discovered that credit card customers usually spent more than if they had to pay with cash. Additionally, retailers found that handling bank-issued cards was less costly than maintaining their own credit card programs.

Visit Vault at **www.vault.com** for insider company profiles, expert advice, career message boards, expert resume reviews, the Vault Job Board and more.

VAULT CAREER LIBRARY   83

The association and the Master

Bank of America masterminded credit card innovations in the 1960s with the introduction of the bank card association. In 1965, Bank of America began issuing licensing agreements that allowed other banks to issue BankAmericards. To compete with the BankAmericard, four banks from California formed the Western States Bankcard Association and introduced the MasterCharge. By 1969, most credit cards had been converted to either the MasterCharge (which changed its name to MasterCard in 1979) or the BankAmericard (which was renamed Visa in 1977).

Cutting the cost of transaction processing and decreasing credit card fraud were the next innovations introduced to the industry. Electronic authorizations, begun in the early 1970s, allowed merchants to approve transactions 24 hours a day. By the end of the decade, magnetic strips on the backs of credit cards allowed retailers to swipe the customer's credit card through a dial up terminal, which accessed the issuing bank cardholder's information. This process gave authorizations and processed settlement agreements in a matter of minutes. In the 1980s, the ATM (automatic teller machine) began to surface, giving cardholders 24-hour access to cash.

The debut of the debit, the climb of the cobrand

The 1990s saw the debit card rise in popularity. The debit card grew from accounting for 274 million transactions in 1990 to 8.15 billion transactions in 2002. (And according to 2006's *A Guide to the ATM and Credit Card Industry*, a report compiled by the Federal Reserve Bank of Kansas City, the amount of debit card transactions rose to 2.6 trillion in 2006.) The 1990s also witnessed the surge of cobranded and affinity cards, which match up a credit card company with a retailer to offer discounts for using the card (think Citibank's AAdvantage cards and American Express' Mileage Rewards program). Although cobranded cards took a dip in the late 1990s—according to some industry experts, this was because issuers had exhausted the most lucrative partners—they've recently returned in full force. Consider that in 2003 alone, MBNA, which *BusinessWeek* has called "King of the Plastic Frontier," struck some 400 new deals with various companies such as Merrill Lynch, Royal Caribbean and Air Canada. Additionally, it renewed deals with another 1,400 organizations, including the National Football League and the University of Michigan. And in 2004, MBNA signed agreements with numerous other companies and organizations such as A.G. Edwards & Sons, the Massachusetts Institute of Technology, Arsenal Football Club (U.K.), Starwood Hotels and Resorts, and Charles Schwab.

And then there were four

In September 2003, a federal court upheld a lower court ruling that cost credit card powerhouses Visa and MasterCard a combined $3 billion. The court found Visa and MasterCard rules preventing the companies' member banks from also issuing American Express and Morgan Stanley's Discover cards to be illegal and harmful to competition. MasterCard was forced to pay $2 billion in damages and Visa paid $1 billion.

In October 2004, the U.S. Supreme Court decided not to hear Visa and MasterCard's appeal in the government's antitrust suit against them, effectively ending the two companies' rules that have prevented banks from issuing cards on rival networks. As a result, Amex and Discover became free to partner with the thousands of banks that issue Visa and MasterCard, which should allow these two companies to gain ground on the two credit powerhouses.

Upon the initial ruling in September 2003, Amex CEO Kenneth I. Chenault said, "We plan to add more partnerships with other issuers on a selective basis, ensuring they are a strategic fit for our brand and can drive more high-spending customers to the merchants on our network." In 2004, David W. Nelms, chairman and CEO of Morgan Stanley's Discover Financial Services unit, told *BusinessWeek* that the ruling "will create competition in our industry for the first time."

That competition is expected to be intense, say insiders. According to *BusinessWeek*, U.S. consumers use cash or checks to pay for about 59 percent of their $8.2 trillion in transactions each year. That leaves $4.8 trillion in cash outlays for credit card companies to capture. *The Nilson Report* estimates that debit and credit card spending will grow 13 percent a year from 2005 to 2008. "You're talking about the most profitable retail banking product in the world," *Nilson* publisher David Robertson told *BusinessWeek* in August 2004. "The competition among the titans is going to be fierce." He added, "They are already clobbering each other."

Re-Discovering the possibilities

In the midst of Morgan Stanley's great personnel exodus of March 2005, the firm announced plans to spin off its Discover credit card unit. The reason for the plan, according to former Morgan Stanley CEO Philip Purcell, was Discover "will be more properly valued as a stand-alone entity" than as a piece of Morgan Stanley. Soon after the announcement, analysts began estimating the Street value of the huge credit card unit. The range fell anywhere between $9 billion and $16 billion. Analysts also disagreed over whether or not the spin-off would maximize shareholder value.

However, new CEO John Mack's first big move at the helm after taking over the reins in mid-2005 was to reverse course on the Discover business, which predecessor Purcell had talked of selling off. "Discover is not only a strong business, but also an attractive asset for Morgan Stanley," Mack said in a statement. "It is a unique, successful franchise with growth opportunities that gives Morgan Stanley a consistent stream of stable, high-quality earnings and substantial cash flow, diversifies the company's earnings and broadens our scale and capital base."

But despite the kind words, there was ultimately a change of heart for Morgan Stanley. Although Discover delivered record before-tax earnings of $16 billion in 2006, Morgan Stanley announced that year that it plans to spin off Discover, which some analysts say will allow both businesses to grow more quickly.

The big buy

In June 2005, BofA went big again, following its $49 billion purchase of FleetBoston Financial in 2003 with the announcement that it would acquire credit card behemoth MBNA in a deal worth $35 billion. The purchase made Bank of America one of the largest card issuers in the U.S., with $143 billion in managed outstanding balances and 40 million active accounts. Bank of America will add more than 20 million new customer accounts as well as affinity relationships with more than 5,000 partner organizations and financial institutions. Bank of America expects to achieve overall expense efficiencies of $850 million after tax, which would be fully realized in 2007, and anticipates a restructuring charge of $1.25 billion after tax. Cost reductions will come from a range of sources, including laying off 6,000 employees. And in November 2006, BofA announced that it had agreed to acquire US Trust, the wealth management subsidiary of Charles Schwab Corporation. In February 2007, the parties said the deal would close later than expected (in the third quarter of 2007, not the second) because BofA and Charles Schwab need more time to coordinate their computer systems. The $3.3 billion acquisition will help BofA strengthen its capabilities in serving high-net-worth clients, and will also increase its assets under management.

The big IPO

At the end of August 2005, MasterCard, which became a private share corporate in 2002, announced that it planned to become a publicly traded company. On May 25, 2006, MasterCard went public, and began trading on the New York Stock Exchange under the ticker MA.

As part of the IPO, the firm adopted new corporate governance and an open ownership structure that included the appointment of a new board of directors, comprised mostly of independent directors, and the establishment of a charitable foundation. Under the new corporate governance and ownership structure, MasterCard's former shareholders, approximately 1,400 financial institutions worldwide, retained a 41 percent equity interest in MasterCard through their ownership of nonvoting

Visit Vault at **www.vault.com** for insider company profiles, expert advice, career message boards, expert resume reviews, the Vault Job Board and more.

V∆ULT CAREER LIBRARY   **85**

Class B common stock. In addition, shareholders received Class M common stock that have no economic rights but provide them with certain rights, including the right to elect several directors from financial institutions around the world.

"Listing on the NYSE marks a major milestone for MasterCard and reinforces our commitment to continued growth and building value for our customers and stockholders," Robert Selander, the company's president and chief executive officer, told Associated Press. The market had expected the issue to open in the $40 to $43 range, but MasterCard was at $39 after a series of setbacks delayed the process. By most accounts, though, the IPO has been a huge success. Since the firm went public, the stock has zoomed to over $140 per share as of June 2007, making MasterCard one of the most successful IPOs of 2006.

No contact credit

"Contactless" cards and finger-swiping systems are the latest advances in the world of plastic purchasing. By the end of 2006, banks had issued 27 million debit and credit cards that do not need to be run through a machine but simply scanned via a radar-like beam. Already, these cards can be used at retailers like McDonald's, 7-Eleven and CVS.

The popularity of contactless credit and debit cards is only expected to skyrocket—according to market research firm Packaged Facts, there will be approximately 109 million in circulation by 2011. Other than not having to run the cards through a machine, one benefit is for purchases less than $25, signing isn't required.

Another no contact credit payment system is now in place: the pay-by-finger system, in which individuals' fingers are scanned and linked to their payment information. All you have to do is press your finger (its print) against a device, enter some personal information, such as your phone number, on a keypad and your payment is made; fingerprints are linked up with credit or debit cards. The system is already in place at hundreds of U.S. supermarkets such as Albertsons and Piggly Wiggly.

An eye to the future

But the credit card industry has also been forced to confront a few profitability issues as of late. The exponential cost of credit cards offering rewards programs is concerning the industry, especially with the burgeoning popularity of debit card use, according to a 2006 Booz Allen Hamilton report. The industry is also dealing with the problem of sluggish receivables growth, the report said. To continue to attract customers, card issuers have employed a variety of strategies, including mergers and acquisitions and rewards across cards that tend to trigger more customer spending. Ultimately, the report said, companies need to examine their most profitable sectors, and develop cost allocations and new incentives for customers from there.

Ratings

Making the grade

Credit ratings are another sector of the financial services industry that serve a highly specific purpose. Founded by John Knowles Fitch as the Fitch Publishing Company in 1913, Fitch was one of the early leaders in providing financial statistics. The Fitch rating system of "AAA" to "D," introduced in 1924, has become the standard for the financial community. Fitch, one of the four major credit-rating agencies (the others are Moody's, Standard & Poor's and DBRS), is the leader in providing ratings on debt issued by companies, covering entities in more than 80 countries.

Moody's Investors Service, founded in 1900, is one of the most prominent and widely utilized sources for credit ratings, research and risk analysis on debt instruments and securities. In addition, Moody's provides corporate and government credit assessment and training services, credit training services and credit software to financial institutions, with 9,000 accounts at 2,400 institutions worldwide. The firm's ratings and analyses track 100 sovereign nations, 11,000 company insurers, 25,000 public finance issuers and 70,000 structured finance obligations. Moody's ratings business consists of four groups: structured finance, corporate finance, financial institutions and sovereign risk, and public finance. The firm's primary clients include corporate and government issuers as well as institutional investors, banks, creditors and commercial banks.

Standard & Poor's operates through six main divisions: credit ratings, data services, equity research, funds, indices and risk solutions. Over $1 trillion in investor assets is directly tied to S&P indices, more than all other indices combined. The firm has the world's largest network of credit ratings analysts, and its equity research division is the world's largest producer of independent equity research. More than 1,000 institutions—including 19 of the top-20 securities firms, 13 of the top-20 banks, and 11 of the top-20 life insurance companies—license their research for their investors and advisors.

DBRS, an international ratings agency, is headquartered in Toronto and gives ratings to borrowing entities. The company is split into corporate, financial institutions, public finance and structured finance divisions. The firm prides itself on being "the leading rating agency in Canada" as well as being the first rating agency to have a full-service web site for customers.

Visit Vault at **www.vault.com** for insider company profiles, expert advice, career message boards, expert resume reviews, the Vault Job Board and more.

VAULT CAREER LIBRARY   87

Employer Directory

Aflac (American Family Life Assurance Company)
1932 Wynnton Road
Columbus, GA 31999
Phone: (706) 323-3431
Fax: (706) 324-6330
www.aflac.com

Alliance Data Systems Corporation (Alliance Data)
17655 Waterview Parkway
Dallas, TX 75252
Phone: (972) 348-5100
Fax: (972) 348-5335
www.alliancedata.com

The Allstate Corp.
2775 Sanders Road
Northbrook, IL 60062-6127
Phone: (847) 402-5000
Fax: (847) 326-7519
www.allstate.com

American Express
World Financial Center
200 Vesey Street
New York, NY 10285
Phone: (212) 640-2000
www.americanexpress.com

American International Group Inc. (AIG)
70 Pine Street
New York, NY 10270
Phone: (212) 770-7000
Fax: (212) 509-9705
www.aig.com

AmeriCredit
801 Cherry Street, Suite 3900
Fort Worth, TX 76102
Phone: (817) 302-7000
Toll Free: (800) 284-2271
www.americredit.com

Aon Corp.
Aon Center
200 E. Randolph Street
Chicago, IL 60601
Phone: (312) 381-1000
Fax: (312) 381-6032
www.aon.com

Arthur J. Gallagher & Co.
The Gallagher Centre
2 Pierce Place
Itasca, IL 60143-3141
Phone: (630) 773-3800
Fax: (630) 285-4000
www.ajg.com

Berkshire Hathaway Inc.
1440 Kiewit Plaza
Omaha, NE 68131
Phone: (402) 346-1400
Fax: (402) 346-3375
www.berkshirehathaway.com

Capital One Financial
1680 Capital One Drive
McLean, VA 22012
Phone: (703) 720-1000
www.capitalone.com

CB Richard Ellis Group, Inc.
100 N. Sepulveda Boulevard
Suite 1050
El Segundo, CA 90245
Phone: (310) 606-4700
Fax: (949) 809-4357
www.cbre.com

The Chubb Corporation
15 Mountain View Road
Warren, NJ 07059
Phone: (908) 903-2000
Fax: (908) 903-2027
www.chubb.com

CIT Group
505 Fifth Avenue
New York, NY 10017
Phone: (212) 771-0505
www.cit.com

Citigroup
399 Park Avenue
New York, NY 10043
Phone: (800) 285-3000
Fax: (212) 793-3946
www.citigroup.com

Countrywide Financial Corp.
4500 Park Granada
Calabasas, CA 91302-1613
Phone: (818) 225-3000
Fax: (818) 225-4051
www.countrywide.com

DaimlerChrysler Financial Services
Eichhornstraße 3
10875 Berlin
Germany
Phone: +49-30-2554-0
Fax: +49-30-2554-2525
www.daimlerchrysler-financialservices.com

27777 Inkster Road
Farmington Hills, MI 48334
Phone: (248) 427-6300
Fax: (248) 427-6600
www.daimlerchrysler-financialservices.com/na

DST Systems
333 W. 11th Street
Kansas City, MO 64105
Phone: (816) 435-1000
Fax: (816) 435-8618
www.dstsystems.com

Employer Directory, cont.

The Dun & Bradstreet Corporation
103 JFK Parkway
Short Hills, NJ 07078
Phone: (973) 921-5500
Fax: (973) 921-6056
www.dnb.com

Equifax
1550 Peachtree Street NW
Atlanta, GA 30309
Phone: (404) 885-8000
Fax: (404) 885-8055
www.equifax.com

Fannie Mae
3900 Wisconsin Avenue NW
Washington, DC 20016-2892
Phone: (202) 752-7000
Fax: (202) 752-6014
www.fanniemae.com

Fidelity National Financial
601 Riverside Avenue
Jacksonville, FL 32204
Phone: (888) 934-3354
www.fnf.com

First Data Corporation
6200 S. Quebec Street
Greenwood Village, CO 80111
Phone: (303) 967-8000
Fax: (303) 967-6701
www.firstdata.com

Fiserv
255 Fiserv Drive
Brookfield, WI 53045
Phone: (262) 879-5000
Fax: (262) 879-5013
www.fiserv.com

Fitch Ratings
1 State Street Plaza
New York, NY 10004
Phone: (212) 908-0500
Fax: (212) 480-4435
www.fitchratings.com

Ford Motor Credit Company
The American Road
Dearborn, MI 48126
Phone: (313) 322-3000
Fax: (313) 323-2959
www.fordcredit.com

Freddie Mac
8200 Jones Branch Drive
McLean, VA 22102-3110
Phone: (703) 903-2000
www.freddiemac.com

Genworth Financial Inc.
6620 W. Broad Street
Richmond, VA 23230
Phone: (804) 281-6000
Fax: (804) 662-2414
www.genworth.com

GMAC LLC
200 Renaissance Center
Detroit, MI 48265
Phone: (313) 556-5000
Fax: (313) 556-5108
www.gmacfs.com

Hartford Financial Services
Hartford Plaza
690 Asylum Avenue
Hartford, CT 06115-1900
Phone: (860) 547-5000
Fax: (860) 547-2680
www.thehartford.com

Leucadia National Corporation
315 Park Avenue South
New York, NY 10010-3607
Phone: (212) 460-1900
Fax: (212) 598-4869
www.leucadia.com

Liberty Mutual
175 Berkeley Street
Boston, MA 02116
Phone: (617) 357-9500
Fax: (617) 350-7648
www.libertymutual.com

Loews Corporation
667 Madison Avenue
New York, NY 10021-8087
Phone: (212) 521-2000
Fax: (212) 521-2525
www.loews.com

Marsh & McLennan Companies, Inc.
1166 Avenue of the Americas
New York, NY 10036-2774
Phone: (212) 345-5000
Fax: (212) 345-4838
www.mmc.com

MassMutual Financial Group
1295 State Street
Springfield, MA 01111-0001
Phone: (413) 744-1000
Fax: (413) 744-6005
www.massmutual.com

MasterCard
2000 Purchase Street
Purchase, NY 10577
Phone: (914) 249-2000
Fax: (914) 249-4206
www.mastercardintl.com

MetLife
200 Park Avenue
New York, NY 10166-0188
Phone: (212) 578-2211
Fax: (212) 578-3320
www.metlife.com

Moody's Corp.
99 Church Street
New York, NY 10007
Phone: (212) 553-0300
Fax: (212) 553-4820
www.moodys.com

Nationwide Financial Services
1 Nationwide Plaza
Columbus, OH 43215-2220
Phone: (614) 249-7111
Fax: (614) 854-5036
www.nationwidefinancial.com

Visit Vault at **www.vault.com** for insider company profiles, expert advice, career message boards, expert resume reviews, the Vault Job Board and more.

VAULT CAREER LIBRARY   89

Employer Directory, cont.

New Century Financial Corp.
18400 Von Karman Avenue
Suite 1000
Irvine, CA 92612
Phone: (949) 440-7030
Fax: (949) 440-7033
www.ncen.com

New York Life Insurance Company
51 Madison Avenue
New York, NY 10010
Phone: (212) 576-7000
Fax: (212) 576-8145
www.newyorklife.com

Northwestern Mutual
720 E. Wisconsin Avenue
Milwaukee, WI 53202-4797
Phone: (414) 271-1444
Fax: (414) 665-9702
www.nmfn.com

The Progressive Corporation
6300 Wilson Mills Road
Mayfield Village, OH 44143
Phone: (800) 766-4737
www.progressive.com

Prudential Financial
751 Broad Street
Newark, NJ 07102-3777
Phone: (973) 802-6000
Fax: (973) 802-4479
www.prudential.com

Sallie Mae
12061 Bluemont Way
Reston, VA 20190
Phone: (703) 810-3000
Fax: (703) 984-5042
www.salliemae.com

Scottrade, Inc.
12800 Corporate Hill Drive
St. Louis, MO 63131-1834
Phone: (314) 965-1555
Fax: (314) 543-6222
www.scottrade.com

Standard & Poor's
55 Water Street
New York, NY 10041
Phone: (212) 438-2000
Fax: (212) 438-7375
www.standardandpoors.com

State Farm
1 State Farm Plaza
Bloomington, IL 61710
Phone: (309) 766-2311
Fax: (309) 766-3621
www.statefarm.com

SunGard Data Systems
680 East Swedesford Road
Wayne, PA 19087-1586
Phone: (800) 825-2518
www.sungard.com

Thornburg Mortgage
150 Washington Avenue
Suite 302
Santa Fe, NM 87501
Phone: (505) 989-1900
Fax: (505) 989-8156
www.thornburgmortgage.com

Toyota Financial Services
19001 S. Western Avenue
Torrance, CA 90509
Phone: (310) 468-1310
Fax: (310) 468-7829
www.toyotafinancial.com

The Travelers Companies, Inc.
385 Washington Street
St. Paul, MN 55102
www.travelers.com

Unum
1 Fountain Square
Chattanooga, TN 37402
Phone: (423) 294-1011
Fax: (423) 294-3962
www.unum.com

USAA
9800 Fredericksburg Road
San Antonio, TX 78288
Phone: (210) 498-2211
Fax: (210) 498-9940
www.usaa.com

Visa USA
900 Metro Center Boulevard
Foster City, CA 94404
Phone: (650) 432-3200
Fax: (650) 432-3631
www.usa.visa.com

Government and Politics

Washington, D.C. has largely been an untapped source of career opportunities for business school students and MBAs. However, several recent trends indicate that MBAs may start looking to Washington for positions not available elsewhere. These trends include a heightened interest in employment with nonprofits and a burgeoning effort by some federal agencies to recruit MBAs. Additionally, there are MBA employers that exist only in Washington, such as the World Bank.

Despite increased interest in hiring MBAs by many of these employers, in general, these organizations have limited and spotty recruiting efforts on business school campuses. The onus remains on interested students to research appropriate opportunities and network with individuals with similar interests. The section below contains a guide to several of the employment options for MBAs in Washington along with advice on how to identify opportunities and successfully apply for positions.

Federal Government

Washington, D.C. is slowly, but increasingly, becoming more aware of the benefits of the MBA as well as the need to bring in qualified managers with more than just government experience. When George W. Bush was sworn in as the 43rd President of the United States, he was commonly referred to as the "MBA President," since, as a graduate of the Harvard Business School, he is the first chief executive of the United States to hold the degree. Several of his appointments to fill key administration posts were also MBAs, including Elaine Chao, the Secretary of Labor, who received her MBA from the Harvard Business School and Don Evans, the Secretary of Commerce, who received an MBA from the University of Texas. Many other of his top appointments were culled from the world of business, including Paul O'Neil, his first Secretary of the Treasury and former CEO of Alcoa, as well as his replacement, John Snow, who was the head of CSX Corp.

The change at the top has not yet translated into widespread opportunities for MBAs, but the government has grown more receptive to MBAs as it begins to appreciate the skills and capabilities they bring to bear. For example, there have been recent efforts to recruit on MBA campuses. In the 2003 recruiting season, the U.S. Department of the Treasury visited select campuses seeking to fill internships and full-time positions. At times, the CIA has promoted opportunities with MBA programs and advertised for MBAs as part of its financial analysis teams on popular job posting sites, such as HotJobs.com and *The Washington Post*.

In 2002, Secretary Chao of the U.S. Department of Labor launched an initiative specifically to recruit MBAs to the department. With a large proportion of senior department personnel scheduled to retire in the coming years, Secretary Chao moved aggressively to create a new pipeline of talent and specifically identified hiring MBAs as the future of the department.

Finding a position with the federal government

As would be expected with the federal government, bureaucracy rules the hiring process. However, as with any organization, there are paths around the human resources quagmire. MBAs interested in finding an appropriate position with the federal government should apply the tools emphasized by any career counseling office: identify your interests, find out the general requirements for position, network, and utilize internships.

Since the federal government is required to post nearly all vacancies, one potential resource to use in identifying appropriate opportunities is its career listing web site, www.usacareers.com. However, a word of warning: while the site provides a useful starting point and a valuable research tool, using it exclusively for a job search with the federal government would sell your efforts short. Instead, for MBAs it can be best used as means to examine the types of positions available and the general salary ranges. Still, even the position descriptions can be overly bureaucratic, and therefore the site should only be considered a starting point in the research process.

Visit Vault at **www.vault.com** for insider company profiles, expert advice, career message boards, expert resume reviews, the Vault Job Board and more.

VAULT CAREER LIBRARY 91

According to several MBAs employed by the federal government in Washington, the best way to identify opportunities is by networking with those already working in the federal government and with those in the nonprofits and other entities that regularly partner or interact with the federal agencies. Two good ways to make such contacts are through MBA alumni networks and student- or school-sponsored conferences focusing on the public sector and nonprofit management.

Applying for positions can also be highly bureaucratic, and again, interested applicants are well advised to use their networks to begin the application process. While all applicants must eventually go through the human resources department to determine whether they are qualified and if so, their pay level, it is far more fruitful to begin the application process with the office one wishes to join than with the human resources department. This is where networking can pay off, since ultimately hiring decisions are made within a specific office for high-level candidates. In fact, many government managers already have an applicant in mind before a position is posted.

One MBA graduate who returned to the federal government after graduation says that while finding government position can take effort, the MBA is definitely seen as a benefit. "There are a lot of hiring managers who will be receptive to talking with MBAs simply because they hold the credential," he says. "MBAs with a specific interest should seek out managers in the federal government, send them their resumes, and then try to follow up."

The insider also confirmed that there is a growing awareness of the value of an MBA, but that the government hasn't been fast enough to quickly establish the right recruiting policies to bring more business students into the federal workforce. "The fact of the matter is that the government just doesn't pay what the private sector does," he says. "But, for those with a strong interest in government work, there are many ways in and many rewarding career paths."

Areas of Interest to MBAs

Since most MBAs aren't interested in becoming lifetime bureaucrats, they usually consider specific opportunities in order to gain the experience they need to advance in their chosen professions. The following are areas of the federal government that provide career enhancing opportunities.

Community and economic development

Community and economic development is an area that has captured the interest of MBAs. Since community and economic development is often the result of cooperation among public sector, private sector and nonprofit entities, a position with the federal government can be an effective way to build experience, gain contacts within the development community and gain an understanding of the government's role in community and economic development and the resources it makes available.

There are several agencies within the federal government that have community and economic development functions. These include the U.S. Department of Treasury, the U.S. Department of Commerce and the Small Business Administration. Since roles within each agency will vary with the specific mission of the department, interested candidates should try to learn about each department's operations and opportunities through networking with organizations such as Net Impact, alumni, and by contacting hiring managers directly to discuss opportunities.

Management

There are many opportunities within the federal government for MBAs to gain management experience. However, these opportunities must be ferreted out, and will depend on what the MBA hopes to gain by joining the federal government. For example, an MBA with an interest in the federal budget process could attempt to locate an analyst position with the Office of Management and Budget. Another potential source of management positions will be the Department of Homeland Security. Since the Homeland Security Department is free of some of the federal employment regulations imposed on virtually every other federal entity, there may be more opportunities for MBAs to utilize their management abilities to a greater degree than elsewhere in the federal bureaucracy. MBAs need to think creatively about how their skills relate to government management.

One avenue for MBAs into the federal government is through the Presidential Management Internship (PMI) program, which is open to all students pursuing master's or doctoral degrees. To be considered for the program, students must submit an application and be nominated by the dean, chairperson or program director of their academic program. Once accepted, PMIs must find an appropriate position within the federal government. The program lasts two years, with PMIs beginning at the GS-9 level (approximately $35,500 to $46,100). After one year, they are eligible for promotion to the GS-11 level ($42,900 to $55,800). At the end of the program, PMI program participants may be converted to a permanent position with the federal government and are eligible for the GS-12 grade level ($51,500 to $66,900). For detailed information on the program, see its web site at www.pmi.opm.gov.

Additionally, the Department of Labor has begun to actively recruit MBAs for general management positions with strong results. For 2002, its first year in operation, the department's MBA recruitment program reported receiving more than 250 applications for 30 openings. While MBAs start at the GS-9 level, the department is offering other incentives, including recruitment bonuses and loan forgiveness programs.

Upon acceptance into the program, MBAs will be allowed to rotate through several different assignments before being placed in a permanent position. The permanent assignments are based on the needs of the department and the long-term interests of each participant.

A senior official working on the program glows about its initial results: "We didn't know what to expect when we fist put the program into place, but we have been very pleased with the results. In fact, several other offices within the federal government have approached us about putting up similar recruitment programs for themselves."

Application information is available on the department's web site at www.dol.gov.

International development

The federal government also provides options for MBA students interested in international development, a field that has traditionally and still remains dominated by economists.

Since there are no formal recruitment programs in place for MBAs for international development positions with the federal government, interested students will have to network with both on-campus and outside organizations to uncover opportunities.

The U.S. Department of Treasury's Office of International Affairs often recruits MBAs for financial analysis positions covering such issues as debt policy or international trade. It is particularly interested in MBAs with strong experience in the banking and financial service sector, as well as international experience. The office's recruitment efforts include posting position openings with MBA career offices and general advertising.

Visit Vault at **www.vault.com** for insider company profiles, expert advice, career message boards, expert resume reviews, the Vault Job Board and more.

VAULT CAREER LIBRARY   93

Employer Directory

Central Intelligence Agency
CIA Headquarters Building
Washington, DC 20505
Phone: (703) 482-1100
Fax: (703) 482-1739
www.cia.gov

**Democratic National
Committee**
430 S. Capitol Street SE
Washington, DC 20003
Phone: (202) 863-8000
www.democrats.org

**Democratic Senatorial
Campaign Committee**
120 Maryland Avenue NE
Washington, DC 20002
Phone: (202) 224-2447
www.dscc.org

**Federal Bureau of
Investigation**
J. Edgar Hoover FBI Building
935 Pennsylvania Avenue NW
Washington, DC 20535
Phone: (202) 324-3000
www.fbi.gov

**Financial Management
Professional Training Program
(NAVY)**
153 Ellyson Avenue, Suite A
Pensacola, FL 32508-5245
Phone: (850) 452-3783
www.navyfmtp.com

**National Republican Senatorial
Committee**
425 Second Street NE
Washington, DC 20002
Phone: (202) 675-6000
www.nrsc.org

**National Republican
Congressional Committee**
320 First Street, SE
Washington, DC 20003
Phone: (202) 479-7000
www.nrcc.org

**Office of Budget and
Management Services**
810 7th Street NW
Washington, DC 20531
Phone: (202) 307-5980
www.ojp.usdoj.gov/obms

**Republican National
Committee**
310 First Street SE
Washington, DC 20003
Phone: (202) 863-8500
www.rnc.org

Small Business Administration
409 Third Street SW
Washington, DC 20416
Phone: (800) U-ASK-SBA
www.sba.gov

**U.S. Department of
Commerce**
1401 Constitution Avenue NW
Washington, DC 20230
Phone: (202) 482-2000
www.commerce.gov

U.S. Department of Education
400 Maryland Avenue SW
Washington, DC 20202
Phone: (800) USA-LEARN
www.ed.gov

**U.S. Department of Health
and Human Services**
200 Independence Avenue SW
Washington, DC 20201
Phone: (202) 619-0257
www.hhs.gov

U.S. Department of Justice
950 Pennsylvania Avenue NW
Washington, DC 20530-0001
Phone: (202) 353-1555
www.justice.gov

U.S. Department of Labor
Frances Perkins Building
200 Constitution Avenue NW
Washington, DC 20210
Phone: (866) 487-2365
www.dol.gov

U.S. Department of State
2201 C Street NW
Washington, DC 20520
Phone: (202)-647-6575
www.careers.state.gov

**U.S. Environmental Protection
Agency**
1200 Pennsylvania Avenue NW
Washington, DC 20460
Phone: (202) 272-0167
www.epa.gov

Health Care

Industry Overview

An industry in flux

You can't live with it and you can't live without it—this pretty much sums up the attitude many Americans have toward today's health care industry. The sector is a veritable Rube Goldberg machine of providers of patient care, manufacturers, middlemen and insurance companies. It's no secret that the sector is a volatile one: despite making up around 16 percent of the nation's gross domestic product (GDP). U.S. health care spending totaled $1.99 trillion in 2005, more than what people spent on housing or food. Despite the awesome quantities of money involved in the industry, industry players have a tough time figuring out how to turn a profit in such a way that benefits both providers and patients—not to mention shareholders. Economists predict health care spending will make up 18.7 percent of the country's GDP in 2014, a percentage considered unsustainable by many analysts. It is estimated that the public sector will pay for nearly half of all health spending in the U.S. by that year—not a healthy number.

Big trouble

Another unhealthy number is the growing number of people who will need medical attention in the coming decades, due to the increasing prevalence of bariatric and geriatric patients. In 2006, census data revealed that Americans were the fattest people on the planet. Two thirds of adults are overweight, to varying degrees, due to increasingly sedentary lifestyles and a diet liberal with calories. Carrying a few extra pounds won't be listed as a cause of death, but it also doesn't just mean that one's trousers are a tad snug—overweight and obese people are increasingly at risk for disorders like heart disease, stroke, osteoarthritis, type II diabetes, certain types of cancer, and a number of other long-term (and expensive) conditions. Economists are continually trying to figure the economic impact of overweight and obese Americans. In 2006, researchers estimated that obesity cost insurers around $80 billion per annum, and the number is rising. However, the term overweight is difficult to define consistently; additionally, there are a number of subtle effects, like depressed wages from weight discrimination and missed productivity due to disability, that can have profound economic consequences. More worryingly, the incidence of obesity in children has tripled since the 1970s, according to data from the Centers for Disease Control and Prevention; studies have shown that children who were overweight had an 80 percent chance of growing up to be obese adults.

Having a senior moment

Speaking of adults, according to the American Association of Retired Persons (AARP), by the year 2050, seniors will outnumber children for the first time ever. With approximately one million people turning age 60 each month worldwide, the phenomenon known as "global aging" promises to have a profound effect on the demand for and delivery of health care services. This shift is sparking interest in all issues affecting senior health, from preventive care to programs promoting home care and assisted living as alternatives to merely shunting the elderly to oft-dreaded nursing home care.

The United States' aging population is also putting pressure on the nation's reimbursement system for seniors and low-income patients. The Medicaid program is funded by the federal government but administered by the states, serving low-income individuals who do not have access to health care through their employers, while the Medicare program serves people over the age of 65. Because of this, the federal government looms large in health care. In fact, ranked by sales, the government's own Centers for Medicare & Medicaid Services (CMS) is No. 1 provider in the insurance industry, covering around one in four people, and distributing $554 billion in benefits in 2006—more than a fifth of the spending of the federal government. Expenditures from the program are expected to rise to 11 percent of GDP by 2008.

Visit Vault at www.vault.com for insider company profiles, expert advice, career message boards, expert resume reviews, the Vault Job Board and more.

VAULT CAREER LIBRARY   95

As the 77 million members of the baby boom reach age 65 and sign up for Medicare, the government will foot an even larger share of the health care bill. In 2007, Ben Bernanke, chairman of the Federal Reserve, warned in a Senate hearing that the spiraling costs of Social Security and government-funded health care could precipitate a budgetary crisis if not swiftly addressed. He predicted that the programs, burdened by the Baby Boomers, could increase publicly-held government debt from 37 percent of the GDP in 2007 to 100 percent of GDP in 2030, and that it would increase astronomically thereafter, requiring large increases in taxes and deep cuts in government spending.

Let's go to Plan D

The solution to this problem, of course, is to expand the benefits offered by Medicare. In 2006, Part D, a prescription drug benefit plan, was rolled out. (Medicare parts A, B and C govern hospital stays, doctor's visits and plans offered through other insurers, respectively.) The Bush administration has made several attempts to tweak the program, with mixed results. The revised Medicare drug plan known as Medicare Part D, which came into effect in 2006, provided seniors with a flurry of plan options provided by various private insurance companies. But the Byzantine regulations for the program left many seniors confused and worried they were not getting the coverage they needed. Befuddled seniors notwithstanding, insurance companies have posted record profits from administering Part D.

New regulations, which took effect in 2007, refigured the rates at which Medicare compensates hospitals and physicians for various procedures. Compensation for surgeries, such as hip and knee replacements and various cardiac procedures, will be cut by as much as a third. In response, the American Medical Association (AMA) announced that if compensation for Medicare patients is reduced, physicians will be forced to restrict the number of such cases they can handle. This legislation represents the opening salvo in a series of laws that will try to rein in Medicare spending by 34 percent over the next decade. Further economic fallout may include hospitals seeking higher reimbursement from insurance companies, which will then raise premiums, further increasing the cost of health care.

Flying without a safety net

Then there is the problem of the remaining 86 percent of the population, who aren't eligible for Medicare or Medicaid, and either must buy private insurance on their own, get it through an employer or just go without and hope for the best. An alarming number of Americans, including many children, are uninsured—15 percent of the population at last count, or some 48 million people.

What's more, this number, along with the number of those who must purchase insurance on their own, will grow. As generally healthy people opt not to pay for health insurance—the cost of which increased at twice the rate of inflation in 2006—the pools of people buying insurance increasingly consists of people with expensive, chronic conditions or those who think they will imminently need expensive medical care—an actuarial nightmare that's driving up premiums. At such high costs, employers are increasingly unwilling or unable to pay to insure their employees, further enlarging the ranks of the uninsured.

Uninsured individuals increase pressure on the price of health care in other ways as well. They are less likely to get regular checkups and treat minor medical problems before they become major issues, causing many to end up seeking treatment in the emergency room. Since many of the uninsured don't have the financial reserves to buy health insurance in the first place, a hospital stay can be devastating, and many default on their debts or are forced into bankruptcy by medical bills. In order to defray the costs of essentially providing free medical care, hospitals must charge higher prices. Reports also indicate that health care is more expensive overall for the uninsured. For example, hospitals bill uninsured clients a higher rate for the same procedures provided to those with health coverage, since big insurance companies are able to negotiate discounts with providers.

The solution to America's health care woes is not as simple as forcing everyone to purchase insurance, however. The fragmented nature of the industry, with so many different players jockeying for their slice of profits, has played a role in increasing the amount that patients must pay for care, since administrative costs only drive up the price of services.

The situation isn't so rosy for consumers fortunate enough to have coverage, either. As the cost of providing health care coverage continues to rise, many employers are finding they can no longer afford this benefit, and are passing more of the costs on to employees in the form of higher premiums, deductibles and stingier reimbursement plans.

Instead of pointing fingers or complaining about the situation, some people are doing something about high health care costs. Seattle's Virginia Mason Medical ran into trouble when the insurance companies that referred patients there pointed out that, despite the stellar quality of the care it delivered, it cost significantly more than other hospitals in the area. Virginia Mason went on a cost-cutting campaign, eliminating pricey medical equipment and specialists. Oddly, the hospital kept losing money, due to the skewed way insurers reimburse procedures. High-tech options, like MRI scans, net big checks from insurers, while simple, equally effective procedures, which cost far less, may cause hospitals to lose money.

In short, insurers are paying caregivers based on how much they do to a patient, as opposed to how effective—or even necessary—the treatments are. The doctors at Virginia Mason and the insurance companies reworked the payment scheme for the hospital, so that patients were treated more efficiently. Instead of seeing scads of specialists for back pain, getting an MRI and finally going to physical therapy, patients are now sent directly to physical therapy, which costs much less, and immediately starts to alleviate the patient's pain.

The quest for reform

Lately, the health care crisis has been getting a lot of buzz, but legislators have been notably reluctant to deal with the issue ever since Hillary Clinton's attempt to create a universal coverage plan was shot down early in her husband's tenure as president. In 2007, however, California Governor Arnold Schwarzenegger outlined a plan to insure the 36 million residents of his state. Individuals would be required to purchase insurance, either privately or through their employers, and health insurance companies would be obliged to cover them. Employers not offering insurance would pay 4 percent of payroll into a state fund for coverage; government assistance in purchasing this insurance would be given to people below a certain income level. To defray future costs, the state will sponsor initiatives against obesity and diabetes, and will levy a fee of 4 percent of gross revenue on hospitals and 2 percent on doctors to pay for it all. Needless to say, many groups oppose the plan. Business owners say that mandated coverage is a sneaky form of tax and will stunt economic growth in the state a nurses' group says it panders to insurance companies, conservatives cry socialism and liberals claim Schwarzenegger stole their idea. With so few groups happy with the plan, it just might work.

The need for heath care reform was also addressed by President Bush in his State of the Union address in January 2007. He proposed a tax break for people who have to purchase their own insurance, in order to make it more affordable, while taxing employer-provided plans as income. The plan, which reveals the current administration's belief that tax cuts will cure all ills, is expected to make coverage affordable for a few million people at best. Critics have rushed to point out the flaws in the proposal. It does not take into account that smaller groups of people, or worse yet, groups of elderly or sick people, are a greater actuarial risk than larger groups, and premiums increase to reflect that. They also point out that this tax scheme would have the effect of driving people towards less expensive plans (which offer skimpier coverage, naturally) in order to reduce spending on unnecessary procedures. Furthermore, it dangerously destabilizes the system under which workers receive health insurance through their employers, the only part of the nation's health insurance plan that could be remotely described as functional. The president also proposed federal funding for states that are creating ways to cover their uninsured populations.

Visit Vault at **www.vault.com** for insider company profiles, expert advice, career message boards, expert resume reviews, the Vault Job Board and more.

VAULT CAREER LIBRARY   97

CDHC—the new wave of care?

Another plan for health care that has generated a buzz in the Bush administration is the idea of "consumer-driven health care," or CDHC. The idea is elegant in theory: if consumers can control their own health care spending, providers and insurers will be forced to compete for business, thus (hopefully) increasing quality of care while driving down costs. At the crux of CDHC are health savings accounts (HSAs), or tax-free accounts offered along with low-cost, high-deductible insurance plans. Either employee or employer (or both) stow away a certain amount of money in the HSA each year, which consumers can spend on virtually any health treatment or medication they want; whatever is unused remains in the account for any future health-related expenses.

Proponents of CHDC point out that the cost of plastic surgery and other elective procedures not covered by insurance has effectively kept pace with inflation, since consumers can shop around and find the best care for the best price. Since 1998, the average price of a tummy tuck has risen 19 percent, only slightly higher than inflation, and far below the 49 percent rise in per capita spending on health care for the same period. Opponents of the plan suggest that employers will use CDHC as a cover to reduce employee compensation. What CDHC plans do not take into account is that the bulk of the cost of health care spending is not from overconsumption of medical care by people who can afford it, but rather from treating people with chronic conditions, which can easily require in excess of thousands of dollars per year to manage. CDHC also fails to take into account that competitive pricing only works when one is in a position to make rational, informed decisions about which doctors to visit; in the event of a medical emergency, a severely wounded, unconscious or similarly incapacitated person is in no position to comparison shop.

Liability looms

Another type of reform that gets plenty of congressional buzz is medical malpractice liability, which the powerful AMA has made its top priority. The association has taken to identifying states that are in a "medical liability crisis" owing to exploding insurance premiums and the aftereffects of those costs—namely, that some providers are limiting or halting certain services because of liability risks. As of July 2006, there were 22 states on the AMA's list. One such state, Massachusetts, is a case in point: according to Massachusetts Medical Society research, 50 percent of the state's neurosurgeons, 41 percent of orthopedic surgeons and 36 percent of general surgeons had been forced to limit their scopes of practice due to insurmountable medical liability costs.

The Bush administration said an end to "junk lawsuits" was one of its primary goals for the president's second term, calling for "medical liability reform that will reduce health care costs and make sure patients have the doctors and care they need." In the early months following his January 2005 inauguration, Congress passed Bush-backed legislation to restrain class-action lawsuits and overhaul bankruptcy laws. However, Bush's influence has not fared as well for the "med-mal" bill, which was passed through the House but not the Senate. Bush's proposal would have limited the amount a health provider could be required to pay a patient for "pain and suffering" to $250,000 beyond actual cost of medical services; the proposal also provided for payout of judgments over time instead of in a lump sum.

It's a seemingly unending loop: multimillion-dollar judgments against providers, brought by a solid industry of trial lawyers devoted to representing mistreated patients, make headlines regularly. These judgments then cause liability insurers to panic, with many refusing to cover health care providers at all. As such, the insurers who have stayed in the medical liability market charge a premium providers increasingly can't afford to pay.

For lawmakers, the issue is a tough one: how do you set a cap on the amount a plaintiff can receive for the preventable death of a loved one? Patient advocates frame the issue as a David vs. Goliath scenario, charging that the monolithic medical community wants to limit consumers' rights to sue providers for poor care. Meanwhile, as the industry waits for the federal government to come up with a solution, states have begun to tackle the issue themselves by setting their own limits on the amount of money a malpractice judgment can reap for the plaintiff. Voters in the state of Texas, which was listed on the

AMA's liability list, recently approved a constitutional amendment capping awards for noneconomic damages at $250,000. (Similar measures are in place in West Virginia and Ohio.) Though these states' actions are a far cry from the national reform physicians and insurers desire, it is at least a start in a definitive direction.

Hot hospitals

In 2005, $616 billion was spent on care in hospitals. Growing demand for hospital services, along with higher rates from private insurers, have led to an increase in capital expended in this area. Among the approximately 6,100 hospitals in the U.S., a few tower over the rest. Each year, *U.S. News & World Report* publishes a ranking of the nation's top hospitals, surveying doctors around the country about hospitals' reputations in 17 medical specialties as well as other factors like staffing, morbidity rates and technology. In 2006, the magazine's list named Baltimore's Johns Hopkins Hospital No. 1 overall—a position the institution has held for 16 years running. The Mayo Clinic came in second, followed by the Cleveland Clinic and Massachusetts General.

MBAs in Health Care

What is health care management?

Health care management, also known as health care administration encompasses a wide range of jobs in a variety of organizations. Health care managers are involved in the delivery of health care and the development of public policy regarding financing of and access to care. It is a field that has evolved over the last 50 years and continues to evolve as the health care delivery system changes. Health care managers work for organizations and individuals that we encounter on a daily basis from physician groups to hospitals, insurance companies and government agencies. Their roles are diverse as well, ranging from line supervisors to directors and middle managers, to executives.

As the health care field has grown so have the number of disciplines that health care managers oversee. In addition to expanding clinical areas requiring managers, such as imaging centers, ambulatory surgery centers, home care, occupational health, assisted living and adult day care to name a few, disciplines in need of professional management have developed. These include specialists in the realm of financial management, reimbursement, revenue cycle management, planning, fundraising and development, performance improvement, medical management and business development.

The health care field has been cited as one of the most rapidly growing in the United States today. An aging population, longer life expectancy and new technology, treatments and medication are major contributors to this growth. As such, the need for health care professionals, including managers at all levels, will increase. The roles and responsibilities of health care managers may change as the health care system continues to do so. However, one objective, which is the primary objective of management, will remain constant: "designing and maintaining an environment within an enterprise in which individuals working together in groups can accomplish selected missions and objectives" (Weihrich and Koontz).

Who are health care managers and what do they do?

Health care managers come from a large number of professions. In addition to those who graduate from programs in health care administration, public administration or business administration there are clinical mangers, financial managers, information systems managers, and public relations and marketing managers. Individuals with undergraduate or graduate degrees in management generally enter the field after the completion of their training with the goal of obtaining a middle management or upper-level management position in a health care organization. Managers in professions such as finance, often have worked in another field, have developed their skills and transfer these skills to the health care environment. Clinical managers, including nurses and physicians, may work as clinicians for a period of time before entering management.

Visit Vault at **www.vault.com** for insider company profiles, expert advice, career message boards, expert resume reviews, the Vault Job Board and more.

VAULT CAREER LIBRARY   99

The organizations in which health care managers work include those that provide direct patient care and those that support the provision of care and services. Along what is referred to as the continuum of care, organizations provide different levels of direct care.

The highest level of care is provided in acute care hospitals. Hospitals are large complex organizations with hundreds or even thousands of employees and dozens or hundreds of supervisory and management personnel. Hospitals may be freestanding or part of a health system. They are classified according to ownership and control, number of beds, by the levels and types of services they provide and whether they have physician training programs, research programs and academic affiliations.

The next level of care on the continuum is called long-term acute care (LTAC). These are hospitals either freestanding or units within an acute care hospital that provide care to patients with chronic conditions. This is a relatively new level of care that is in a growth mode as units and facilities open throughout the country.

Sub acute care is provided in hospital and nursing homes. Hospital units are often referred to as transitional care units in which patients receive intense rehabilitation. Nursing homes operate sub acute or short-term units in which patients discharged from the hospital receive rehabilitation and other clinical services. Nursing homes or skilled nursing facilities provide care to the elderly and disabled and others requiring long-term care. Nursing homes may be freestanding, part of a regional or national company or hospital based.

Assisted living facilities provide a lower level of care than nursing homes. These facilities are generally for elderly residents who are unable to live on their own who require supervision and assistance with activities of daily living. Adult day care programs may be a medical model or social model. These programs provide socialization and medical services in the case of the medical model to elderly individuals who live in the community.

Other levels include home health care and ambulatory care. These services are provided by a variety of organizations and individuals including hospitals, physicians, nurses, therapists and technologists.

Organizations that support the provision of care may be classified into the following categories:

• Managed care organizations and insurance companies
• Management services organizations
• Consulting firms
• Public health and community health organizations
• Health care information services organizations
• Health related companies
• Research organizations, associations and educational institutions
• Regulatory and government agencies

Each of these entities plays a role in the delivery, financing and regulation of health care services. Managers in these organizations may have worked for a direct care provider previously or in another field.

Levels of health care management

As in any organization, there are different levels of management in health care. Entry-level management positions are generally referred to as a line supervisor. This type of individual supervises the day-to-day activities of a group of employees. Examples of this type of position are a chemistry lab supervisor in a hospital, a nursing supervisor in a nursing home, a food services supervisor in an assisted living facility and a case management supervisor in a managed care company. Many of these individuals are trained in a clinical or technical field and have come up through the ranks.

The next management level is department manager, or department head. These individuals are responsible for an entire department in a hospital nursing home or other health care organization. An environmental services manager in a nursing home, a health information management (also known as medical records) department head in a hospital, and a project manager in a consulting firm are all at this management level. Many of these individuals have formal management training (a bachelor's or master's degree or other training program) and/or certification in their specific discipline.

The level above department manager is often called director although some organizations refer to their managers as directors. Director usually implies the management of a broad function in the company, such as director of public relations or director of staff development. Managers in these roles may have clinical or technical experience, management training and specific training and certification in their area of expertise. In health care systems with corporate structures the director title is utilized for individuals with corporate or system wide responsibility for a function such as the director of materials management or the director of managed care.

There are physicians in management roles as well. These include the head of a clinical department in a hospital (medicine, surgery, obstetrics), the head of a clinical section in a large hospital (e.g., cardiology, urology) and various positions that are administrative in nature. The administrative type roles include medical director, chief medical officer, director of performance improvement, director of clinical effectiveness and medical director of a managed care organization. Many of these physician executives obtain management degrees and attend management training courses.

There are several designations for the executive-level management in health care organizations. One title sequence uses administrator to signify the highest management level. In this scheme there are associate administrators and assistant administrators. In hospitals and nursing homes that utilize these titles, the administrator is the highest ranking executive responsible for the entire organization. Associate administrators and assistant administrators report to this individual and are responsible for multiple departments and/or large functional areas. A common variation of this structure is the president and chief executive officer, executive and senior vice president and vice presidents. For the most part, the roles and responsibilities of these individuals correspond to the first set of titles. Another set of titles utilizes executive director to signify the top person and associate and assistant executive director for the top managers reporting to this individual. Those who hold these positions may have worked their way up through the management ranks and almost always have graduate degrees in health care management, business administration or a similar discipline.

In health systems and academic medical centers, there is also a corporate management level. These executives have system responsibilities for multiple facilities and usually have the title corporate director or vice president. There is also a corporate president or chief executive officer and a corporate chief financial officer. These companies may be regional, national or international and either for profit or not for profit. They may be comprised of one type of health care facility, such as a nursing home, or many types, such as hospitals, physician practices and insurance companies.

In the academic setting, there are often deans and university vice presidents who are have overall responsibilities for the hospitals and other health care facilities in the organization. The health care executives at the hospital or health care facilities report to these individuals.

A number of other roles and titles exist in both direct care and non-direct care health care from directors and coordinators in performance improvement organizations to managers in home health care agencies and supervisors in public health agencies.

Functional areas

There are numerous functional areas in which health care managers work. These include strategic planning, day-to-day operations, finance, business development, information services, marketing, planning, human resources and performance improvement. At one time, health care executives were for the most part generalists with knowledge and experienced in all or most of these areas. As the field and organizations became more complex, specialists in these areas and others emerged.

Visit Vault at **www.vault.com** for insider company profiles, expert advice, career message boards, expert resume reviews, the Vault Job Board and more.

VAULT CAREER LIBRARY   **101**

Today, although the chief executive officer of a health care organization has a general understanding of these functional areas, she is supported by experts with education, training and in-depth knowledge of their respective disciplines.

New health care management roles developed with the growth of managed care and health systems. Managed care executives, managers of physician practices, preferred provider organizations (PPOs), physician hospital organizations, ambulatory surgery centers, imaging centers and joint ventures appeared on the scene. In response to the increase in law suits and legal issues, risk managers, in-house attorneys and insurance manager roles were introduced. In the area of finance, revenue cycle managers and consultants responded to the complexities of government and managed care reimbursement for services. With the growth of government and accrediting agency regulations, government relations and regulatory affairs professionals emerged. Pressure to control cost and resource consumption prompted the introduction of medical management and disease management.

New roles and positions continue to evolve. Administrators and managers for organizational effectiveness, and managers of clinical effectiveness are two examples.

There is good reason to believe that as the health care system continues to evolve, new roles for managers will be created. These positions may be in areas of outcomes management, health education, information systems and ambulatory services. Alternatives to institutional long-term care will also have an impact. New models for the provision of care to the growing elderly population are being developed and tested.

Government policy and regulation will play a major role in shaping new management positions. All of these factors contribute to field that is expected to expand and diversify for years to come.

Employer Directory

Aetna Inc.
151 Farmington Avenue
Hartford, CT 06156
Phone: (860) 273-0123
Toll Free: (800) 872-3862
Fax: (860) 273-3971
www.aetna.com

Amerigroup Corporation
4425 Corporation Lane
Virginia Beach, VA 23462
Phone: (757) 490-6900
Fax: (757) 490-7152
www.amerigrp.com

Applera Corporation
301 Merritt 7
Norwalk, CT 06856-5435
Phone: (203) 840-2000
Fax: (203) 840-2312
www.applera.com

Beckman Coulter, Inc.
4300 N. Harbor Boulevard
Fullerton, CA 92834-3100
Phone: (714) 871-4848
Fax: (714) 773-8283
www.beckman.com

Beverly Healthcare
1000 Fianna Way
Fort Smith, AR 72919
Phone: (479) 201-2000
Fax: (479) 201-1101
www.beverlyhealthcare.com

Blue Cross and Blue Shield Association
225 N. Michigan Avenue
Chicago, IL 60601-7680
Phone: (312) 297-6000
Fax: (312) 297-6609
www.bcbs.com

Boston Scientific Corporation
1 Boston Scientific Place
Natick, MA 01760-1537
Phone: (508) 650-8000
Fax: (508) 647-2393
www.bostonscientific.com

Caremark Pharmacy Services
211 Commerce Street, Suite 800
Nashville, TN 37201
Phone: (615) 743-6600
Fax: (205) 733-9780
www.caremark.com

CIGNA
2 Liberty Place, 1601 Chestnut Street
Philadelphia, PA 19192
Phone: (215) 761-1000
Fax: (215) 761-5515
www.cigna.com

Community Health Systems, Inc.
4000 Meridian Boulevard
Franklin, TN 37067
Phone: (615) 465-7000
www.chs.net

Coventry Health Care, Inc.
6705 Rockledge Drive
Suite 900
Bethesda, MD 20817
Phone: (301) 581-0600
Fax: (301) 493-0731
www.cvty.com

DaVita, Inc.
601 Hawaii Street
El Segundo, CA 90245
Phone: (310) 536-2400
Fax: (310) 536-2675
www.davita.com

Express Scripts, Inc.
1 Express Way
St. Louis, MO 63121
Phone: (314) 996-0900
www.express-scripts.com

Fresenius Medical Care AG
Else-Kröner-Straße 1
Germany
Phone: +49-6172-608-0
Fax: +49-6172-608-2488
www.fmc-ag.com

Guidant Corporation
111 Monument Circle, 29th Floor
Indianapolis, IN 46204
Phone: (317) 971-2000
Fax: (317) 971-2040
www.guidant.com

HCA, Inc.
1 Park Plaza
Nashville, TN 37203
Phone: (615) 344-9551
Fax: (615) 344-2266
www.hcahealthcare.com

Health Management Associates, Inc.
5811 Pelican Bay Boulevard, Suite 500
Naples, FL 34108-2710
Phone: (239) 598-3131
Fax: (239) 598-2705
www.hma-corp.com

Health Net, Inc.
21650 Oxnard Street
Woodland Hills, CA 91367
Phone: (818) 676-6000
Fax: (818) 676-8591
www.healthnet.com

HealthSouth Corporation
1 HealthSouth Parkway
Birmingham, AL 35243
Phone: (205) 967-7116
Fax: (205) 969-6889
www.healthsouth.com

Henry Schein
135 Duryea Road
Melville, NY 11747
Phone: (631) 843-5500
Fax: (631) 843-5658
www.henryschein.com

Hillenbrand Industries, Inc.
700 State Route 46 East
Batesville, IN 47006-8835
Phone: (812) 934-7000
Fax: (812) 934-7371
www.hillenbrand.com

Visit Vault at **www.vault.com** for insider company profiles, expert advice, career message boards, expert resume reviews, the Vault Job Board and more.

VAULT CAREER LIBRARY   103

Employer Directory, cont.

Humana Inc.
The Humana Building
500 W. Main Street
Louisville, KY 40202
Phone: (502) 580-1000
Fax: (502) 580-3677
www.humana.com

Johns Hopkins Health System Corporation
600 N. Wolfe Street
Baltimore, MD 21287
Phone: (410) 955-5000
Fax: (410) 955-0890
www.hopkinshospital.org

Kaiser Permanente
1 Kaiser Plaza, Suite 2600
Oakland, CA 94612-3673
Phone: (510) 271-5800
Fax: (510) 267-7524
www.kaiserpermanente.org

Kindred Health Care
680 S. 4th Street
Louisville, KY 40202-2412
Phone: (502) 596-7300
Fax: (502) 596-4170
www.kindredhealthcare.com

Laboratory Corporation of America
358 S. Main Street
Burlington, NC 27215
Phone: (336) 229-1127
Fax: (336) 436-1205
www.labcorp.com

Magellan Health Services, Inc.
55 Nod Road
Avon, CT 06001
Phone: (860) 507-1900
Toll Free: (800) 410-8312
Fax: (860) 507-1990
www.magellanhealth.com

Manor Care, Inc.
333 N. Summit Street
Toledo, OH 43604-2617
Phone: (419) 252-5500
Fax: (419) 252-5596
www.hcr-manorcare.com

Mariner Health Care, Inc.
1 Ravinia Drive, Suite 1500
Atlanta, GA 30346
Phone: (678) 443-7000
Fax: (770) 393-8054
www.marinerhealth.com

Mayo Foundation for Medical Education and Research
200 1st Street SW
Rochester, MN 55905
Phone: (507) 284-2511
Fax: (507) 284-0161
www.mayo.edu

Medco Health Solutions
100 Parsons Pond Drive
Franklin Lakes, NJ 07417-2604
Phone: (201) 269-3400
Fax: (201) 269-1109
www.medco.com

Medical Mutual of Ohio
2060 E. 9th Street
Cleveland, OH 44115-1300
Phone: (216) 687-7000
Fax: (216) 687-6044
www.mmoh.com

Medtronic, Inc.
710 Medtronic Parkway NE
Minneapolis, MN 55432-5604
Phone: (763) 514-4000
Fax: (763) 514-4879
www.medtronic.com

PacifiCare Health Systems, Inc.
5995 Plaza Drive
Cypress, CA 90630
Phone: (714) 952-1121
Fax: (714) 226-3581
www.pacificare.com

Quest Diagnostics Incorporated
1290 Wall Street West
Lyndhurst, NJ 07071
Phone: (201) 393-5000
Fax: (201) 729-8920
www.questdiagnostics.com

Sierra Health Services, Inc.
2724 N. Tenaya Way
Las Vegas, NV 89128
Phone: (702) 242-7000
Fax: (702) 242-9711
www.sierrahealth.com

St. Jude Medical, Inc.
1 Lillehei Plaza
St. Paul, MN 55117-9983
Phone: (651) 483-2000
Fax: (651) 482-8318
www.sjm.com

Stryker Corporation
2825 Airview Boulevard
Kalamazoo, MI 49002-1802
Phone: (269) 385-2600
Fax: (269) 385-1062
www.stryker.com

Sun Healthcare Group, Inc.
18831 Von Karman, Suite 400
Irvine, CA 92612
Phone: (949) 255-7100
Fax: (949) 255-7054
www.sunh.com

Employer Directory, cont.

Tenet Healthcare
13737 Noel Road
Dallas, TX 75240
Phone: (469) 893-2200
Fax: (469) 893-8600
www.tenethealth.com

UnitedHealth Group Inc.
UnitedHealth Group Center
9900 Bren Road East
Minnetonka, MN 55343
Phone: (952) 936-1300
Fax: (952) 936-7430
www.unitedhealthgroup.com

Universal Health Services
Universal Corporate Center
367 S. Gulph Road
King of Prussia, PA 19406-0958
Phone: (610) 768-3300
Fax: (610) 768-3336
www.uhsinc.com

WellPoint, Inc.
120 Monument Circle
Indianapolis, IN 46204
Phone: (317) 488-6000
Fax: (317) 488-6028
www.wellpoint.com

Visit Vault at **www.vault.com** for insider company profiles, expert advice, career message boards, expert resume reviews, the Vault Job Board and more.

VAULT CAREER LIBRARY   105

Hedge Funds

What is a Hedge Fund?

In a recent article by *The Wall Street Journal*, Tremont Advisors reported that hedge funds took in approximately $72.2 billion in assets in 2003 and that worldwide hedge fund investment is now as high as $750 billion in assets.

Hedge funds are considered an "alternative investment" vehicle. The term "alternative investment" is the general term under which unregulated funds operate; this includes private equity and real estate funds. The total "alternative" category (including private equity and real estate) is not covered within the scope of this section but it is useful to know that often people refer to hedge funds as alternative investments. Mainstream funds are investment funds that everyday investors can purchase, mutual funds are the prime example of a mainstream fund.

Over the past decade, hedge funds have grown tremendously in terms of assets under management and also garnered a lot of media attention. Although, despite their growth and popularity, hedge funds still remain a mystery to many people who do not understand exactly what they are and how they work. So what exactly is a hedge fund?

A Concise Definition of "Hedge Fund"

A "private unregistered investment pool" encompassing all types of investment funds, companies and private partnerships that can use a variety of investment techniques such as borrowing money through leverage, selling short, derivatives for directional investing and options.

During the early years of the hedge fund industry (1950s to 1970s), the term "hedge fund" was used to describe the "hedging" strategy used by managers at the time. "Hedging" refers to the hedge fund manager making additional trades in an attempt to counterbalance any risk involved with the existing positions in the portfolio. Hedging can be accomplished in many different ways but the most basic technique is to purchase a long position and a secondary short position in a similar security. This is used to offset price fluctuations and is an effective way of neutralizing the effects of market conditions.

Today, the term "hedge fund" tells an investor nothing about the underlying investment activities, similar to the term "mutual fund." So how do you figure out what the hedge fund manager does? You are able to figure out a little more about the underlying investment activities by understanding the trading/investment strategies that the hedge fund manager states he trades. The "investment strategy" is the investment approach or the techniques used by the hedge fund manager to have positive returns on the investments. If a manager says he trades long/short equity then you know he is buying undervalued equities and selling overvalued equities. Although this description is the long/short equity strategy at its most basic, it is important to understand the strategies that the manager says he employs. For more information on specific hedge fund investment strategies, see the *Vault Career Guide to Hedge Funds*.

Visit Vault at **www.vault.com** for insider company profiles, expert advice, career message boards, expert resume reviews, the Vault Job Board and more.

VAULT CAREER LIBRARY 107

Distinguishing Characteristics

So now that you have reviewed some of the basic terminology in the industry, we will explain the key points in depth. The main distinguishing characteristics of hedge funds are the following:

• Hedge funds can "hedge" their portfolio

• Hedge funds use derivatives

• Hedge funds can short sell

• Hedge funds have the ability to use leverage

These characteristics make hedge funds different from most other investment funds, especially mutual funds. To get a good understanding of how a hedge fund manager operates, it is very important to understand these concepts. The four concepts are now defined in detail.

Hedging

Hedging can be accomplished in many different ways, although the most basic technique is to purchase a long position and a secondary short position in a similar security (see Gap example). This is used to offset price fluctuations and is an effective way of neutralizing the effects of market conditions.

Hedging Example

Courtney is a hedge fund manager who invested in the Gap stores. Here we will see how he hedges his risk. Courtney is "long" (he's bought) 100 shares of Gap stores but he now believes the retail industry may be vulnerable to a down turn in the market. He wants to hedge this risk and does this by going "short" (selling) Abercrombie & Fitch, which is in the same retail industry.

Q. What would happen if the retail industry did poorly?
A. The share prices of both Gap and Abercrombie & Fitch might decline.

Q. How would this affect any money Courtney makes?
A. Since Courtney is long on Gap (he owns it) he would lose money on this trade. Since Courtney is also short (he has already sold it) Abercrombie & Fitch, he would make money on that trade. Therefore he can offset some of his losses from Gap with gains from Abercrombie & Fitch. He reduces his risk of Gap by hedging with Abercrombie & Fitch.

Q. When you say Courtney gains from the Abercrombie & Fitch trade, what does this mean?
A. When Courtney goes short A&F, it means he has sold it before he owns it. So say he sells 100 A&F shares short for $50 each. He receives $5,000 cash for doing so. This transaction is conducted through his broker and he now owes 100 A&F shares to his broker, to be paid back at some time the future. As time goes by, the retail industry does poorly and the share price of A&F falls to $40.

Q. If the stock price of A&F falls to $40, what does this mean for Courtney's profits?
A. Since Courtney owes 100 A&F shares to his broker, he can now go out and buy the 100 shares for $40 each, costing him a total of $4,000. Therefore, Courtney has made $1,000 profit. (He receives $5,000 from the original short sale and then pays $4,000 to buy A&F, so his profit is $1,000)

Derivatives

Derivatives that are used by hedge funds can take on many forms, and the more complex derivatives (interest rate swaps, foreign currency swaps, contract for differences, total return swaps, etc.) are not covered in this book. Discussed now are the most basic forms of derivatives: "put" and "call" options on stocks.

Option Definitions

Put option

A "put" option gives the holder the right to sell the underlying stock at a specified price (strike price) on or before a given date (exercise date).

Call option

A "call" option gives the holder the right to buy the underlying stock at specified price (strike price) on or before a given date (exercise date).

Option writer

The seller of these options is referred to as the "writer"—many hedge funds will often write options in accordance with their strategies. This is the person who originates an option contract by promising to perform a certain obligation in return for the price or premium of the option. Any investor can sell options (write options) provided they have answered an options questionnaire provided to them by their broker. This would determine the knowledge of the investor and whether they understand the risks associated with writing options.

How does a hedge fund manager use options to reduce risk?

Consider Kristin, a long/short hedge fund manager, who in January 2004 owns 1,000 Wal-Mart shares. The current share price is $73 per share. Kristin is concerned about developments in Wal-Mart's illegal immigrant lawsuit that may cause the share price to decline sharply in the next two months and wants to protect herself from this risk. The process that Kristin would go through to hedge the risk of Wal-Mart's share price falling would be:

- Kristin could buy 10 July "put" options with a strike price of $65 on the Chicago Board Options Exchange (www.cboe.com).

- This "put" option gives Kristin the right to sell 1,000 shares for $65 per share at any time before it expires in July. If the market price of Wal-Mart falls below $65, the options can be exercised so that Kristin received $65,000 for the entire holding. When the cost of the options is taken into account, the amount realized is $62,500.

- If the quoted option price is $2.50, each option contract would cost $250. Since each option contract is valued per 100 shares, the total cost of the hedging strategy would be 10*$250 = $2,500.

- Although this strategy costs $2,500, it guarantees that the shares can be sold for at least $65 per share for the life of the option (it expires in July).

- But if the market price stays above $65, the options are not exercised because Kristin can make more money by just selling the shares for market price.

Visit Vault at **www.vault.com** for insider company profiles, expert advice, career message boards, expert resume reviews, the Vault Job Board and more.

VAULT CAREER LIBRARY   **109**

The Chicago Board Options Exchange (CBOE)

The CBOE created an orderly market with well-defined contracts on 16 stocks when it began trading call option contracts in 1973. The exchange began trading put options in 1977. The CBOE now trades options on over 1,200 stocks and many different stock indices. Many other exchanges throughout the world also trade option contracts. To learn more, visit the exchange's web site at www.cboe.com.

Short selling (going "short")

Short selling involves the selling of a security that the seller does not own. Short sellers believe that the stock price will fall and that they will be able to repurchase the stock at a lower price in the future. Thus, they will profit from selling the stock at a higher price, then buy it in the future at a lower price. (The opposite of going "short" is going "long," when investors buy stocks they believe will rise.)

Short Selling Example

Jimmy believes that McDonald's is overvalued and that he can profit by selling short "MCD." Jimmy sells short 100 shares at $50 which means he has sold stock that he does not yet own, this is a stock loan. In the future he has to buy the stock to repay the stock loan he entered into when shorting the stock. But, McDonald's price continues to rise to $75, this means that in order to buy the stock (this is called "covering" his stock loan), Jimmy pays $75 per share, which results in him losing $2,500 (100*$25)

Before Jimmy enters into the short sale, he must ensure that he is able to borrow the stock (get a stock loan), usually through its prime broker. Jimmy will call the stock loan department of the prime broker to see if the prime broker has the stock available to lend to him. If the stock loan department has the stock to lend, then Jimmy can short sell the stock (borrowing it from the prime broker). If the stock is not available for borrow, Jimmy cannot sell short the security.

Leverage

Leverage measures the amount of assets being borrowed for each investment dollar. Leverage (borrowing additional funds) is utilized by hedge fund managers when they believe that the cost of the borrowed funds will be minimal compared to the returns of a particular position. It can be a key component to hedge fund management since it gives the hedge fund managers the ability to have higher returns (and potentially lose more) with borrowed funds.

Typical hedge fund leverage depends on the type of financial instruments that the hedge fund trades. Fixed income has lower risk levels so it is not uncommon to have four or five times the value of the fund borrowed. Equities have a higher risk profile and therefore typical leverage is one and a half to two times the value of the fund. However, hedge funds are usually comprised of long and short positions, so a large market rise or fall has little impact if their profitable positions were equally balanced by their losing positions.

The simplest examples in everyday life of leverage are house mortgages and car loans. The bank manager uses the house or the car as collateral for the loan from the bank. The bank manager can then sell the house or the car if you default on your loan. Similarly, the hedge fund manager uses the financial instruments in his account as collateral for the funds they have borrowed from their bank (prime broker). The primary sources of leverage are financial institutions and banks. If the hedge fund manager cannot pay the loan back, the financial institution can then sell the collateral (the financial instruments in the account) to pay back the loan.

Leverage Calculation Example

If the hedge fund has $1 million of invested money and is borrowing another $2 million, to bring the total dollars invested to $3 million, then the leverage used is 200 percent. The amount of leverage typically used by the fund is shown as a percentage of the fund.

Organizational Structure of a Typical Hedge Fund

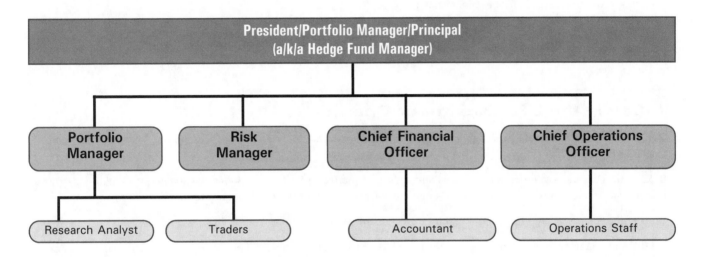

So what exactly are hedge fund managers and what do they do? A hedge fund manager is normally the founder and the key person in charge of overseeing the whole operation of the hedge fund. This means that he/she is responsible for overseeing the portfolio, often making trading decisions, hiring personnel, monitoring the risk of the portfolio and ensuring that the accounting and operations departments are in order. The hedge fund manager is often referred to as the principal or president and can often also be called the portfolio manager.

Hedge funds vary in size from assets under management from as little as $1 million to over $10 billion. Unlike a typical investment bank, the roles of the employees at hedge funds are not the same for each hedge fund. Someone entering an investment bank as a trader will likely have a similar role to someone else entering another investment bank as a trader. Traders at hedge funds are likely to have different responsibilities, which are usually determined by the size of the fund. At a smaller fund the trader is much more likely to be involved with the operations of the trade, whereas a larger hedge fund would have a separate operations person to handle this element. A smaller hedge fund may have three or four employees, whereas a larger hedge fund may employ over 300 people.

A typical hedge fund will have various departments: operations, accounting, trading, and risk and investor relations. These departments support the trading decisions and operations of the hedge fund. Since the size of hedge funds vary dramatically, the number of people in each department can range from one to over 20. As a hedge fund grows in size (manages more money), more personnel are added to support the increased trading volume.

In the next few pages, we will attempt to clearly outline the different departments at hedge funds and the distinct roles within each department. While you read through the different roles, it is very important to note that specific job titles are not important at hedge funds. This is because one role (job) can have many different titles depending on the hedge fund. For example, an operations analyst can also be called portfolio analyst, trading assistant or accountant depending on the size and environment of the fund.

Visit Vault at **www.vault.com** for insider company profiles, expert advice, career message boards, expert resume reviews, the Vault Job Board and more.

VAULT CAREER LIBRARY   111

In addition, due to the varying sizes of hedge funds, employees tend to have a more diverse range of responsibilities, which may overlap between several different departments. This unique nature of the hedge fund job requires superior teamwork skills and the ability to deal with a variety of people.

Director of Operations

Most individuals carrying this title either have several years of experience in the same capacity, a MBA or both. At this stage one generally has a staff of 2 to 10 people who are direct reports. The job functions are similar to the operations specialist although there is much more responsibility for the employees working under you as well as maintaining relationships between prime broker, banks and offshore administrators.

This position will generally pay between $100,000 and $250,000 depending on experience, background and size of hedge fund.

A Day in the Life: Director of Operations

7:30 a.m.: Arrive at the office and log onto the computer, along will various back office and portfolio systems such as DTC.

8:15 a.m.: Go over exception reports (available only to a manager) that show trades that have not settled and any margin calls for accounts and speak to the member of staff who works on it to get status on the item.

9:00 a.m.: Have weekly team meeting and go over team workload and coverage for the week.

10:00 a.m.: Get on a call with a manager in the prime broker because a large wire needs to be sent out for management fees and there needs to be extra attention give to it to make sure it goes through properly. The prime broker department at an investment bank offers products, technology and clearing services to a hedge fund.

11:00 a.m.: Have a meeting with the head trader on the convertible trading desk who does not agree with the final position on a particular security. Go over each transaction and see if anything was incorrectly booked. Have one of the staff members print all transaction reports internally and ask the prime broker to find a solution to this problem as it may involve large losses for the desk.

1:00 p.m.: Have lunch at the desk while browsing through some stories on Bloomberg.

2:00 p.m.: Field calls and help the staff resolve any pending problems.

4:00 p.m.: Re-review all reports from the morning and make sure all highlighted discrepancies are resolved otherwise jot them down as "open items."

5:00 p.m.: Create a list of agenda items for the next day and look at the calendar of any meetings.

6:00 p.m.: Leave work and meet the prime broker for dinner who is taking the operations team out.

7:00 p.m.: Discuss rates with the prime broker over dinner and get to know them better.

10:00 p.m.: Head home and try to get the motivation to go to the gym before crashing.

Risk Management

The risk department proactively monitors each hedge fund, identifying potential risks and then determining and understanding the importance of various types of risks. This department uses various propriety or vendor tools and methodologies for risk management and implements strategies to prevent any risk completely or to deal with them if they occur.

At a hedge fund, a risk management role can vary depending on the size of the fund. At a small fund, generally the principals or the trading group may monitor the risk and there are no specific risk personnel; while at a larger fund, there is a group who is solely responsible for monitoring risk. Many hedge funds are also known to outsource their risk controls through third party vendors specialized in providing this service to corporations, hedge funds, mutual funds, etc. Many investment banks also provide such added value service through their prime broker departments.

Fund of funds are known to have a very large risk teams because of two reasons. Firstly, due to the way fund of funds operate they are dealing with a large variety of securities product base; and secondly, the risk group plays a large role in alleviating concerns of existing and potential investors.

Risk Associate

This associate level position will play a supporting role in the risk department. Many hedge funds don't have a separate risk department but this position would be available at an investment bank's prime broker department.

In a prime broker department, the risk associate will perform the same duties, except he will be monitoring risk for several hedge funds that are prime broker clients. This position generally requires a minimum of a bachelor's degree and a few years of relevant experience. A thorough understanding of a variety of trading products (i.e., options, fixed income, mortgage backed securities, swaptions), options risks (i.e., delta, gamma, vega, rho and theta) and strong analytical skills are strongly recommended. The daily job duties include but are not limited to maintaining value at risk (VAR) data, back-testing and stress-testing securities within a portfolio and reporting the analyzed data to senior risk management.

For example, Heather works with the trading group to monitor risk. The hedge fund where she works subscribes/utilizes a risk monitoring system designed by a large investment bank. Every morning she will perform analysis to the short portfolio measuring how minor changes in the stock market, such as the Dow Jones Industrial Average decreasing substantially in one day, could affect the value of the portfolio. Heather does not have to compute everything manually because the risk system has built in mathematical models to attribute for different scenarios, although Heather needs to understand what the output of results mean and be able to verbally communicate those clearly to the traders and portfolio mangers along with having spreadsheets and graphs as back up of her analysis.

This position generally pays from $50K to $70K, depending on geographical location, previous experience, education skills and size of the corporation. The risk position could potentially have interaction with clients (investors) depending on the size of the fund. Some hedge funds have a designated investor relations employee whose sole responsibility is to field calls from investors. Although, in smaller funds investors may call the risk group directly to state and address any risk concerns. It is important that a hedge fund has a strong risk monitoring system because this reduces the likelihood of error and losses in the fund and will also help alleviates the investor's worries.

Risk jobs are found through job agencies or through connections. Generally, traders are also well aware of job openings in the risk groups and can be a good source of contact/network.

Visit Vault at **www.vault.com** for insider company profiles, expert advice, career message boards, expert resume reviews, the Vault Job Board and more.

V/\ULT CAREER LIBRARY   **113**

A Day in the Life: Risk Analyst at a Large Hedge Fund

7:30 a.m.: Get into the office and check e-mail. Chat with colleagues about interesting stories in the *WSJ*.

8:00 a.m.: Daily risk conference call with traders, portfolio manager and principals

9:30 a.m.: Monitoring the portfolios on one screen while looking at the markets affecting the various securities on another screen. Quantify illiquid positions and valuations risk and compare margin requirements of all positions with the custodian/prime broker making sure you are in agreement.

10:00 a.m.: Call the prime broker risk department and discuss risks involved in utilizing more leverage for a particular option arbitrage fund. Write up a report based on the call to present to the principals.

11:00 a.m.: Compile statistics for the ongoing exception report for non-investment risk issues such as trade settlement, particular trader leaving the organization, etc.

12:00 p.m.: Making sure that the portfolio is maintained within established risk parameters

1:00 p.m.: Eat lunch at the desk while preparing for the 1:30 meeting with potential investors of the hedge fund who want to discuss business and corporate structure of the hedge fund and its links to the investment manger.

1:30 – 2:30 p.m.: Meeting with investors in a conference room. Emphasize the safety of assets to the investor because of proper risk monitoring.

2:30 p.m.: Recap the meeting with principals, see how it went and make a list of items to follow up with the investor. It is very important that the risk manager gets rid of any potential investors concerns of sudden losses.

4:00 p.m.: Work with the CFO to have him clarify a problem you noticed on last month's audit.

5:00 p.m.: Field calls and answer e-mails on all risk and portfolio inquiries to internal and external people.

7:00 p.m.: Look over notes from today and jot down any items that needs to be addressed tomorrow.

7:15 p.m.: Review schedule for next day.

7:30 – 8 p.m.: Head home and get to bed early for a good night's sleep.

Employer Directory

AIG Global Investment Group
70 Pine Street
New York, NY 10270
Phone: (800) 706-6661
Fax: (212) 770-9491
www.aiginvestments.com

Andor Capital Management
1 American Lane, 3rd Floor
Greenwich, CT 06831
Phone: (203) 742-7200
www.andorcap.com/index.html

Angelo, Gordon & Co.
245 Park Avenue
New York, NY 10167
Phone: (212) 692-2000
Fax: (212) 867-9328
www.angelogordon.com

Arden Asset Management
375 Park Avenue, 32nd Floor
New York, NY 10152
Phone: (212) 751-5252
Fax: (212) 751-8546
www.ardenasset.com

Atticus Capital
152 W. 57th Street
New York, NY 10019
Phone: (212) 373-0800

Avenue Capital
535 Madison Avenue
New York, NY 10022
Phone: (212) 878-3535
www.avenuecapital.com

Bank of America
100 N. Tryon Street
Bank of America Corporate Center
Charlotte, NC 28255
Phone: (704) 386-5681
Fax: (704) 386-6699
www.bankofamerica.com

Blackstone Alternative Asset Management
345 Park Avenue, Floor 30
New York, NY 10154
Phone: (212) 583-5000

Brevan Howard Asset Management
590 Madison Ave Fl 9
New York, NY 10022-2524
Phone: (212) 418-8200
www.brevanhoward.com

Bridgewater Associates
One Glendinning Place
Westport, CT 06880
Phone: (203) 226-3030
Fax: (203) 291-7300
www.bwater.com

Campbell & Co.
210 West Pennsylvania Avenue
Suite 770
Towson, MD 21204
Phone: (800) 698-7235
Fax: (410) 296-3311
www.campbell.com

Caxton Associates
500 Park Ave
New York, NY 10022-1606
Phone: (212) 418-8300
www.caxton.com

Cerberus Capital Management
299 Park Avenue
New York, NY 10171
Phone: (212) 891-2100
Fax: (212) 891-1540
www.cerberuscapital.com

Citadel Investment Group
131 S. Dearborn Street
Chicago, IL 60603
Phone: (312) 395-2100
Fax: (312) 977-0270
www.citadelgroup.com

CSFB Alternative Capital (Credit Suisse)
Credit Suisse
Eleven Madison Avenue
Phone: (212) 325-2000
www.csfb.com/investment_management/private_equity/index.shtml

D. E. Shaw & Co.
120 W. 45th Street, 39th Floor
Tower 45
New York, NY 10036
Phone: (212) 478-0000
Fax: (212) 478-0100
www.deshaw.com

Davidson Kempner Capital Management
65 E 55th Street, Floor 19
New York, NY 10022-3355
Phone: (212) 371-3000

DB Absolute Return Strategies
Phone: (212) 454-2118
ars.db.com/arsportal/index.jsp

EIM
750 Lexington Avenue
New York, NY 10022
Phone: (212) 371-9000
Fax: (212) 371-9111
www.eimgroup.com

ESL Investments
200 Greenwich Avenue
Greenwich, CT 06830
Phone: (203) 861-4600

Fortress Investment Group
1345 Avenue of the Americas
New York, NY 10105
Phone: (212) 798-6100
www.fortressinv.com

Goldman Sachs Asset Management
1 New York Plaza
New York, NY 10004
Phone: (800) 292-4726
goldmansachs.com

Visit Vault at **www.vault.com** for insider company profiles, expert advice, career message boards, expert resume reviews, the Vault Job Board and more.

VAULT CAREER LIBRARY 115

Employer Directory, cont.

Grosvenor Capital Management
900 North Michigan Avenue
Suite 1100
Chicago, IL 60611

Harris Alternatives
227 W Monroe Street, Floor 60
Chicago, IL 60606-5055
Phone: (312) 762-6700
www.harrisalternatives.com

HBK Capital Management
300 Crescent Court
Dallas, TX 75201-1836
Phone: (214)758-6100
www.hbk.com

Ivy Asset Management
1 Jericho Plaza, Suite 304
Jericho, NY 11753
Phone: (516) 2286500
Fax: (516) 228-6515
www.ivyasset.com

J.P. Morgan Alternative Asset Management
245 Park Avenue
New York, NY 10167
Phone: (212) 483-2323
im.jpmorgan.com

Lehman Brothers Alternative Investment Management
399 Park Avenue
New York, NY 10022-4614
Phone: (212) 526-9166

Man Investments
123 N Wacker Drive, Floor 28
Chicago, IL 60606-1749
Phone: (312) 881-6800

Mesirow Advanced Strategies
350 N. Clark Street
Chicago, IL 60610
Phone: (312) 595-6000
Toll Free: (800) 453-0600
Fax: (312) 595-4246
www.mesirowfinancial.com

Oaktree Capital Management, LLC
333 S. Grand Avenue, 28th Floor
Los Angeles, CA 90071
Phone: (213) 830-6300
Fax: (213) 830-6393
www.oaktreecapital.com

Och-Ziff Capital Management
9 W 57th Street, Floor 39
New York, NY 10019
Phone: (212) 790-0120

Pacific Alternative Asset Management Co.
19540 Jamboree Road, Suite 400
Irvine, CA 92612
Phone: (949) 261-4900
Fax: (949) 261-4901
www.paamco.com

Pequot Capital Management
500 Nyala Farm Road
Westport, CT 06880
Phone: (203) 429-2200
Fax: (203) 429-2400
www.pequotcap.com

Permal Group
900 3rd Avenue, Floor 28
New York, NY 10022
Phone: (212) 418 6500
www.permal.com

Perry Capital
3113 Woodcreek Drive
Downers Grove, IL 60515-5412
Phone: (630) 719-7800
www.perrycap.com

Pirate Capital LLC
200 Connecticut Avenue, 4th Floor
Norwalk, CT 06854
Phone: (203) 854-1100
www.piratecapitalllc.com

Quellos Capital Management
601 Union Street, Suite 5600
Seattle, WA 98101-4059
Phone: (206) 613-6700; (866) 613-6700
www.quellos.com

RBS Asset Management
71 S Wacker Drive, Floor 28
Chicago, IL 60606-4637
Phone: (312) 777-3500

Renaissance Technologies Corp.
800 3rd Avenue, 33rd Floor
New York, NY 10022
Phone: (212) 486-6780
Fax: (212) 758-7136
www.rentec.com

SAC Capital Advisors
72 Cummings Point Road
Stamford, CT 06902-7912
Phone: (203) 614-2000

Soros Fund Management
888 7th Avenue, 33rd Floor
New York, NY 10106
Phone: (212) 262-6300
Fax: (212) 245-5154

Superfund Group
489 Fifth Avenue
New York, NY 10017
Phone (212) 750-6300
Fax: (212) 750-2206
www.superfund.net

Tremont Capital Management
555 Theodore Fremd Avenue
Rye, NY 10580
Phone: (914) 925-1140
Fax: (914) 921-3499
www.tremont.com

Tudor Investment Corporation
1275 King Street
Greenwich, CT 06831
Phone: (203) 863-6700
Fax: (203) 863-8600
www.tudorfunds.com

UBS Global Asset Management
51 W. 52nd Street, Floor 22
New York, NY 10019-6119
Phone: (212) 713-2000

High Tech

Technology is Everywhere

Information Technology (IT) is a huge, ever-changing field. It encompasses the products and services necessary to store, convert, and deliver information electronically. This includes the entire computer infrastructure of an organization: computer hardware, packaged software, computer system architecture, documents outlining technical procedures, many other computer-related products, and lots and lots of people.

Computers and IT continue to have an explosive impact of on life and business. More than ever, companies must rapidly evolve, incorporating new technologies into their daily operations to remain competitive. From one-man sales companies to international medical labs, almost every type of business utilizes an IT infrastructure to run, to expand and, occasionally, to simply comply with the law.

IT is essential to business because it allows people to communicate faster, more efficiently, and with more capabilities than older technologies. A lone costume maker in Illinois can suddenly turn her enterprise into an international business by putting up a web site. A corporate executive can instantaneously deliver vital information to associates in Japan, South Africa and England through the power of a secure network. A student whose laptop gets stolen can immediately retrieve all of his lost information from a backup database server. A doctor can use a computer program that makes all of his patients' correspondences and information secure from prying eyes. There is power in IT.

Since technology issues are so critical to a company's health, a significant portion of business is involved with IT. In fact, one in every 14 jobs in America is an IT or IT-related position. IT careers cover a broad range of businesses, skill paths, office sizes and backgrounds.

The scope of IT

Today, IT is integral in most businesses, and its definition is still being redefined. Although most job seekers know that IT involves widespread technologies, few trying to enter the field probably know just which technologies or which jobs it encompasses.

Authorities describing IT demonstrate how widespread yet "blurry" the field is. First of all, "There is not a government-wide definition of who is classified as an information technology worker," says Roger Moncarz, an economist for the U.S. Bureau of Labor Statistics. "There's a wide sampling of estimates out there for exactly how to define an information technology worker."

Moncarz continues, "Based on our definition of information technology workers, and based on government occupational surveys, we come up with 3.3 million to 3.5 million IT workers in America. The Information Technology Association of America (ITAA), in it's recently released study, says there are 10.4 million IT workers. So there's wide discrepancy."

Regardless of who may define it, one thing is certain: IT is everywhere. Offices large and small must maintain, utilize and upgrade IT infrastructures to be effective in the marketplace. Because of the ubiquitous and demanding nature of the technology, IT jobs run the gamut from entry-level, low-tech positions to tech-savvy engineering managers.

The MBA in Tech

So you're in IT and you decided to get an MBA. Perhaps your degree even came with a technology specialty, which is an increasingly common option. Where will your degree get you?

Visit Vault at **www.vault.com** for insider company profiles, expert advice, career message boards, expert resume reviews, the Vault Job Board and more.

V/\ULT CAREER LIBRARY 117

Despite the lore of the 1970s-era computer "hackers" who revolutionized personal computing by working out of garages, many other people even then were studying for MBA degrees and were interested in technology. In the five-year period from 1976 to 1981, Harvard Business School produced Dan Bricklin (VisiCalc), Scott Cook (Intuit), Donna Dubinsky (Palm), Meg Whitman (eBay), and many others. Bricklin was an MIT-educated engineer, but has stated that he thought of many core ideas for the electronic spreadsheet while in business school.

Today, working in IT or working at a technology manufacturer offers many opportunities for MBAs to advance. Some of the popular fields are consulting, director-level positions, finance, law, marketing, project management, sales, training and the ultimate, which is C-level leadership.

Project management

As a project (or product) manager, you have a very specific set of goals to meet. They typically include detailed technology specifications to follow, deadlines to make and, of course, a budget to stick with. Maybe you'd be put in charge of an IT department's rollout of a new software product for internal users, or in charge of a certain operating system version of a certain piece of hardware. Either way, acquiring an MBA as a project/product manager can lead to doing the same job but with a bigger company, or to a position with a VP title. As in marketing, project/product managers need a very wide range of skills and knowledge, so having your MBA can only help. If you're a hardcore engineer or programmer, the MBA will help you break into project/product management.

Marketing

If the intensity of the IT lifestyle makes you feel burned out, and you have some creative DNA, then you may be a good fit for a position in technology marketing. The field involves dealing with advertising, partners, the press and anything related to corporate outreach. In technology marketing, more so than in other fields, you will be expected to know quite a bit about the technology in question. By getting that MBA you can also understand the technology's business strategic situation, and have a good chance at moving up into upper management.

Tech consulting

Many tech consultants are former successful technologists who desire to share what they've learned with others. With just IT experience, you can get an entry-level consulting job, which means interfacing with your client's own IT staff about their special needs. With a few years of experience and the addition of an MBA degree, you can open your own consulting firm, be invited to participate in panels at trade shows, or perhaps move from out of consulting and into the exciting world of venture capital. (To be a VC, you need to excel at understanding business and technology hand-in-hand, just as good consultants do.) You can also become an in-house consultant for a very large company, which may involve more deadlines and politics to play, but leaves you not having to worry about finding new customers.

Director jobs

If you work for a company that makes technology products, instead of working in the IT department of a company that simply utilizes technology, then possessing an MBA degree will often lead you into a "director" level job. For example, you might become the director of printers for a company that makes business technology, or the director of R&D for a military software contractor. As a director, your role is a notch below the division vice president and a notch above the various product managers. Product managers work on just one thing, but as director you're also working on a technology group's sales, marketing, manufacturing, etc.

Finance and law

Finance and law positions in an IT department or at a technology vendor have some aspects that are unique compared to working in other fields. You may have to deal with patent issues, foreign employee visas, international licensing laws, making sure the IT staff follows legal compliance rules for backing up data, and working with multiple layers of distributors, partners and resellers. By getting an MBA degree as well, you are in good position to become a company's operations director, or even to get a C-level position if you have extensive sales or technology experience as well.

Sales

In sales the job description is very clear: generate revenue for the company. By having an MBA you can manage entry-level staff, get the best and biggest clients, get into working with partners and resellers, or even enter the field of "competitive intelligence," which is a nice way of saying corporate espionage.

Training

As an IT trainer you have many career options. You can work in a classroom setting, manage advanced customer support, become involved with technical writing, educate the sales staff or work with your company's technology partners. With an MBA degree you can become a manager and get a title such as call center director or VP of user experience.

Upper management

Last, and the hardest job to get, is technology upper management. To become a CIO, CTO or even a CEO in the technology field, an MBA degree is almost a requirement, especially at large companies. There are a lucky few who become business leaders straight out of core technology jobs (and with a lot of natural talent)—the world's richest person, Bill Gates, never even finished his undergraduate degree. But for mere mortals, if you want to become an IT business leader, you can't go wrong with an MBA: it will help you close big sales, manage your company's logistics, strategize for growth and prepare you for the executive suite.

Tech Experience and the MBA

Of course, getting an MBA is not enough for a successful career in tech. "My gut reaction is, get the real-world experience," says Paul Buonaiuto, director of recruiting for Computer Associates International Inc., the Islandia, NY company specializing in business management software. The problem with classroom experience alone, he says, is that "Unless you're really out in the trenches, it's difficult to implement sometimes what you read in a book. Real-world experience I hold in more high regard." And even when a rookie MBA gets hired, there is usually the need for some amount of retraining, as "a lot of the [MBA] case studies are dot-com [or] an Enron or a latest-greatest merger," Buonaiuto explains.

To really stand out in the hiring process, the ideal job candidate should also have some kind of hands-on technology experience, Buonaiuto said. Candidates that well rounded come along "almost never," he says. When a pure MBA interviews in technology, "What's sorely lacked in those folks looking for a job is research skills. It becomes painfully evident in the interview" that they know about CA's stock performance but know nothing about its technology other than what's on the web site, he said.

Many future executive candidates start out as technical employees or lower-level managers. For them, many companies will pay for a portion of their MBA educations. There are a wide range of choices for where to get it—a traditional MBA program gives you the recognition that business is business and profits are profits, regardless of your industry, while a specialized technology MBA program (such as in e-commerce or systems management) will make you stand out but can be risky if your

Visit Vault at www.vault.com for insider company profiles, expert advice,
career message boards, expert resume reviews, the Vault Job Board and more.

VAULT CAREER LIBRARY   119

chosen specialty market has a downturn. Magazines like *Computerworld*, *BusinessWeek* and *U.S. News & World Report* sometimes publish features dedicated to ranking the graduate programs. The relative newness of specialized degrees is another common point of debate: it's been noted many times before that the leading rankings often wildly disagree.

Vault Q&A: Catherine Wang, Intuit

Prior to attending the Stanford Graduate School of Business, Catherine Wang had little experience in high tech. While at Stanford, however, she landed an internship at Silicon Valley stalwart Intuit and took a position as a marketing manager upon graduating in 2005. Wang took some time out from her busy schedule to talk to Vault about her experience as an MBA at a tech company.

Vault: Tell me a little about your experience prior to business school

Wang: I was in consulting at McKinsey for two years and then worked with Charles Schwab for two years before going to business school.

Vault: Did you know going into business school that you wanted to move into high-tech marketing?

Wang: I actually wanted to do marketing in general, so technology was less important. I chose Intuit less because Intuit is a software company, but more because of Intuit's approach to customers. Intuit is definitely not a technology company for the sake of being a technology company. It just happens that they use technology to solve their customer's needs. Frankly, I didn't interview with many tech companies, but was interested in Intuit's strong marketing organization.

I did my summer internship at Intuit. You can do either marketing or product development on the MBA side. The internship was very structured—lots of meetings with senior executives of the company, intern events, things like that.

Vault: Were there a lot of MBAs that joined Intuit at the same time you did?

Wang: There really isn't an MBA class my year; Intuit kind of hires MBAs as needed. That said, there's tons of MBAs at Intuit and there's tons of Stanford MBAs at Intuit.

There are many people who have very very similar backgrounds to you. We are a big company, but the culture at Intuit is very collaborative, it's very much about helping people out, getting to know people. You don't really have to be very proactive in networking, a lot of people reach out to get to know you. It's part of the company culture to make sure you have the mentors you need that you have the network that you need.

Vault: Tell me about your current position at Intuit.

Wang: I'm a marketing manager, working on our payroll service, which is a small business solution that enables small businesses to do payroll in house. It's a service within the Quickbooks product.

Vault: How is it delivered? Is it a CD or through the Web?

Wang: It's functionality that we turn on in Quickbooks. Think about your cable TV, and how there are different packages. If you pay more, you get HBO versus if you didn't pay for it. It's kind of like that—we turn it on for you. Quickbooks itself can be downloaded from the Web or you can buy it off the shelf and install it.

Vault: So what does it mean to be a marketing manager at Intuit?

Wang: So marketing manager is comparable to a brand management position. What I manage is one of our channels, the phone channel. I work a lot through our call centers, to make sure that they have the materials they need. Our main call centers are in Tucson and Reno, so I go to each of them about once a month. Right now, I'm in Tucson.

We have a group of 12 marketing folks within payroll. For example, there's someone focused on retail, so packaging is a more important part of her responsibilities than it is for me. We also have someone who focuses on the web channel who's responsible for the content displayed on the Web.

Vault: What is your impression of how marketing management at Intuit and other high-tech companies compares to brand management at traditional packaged goods companies?

Wang: My perception is that with many consumer packaged goods companies, there's more of a focus on marketing. I would say it's less so that way here, because technology plays an important role. It's more of a balance.

I think a big difference between Intuit and a lot of other tech companies, however, is that marketing is very important. I did interview at tech companies where the folks I was interviewing with would say, "Honestly, we have some products that have certain functionality because the engineers thought it was cool." Here, the focus is on the customer and so I don't think you have that tension between engineering and marketing.

Vault: In brand management at traditional packaged goods companies, brand managers interface with a wide variety of departments in an organization. Who are you working with mainly?

Wang: People from all levels, starting from sales managers to coaches who lead a team of about 15 agents. We're very customer focused, so I spend a lot of time listening on calls to agents, to see who what our customers are saying, or doing agent focus groups.

For example, we did six focus groups around what types of marketing messages we should emphasize. This starts with identifying what are the benefits that customers really value, that has implications that they really sell—so if customers are saying that a benefit is not important, the salespeople aren't going to focus on that.

Vault: What about getting customers in the door in the first place?

Wang: So I also deal with lead generation—getting calls into the call center. That involves working with our managers who manage Quickbooks.com or Payroll.com, as well as working with our direct marketing organization. Direct marketing is a centralized function at Intuit, so all marketing managers coordinate with that team.

Vault: What other responsibilities do you have?

Wang: Although we're largely structured by channels, we also spend some time on different issues that affect all channels. For me, beyond telesales, I work on pricing promotion across channels. These promotions must be coordinated with other channels.

Vault: Was there a particular reason that pricing promotion fell under your oversight? Does it have particular relevance to the telesales channel?

Wang: No, it was just how things were divided up.

Vault: So are you frequently interacting with the marketing managers overseeing other channels?

Wang: Yes, definitely—every day, if not more frequently. Things that we do in one channel affect other channels. If we do a promotion on the Web, we know not everyone is going to order through the Web, some will call. If we are trying to grow sales of one particular product, that affects all channels.

Visit Vault at **www.vault.com** for insider company profiles, expert advice, career message boards, expert resume reviews, the Vault Job Board and more.

V∧ULT CAREER LIBRARY   **121**

Vault: Are you often in contact with the engineers building the products?

Wang: Not so much. We interface more with the product marketing folks. Of the four Ps in marketing, the marketing side is really focused on the pricing, promotions and placement. The product piece is really the ownership of the product managers. The product managers are the ones who take customer requirements, find out what functionality is missing, and they work with engineers with the product themselves.

The product managers and engineers work on future functionality, the marketing group focuses on selling current functionality.

Employer Directory

3Com
350 Campus Drive
Marlborough, MA 01752-3064
Phone: (508) 323-5000
Fax: (508) 323-1111
www.3com.com

Advanced Micro Devices, Inc.
One AMD Place
P.O. Box 3453
Sunnyvale, CA 94088-3453
Phone: (408) 749-4000
Fax: (508) 323-1111
www.amd.com

Agilent Technologies
395 Page Mill Road
Palo Alto, CA 94306
Phone: (650) 752-5000
Fax: (650) 752-5300
www.agilent.com

Analog Deivces, Inc.
1 Technology Way
Norwood, MA 02062-9106
Phone: (781) 329-4700
Fax: (781) 461-3638
www.analog.com

Apple Computer, Inc.
1 Infinite Loop
Cupertino, CA 95014
Phone: (408) 996-1010
Fax: (408) 974-2113
www.apple.com

Applied Materials, Inc.
3050 Bowers Avenue
Santa Clara, CA 95054-8039
Phone: (408) 727-5555
Fax: (408) 748-9943
www.appliedmaterials.com

Ariba Inc.
807 11th Avenue
Sunnyvale, CA 94089
Phone: (650) 390-1000
Fax: (650) 390-1100
www.ariba.com

The Boeing Company
100 N. Riverside Plaza
Chicago, IL 60606-2609
Phone: (312) 544-2000
Fax: (312) 544-2082
www.boeing.com

Bose Corp.
The Mountain
Framingham, MA 01701
Phone: (508) 879-7330
Fax: (508) 766-7543
www.bose.com

Cisco Systems, Inc.
170 West Tasman Drive
San Jose, CA 95134
Phone: (408) 526-4000
www.cisco.com

Computer Associates International, Inc.
1 Computer Associates Plaza
Islandia, NY 11749
Phone: (631) 342-6000
Fax: (631) 342-5329
www.ca.com

Compuware Corporation
1 Campus Martius
Detroit, MI 48266-5099
Phone: (313) 227-7300
Fax: (248) 737-7108
www.compuware.com

Cypress Semiconductor Corporation
3901 N. 1st Street
San Jose, CA 95134-1599
Phone: (408) 943-2600
Fax: (408) 943-6841
www.cypress.com

Dell Inc.
One Dell Way
Round Rock, TX 78682
Phone: (512) 338-4400
Fax: (512) 728-3653
www.dell.com

EMC Corporation
176 South Street
Hopkinton, MA 01748
Phone: (508) 435-1000
Toll Free: (877) 362-6973
Fax: (508) 497-6912
www.emc.com

Gateway, Inc.
7565 Irvine Center Drive
Irvine, CA 92618
Phone: (949) 471-7000
Fax: (949) 471-7041
www.gateway.com

Hewlett-Packard Company
3000 Hanover Street
Palo Alto, CA 94304
Phone: (650) 857-1501
Fax: (650) 857-5518
www.hp.com

Intel Corporation
2200 Mission College Boulevard
Santa Clara, CA 95052
Phone: (408) 765-8080
Fax: (408) 765-9904
www.intel.com

International Business Machines Corporation (IBM)
New Orchard Road
Armonk, NY 10504
Phone: (914) 499-1900
Fax: (914) 765-7382
www.ibm.com

Intuit Inc.
2632 Marine Way
Mountain View, CA 94043
Phone: (650) 944-6000
Fax: (650) 944-3699
www.intuit.com

LSI Logic Corporation
1621 Barber Lane
Milpitas, CA 95035
Phone: (408) 433-8000
Fax: (408) 954-3220
www.lsilogic.com

Visit Vault at **www.vault.com** for insider company profiles, expert advice,
career message boards, expert resume reviews, the Vault Job Board and more.

VAULT CAREER LIBRARY   123

Employer Directory, cont.

Microsoft Corporation
1 Microsoft Way
Redmond, WA 98052-6399
Phone: (425) 882-8080
Fax: (425) 936-7329
www.microsoft.com

Motorola, Inc.
1303 E. Algonquin Road
Schaumburg, IL 60196
Phone: (847) 576-5000
Fax: (847) 576-5372
www.motorola.com

NCR Corporation
1700 S. Patterson Boulevard
Dayton, OH 45479
Phone: (937) 445-5000
Toll Free: (800) 225-5627
Fax: (937) 445-1682
www.ncr.com

Oracle Corporation
500 Oracle Parkway
Redwood City, CA 94065
Phone: (650) 506-7000
Fax: (650) 506-7200
www.oracle.com

Rockwell Collins
400 Collins Road NE
Cedar Rapids, IA 52498
Phone: (319) 295-1000
Fax: (319) 295-5429
www.rockwellcollins.com

SAP Aktiengesellschaft
Dietmar Hopp Allee 16
69190 Walldorf
Germany
Phone: +49-6227-7-47474
Toll Free: (800) 225-5627
Fax: +49-6227-7-57575
www.sap.com

**Science Applications
International Corporation
(SAIC)**
10260 Campus Point Drive
San Diego, CA 92121
Phone: (858) 826-6000
Fax: (858) 826-6800
www.saic.com

Siebel Systems, Inc.
2207 Bridgepointe Parkway
San Mateo, CA 94404
Phone: (650) 295-5000
Fax: (650) 295-5111
www.siebel.com

Siemens AG, Inc.
Wittelsbacherplatz 2
D-80333 Munich
Germany
Phone: +49-89-636-00
Fax: +49-89-636-52-000
www.siemens.com

Sony Corporation
7-35, Kitashinagawa, 6-chome,
Shinagawa-ku
Tokyo, 141-0001
Japan
Phone: +81-3-5448-2111
Fax: +81-3-5448-2244
www.sony.net

Sun Microsystems, Inc.
4150 Network Circle
Santa Clara, CA 95054
Phone: (650) 960-1300
Fax: (408) 276-3804
www.sun.com

Sybase Inc.
1 Sybase Drive
Dublin, CA 94568
Phone: (925) 236-5000
Fax: (925) 236-4321
www.sybase.com

Symantec Corporation
20330 Stevens Creek Boulevard
Cupertino, CA 95014-2132
Phone: (408) 517-8000
Fax: (408) 253-3968
www.symantec.com

**Texas Instruments
Incorporated**
12500 TI Boulevard
Dallas, TX 75266-4136
Phone: (972) 995-2011
Toll Free: (800) 336-5236
Fax: (972) 995-4360
www.ti.com

Unisys Corporation
Unisys Way
Blue Bell, PA 19424
Phone: (215) 986-4011
Fax: (215) 986-2312
www.unisys.com

Xerox Corporation
800 Long Ridge Road
Stamford, CT 06904
Phone: (203) 968-3000
Fax: (203) 968-3218
www.xerox.com

Human Resources

Every organization has people, which means every organization needs human resources (HR) professionals. HR helps manage and develop the people in an organization. Sometimes called "personnel" or "talent management," HR is the function in charge of an organization's employees, which includes finding and hiring employees, helping them grow and learn in the organization, and managing the process when an employee leaves. Human resources takes care of people from the time they're interested in the organization to long after they leave.

The History of Human Resources

Now a thriving, growing profession, human resources wasn't always a key part of most organizations—if at all. Until the early 1900s, all human resources functions were typically handled by the workers themselves or their bosses (often called master craftsmen). As more workers were needed, master craftsmen would just go out and find them (talk about the birth of recruiting!).

When the 1900s brought inventions and changes in the workplace, like machines that automated production, human resources began to take shape. The addition of machines made factories run more quickly and smoothly, but also meant that the workers had to learn how to use them, and forced factory managers to introduce rules and procedures on the factory floor.

Frederick Taylor, a businessman and researcher, first introduced the concept of scientific management. Taylor's theory took workplace rules and procedures one step further, declaring that there was only one best way to do a job. He spent years collecting data on the tasks making up specific jobs and then researching the workers who performed each small task. Workers who performed well, following tasks to the letter, remained employed and were paid well. Those who didn't were among the first to hear "you're fired."

Taylor's research was the first to increase worker productivity, but his robotic approach didn't prove to be an effective management tool. Still, his work showed the importance of managing workers to increase a company's success. While Taylor's work focused more on company success than that of the worker, it propelled many companies to begin to personalize the workplace, anticipating the first appearance of HR. One of the earliest HR roles was that of a welfare secretary, whose role was to look out for the welfare of the workers. An ancestor of what's now called a benefits manager, welfare secretaries created libraries and recreation areas in the workplace as well as primitive medical and health programs.

But HR really took shape in the 1930s when a company called Western Electric asked a team of researchers to figure out how to increase workers' productivity at one of their plants in Chicago. The Hawthorne Studies, taking their name after the targeted plant, set out to determine whether changing the lighting in the plant could help the employees work faster. What they found instead was how important it was for plant managers to pay attention to the workers, reward them for a good job and make sure they were satisfied. The idea of happy workers being productive workers took hold and still remains true today. If a company wants to perform well, it has to create and manage a content workforce. HR plays a critical role in making sure that happens.

The Hawthorne Studies fueled the study of worker behavior in organizations, and what was called behavioral science. The growth of behavioral science as a field studied how jobs and the workplace affect workers and how workers affect the performance of a company.

The study of behavioral science reinforced the importance of welfare secretaries. The secretaries' jobs became more and more complex as governments introduced labor laws to keep up with the changing workplace. These laws, restricting the rights of both employers and employees, required the welfare secretaries to keep paper records of employees and their activities. One of the first human resources laws, the Fair Labor Standards Act (FLSA) created a minimum wage, set rules for child labor and required employers to treat employees fairly with regard to wage and hours worked.

Visit Vault at **www.vault.com** for insider company profiles, expert advice, career message boards, expert resume reviews, the Vault Job Board and more.

VAULT CAREER LIBRARY 125

In many industries, workers also began organizing into unions—groups of workers banding together to lobby for rights in the workplace. New laws around union activity also required companies and welfare secretaries to understand and comply with the laws.

Many companies began hiring multiple welfare secretaries—one responsible for hiring employees, another responsible for employee benefits and perhaps another to train employees on the factory floors. These specialty areas evolved into the specialty areas of the human resources profession today.

Human Resources Today

Today, human resources is essential to the success of business. The level of importance HR holds does differ from organization to organization, but businesses consistently rely on HR professionals to help them through high-growth times and periods of turmoil. Regardless of how successful (or not) an organization is, there is always a need for HR staff. The welfare secretary title may be long gone, but the idea of having human resources professionals focus on specific areas of managing and developing a company's workers has remained. Now, in most organizations, there are HR professionals who focus specifically on hiring, training, benefits, labor relations, health and safety and more.

While it's important to like working with and wanting to help people to be successful in HR, that's definitely not the only skill or attribute you need to be a successful HR professional. HR is about creating systems, processes and environments where employees perform better and are satisfied, and there are many different career paths and opportunities in the profession. For example, HR professionals can take center stage as a recruiter or trainer. In these roles, you're interacting with people all day long, whether conducting interviews or running a training course. But HR professionals can also serve behind the scenes, administering payroll, tracking HR metrics (statistics about company workers) or running an organization's human resource information system (HRIS), technical databases where all employee data is stored and managed.

While HR continues to grow as a function, in many companies it does not carry the importance or value of its colleagues in finance, sales or marketing. Know that as satisfying as an HR career can be, the profession still struggles to gain respect in many places.

What Do HR Professionals Do?

Typical HR responsibilities are focused in major areas such as recruiting and staffing, compensation and benefits, training and learning, labor and employee relations, and organization development. Most HR professionals have experience in one or more of these specialty areas. These areas all deal with helping employees in an organization perform more effectively and satisfactorily on the job.

Recruiting and staffing

You're either in or you're out. When an employee leaves and a job opens up or new jobs are created, HR is usually in charge of the process. Recruiting and staffing is one of the largest areas of HR. Recruiters start the process—working with specific departments to write job descriptions and understand what skills and abilities the new employee should have. Then they're off and running—responsible for finding candidates, determining who might be a good fit, conducting interviews and making job offers. While recruiters involve department employees in the process to interview and make the hiring decisions, it's the recruiters who are usually in charge of finding the talent, managing interview scheduling, negotiating offers and making sure departments have all the information they need to make the best hiring decisions possible.

While recruiters work to find and hire the talent, staffing experts determine who should go where. They strategize with different departments to anticipate hiring needs and help determine where a new employee might best fit in an organization.

Staffing professionals are heavily relied on in high-growth companies to make sure the company is prepared to hire enough new employees to grow the company, and that employees are in the right positions.

Recruiting and staffing professionals are also called upon to help an organization market to prospective employees. This can include creating and managing recruiting events, designing marketing pieces, such as company brochures and commercials, and staffing career fairs to educate prospective employees about open opportunities. Many organizations also have recruiting and staffing professionals dedicated to working with universities. These roles are focused on finding talent on undergraduate and graduate school campuses and can include a great deal of travel and campus presentations.

Compensation and benefits

Finding talent is important, but employees also have to be paid. HR, specifically compensation and benefits professionals, are in charge of making sure new employees are given an appropriate salary and benefits, and current employees continually receive their salary and benefits.

Compensation experts focus on the money. This includes processing regular payroll (making sure that the check is in the mail) and payroll changes, including raises and tax changes. Compensation experts also work closely with an organization's finance department to ensure salaries stay within each department's budget, as well as conducting and researching salary surveys to make sure they're paying the going rate.

Benefits professionals also have to make sure employees are taken care of—they specialize in helping employees with medical and other company benefits. This may include teaching new employees about their medical plan choices, implementing and managing the plans offered by the company, and managing the cost of benefits for the company.

Compensation and benefits professionals are also often tasked with communicating salary and benefits information to employees. This may include marketing and promoting new benefits offerings to a company or managing an company's open enrollment period—a brief period of time where employees can change medical plans and other benefit options.

One-on-one counseling may also be part of the job. If an employee leaves an organization, the benefits manager may counsel the employee on access to health insurance available after departure. Employees also often seek guidance on understanding their compensation packages, making changes to employment tax forms or managing a difficult medical insurance claim.

Training and learning

Part teacher, part manager, part leader—that's a training professional. Helping employees become oriented to a new job or company is just one of the many responsibilities of training and learning professionals. Sometimes called training, or learning and development, it's helping both new and tenured employees develop and grow as professionals both on and off the job.

Training and learning professionals are typically responsible for running programs designed to educate and develop employees. This can include programs for an entire employee population, such as new hire orientation or ethics training, but also includes more specialized programs for different groups of workers within a company, like online training courses, in-class instruction or on-the-job training.

Training managers, for example, are called upon to do everything from registering and tracking training courses to developing new courses and evaluating the effectiveness of training programs after they happen. This may include designing surveys or determining if newly trained employees perform better than they did before the training. They may also be responsible for providing information to employees on training classes and programs outside the company.

In some organizations, training and learning professionals actually deliver the training courses. They might create a presentation skills course and then send trainers on the road to teach the new course to employees around the country. Since it's often cheaper to train current employees rather than hire new ones, training and learning is becoming increasingly

Visit Vault at **www.vault.com** for insider company profiles, expert advice, career message boards, expert resume reviews, the Vault Job Board and more.

VAULT CAREER LIBRARY 127

important in the business world. A company's strong commitment to training and development is also a boost to its workers' morale.

Labor and employee relations

Just like welfare secretaries responded to new laws in the early 1900s, labor and employee relations professionals ensure that anything dealing with employee contracts, rights, responsibilities and complaints is taken care of right quick.

Labor relations is a function typically found in companies whose employees are members of unions. Labor relations professionals are called upon to deal directly with unions, doing everything from interpreting current union contracts to negotiating new ones. They also analyze and monitor union activity and work with unions during organizing campaigns— the time when unions recruit new members.

Employee relations professionals need to be familiar and comfortable with the law; they are also responsible for equal employment opportunity and affirmative action programs. For government agencies or companies that do work for the government, this may include creating reports to demonstrate a company is complying with the law and making an effort to hire and retain employees from underrepresented ethnicities. Other key responsibilities may include counseling or conflict resolution within an organization, helping employees who are dealing with disagreements in the workplace or have issues preventing them from doing their jobs.

Labor and employee relations is not found in every human resources department. Organizations that don't have government contracts or unionized employees may rely on outside attorneys or consultants to deal with any legal issues or employee conflicts that arise.

Organization development

While developing employees is important, perhaps just as important is developing an organization. A relatively new field, organization development (OD) focuses on evaluating how a company is structured and how employees work together to see where improvements can be made. Also referred to as organization effectiveness, this might include helping to restructure the chain of command in a department to helping employees cope with a major change, such as the introduction of a new companywide technical system.

OD professionals are experts in understanding behavior and psychology. They often act as internal consultants, helping their fellow employees understand how a new company program might affect the employees' behavior.

They often work closely with training professionals to address development needs for the company. OD professionals may develop companywide team-building activities or introduce new programs for leadership development.

OD specialists often manage the performance review process, making sure that employees are evaluated and moved within the organization based on how well they're working. OD specialists may also help companies develop succession plans (determining who is in line to be the next person in a leadership position, such as CEO or CFO) and mentoring programs, making sure less experienced employees can learn from their more experienced comrades. OD professionals may also be called upon to help an employee address individual issues through executive coaching, or a department address a leadership or performance challenge.

Less common OD work may include coaching or career development. Coaches, common at the executive level, help employees overcome poor teamwork or management skills. Many large firms are hiring external coaches, or creating coaching functions in order to help valuable employees deal with singular issues that may prevent them from being promoted.

Health and safety

Factory machines, hazardous chemicals and construction sites are all potentially dangerous situations for workers. This is where health and safety professionals come in. One of the oldest HR specialties, health and safety professionals are responsible for ensuring a safe working environment for all workers—this is more of an issue in industries with risky work settings such as manufacturing, health care and construction. While all organizations must protect the safety of their employees while at work, it is more complicated in industries that have worksites beyond a typical office environment.

One of the major components of the role of a health and safety professional is to be proactive—assessing a work environment to anticipate where the dangers might be and correcting them before an injury occurs. This might include periodic tours of a worksite, or research into the latest workplace safety options.

Health and safety professionals are also responsible for reacting to issues, concerns or problems related to the workplace environment. They might handle a complaint from a worker about a dangerous factory machine or an on-site injury. They work closely with compensation and benefits professionals to handle any injuries and determine how to prevent future injuries from occurring.

Working with an organization's legal team and employee law specialists is also part of the role. Health and safety professionals are responsible for following federal and state rules governing workplace safety including, in some industries, submitting reports that demonstrate a company's compliance with the law.

Why HR?

While HR professionals have varying degrees of interaction with an organization's employees, all HR people can enjoy the satisfaction of knowing that the work they do has a direct impact on people every day. HR professionals like helping employees navigate through tough problems and get back to normal on the job. Whether it's helping an employee overcome a performance problem or fix an expensive and stressful medical claim, there is an inherent satisfaction in these types of tasks.

They also enjoy the ability to interact with different groups of people; HR professionals may be working with employees in many different parts of the company. Organization development specialists may act like internal consultants helping different departments in a company work better together. This means they might be working with a sales team one week and a product design team the next. So there is a ton of variety in their day-to-day tasks.

In his role at Bank of America, Phil Skeath likes the diversity of projects. "Each time I am on a new project," he says, "I find myself identifying general concepts I learned in my educational experience, adapting them, and applying them to a specific issue in the bank."

They also like contributing to the business and bottom line. For example, one of the most common issues CFOs are facing in 2005 (according to *CFO Magazine*) is the rising cost of healthcare. HR and benefits professionals who analyze how to lower these costs can save a company millions of dollars. Talk about making an impact.

Why not?

For most HR professionals, the positives of working in HR (such as extending a job offer to a very excited job candidate) are enough to outweigh the drawbacks (in the opposite category, downsizing or laying off employees). Otherwise, they wouldn't be there in the first place. But no job is perfect. Even rock stars have to deal with annoying paparazzi and screaming fans. While it's highly unlikely you'll be chased by reporters working in HR, you may be chased by unhappy employees. One of the toughest things about working in HR is providing a service many employees take for granted. No one says "Thanks, HR" every time they get a paycheck. But if something goes wrong, if employees don't get paid, if benefits disappear or new employees aren't trained properly, you may end up with a mailbox full of angry callers to contend with.

Visit Vault at **www.vault.com** for insider company profiles, expert advice, career message boards, expert resume reviews, the Vault Job Board and more.

VAULT CAREER LIBRARY 129

Like many professions, starting out in HR you may also have your fair share of administrative work. Many HR careers may begin with processing paperwork for new employees, or entering and maintaining resumes in an online database. This might seem like menial work, especially if you've just received a college degree, but don't walk away too quickly. These roles, while tedious, provide a great learning opportunity and a chance to prove you're ready for more responsibilities.

HR also suffers from some common misconceptions, like being a touchy-feely profession or being female-dominated; we'll go into some of these misconceptions and how to deal with them later in this guide.

Ready to help your colleagues and organization perform better? Before you determine what type of HR role you might best be cast in, it's important to understand that HR as a function isn't the same in every organization.

Human Resource Management (HRM)

Human resource management (HRM) is the set of traditional HR activities that manage or support the people in the organization, and every working organization has to have at least one person responsible for HRM. The major areas of HRM include:

- Recruiting and staffing
- Compensation and benefits
- Labor and employee relations
- Health and safety

In HRM roles, professionals need to keep the HR motor humming and wheels turning. Imagine if you stopped receiving your paycheck or if your company stopped recruiting altogether. HRM functions are key to keeping organizations running smoothly, and HRM professionals are responsible for preventing any interruption in services that employees expect.

HRM professionals are also responsible to the organization as a whole. Running all of these processes can cost a lot of money, and it is up to HRM professionals to make decisions that help save the company money and make sure employees are well-served. In each of the major areas of HRM, professionals are continually evaluating processes and implementing new programs and systems to better serve the organization. Examples include:

- Recruiting and staffing: recruiting management systems (RMS) or applicant tracking systems (ATS) are the latest trend in electronically managing the influx of resumes during busy recruiting times. These systems save organizations money by streamlining the recruiting process and requiring fewer staff members to manage employee records.

- Labor and employee relations: legal training for managers on topics such as sexual harassment and workplace law is becoming more and more common, in order to proactively reduce lawsuits related to workplace behavior.

- Health and safety: while injuries at plants and hazardous sites are common, HR professionals are also recognizing the increase in office injuries; many health and safety professionals are introducing ergonomically correct office furniture. While these fancy chairs and glare-reducing computer screens may be expensive, such investments can prevent future injuries and their associated costs.

- Compensation and benefits: benefits outsourcing is a popular way to reduce costs and responsibility for an organization. Some compensation and benefits professionals work with outside vendors to manage programs such as an employee stock purchase plan. Since these outside vendors already have the expertise and systems in place to manage these programs, it saves the company the expense of creating them from scratch.

Companies such as The Home Depot are well known for their HR practices, and are consistently looking for ways to ease and automate the function in order to serve customers, and ultimately the organization, better. The Home Depot has become more recently renowned for creatively recruiting veterans who have recently finished their military careers. Since advertising on online job boards can be expensive, finding new channels to recruit prospective employees is an important way to save valuable recruiting dollars.

As a human resources VP for a consulting firm professes, improving the way employees are served is an important part of the job. "In the last five years, over 75 percent of our HR transactions have been automated to better serve our customers. We created a company Intranet and put our benefits elections process online as well as all of our employee policies and procedures. No more paper!"

HRM professionals are also often charged with reporting HR's return on investment (ROI) to the company through tracking HR metrics (statistics on how a company's employees are performing) and demonstrating the value HR brings to the company. Compensation and benefits professionals might track how much employees are spending on health care costs and seek ways to reduce them. On the other hand, an employee relations professional might track statistics on how many minorities are employed in an organization for an affirmative action report. Measuring such activity is important for HRM professionals to show their commitment to an organization's bottom line.

HR management professionals must continually be thinking about ways to better serve and save a company money at the same time.

Common Human Resource Management (HRM) Roles

Common HRM roles include:

- Compensation manager
- Senior recruiter
- Health and safety manager
- Employment lawyer

- Labor relations specialist
- Benefits specialist
- HR generalist

Human Resource Development (HRD)

Human resource development (HRD) is the second part (albeit much smaller) of the HR world. If HRM professionals are keeping the wheels turning smoothly, HRD professionals are helping them turn faster and better. Human resource development refers to the activities in an organization that help develop and grow employees. Many organizations simply refer to HRD as training or learning and development but in reality, it's much more than that. HRD includes:

- Training and learning
- Organization development, which includes:
  - Succession planning (determining who is next in line for a CEO or other senior job)
  - Coaching (helping employees overcome on-the-job problems)
  - Performance management (those pesky performance reviews)

HRD is the area of HR that is growing most quickly as organizations recognize the need to go way beyond simply managing their workforce. While smaller organizations often have HR generalists assume the responsibility for training alongside other HR tasks, large companies such as Medtronic, Bank of America and Texas Instruments have entire functions devoted to subsets of HRD such as organization development.

"Organization development is a key part of human resources," says Phil Skeath, a performance improvement consultant at Bank of America. "We are business partners who support our line managers' needs, but we are also an integral part in driving the company's strategy."

Visit Vault at **www.vault.com** for insider company profiles, expert advice, career message boards, expert resume reviews, the Vault Job Board and more.

VAULT CAREER LIBRARY 131

HRD professionals may be responsible for a certain subset of the workforce (such as training the sales force), or may serve as internal consultants working on projects as they arise, such as helping to restructure a department or working on the succession plan for an entire division. Other HRD responsibilities include employee performance evaluations, training new employees and helping companies deal with changes as the result of a new program, technology, merger or acquisition.

HRD careers are growing every year. Training and development is one area in which the Bureau of Labor Statistics (BLS) predicts growth in 2005 and beyond. This is due not only to how complex jobs are becoming, but also the aging of the workforce, and the many changes in technology requiring more and more training and development programs for workers. What does this mean for HR professionals? HRD might well be an increasingly popular career path.

Because HRD is not only growing, but is also structured very differently from organization to organization, if you see HRD as a viable career path, it's important to research where it fits in specific companies. Organizations that only have a training and learning function may not see as much value in HRD as a company that has a specific organization development function.

Employer Directory

Buck Consultants
One Pennsylvania Plaza
New York, NY 10119
Phone: (212) 330-1000
Fax: (212) 695-4184
www.buckconsultants.com

ADP TotalSource Group
10200 Sunset Drive
Miami, FL 33173
Phone: (305) 630-1000
Fax: (305) 630-2006
www.adptotalsource.com

Adecco SA
Sägereistrasse 10
8152 Glattbrugg
Switzerland
Phone: + 41-44-878-8888
Fax: + 41-44-829-8888
www.adecco.com

Convergys
201 E. 4th Street
Cincinnati, OH 45202
Phone: (513) 723-7000
Fax: (513) 421-8624
www.convergys.com

Hay Group
The Wanamaker Building
100 Penn Square East
Philadelphia, PA 19107
Phone: (215) 861-2000
Fax: (215) 861-2111
www.haygroup.com

Hewitt Associates
100 Half Day Road
Lincolnshire, IL 60069
Phone: (847) 295-5000
Fax: (847) 295-7634
www.hewitt.com

Kelly Services, Inc.
999 W. Big Beaver Road
Troy, MI 48084
Phone: (248) 362-4444
Fax: (248) 244-4360
www.kellyservices.com

Manpower Inc.
5301 N. Ironwood Road
Milwaukee, WI 53217
Phone: (414) 961-1000
Fax: (414) 906-7985
www.manpower.com

Mercer Human Resource Consulting
1166 Avenue of the Americas
New York, NY 10036
Phone: (212) 345-7000
Fax: (212) 345-7414
www.mercerHR.com

Paychex, Inc.
911 Panorama Trail South
Rochester, NY 14625-2396
Phone: (585) 385-6666
Fax: (585) 383-3428
www.paychex.com

Robert Half International Inc.
2884 Sand Hill Road
Menlo Park, CA 94025
Phone: (650) 234-6000
Fax: (650) 234-6999
www.rhi.com

Spherion
2050 Spectrum Boulevard
Fort Lauderdale, FL 33309
Phone: (954) 308-7600
Fax: (954) 308-7666
www.spherion.com

Towers Perrin
263 Tresser Boulevard
Stamford, CT 06901
Phone: (203) 326-5400
www.towersperrin.com

Watson Wyatt Worldwide
901 North Glebe Road
Arlington, VA 22203
Phone: (703) 258-8000
Fax: (703) 258-8585
www.watsonwyatt.com

Visit Vault at **www.vault.com** for insider company profiles, expert advice, career message boards, expert resume reviews, the Vault Job Board and more.

VAULT CAREER LIBRARY   133

limitless potential

[**MERRILL LYNCH**]

growth and momentum

inspiring colleagues

Merrill Lynch offers you unparalleled opportunities to build your career. Our premier brand and global capabilities create a strong foundation for you to explore a range of diverse career options. Working within a dynamic environment, you will contribute to our company's business growth and momentum. It's a great time to join us.

Work alongside industry-leading professionals to deliver exceptional solutions to our clients. Expect to be a contributor, a collaborator, and a colleague.

For more information or to apply online, visit **ml.com/careers**

Merrill Lynch is an equal opportunity employer.

ml.com/careers

 **Merrill Lynch**

Investment Banking

What is investment banking? Is it investing? Is it banking? Really, it is neither. Investment banking, or I-banking as it is often called, is the term used to describe the business of raising capital for companies and advising them on financing and merger alternatives. Capital essentially means money. Companies need cash in order to grow and expand their businesses; investment banks sell securities to public investors in order to raise this cash.

The Firms

The biggest investment banks include Goldman Sachs, Merrill Lynch, Morgan Stanley, Credit Suisse First Boston, Salomon Smith Barney, JPMorgan Chase and Lehman Brothers, among others. Of course, the complete list of I-banks is more extensive, but the firms listed above compete for the biggest deals both in the U.S. and worldwide.

You have probably heard of many of these firms, and perhaps have a brokerage account with one of them. While brokers from these firms cover every major city in the U.S., the headquarters of every one of these firms is in New York City, the epicenter of the I-banking universe. It is important to realize that investment banking and brokerage go hand-in-hand, but that brokers are one small cog in the investment banking wheel. As we will cover in detail later, brokers sell securities and manage the portfolios of "retail" (or individual) investors.

Many an I-banking interviewee asks, "Which firm is the best?" The answer, like many things in life, is unclear. There are many ways to measure the quality of investment banks. You might examine a bank's expertise in a certain segment of investment banking. Those who watch the industry pay attention to "league tables," which are rankings of investment banks in several categories (e.g., equity underwriting or M&A advisory). The most commonly referred to league tables are published quarterly by Thomson Financial Securities Data (TFSD), a research firm based in Newark, NJ. TFSD collects data on deals done in a given time period and determines which firm has done the most deals in a given sector over that time period. Essentially, the league tables are rankings of firm by quantity of deals in a given area.

Corporate Finance

Stuffy bankers?

The stereotype of the corporate finance department is stuffy, arrogant (white and male) MBAs who frequent golf courses and talk on cellphones nonstop. While this is increasingly less true, corporate finance remains the most white-shoe department in the typical investment bank. The atmosphere in corporate finance is, unlike that in sales and trading, often quiet and reserved. Junior bankers sit separated by cubicles, quietly crunching numbers.

Depending on the firm, corporate finance can also be a tough place to work, with unforgiving bankers and expectations through the roof. Although decreasing, stories of analyst abuse abound, and some bankers come down hard on new analysts to scare and intimidate them. The lifestyle for corporate finance professionals can be a killer. In fact, many corporate finance workers find that they literally dedicate their lives to the job. Social life suffers, free time disappears and stress multiplies. It is not uncommon to find analysts and associates wearing rumpled pants and wrinkled shirts, exhibiting the wear and tear of all-nighters. Fortunately, these long hours pay remarkable dividends in the form of six-figure salaries and huge year-end bonuses.

Personality-wise, bankers tend to be highly intelligent, motivated and not lacking in confidence. Money is important to the bankers, and many anticipate working for just a few years to earn as much as possible, before finding less demanding work. Analysts and associates tend also to be ambitious, intelligent and pedigreed. If you happen to be going into an analyst or

Visit Vault at **www.vault.com** for insider company profiles, expert advice,
career message boards, expert resume reviews, the Vault Job Board and more.

VAULT CAREER LIBRARY 135

associate position, make sure to check your ego at the door but don't be afraid to ask penetrating questions about deals and what is required of you.

The deal team

Investment bankers generally work in deal teams which, depending on the size of a deal, vary somewhat in makeup. In this chapter we will provide an overview of the roles and lifestyles of the positions in corporate finance, from analyst to managing director. (Often, a person in corporate finance is generally called an I-banker.) Because the titles and roles really do not differ significantly between underwriting to M&A, we have included both in this explanation. In fact, at most smaller firms, underwriting and transaction advisory are not separated, and bankers typically pitch whatever business they can scout out within their industry sector.

The Players

Analysts

Analysts are the grunts of the corporate finance world. They often toil endlessly with little thanks, little pay (when figured on an hourly basis), and barely enough free time to sleep four hours a night. Typically hired directly out of top undergraduate universities, this crop of bright, highly motivated kids does the financial modeling and basic entry-level duties associated with any corporate finance deal.

Modeling every night until 2 a.m. and not having much of a social life proves to be unbearable for many an analyst and after two years many analysts leave the industry. Unfortunately, many bankers recognize the transient nature of analysts, and work them hard to get the most out of them they can. The unfortunate analyst that screws up or talks back too much may never get quality work, spending his days bored until 11 p.m. waiting for work to come, stressing even more than the busy analyst. These are the analysts that do not get called to work on live transactions, and do menial work or just put together pitchbooks all the time.

When it comes to analyst pay, much depends on whether the analyst is in New York or not. In NYC, salary often begins for first-year analysts at $45,000 to $55,000 per year, with an annual bonus of approximately $30,000. While this seems to be a lot for a 22-year-old with just an undergrad degree, it's not a great deal if you consider per-hour compensation. At most firms, analysts also get dinner every night for free if they work late, and have little time to spend their income, often meaning fat checking and savings accounts and ample fodder to fund business school or law school down the road. At regional firms, pay typically is 20 percent less than that of their New York counterparts. Worth noting, though, is the fact that at regional firms (1) hours are often less, and (2) the cost of living is much lower. Be wary, however, of the small regional firm or branch office of a Wall Street firm that pays at the low end of the scale and still shackles analysts to their cubicles. While the salary generally does not improve much for second-year analysts, the bonus can double for those second-years who demonstrate high performance. At this level, bonuses depend mostly on an analyst's contribution, attitude and work ethic, as opposed to the volume of business generated by the bankers with whom he or she works.

Associates

Much like analysts, associates hit the grindstone hard. Working 80- to 100-hour weeks, associates stress over pitchbooks and models all night, become experts with financial modeling on Excel, and sometimes shake their heads wondering what the point is. Unlike analysts, however, associates more quickly become involved with clients and, most importantly, are not at the bottom of the totem pole. Associates quickly learn to play quarterback and hand-off menial modeling work and research projects to analysts. However, treatment from vice presidents and managing directors doesn't necessarily improve for associates versus analysts, as bankers sometimes care more about the work getting done, and not about the guy or gal working away all night to complete it.

Usually hailing directly from top business schools (sometimes law schools or other grad schools), associates often possess only a summer's worth of experience in corporate finance, so they must start almost from the beginning. Associates who worked as analysts before grad school have a little more experience under their belts. The overall level of business awareness and knowledge a bright MBA has, however, makes a tremendous difference, and associates quickly earn the luxury of more complicated work, client contact and bigger bonuses.

Associates are at least much better paid than analysts. An $80,000 starting salary is typical, and usually bonuses hit $25,000 and up in the first six months. (At most firms, associates start in August and get their first prorated bonus in January.) Newly minted MBAs cash in on signing bonuses and forgivable loans as well, especially on Wall Street. These can amount to another $25,000 to $30,000, depending on the firm, providing total first-year compensation of up to $150,000 for top firms. Associates beyond their first year begin to rake it in, earning $250,000 to $400,000 and up per year, depending on the firm's profitability and other factors.

Vice presidents

Upon attaining the position of vice president (at most firms, after four or five years as associates), those in corporate finance enter the realm of real bankers. The lifestyle becomes more manageable once the associate moves up to VP. On the plus side, weekends sometimes free up, all-nighters drop off, and the general level of responsibility increases—VPs are the ones telling associates and analysts to stay late on Friday nights. In the office, VPs manage the financial modeling/pitchbook production process in the office. On the negative side, the wear and tear of traveling that accompanies VP-level banker responsibilities can be difficult. As a VP, one begins to handle client relationships, and thus spends much more time on the road than analysts or associates. You can look forward to being on the road at least two to four days per week, usually visiting clients and potential clients. Don't forget about closing dinners (to celebrate completed deals), industry conferences (to drum up potential business and build a solid network within their industry), and, of course, roadshows. VPs are perfect candidates to baby-sit company management on roadshows.

Directors/managing directors

Directors and managing directors (MDs) are the major players in corporate finance. Typically, MDs set their own hours, deal with clients at the highest level, and disappear whenever a drafting session takes place, leaving this grueling work to others. MDs mostly develop and cultivate relationships with various companies in order to generate corporate finance business for the firm. MDs typically focus on one industry, develop relationships among management teams of companies in the industry and visit these companies on a regular basis. These visits are aptly called sales calls.

Pay scales for vice presidents and managing directors

The formula for paying bankers varies dramatically from firm to firm. Some adhere to rigid formulas based on how much business a banker brought in, while others pay based on a subjective allocation of corporate finance profits. No matter how compensation is structured, however, when business is slow, bonuses taper off rapidly. For most bankers, typical salaries may range from $100,000 to $200,000 per year, but bonuses can be significantly greater. Total packages for VPs on Wall Street often hit over $500,000 level in the first year—and pay can skyrocket from there.

Top bankers at the MD level might be pulling in bonuses of up to $1 million or more a year, but slow markets (and hence slow business) can cut that number dramatically. It is important to realize that for the most part, MDs act as relationship managers, and are essentially paid on commission. For top performers, compensation can be almost inconceivable.

Visit Vault at **www.vault.com** for insider company profiles, expert advice, career message boards, expert resume reviews, the Vault Job Board and more.

VAULT CAREER LIBRARY   137

A Day in the Life: Associate, Corporate Finance

We've asked insiders at leading investment banks to offer us insight into a day in the life of their position. Here's a look at a day of an associate I-banker at Goldman Sachs.

8:15 a.m.: Arrive at 85 Broad Street. (Show Goldman ID card to get past the surly elevator guards.)

8:25 a.m.: Arrive on 17th Floor. Use "blue card" to get past floor lobby. ("Don't ever forget your blue card. Goldman has tight security and you won't be able to get around the building all day.")

8:45 a.m.: Pick up work from word processing department, review it, make changes.

9:00 a.m.: Check voicemail, return phone calls.

9:30 a.m.: Eat breakfast; read *The Wall Street Journal*. ("But don't let a supervisor see you with your paper sprawled across your desk.")

10:00 a.m.: Prepare pitchbooks, discuss analysis with members of deal team.

12:00 p.m.: Conference call with members of IPO team, including lawyers and client.

1:00 p.m.: Eat lunch at desk. ("The Wall Street McDonald's delivers, but it's the most expensive McDonald's in New York City; Goldman's cafeteria is cheaper, but you have to endure the shop talk.")

2:00 p.m.: Work on restructuring case studies; make several document requests from Goldman library.

3:00 p.m.: Start to prepare analysis; order additional data from DRG (data resources group).

5:00 p.m.: Check in with vice presidents and heads of deal teams on status of work.

6:00 p.m.: Go to gym for an abbreviated workout.

6:45 p.m.: Dinner. ("Dinner is free in the IBD cafeteria, but avoid it. Wall Street has pretty limited food options, so for a quick meal it's the Indian place across the street that's open 24 hours.")

8:00 p.m.: Meet with VP again. ("You'll probably get more work thrown at you before he leaves.")

9:45 p.m.: Try to make FedEx cutoff. Drop off pitchbook to document processing department on the 20th Floor. ("You have to call ahead and warn them if you have a last-minute job or you're screwed.")

10:00 p.m.: Order in food again. ("It's unlikely that there will be any room left in your meal allowance—but we usually order in a group and add extra names to bypass the limit.")

11:00 p.m.: Leave for home. ("Call for a car service. Enjoy your nightly 'meal on wheels' on the way home.")

Employer Directory

Credit Suisse

11 Madison Avenue
New York, NY 10010
www.credit-suisse.com/standout

Active in over fifty countries and employing more than 45,000 people, Credit Suisse provides investment banking, private banking and asset management services to companies, institutional clients and high-net-worth individuals. In 2006, we announced record profits and launched an integrated banking platform. Now there are exceptional opportunities for further growth in new product areas and emerging markets; there are equally exceptional opportunities for people who can help deliver that growth.

We typically recruit MBAs to specialize in investment banking, fixed Income, equities, alternative investments, private banking and asset management. More information is available at www.credit-suisse.com/careers

Business Schools Credit Suisse Recruits From: University of Chicago GSB, Columbia University GSB, Cornell University-Johnson School of Management, Harvard Business School, New York University Stern School of Business, University of Michigan Business School, Wharton Graduate School (University of Pennsylvania), as well as many other top business programs.

Goldman, Sachs and Co.

85 Broad Street
New York, NY 10004
MBA Recruiting Contact: (212) 902-1000
www.gs.com/careers

Goldman Sachs is a leading global investment banking, securities and investment management firm that provides a wide range of services worldwide to a substantial and diversified client base that includes corporations, financial institutions, governments and high-net-worth individuals. Founded in 1869, it is one of the oldest and largest investment banking firms. The firm is headquartered in New York and maintains offices in London, Frankfurt, Tokyo, Hong Kong and other major financial centers around the world. Please visit our careers site for information about applying online and our recruiting process.

Schools Goldman recruits from

The following is a list of our primary cross-divisional target schools. The firm also hires from a number of additional schools on a divisional basis, and welcomes online applications from all business schools.

University of Chicago,Columbia University, Cornell University (Johnson), Dartmouth (Tuck), Duke University (Fuqua), Harvard University, Indiana University (Kelley), University of Michigan (Ross), MIT (Sloan), Northwestern University (Kellogg), NYU (Stern), Stanford University, University of Texas (Rice), UCLA (Anderson), University of North Carolina (Kenan-Flagler), University of Pennsylvania (Wharton), University of Virginia (Darden), Vanderbilt University (Owen), Yale University

Visit Vault at **www.vault.com** for insider company profiles, expert advice, career message boards, expert resume reviews, the Vault Job Board and more.

VAULT CAREER LIBRARY   **139**

Employer Directory, cont.

Merrill Lynch

250 Vesey Street
New York, NY 10080
www.ml.com/careers

Merrill Lynch is one of the world's leading wealth management, capital markets and advisory companies, with offices in 38 countries and territories and total client assets of almost $2 trillion.

Merrill Lynch has two core businesses--Global Markets & Investment Banking and Global Wealth Management--offering a range of services for private clients, small businesses, and institutions and corporations.

As an investment bank, it is a leading global trader and underwriter of securities and derivatives across a broad range of asset classes and serves as a strategic advisor to corporations, governments, institutions and individuals worldwide.

Merrill Lynch owns approximately half of BlackRock, one of the world's largest publicly traded investment management companies with more than $1 trillion in assets under management.

We're growing our business by helping clients grow theirs.
Our client relationships are among our greatest competitive assets. We deepen and enrich these relationships through disciplined growth, innovation, and seamless execution.

Business schools Merrill recruits from
Merrill recruits from a variety of top tier graduate business schools.

Corporate Snapshot

Founded: 1914 (Charles E. Merrill & Co)
Employees: 62,000
Q3 2006 Net Revenue: $9.7 billion
Total Client Assets: Almost $2 trillion
Total Stockholders' Equity: $42.2 billion
Fortune 500: Ranked No.34
Stock Symbol: MER
Global Markets: 38 countries.

As of quarter-end, Q2 2007.

Allen & Co.
711 Fifth Avenue
9th Floor
New York, NY 10022
Phone: (212) 832-8000
Fax: (212) 832-8023

Bank of America, Global Corporate & Investment Banking Division
9 West 57th Street
New York, NY 10019
Phone: (212) 583-8900

100 N. Tryon Street
Charlotte, NC 28255
Phone: (800) 432-1000
www.bankofamerica.com

Bank of New York
1 Wall Street
New York, NY 10286
Tel: (212) 495-1784
Fax: (212) 809-9528
www.bankofny.com

Barclays Capital
5 The North Colonnade
Canary Wharf
London, E14 4BB
United Kingdom
Phone: +44-20-7623-2323

200 Park Avenue
New York, NY 10166
Phone: (212) 412-4000
www.barcap.com

Bear Stearns
383 Madison Avenue
New York, NY 10179
Phone: (212) 272-2000
Fax: (212) 272-4785
www.bearstearns.com

The Blackstone Group
345 Park Avenue
New York, NY 10154
Phone: (212) 583-5000
Fax: (212) 583-5712
www.blackstone.com

BNP Paribas
3, rue d'Antin
Paris 75002
France
Phone: +33-1-4014-4546
Fax: +33-1-4014-6973
www.bnpparibas.com

Employer Directory, cont.

Brown Brothers Harriman & Co.
140 Broadway
New York, NY 10015-1101
Phone: (212) 483-1818
Fax: (212) 493-8545
www.bbh.com

CIBC World Markets
300 Madison Avenue
New York, NY 10017
Phone: (212) 856-4000
www.cibcwm.com

Citigroup Inc.
399 Park Avenue
New York, NY 10043
Phone: (800) 285-3000
Fax: (212) 793-3946
www.citigroup.com

Cowen and Company, LLC
1221 Avenue of the Americas
New York, NY 10020
Phone: (646) 562-1000
Fax: (646) 562-1741
www.cowen.com

Deutsche Bank
60 Wall Street
New York, NY 10005
Phone: (212) 250-2500
www.db.com

Dresdner Kleinwort
1301 Avenue of the Americas
New York, NY 10019
Phone: (212) 969-2700
www.dresdnerkleinwort.com

Evercore Partners
55 East 52nd Street
43rd Floor
New York, NY 10055
Phone: (212) 857-3100
Fax: (212) 857-3101
www.evercore.com

Friedman, Billings, Ramsey Group
1001 19th Street North
Arlington, VA 22209
Phone: (703) 312-9500
Fax: (703) 312-9501
www.fbr.com

Gleacher Partners
660 Madison Avenue
19th Floor
New York, NY 10021
Phone: (212) 418-4200
Fax: (212) 752-2711
www.gleacher.com

Greenhill & Co.
300 Park Avenue
New York, NY 10022
Phone: (212) 389-1500
www.greenhill-co.com

HSBC Holdings
8 Canada Square
London, E14 5HQ
United Kingdom
Phone: +44-020-7991-8888
Fax: +44-020-7992-4880
www.hsbc.com

Houlihan Lokey Howard & Zukin
1930 Century Park West
Los Angeles, CA 90067
Phone: (310) 553-8871
Fax: (310) 553-2173
www.hlhz.com

Jefferies & Company, Inc.
520 Madison Avenue
12th Floor
New York, NY 10022
Phone: (212) 284-2550
www.jefferies.com

JPMorgan
270 Park Avenue
New York, NY 10017
Phone: (212) 270-6000
Fax: (212) 270-2613
www.jpmorgan.com

Keefe, Bruyette & Woods
The Equitable Building
787 Seventh Avenue, 4th Floor
New York, NY 10019
Phone: (212) 887-7777
www.kbw.com

Lazard
30 Rockefeller Plaza
New York, NY 10020
Phone: (212) 632-6000
www.lazard.com

Lehman Brothers
745 Seventh Avenue
New York, NY 10019
Phone: (212) 526-7000
Fax: (212) 526-8766
www.lehman.com

Macquarie Group
125 West 55th Street
New York, NY 10019
Phone: (212) 231-1000
Fax: (212) 231-1010
www.macquarie.com/us

Morgan Keegan
Morgan Keegan Tower
50 Front Street, 17th Floor
Memphis, TN 38103
Phone: (901) 524-4100
Fax: (901) 579-4406
www.morgankeegan.com

Morgan Stanley
1585 Broadway
New York, NY 10036
Phone: (212) 761-4000
Fax: (212) 762-0575
www.morganstanley.com

Visit Vault at **www.vault.com** for insider company profiles, expert advice, career message boards, expert resume reviews, the Vault Job Board and more.

VAULT CAREER LIBRARY   **141**

Employer Directory, cont.

Nomura Holdings
2 World Financial Center
Building B
New York, NY 10281-1198
Phone: (212) 667-9300
Fax: (212) 667-1058
www.nomura.com

Peter J. Solomon Company
520 Madison Avenue
New York, NY 10022
Phone: (212) 508-1600
Fax: (212) 508-1633
www.pjsc.com

Piper Jaffray & Co.
800 Nicollet Mall
Suite 800
Minneapolis, MN 55402-7020
Phone: (612) 303-6000
Fax: (612) 303-8199
www.piperjaffray.com

Raymond James Financial
880 Carillon Parkway
St. Petersburg, FL 33716
Phone: (727) 567-1000
Fax: (727) 567-5529
www.rjf.com

RBC Capital Markets
Royal Bank Plaza
200 Bay Street
Toronto, Ontario, M5J 2W7
Canada
Phone: (416) 842-2000
Fax: (416) 842-8033

One Liberty Plaza
165 Broadway
New York, NY 10006
Phone: (212) 858-7000
www.rbccm.com

Robert W. Baird & Co. (Baird)
777 East Wisconsin Avenue
Milwaukee, WI 53202
Phone: (414) 765-3500
Fax: (414) 765-3633
www.rwbaird.com

Rothschild
New Court, St. Swithin's Lane
London, EC4P 4DU
United Kingdom
Phone: +44-20-7280-5000
Fax: +44-20-7929-1643
www.rothschild.com

Rothschild North America
1251 Avenue of the Americas
51st Floor
New York, NY 10020
Phone: (212) 403-3500
Fax: (212) 403-3501
www.rothschild.com

Sandler O'Neill + Partners, L.P.
919 Third Avenue
6th Floor
New York, NY 10022
Phone: (212) 466-7800
www.sandleroneill.com

Thomas Weisel Partners
One Montgomery Street
San Francisco, CA 94104
Phone: (415) 364-2500
Fax: (415) 364-2695
www.tweisel.com

UBS Investment Bank
299 Park Avenue
New York, NY 10171
Phone: (212) 821-3000

677 Washington Boulevard
Stamford, CT 06901
Phone: (203) 719-3000
www.ibb.ubs.com

William Blair & Company
222 West Adams Street
Chicago, IL 60606
Phone: (312) 236-1600
Fax: (312) 368-9418
www.williamblair.com

WR Hambrecht + Co
539 Bryant Street, Suite 100
San Francisco, CA 94107
Phone: (415) 551-8600
Fax: (415) 551-8686
www.wrhambrecht.com

Investment Management

How many industries can you think of that impact households all over the world? Very few. That is one of the many exciting aspects of the asset management industry—more people than ever before are planning for their future financial needs, and as a result, the industry is more visible and important than ever. The asset management community seeks to preserve and grow capital for individuals and institutional investors alike.

Investment management vs. asset management

A quick note about the terms **investment management** and **asset management**: these terms are often used interchangeably. They refer to the same practice—the professional management of assets through investment. Investment management is used a bit more often when referring to the activity or career (i.e., "I'm an investment manager" or "That firm is gaining a lot of business in investment management"), whereas "asset management" is used more with reference to the industry itself (i.e., "The asset management industry").

More stability

Because of the stability of cash flows generated by the industry, investment management provides a relatively stable career when compared to some other financial services positions (most notably investment banking). Investment management firms are generally paid a set fee as a percentage of assets under management. (The fee structure varies, and sometimes is both an asset-centered fee plus a performance fee, especially for institutional investors.) Still, even when investment management fees involve a performance incentive, the business is much less cyclical than cousins like investment banking. Banking fees depend on transactions. When banking activities such as IPOs and M&A transactions dry up, so do fees for investment banks, which translates into layoffs of bankers. In contrast, assets are quite simply always being invested.

History

To better understand why asset management has become such a critical component of the broader financial services industry, we must first become acquainted with its formation and history.

The beginnings of a separate industry

While the informal process of managing money has been around since the beginning of the 20th century, the industry did not begin to mature until the early 1970s. Prior to that time, investment management was completely relationship-based. Assignments to manage assets grew out of relationships that banks and insurance companies already had with institutions— primarily companies or municipal organizations with employee pension funds—that had funds to invest. (A pension fund is set up as an employee benefit. Employers commit to a certain level of payment to retired employees each year and must manage their funds to meet these obligations. Organizations with large pools of assets to invest are called institutional investors.)

These asset managers were chosen in an unstructured way—assignments grew organically out of pre-existing relationships, rather than through a formal request for proposal and bidding process. The actual practice of investment management was also unstructured. At the time, asset managers might simply pick 50 stocks they thought were good investments—there was not nearly as much analysis on managing risk or organizing a fund around a specific category or style. (Examples of different investment categories include small cap stocks and large cap stocks. We will explore the different investment categories and

Visit Vault at **www.vault.com** for insider company profiles, expert advice, career message boards, expert resume reviews, the Vault Job Board and more.

VAULT CAREER LIBRARY 143

styles in a later chapter.) Finally, the assets that were managed at the time were primarily pension funds. Mutual funds had yet to become broadly popular.

ERISA, 401(k) plans and specialist firms

The two catalysts for change in the industry were: (1) the broad realization that demographic trends would cause the U.S. government's retirement system (Social Security) to be underfunded, which made individuals more concerned with their retirement savings, and (2) the creation of ERISA (the Employment Retirement Income Secruity Act) in 1974, which gave employees incentives to save for retirement privately through 401(k) plans. (401(k) plans allow employees to save pretax earnings for their retirement.) These elements prompted an increased focus on long-term savings by individual investors and the formation of what can be described as a private pension fund market.

These fundamental changes created the opportunity for professional groups of money managers to form "specialist" firms to manage individual and institutional assets. Throughout the 1970s and early 1980s, these small firms specialized in one or two investment styles (for example, core equities or fixed income investing).

During this period, the investment industry became fragmented and competitive. This competition added extra dimensions to the asset management industry. Investment skills, of course, remained critical. However, relationship building and the professional presentation of money management teams also began to become significant.

The rise of the mutual fund

In the early to mid 1980s, driven by the ERISA laws, the mutual fund came into vogue. While mutual funds had been around for decades, they were only used by financially sophisticated investors who paid a lot of attention to their investments. However, investor sophistication increased with the advent of modern portfolio theory (the set of tools developed to quantitatively analyze the management of a portfolio; see sidebar on next page). Asset management firms began heavily marketing mutual funds as a safe and smart investment tool, pitching to individual investors the virtues of diversification and other benefits of investing in mutual funds. With more and more employers shifting retirement savings responsibilities from pension funds to the employees themselves, the 401(k) market grew rapidly. Consequently, consumer demand for new mutual fund products exploded (mutual funds are the preferred choice in most 401(k) portfolios). Many specialists responded by expanding their product offerings and focusing more on the marketing of their new services and capabilities.

Modern Portfolio Theory

Modern Portfolio Theory (MPT) was born in 1952 when University of Chicago economics student Harry Markowitz published his doctoral thesis, "Portfolio Selection," in the *Journal of Finance*. Markowitz, who won the Nobel Prize in economics in 1990 for his research and its far-reaching effects, provided the framework for what is now known as modern portfolio theory. MPT quantifies the benefits of diversification, looking at how investors create portfolios in order to optimize market risk against expected returns. Markowitz, assuming all investors are risk averse, proposed that investors, when choosing a security to add to their portfolio, should not base their decision on the amount of risk that an individual security has, but rather on how that security contributes to the overall risk of the portfolio. To do this, Markowitz considered how securities move in relation to one another under similar circumstances. This is called "correlation," which measures how much two securities fluctuate in price relative to each other. Taking all this into account, investors can create "efficient portfolios," ones with the highest expected returns for a given level of risk

Consolidation and globalization

The dominant themes of the industry in the 1990s were consolidation and globalization. As many former specialists rapidly expanded, brand recognition and advanced distribution channels (through brokers or other sales vehicles) became key success factors for asset management companies. Massive global commercial and investment banks entered the industry, taking business away from many specialist firms. Also, mutual fund rating agencies such as Lipper (founded in 1973, now a part of Reuters) and Morningstar (founded in Chicago in 1984) increased investor awareness of portfolio performance. These rating agencies publish reports on fund performance and rate funds on scales such as Morningstar's four-star rating system.

These factors led to a shakeout period of consolidation. From 1995 to 2001, approximately 150 mergers took place, creating well-established and formidable players such as Capital Group and Citigroup. As opposed to specialist firms, these large financial services firms provide asset management products that run the gamut: mutual funds, pension funds, management for high-net-worth individuals, etc. While many excellent specialist firms continue to operate today, they are not the driving force that they once were.

The Industry Today

Wealth creation in the 1990s has led to even greater demand for money management services today. In the U.S. alone, 2.8 million families have reached millionaire status. Mutual fund demand has continued to increase; as of 2002, there were 8,000 different funds in the market, up from just 3,000 in 1990. In fact, nearly 50 million households invest in mutual funds, with a total worth of $8.5 trillion, up from only $340 billion in 1984 and $1 trillion as recently as 1990.

As the industry has matured, total assets under management (AUMs) in the United States have grown to $20 trillion. Consolidation and globalization have created a diverse list of leading industry players that range from well-capitalized divisions of investment banks, global insurance companies and multinational commercial banks to independent behemoths, such as Fidelity and Capital Group.

The leading players in the industry are located all over the U.S. Working in the industry, unlike other areas of financial services like investment banking, does not require that you live in a particular region of the country.

Portfolio Management

The portfolio management segment of the firm makes the ultimate investment decision; it's the department that "pulls the trigger." There are three jobs that typically fall under this component of the firm: portfolio managers, associate portfolio managers and portfolio manager assistants. Recent college graduates often fill portfolio assistant positions, while individuals with many years of investment experience hold associate and senior portfolio manager assignments. MBAs are not hired as portfolio managers right out of business school unless they have a ton of experience. Typically, MBAs who wish to pursue a career in portfolio management join investment management firms in their investment research divisions. After two years in research, MBAs will then have a choice: either stay in research or leverage their research experience to move into an associate portfolio manager position.

Senior portfolio manager

Portfolio managers are responsible for establishing an investment strategy, selecting appropriate investments and allocating each investment properly. All day long, portfolio managers are presented with investment ideas from internal buy-side analysts and sell-side analysts from investment banks. It is their job to sift through the relevant information and use their judgment to buy and sell securities. Throughout each day, they read reports, talk to company managers and monitor industry and economic trends looking for the right company and time to invest the portfolio's capital.

Visit Vault at **www.vault.com** for insider company profiles, expert advice, career message boards, expert resume reviews, the Vault Job Board and more.

VAULT CAREER LIBRARY   145

The selection of investments must adhere to the style of the portfolio. For instance, a large-capitalization growth manager might be screening for only companies that have a market capitalization in excess of $3 billion and earnings growth characteristics that exceed its industry. Therefore, the portfolio manager would not even consider a $500 million utility stock with a 6 percent dividend yield.

Associate portfolio manager

The associate portfolio manager position requires an MBA, CFA or considerable investment experience. Typically, the job is filled by successful research analysts who have at least three to five years of post-MBA experience. The job itself is very similar to that of the senior portfolio manager with one main exception: associates interact less with clients than senior managers do. Associate portfolio managers are usually assigned smaller, less sophisticated portfolios to manage or serve as lieutenants on large, complicated portfolios.

The role of the associate portfolio manager differs depending on which segment of the market is being served—mutual fund, institutional or high-net-worth. For instance, associate portfolio managers at many mutual fund firms will either act as the lead investor on a sector fund or as second-in-command on a large diversified fund. Depending on the firm, an associate could also act as a lead on a sector fund and a second-in-command on a diversified fund at the same time. Alternatively, on the institutional side, associate portfolio managers typically apprentice with seasoned portfolio managers on the largest and most complicated portfolios. After they have succeeded in that role, the firm will assign them smaller institutional accounts to manage on their own.

Successful associate portfolio managers will usually be promoted to senior portfolio managers within two to five years.

Investment Research

The investment research segment is responsible for generating recommendations to portfolio managers on companies and industries that they follow. Similar to the portfolio management segment, there are three potential positions: senior research analyst, investment research associate and investment research assistant. Senior research analysts typically have two to four years of post-MBA research experience. Research associates are usually recent MBA graduates, while assistants are recent college graduates.

Senior research analyst

Senior research analysts are investment experts in their given industry focus. An equity analyst covers stocks; a fixed income analyst covers bonds.

Their role is to predict the investment potential of the companies in their sector. For instance, take an equity analyst covering computer hardware companies, including Apple Computer. The analyst would be responsible for predicting Apple's future earnings and cash flow, and comparing the fair value of Apple to the expectations of the stock market. To do this, the analyst would build a financial model that included all of the potential variables to derive Apple's earnings and appropriate value (e.g., sales growth and business costs, as well as research and development).

A fixed income analyst focusing on telecom, for example, might be looking at a new high-yield corporate bond issued by Qwest. The main thing the analyst will be looking for is Qwest's ability to pay off that loan—the amount of the bond. The analyst will look at historical cash flows, project future cash flows and look at other debt obligations that might be more senior to the new bond. This will tell the analyst the likelihood that Qwest will be able to pay off the bond.

Analysts spend a considerable amount of time attending industry conferences, meeting with company management and analyzing industry supply and demand trends to derive business forecasts. Many analysts follow 20 to 30 companies and must be an expert on each.

An important part of a senior research analyst's job is to convey their recommendations to the portfolio management teams. Therefore, senior analysts spend considerable time presenting to portfolio managers and issuing investment reports. Because of this, senior research analysts must be articulate and persuasive in their convictions in order to earn respect within the firm.

Senior research analysts typically have served as investment research associates for two to four years, post MBA or CFA, before assuming their position. If successful in their role, many senior analysts move into portfolio management roles later in their careers.

Investment research associate

This is the role for most MBAs or those with equivalent experience. Essentially, investment research associates have the same responsibilities as senior research analysts with one exception: associates are given smaller industries to follow. Typically, the industry assigned to an associate is a component of a broader sector that is already being analyzed by a senior analyst. For instance, a research associate might be assigned HMOs and work closely with the senior analyst in charge of insurance companies.

The associate analyst creates investment recommendations in the same manner as a senior analyst. In general, new associates spend several weeks familiarizing themselves with their industry by reading industry papers, journals and textbooks, and attending industry conferences. A large percentage of a research analyst's time is spent monitoring industry and company trends to predict financial results for the company. Therefore, research associates are constantly speaking with management, customers and suppliers to gauge the current status of the company they are analyzing. Armed with financial models and fundamental company analysis, they develop investment recommendations that they distribute to the firm's portfolio managers.

One of the greatest challenges for a new associate is the steepness of the learning curve. Portfolio managers don't have the patience or the luxury to allow an analyst to be uninformed or consistently incorrect. New associates work extremely hard building trust with portfolio managers.

Obviously, financial acumen and quantitative skills are a must for a research associate, but communication skills are also critical. Research associates need to be able to clearly and persuasively communicate their investment recommendations. These associates must also be able to respond to detailed inquiries from portfolio managers that challenge their ideas—which requires a strong tact and a great deal of patience. Furthermore, associates need to be energetic, diligent and intellectually curious. Research associates are usually promoted to larger industries within two to four years of joining the firm.

Visit Vault at **www.vault.com** for insider company profiles, expert advice, career message boards, expert resume reviews, the Vault Job Board and more.

VAULT CAREER LIBRARY   **147**

Employer Directory

A.G. Edwards
One North Jefferson Avenue
St. Louis, MO 63103
Phone: (314) 955-3000
Fax: (314) 955-5402
www.agedwards.com

AllianceBernstein
1345 Avenue of the Americas
New York, NY 10105
Phone: (212) 969-1000
Fax: (212) 969-2229
www.alliancebernstein.com

Allianz Group
Königinstrasse 28
D-80802 Munich
Germany
Phone: +49-89-3800-0
Fax: +49-89-3800-3425
www.allianz.com

**American Century
Investments**
4500 Main Street
Kansas City, MO 64111
Phone: (816) 531-5575
Fax: (816) 340-7962
www.americancentury.com

Ameriprise Financial
707 2nd Avenue South
Minneapolis, MN 55402
Phone: (612) 671-3131
www.ameriprise.com

**The Asset Management
Division of Credit Suisse**
11 Madison Avenue
New York, NY 10010
Phone: (212) 325-2000
Fax: (212) 538-3395
www.credit-suisse.com/us/en

Bank of America
Bank of America Corporate Center
100 N. Tryon Street
Charlotte, NC 28255
www.bankofamerica.com

**Barclays Global Investors,
N.A.**
45 Fremont Street
San Francisco, CA 94105
Phone: (415) 597-2000
Fax: (415) 597-2171
www.barclaysglobal.com

**Bear Stearns Asset
Management**
383 Madison Avenue
New York, NY 10179
Phone: (212) 272-2000
Fax: (212) 272-4785
www.bearstearns.com

BlackRock
40 East 52nd Street
New York, NY 10022
Phone: (212) 810-5300
www.blackrock.com

Blackstone
345 Park Avenue
New York, NY 10154
Phone: (212) 583-5000
Fax: (212) 583-5712
www.blackstone.com

CalPERS
Lincoln Plaza, 400 P Street
Sacramento, CA 95814
Phone: (916) 795-3829
Fax: (916) 795-4001
www.calpers.ca.gov

Capital Group Companies
333 S. Hope Street, 53rd Floor
Los Angeles, CA 90071
Phone: (213) 486-9200
Fax: (213) 486-9217
www.capgroup.com

Charles Schwab
101 Montgomery Street
San Francisco, CA 94104
Phone: (415) 636-7000
Fax: (415) 636-9820
www.schwab.com

D.E. Shaw & Co., L.P.
120 West 45th Street
39th Floor, Tower 45
New York, NY 10036
Phone: (212) 478-0000
Fax: (212) 478-0100
www.deshaw.com

DC Energy
8065 Leeburg Pike
5th Floor
Vienna, VA 22182
Phone: (703) 506-3901
Fax: (703) 506-3905
www.dc-energy.com

Deutsche Bank
345 Park Avenue
New York, NY 10017
Phone: (212) 454-3600

Taunusanlage 12
60262 Frankfurt am Main
Germany
Phone: +49-69-910-00
Fax: +49-69-910-00
www.db.com

Dreyfus Corporation
200 Park Avenue
New York, NY 10166
Phone: (212) 922-6000
Fax: (212) 922-7533
www.dreyfus.com

Fidelity Investments
82 Devonshire Street
Boston, MA 02109
Phone: (617) 563-7000
Fax: (617) 476-6150
www.fidelity.com

Employer Directory, cont.

E*TRADE FINANCIAL
135 East 57th Street
New York, NY 10022
Phone: (646) 521-4300
www.etrade.com

Edward Jones
12555 Manchester Road
St. Louis, MO 63131
Phone: (314) 515-2000
Fax: (314) 515-2820
www.edwardjones.com

Federated Investors
Federated Investors Tower
1001 Liberty Avenue
Pittsburgh, PA 15222-3779
Phone: (412) 288-1900
Fax: (412) 288-6446
FederatedInvestors.com

Franklin Resources, Inc.
(Franklin Templeton Investments)
1 Franklin Parkway
Building 970, 1st Floor
San Mateo, CA 94403
Phone: (650) 312-2000
Fax: (650) 312 5606
www.franklintempleton.com

GAMCO Investors, Inc.
One Corporate Center
Rye, NY 10580-1422
Phone: (914) 921-5100
Fax: (914) 921-5392
www.gabelli.com

Goldman Sachs
85 Broad Street
New York, NY 10004
Phone: (212) 902-1000
www.gs.com

HSBC North America Holdings
2700 Sanders Road
Prospect Heights, IL 60070
Phone: (847) 564-5000
www.hbscusa.com

ING Investment Management
Prinses Beatrixlaan 15
2595 AK The Hague
Netherlands
Phone: +31-70-378-1781
Fax: +31-70-378-1854
www.ingim.com

INVESCO
30 Finsbury Square
London, EC2A 1AG
United Kingdom
Phone: +44-20-7638-0731
Fax: +44-20-7065-3962
www.amvescap.com

Janus Capital Group
151 Detroit Street
Denver, CO 80206
Phone: (303) 333-3863
Fax: (303) 336-7497
www.janus.com

JPMorgan Investment Management
245 Park Avenue
New York, NY 10017
Phone: (212) 270-6000
Fax: (212) 270-2613
www.jpmorgan.com

Lazard Asset Management
30 Rockefeller Plaza
58th Floor
New York, NY 10112-6300
Phone: (800) 821-6474
www.lazardnet.com

Legg Mason
100 Light Street
Baltimore, MD 21202-1099
Phone: (877) 534-4627
Fax: (410) 454-4923
www.leggmason.com

Lehman Brothers—Investment Management Division
399 Park Avenue
New York, NY 10022
Phone: (212) 526-7000
www.lehman.com

Mellon Financial Corporation
One Mellon Center
Pittsburgh, PA 15258-0001
Phone: (412) 234-5000
Fax: (412) 234-9495
www.mellon.com

Merrill Lynch Global Private Client
4 World Financial Center
250 Vesey Street
New York, NY 10080
Phone: (212) 449-1000
Fax: (212) 449-7357
www.ml.com

MFS Investment Management
500 Boylston Street
Boston, MA 02116
Phone: (617) 954-5000
www.mfs.com

Morgan Keegan—Wealth Management Division
Morgan Keegan Tower
50 Front Street, 17th Floor
Memphis, TN 38103
Phone: (901) 524-4100
Fax: (901) 579-4406
www.morgankeegan.com

Morgan Stanley Investment Management
1585 Broadway
New York, NY 10036
Phone: (212) 761-4000
Fax: (212) 762-0575
www.morganstanley.com

Visit Vault at **www.vault.com** for insider company profiles, expert advice, career message boards, expert resume reviews, the Vault Job Board and more.

VAULT CAREER LIBRARY   149

Employer Directory, cont.

Northern Trust Corporation
50 South LaSalle Street
Chicago, IL 60603
Phone: (312) 630-6000
Fax: (312) 630-1512
www.ntrs.com

Nuveen Investments
333 W. Wacker Drive
Chicago, IL 60606
Phone: (312) 917-7700
Fax: (312) 917-8049
www.nuveen.com

Pacific Investment Management Co. (PIMCO)
840 Newport Center Drive
Suite 300
Newport Beach, CA 92660
Phone: (949) 720-6000
Fax: (949) 720-1376
www.pimco.com

Pequot Capital Management
500 Nyala Farm Road
Westport, CT 06880
Phone: (203) 429-2200
Fax: (203) 429-2400
www.pequotcap.com

Putnam Investments
One Post Office Square
Boston, MA 02109
Phone: (617) 292-1000
www.putnam.com

Raymond James Financial
880 Carillon Parkway
St. Petersburg, FL 33716
Phone: (727) 567-1000
Fax: (727) 567-5529
www.rjf.com

Schroders plc
31 Gresham Street
London, EC2V 7QA
United Kingdom
Phone: +44-207-658-6000
Fax: +44-207-658-6965
www.schroders.com

State Street Corporation
1 Lincoln Street
Boston, MA 02111
Phone: (617) 786-3000
Fax: (617) 664-4299
www.statestreet.com

T. Rowe Price
100 E. Pratt Street
Baltimore, MD 21202
Phone: (410) 345-2000
Fax: (410) 345-2394
www.troweprice.com

TD Ameritrade
4211 S. 102nd Street
Omaha, NE 68127
Phone: (402) 331-7856
Fax: (402) 597-7789
www.amtd.com

TIAA-CREF
730 3rd Avenue
New York, NY 10017
Phone: (212) 490-9000
www.tiaa-cref.org

UBS Financial Services
1285 Avenue of the Americas
New York, NY 10019
Phone: (212) 713-2000
Fax: (212) 713-9818
www.ubs.com

The Vanguard Group
100 Vanguard Boulevard
Malvern, PA 19355
Phone: (610) 648-6000
Fax: (610) 669-6605
www.vanguard.com

Wachovia/Evergreen Investments
301 S. College Street
Suite 4000
One Wachovia Center
Charlotte, NC 28288-0013
Phone: (704) 374-6565
Fax: (704) 374-3425
www.wachovia.com

Wellington Management Co., LLP
75 State Street
Boston, MA 02109
Phone: (617) 951-5000
www.wellington.com

Leveraged Finance

What is Leveraged Finance?

The financial markets can be divided into two major sections: debt and equity. Under this overarching organization structure, think of leveraged finance as the intersection of investment banking, commercial banking, hedge funds, private equity, and sales and trading on the debt side of the financial markets.

Generally speaking, leveraged finance is a platform in all major investment and commercial banks. It is a function that taps into two major financial markets (the high-yield bond market and the leveraged loan market), is accessed by nearly all private equity shops and hedge funds on a regular basis, and has been one of the booming profit centers of Wall Street for the past two decades. For analysts and associates, it has become a prime training ground for the most elite private equity shops and hedge funds. Subsequently, for careers on Wall Street, leveraged finance is one of the most sought-after fields.

Why leveraged finance?

Along with its role as a potential springboard to careers in private equity and hedge funds, leveraged finance is also unique from a career perspective because it provides a vantage point into most of the other areas of investment banking, as well as sales and trading. For analysts and associates, working in leveraged finance allows one to see what else is out there career-wise in the financial markets, without ever having to leave the field.

Another advantage of working in leveraged finance is that in general, it is an area of investment banking that is focused on closing transactions. In a corporate finance role within a coverage team in an investment bank (a team that covers a specific industry and pitches deals to companies in that industry), one analyst might close one or two deals a year in an investment bank. By contrast, in leveraged finance, it's feasible to close 5 to 10 transactions a year. Leveraged finance affords analysts and associates a continually busy pace and good deal and client exposure along the way.

Major deals

One of the great advantages to working in leveraged finance is that you will typically work on notable transactions. As an analyst or associate in a major leveraged finance firm, you may even see at least one of your deals make the cover of *The Wall Street Journal*. Notable brands like RJR Nabisco, Burger King, United Airlines, Domino's Pizza and Sony MGM have all accessed the leveraged finance markets. From multibillion-dollar leveraged buyouts to major corporate restructurings, there are plenty of headline transactions across the field.

Leveraged Finance vs. Corporate Finance/Investment Banking

Are the leveraged finance and investment banking the same animal? Sort of. As leveraged finance was originally a commercial banking function, most of the premier leveraged finance shops can be found within the investment banks of the largest finance institutions, such as JPMorgan Chase, Bank of America and Citigroup. Because of the sheer amount of leveraged finance deal volume at these institutions, there will typically be entire floors and groups dedicated to "originating deals" (proposing deals to existing or new clients), following the capital markets, trading in and out of loan/bond positions, selling these products to investors, and monitoring the firm's exposure to loans and bonds of issuers. Naturally, at pure investment banks such as Goldman Sachs or Lehman Brothers that do not originate as many of these types of debt transactions, there will typically be smaller groups dedicated to following the markets, in more of a debt capital markets generalist role. However, in both types of institutions, the leveraged finance platform is typically part of a debt capital markets group—it just depends on the volume of deals to determine how specific and/or large the groups will be.

Visit Vault at **www.vault.com** for insider company profiles, expert advice, career message boards, expert resume reviews, the Vault Job Board and more.

VAULT CAREER LIBRARY   151

A common misperception is that traditional investment banking only involves providing solutions and advice to companies (such as mergers and acquisitions advice). In this regard, leveraged finance is different from investment banking, since a leveraged finance bank is not only offering advice for a financial problem, but also a product as a solution. However, most people these days broaden their definition of investment banking to include both offering advice to companies, as well as executing a financial transaction, such as an initial public offering (IPO). In this sense, leveraged finance is identical—just as an investment bank covers a company in an industry coverage group and works with its equity capital markets team to structure an IPO, so does it provide the same service for leveraged finance transactions. In the case of a leveraged finance transaction, the investment bank also covers the company and works with people from its debt capital markets team to structure a syndicated loan and/or high-yield bond.

Unlike investment banking, however, there exist a number of other financial institutions, such as General Electric or CIT Group, that arrange these similar financing packages for companies, but do so without a coverage group or an industry platform (which an investment bank would have). These financial institutions still have relationships with companies, but they don't typically provide M&A or IPO advice like an investment bank. The loan market is a private market, and as such is not limited in terms of what type of firm can provide lending solutions. If you're a treasurer of a multibillion dollar company and you need a large loan for an acquisition, you'll go to the firm with the best interest rate, regardless of whether it's an investment bank or not. In this regard, leveraged finance is more similar to commercial lending (e.g., lending to a company so that they can buy copiers, printers, etc.) than it is similar to investment banking.

Different experiences: working in the coverage group of an investment bank vs. leveraged finance

Working in a coverage group or M&A at an investment bank differs greatly from working in a debt capital markets (DCM) or equity capital markets (ECM). There is more execution of deals in a DCM or ECM role. Whereas someone in this role may not be as familiar with every facet of an industry like their counterpart in a coverage group, they will generally have more breadth of financial market knowledge.

This breadth vs. depth trade-off is directly related to the amount of transaction experience offered in leveraged finance. For example, the day-to-day grind might be a little more hectic in a leveraged finance role, as a deal team could potentially be closing two multibillion-dollar transactions on the same day—something that would be quite unlikely in a coverage role. However, this transaction-oriented environment involves substantially less idea generation and pitching of ideas to clients than one would find in an investment banking industry coverage group. That is not to say that someone in leveraged finance will not do any pitching—quite the contrary. While the industry coverage group might come up with and pitch the idea of a syndicated loan or high-yield bond to finance an M&A deal, they will surely bring along the appropriate people from the leveraged finance platform to comment on the markets, comparable transactions and provide other relevant advice.

If you are beginning your career in finance, it is important to think about your long-term career goals when considering a role in investment banking coverage versus leveraged finance. If your goal is to work in a specific industry—let's say running a health care company—you would probably be better served in a health care coverage group at an investment bank. However, if you are interested in working at a hedge fund or private equity shop, working in leveraged finance will give you the opportunity to interact with many of these firms, as you close numerous deals of theirs. Furthermore, you will be trained in certain debt metrics (what's typically called "credit" training), which are useful in understanding the industry and are not typically emphasized in the coverage side of the bank. This is not to say that moving from a coverage group to a private equity shop or hedge fund can't happen—it certainly does, and even the top-tier PE shops and hedge funds seek people with very specific industry knowledge. However, it's definitely the case that your exposure (most likely in late-night financial modeling revisions) to the private equity shops will be higher in leveraged finance groups when compared to your exposure working in an industry coverage group. In an industry where relationships are everything, this exposure will definitely matter.

Types of leveraged finance deals

There are a wide variety of deals executed within leveraged finance. Most common are syndicated loans and high-yield bonds for working capital or general corporate purposes (day-to-day financing needs). However, in leveraged finance you'll also find leveraged buyouts, when private equity shops and financial sponsors use borrowed money to purchase companies. There are also corporate restructurings and DIP (Debtor-in-Possession) facilities, where companies are entering/exiting bankruptcy and are trying to avoid Chapter 7 bankruptcy (liquidation). In this case, the companies will work with both the financial institutions' leveraged finance groups and the federal bankruptcy court to get financing packages in order to stay in business. Leveraged finance also covers dividend transactions, where loans/bonds are used to pay out the owners of a business, recapitalizations, where a company's financial structure is changed, IPO/spin-off financings, where the proceeds of a loan/bond are in tandem with an IPO or a spin-off of a business unit, and even general debt refinancings, where an existing loan/bond is taken out with a new loan/bond.

Opportunities in Leveraged Finance

There are so many different areas within leveraged finance and so many related to the field that there is place for almost everyone. For example, there is deal origination, for the person who enjoys managing numerous processes such as putting together presentations, financial modeling and pitching. There is also capital markets work (for both syndicated loans and high-yield bonds) for the person who enjoys understanding the flow of the markets and conducting research about the market's trends. For the person who enjoys the asset management aspect of managing a firm's exposure to the syndicated loan/high-yield bond markets, there are positions in internal credit/portfolio management work. Finally, there is a sales and trading function for both syndicated loans and high-yield bonds.

However, very generally speaking, leveraged finance refers to the deal origination function—when a team goes out to pitch a client, wins the mandate, structures the loan/bond, markets it to investors, sells it, and then closes and funds the transaction. This role as an analyst or associate caters to the individual who enjoys managing numerous deals throughout this process, who is a jack-of-all-trades from financial modeling to talking to investment firms, and who thrives in the pace of a seemingly never-ending day. Furthermore, when considering if leveraged finance is/is not the field for you, it is important to realize that some firms are organized in a typical investment banking "cubicle/office" atmosphere, whereas some are organized like trading floors. Some people feed off the energy from a football field-sized area crammed with people chatting all day long, while others would prefer the quieter nature of a cube or an office, where personal phone calls are not heard by your neighbors and neighbor's neighbors. This type of setup can make a substantial difference in the day-to-day enjoyment of someone's role in leveraged finance.

The culture of leveraged finance depends almost entirely on the culture of the firm in general. At a pure investment bank such as Goldman Sachs, you might find the culture to be almost entirely opposite from that of the commercial lending arm of a larger financial institution, such as General Electric Commercial Finance. Whereas one might be very rigid and hierarchical, the other might be golf shirt and khakis on Fridays, where an analyst can chat it up with any managing director at any time.

Investment banks: structuring/organization

Within structuring/origination, there are four major roles: managing director, vice president, associate and analyst. As the hierarchy is structured, there are generally more analysts than associates, more associates than VPs, and more VPs than MDs. At most firms, the ratio tends to be one MD for every one to two VPs, two to three associates, and three to four analysts.

Managing director: Sitting at the top of the leveraged finance food chain, the MD generally spends most of his/her time speaking with treasurers and CFOs of companies, in order to assess their financial status and need for debt facilities. The MD

Visit Vault at www.vault.com for insider company profiles, expert advice, career message boards, expert resume reviews, the Vault Job Board and more.

VAULT CAREER LIBRARY   153

is usually the key relationship manager for the bank because of continuous dialogue with the client. As senior members of the deal team, MDs have something of a sales role, and interact with a limited number of clients with whom they have worked throughout the years. The top MDs are group heads, who may have contracts outlining their compensation structure.

Managing directors will spend quite a bit of time pitching ideas to clients, as their salary is typically determined based on the fees they earn from their deal flow. In this sense, it is not uncommon for the best-of-the-best MDs to command multiple-millions of dollars in compensation in good years (think $3 million or more in bonuses). Naturally, it pays to be an MD in a leveraged finance group that executes a high volume of exceptionally profitable LBOs, DIP facilities, and recapitalizations. However, more often than not, the salary of an MD is enough to support his/her basic lifestyle and the bulk of pay comes in the form of a bonus paid with stock options that must vest over a certain period of years. These "golden handcuffs" are usually incentive enough for senior MDs to stay at their current firms for long periods of time, which generally ensures consistency at the most senior ranks.

As for lifestyle, managing directors typically work "market" hours—from 8 a.m. to 7 p.m. However, when working on more complex transactions, they will often work later, reviewing financial presentations and editing offering memorandums. Rarely is a weekend worked from the office, but it is not uncommon for an MD to review materials and make calls from their homes on the weekend or on the train ride home from work. MDs also tend to have access to corporate expense accounts, in order to entertain clients over lunch, dinner, a ballgame or on the golf course.

Vice president: The vice president on a deal team is the right hand man of the MD. Once a mandate has been won, the VP generally takes over and manages the process going forward. From the negotiating and signing of legal documents to the final signoff of the information memorandum, the VP's role is to ensure that everything in the deal goes smoothly. Throughout the deal lifecycle, a VP will often act as the relationship manager, delivering the periodic client update call and subsequently laying the future foundation for his promotion to MD.

Although, like MDs, VPs interact frequently with clients, VPs tend to be salaried and not commission-based they way MDs typically are. The very best VPs are paid extremely well, commanding salaries in the multiple hundreds of thousands of dollars, like their other corporate finance investment banking counterparts. In great years, it is not uncommon for a top performing VP in a very active team to clear $1 million. However, in bad economic times, or working in groups that do not originate many transactions, these VPs tend to make closer to $250K.

The high performing VPs are generally on the fast track to promotion, spending three to four years in the role before becoming a managing director. At some firms a vice president will be referred to as a "principal" or "director"—the main distinction of this role from that of a managing director is a lower salary. VP titles are also quite often awarded to those who spend a good amount of time interacting with clients.

Associate: Either fresh out of a top-tier MBA program or recently promoted from third-year analyst, the associate role is highly soughtafter. For those top-performing analysts fortunate enough to land the analyst-to-associate ("A-to-A") promotion, this position has a lot of upsides. Able to hit the ground running more quickly than their just-out-of-B-school counterparts, these associates stand a much higher chance to be ranked near the top of their class. The downside is that an A-to-A might have trouble separating herself from the day-to-day financial modeling that came with the analyst lifestyle and subsequently, might run the risk of becoming a micromanager. The deal lifecycle is so process-oriented that this can easily become the downfall of an associate.

Associates generally have a very similar lifestyle to that of an analyst. Eager to be promoted to VP, they arrive in the office early. They typically leave late, reviewing work with their analysts to get projects completed. It is not uncommon for even the most senior associates to work 80+ hour workweeks, including nearly every weekend. As is the case with the deal cycle in leveraged finance, there are typically quite a few projects needing to be completed at any given time. This lifestyle lends itself to the never-ending workday.

However, associates are paid accordingly with other corporate finance investment banking associates, which tends to reward them handsomely for their work ethic. With base salaries as high as $95K, signing bonuses in the $25 to 45K range, and full-year bonuses well in excess of $150K, the first-year associate gets paid well for his efforts. The more experienced associates can expect to be compensated very well in the good economic years. This can translate into bonuses near $300K, with salaries clearing $150 to 200K. However, in slower years, this bonus amount can easily be cut in half. Whereas analysts are generally very excited to make their base salary in their bonus in a good year, senior associates are hoping to double their salary amount.

Generally staffed by a VP in their team, analysts and associates are usually placed on a variety of deals, which means that they should not all be "live" or closing at the same time. Inevitably, this is never actually the case. This deal variety helps to ensure that these junior resources will be able to work with different issuers, deal teams and financial products. At first, most junior resources are staffed alongside other seasoned ones.

Investment banks: capital markets/loan sales and distribution

Managing director/vice president: In a capital markets function, the managing director and vice president often have very similar job responsibilities; one's title reflects not job responsibilities but years of experience in the field. As loan sales and distribution is typically grouped with these capital markets professionals (if not one and the same at most firms), these positions are compensated similarly. Managing directors and vice presidents spend most of their time advising deal teams and clients on market conditions, as well as delivering these deals to investors.

With years of relevant experience, these professionals generally hail from origination and structuring teams or another section of the investment bank's corporate finance practice, and are typically compensated on a scale comparable to their managing director and vice president peers in origination and corporate finance. Although their function is not specifically "on the line" (they are not directly responsible for generating revenues for a firm), and this means that their pay scale might not be quite the same as those successful at originating many deals, it is generally very close. However, because the pay for a capital markets MD does not depend as much on fee generation as it does for an origination MD, this can lead to more consistent earnings for the capital markets MD/VP year after year.

In this sense, the capital markets and loan sales teams are like head coaches of professional sports teams: whereas the players (the deal team) are out winning the games, the coach is directing the team during games, drawing up new plays (adjusting the terms of the deal in market), conducting research on other competition (market comparables), talking to fans (investors), and interacting with the team's owners (the client). While marquee players bring in extraordinary financial contracts, the very best coaches are generally not too far behind.

As the firm's eyes and ears of the financial markets, the capital markets and loan sales positions tend to work more "market" hours. In at 7 a.m. and out by 7 p.m. is somewhat typical for these senior professionals. However, even the senior capital markets professionals will commonly find themselves working with origination teams and issuers to structure large deals well into the evenings. Loan sales professionals often work late too, but in a different capacity and outside of the office. Often, they are attending dinners/sporting events with investors and/or clients. Regardless, the lifestyles of senior professionals in both capacities tends to be quite hectic: following the markets, talking to clients, answering questions from investors, and spending the day attached to a BlackBerry. Weekends for these teams are typically freer than origination teams', but there is always occasional work that needs to be done.

Associate/analyst: As part of the corporate finance program, the associate and analyst role within these teams is much like their peers in other groups. On a junior level, in capital markets these tend to be positions that are more geared towards research, while in loan sales these roles are more focused on investment-grade deals and coverage of smaller clients. Because they are paid on the same scale as an origination associate/analyst, it appears on first glance that the capital markets analyst or associate role would offer a better lifestyle than in origination. However, because of the pace of the job, that's not necessarily true.

Visit Vault at **www.vault.com** for insider company profiles, expert advice, career message boards, expert resume reviews, the Vault Job Board and more.

V∧ULT CAREER LIBRARY   **155**

While an origination analyst or associate completes a number of different tasks over the span of a week (such as writing an info memo, adding pages to a credit deck, or completing slides in a pitch), the capital markets associate/analyst usually completes tasks on a daily or hourly basis. The nature of the job is like a sprint, not a marathon, often involving numerous fire drills. For example, deal teams might ask for league tables and credential slides, investors might want to know the spread differential between a particular syndicated loan and a high-yield bond, a senior MD of the bank might want a deck of slides outlining market conditions, and a client might want a set of recent second lien LBO deals. These are all likely requests in the first half of a day for a capital markets associate or analyst.

Therefore, it is not uncommon for an associate/analyst in these groups to spend the entire day at his desk, working through a large list of requests. On the upside (if you can call it that), the day will most likely end before midnight (and usually closer to 9 to 10 p.m.) and resume again promptly at 8 a.m. Although the capital markets have closed and the MD and VPs might have gone home, there are always materials needing preparation for early morning meetings and late-night, last-minute requests from deal teams. This is quite different from origination, where the day of an analyst might not end until 4 a.m., but the next day will not usually start until 10 a.m., as there is less market sensitivity in origination/structuring.

Weekend work for capital markets associates and analysts is usually a regular occurrence. While unlike the weekends of their origination counterparts, weekends for capital markets analysts and associates are usually not spent entirely in the office, the variety of the requests is less predictable than in origination. In origination, there are usually projected deadlines for projects. In capital markets, those deadlines are usually ASAP. As for sales, working on a weekend would be quite out of the ordinary. A quick phone call or BlackBerry message to a client might occur, but not the creation of market update slides or league tables, which usually happens in capital markets.

Investment banks: credit/risk/corporate banking/ratings advisory

These functions are essential to the leveraged finance platform but are not generally aligned with revenue generation. As such, they are typically compensated on a lower pay scale, and the lifestyle in these groups is better.

Managing director/vice president: Similar to other senior resources, the lifestyles of the managing director and vice president roles within these teams is less intense than their coverage counterparts. With the exception of corporate banking, these roles are not usually the primary client contacts for the firm. Also, since they are not usually aligned with revenue generation, they are compensated on a different scale. Whereas an all-star managing director in origination might get the credit for bringing in $25 million of fees for a deal and will be paid in-line with this fee generation (or lack thereof in a bad year), someone in a non-revenue generation role will have more stable earnings. This means that the top-tier ratings advisory managing director will most likely not earn as much as the top-tier origination managing director. However, when it comes to compensation for group/department heads, all bets are off.

In terms of hours, the senior resources in these functions can expect to work even more predictable hours than those senior professionals in origination. Like their counterparts, weekends are usually free and you will not usually find them in the office at 9 p.m. However, as with any other major leveraged finance function, if a large or complex deal is coming to the market, everyone on a deal team usually works well past their "normal" hours.

Associate/analyst: Much like the origination/structuring and capital markets junior resources, these individuals are part of the corporate finance program at the investment banks. However, the ebb-and-flow of workload in these positions tends to be more similar to origination than to capital markets. Their day-to-day will fluctuate based on their group and or deal-flow, but will generally be long hours, marked with long-term projects and firm deadlines, such as the creation of a ratings agency presentation. Also, the pay will generally coincide with the entire corporate finance program. As for weekend work, junior resources in all of these groups can definitely expect it. Usually working intensely on one or two deals, as opposed to three to five in origination, their weekend lifestyle is slightly more predictable.

Commercial banks and commercial finance companies

Organizationally, commercial banks and commercial finance companies tend to set up their leveraged finance platforms in relation to their deal flow. Whereas some of the larger players like GE have dedicated origination teams to cover large cap and small cap issuers, smaller middle-market players might combine all of their origination, capital markets and sales roles. Typically though, the large players are set up in a manner similar to the investment banks, although they will combine the complementary functions such as sales/capital markets and underwriting/credit/risk. At these firms, the titles/hierarchy are similar to that of investment banks, as is the way that pay for each function depends on how closely tied that group is to revenue generation. However, at the commercial banks, pay and lifestyle are often very different than that at an investment bank.

A Day in the Life of a Leveraged Finance Structuring/Origination Associate

7:00 a.m.: It's a little bit early for you to be up, but you want to get a head start on the day. Since it's a Friday and your analyst has been cranking late on an info memo for a new deal, you definitely want to get into the office and review it ASAP. Also, your MD has called a 9 a.m. meeting for this deal and you want to be prepared. So, you grab the BlackBerry and head to the office.

8:15 a.m.: Even as a third-year associate, you still are not used to the early morning hours, which follow long evenings. Although you were at work until 11 p.m., your adrenaline still runs high, as you are now on two live deals. One, a multibillion-dollar refinancing, was just mandated, and the second is in market with a lenders' meeting on Tuesday morning. There's always plenty going on in this job, which is exactly why you love it. You check e-mails and start to review the info memo shell that your top-notch analyst worked on late last night. That kid is definitely going places.

8:40 a.m.: Realizing that you've got 20 minutes until your meeting, you run downstairs to grab a cup of coffee and a bagel.

9:00 a.m.: You finish your bagel at your desk while reading the info memo, and head over to the meeting where the MD outlines the next tasks for the transaction. The MD is exceptionally pleased to know that the info memo was already started and you all talk about the next steps. You set a firm deadline for the info memo to be distributed to lenders, for a lenders' meeting to be held and for sit-downs with the sales and capital markets teams. The MD, always on the BlackBerry, forwards you all a note from senior management, which says how proud they are that the deal team pulled off another successful pitch. As you have been on quite a number of deals, you recognize that this is the calm before the storm and the crunch time before the deal launches.

10:00 a.m.: With some clear deadlines in hand, you quickly debrief with the analyst, dividing up responsibilities. You agree to meet at the office at 10 a.m. tomorrow, to make sure that everything is on track and to review progress. Since the other analyst on your live transaction is out of the office for recruiting, you are doing all of the heavy lifting for the lenders' meeting and will need all of the help possible on this deal. With two live deals in market, things are busy right now. Thankfully your auctions have gone radio silent, while the owners review bids from the private equity shops and financing firms.

10:15 a.m.: You return to your desk to find some investors have already called about the new transaction, even before the lenders' presentation has gone out. You call them back, giving them some information and passing the word along to your sales team. People are definitely excited about this deal.

10:45 a.m.: As soon as you set down the phone, the VP for this deal comes over to your desk, checking in with you about the presentation. Almost on cue, the client calls, asking to review the lenders' presentation slides you sent last night. Since they will be traveling to New York on Monday for the presentation on Tuesday, they'd like to wrap up any major changes before the weekend.

Visit Vault at **www.vault.com** for insider company profiles, expert advice, career message boards, expert resume reviews, the Vault Job Board and more.

VAULT CAREER LIBRARY 157

11:00 a.m.: On the call with the client, you are going slide-by-slide through your newest update to the presentation with the client. You discuss talking points, where you all should meet and any other changes. The client suggests updates to a few slides and you make note of them. Knowing these changes will be made to the info memo, you make note to change those as well. You promise to send them a soft copy of the slides by 4 p.m. so they can print them out before they leave for home.

12:30 p.m.: Immediately after you get off the phone, you begin reviewing the changes. Recognizing that this will take you a few hours, you decide to grab a bite to eat from the cafeteria downstairs, since you know that you can get back to your desk quickly.

12:50 p.m.: While eating lunch at your desk, you start cranking on changes. The VP stops by periodically to ask questions, but otherwise you spend most of the afternoon cranking on the changes and double-checking everything. Since hundreds of investors will be scrutinizing this deck of slides, you want it to be as perfect as possible. Also, since this is going back to the client, you want the work to be topnotch.

3:00 p.m.: With the changes made, you circulate the presentation to the VP and MD to show them what you are sending. Often, the CFO and treasurer will call you directly and vice versa, but you still like to touch base with your deal team. Once you have final approval from them, you send over a copy of the lenders' meeting slides.

3:30 p.m.: Your e-mail to the client has been sent, so now it is time to check in with your other deal team. Meanwhile, the analyst is cranking on the transaction overview section of the info memo and making good progress. You both grab some coffee to take a break, while you discuss the weekend and career stuff.

4:00 p.m.: Once back at your desk, you check e-mails and voicemails. You make some calls to friends, check CNN and the *WSJ*, and catch up on the rest of your day. About this time, the analyst from your deal has arrived back in the office from the high-yield bond roadshow, completely exhausted. You both sit down to update on what has happened with the lenders' presentation, while you strategize what needs to happen before Tuesday's meeting. However, since the final approval for the deck of slides has not yet been given, you are really in a holding pattern on that front. Yet, updates need to be made to that info memo so that it can be sent to investors immediately after the meeting. This will definitely be your weekend work.

5:00 p.m.: Before your MDs leave for the weekend, you check in with each of them to make sure they know where everything stands. The lenders' slides for the first transaction look great, the shell of the info memo for the refinancing transaction is underway and your auctions still remain quiet with no news. From the looks of it, you might actually have something of a weekend. You also make sure to check in with the VPs, since they are leaving shortly too. As one of them is drafting part of a credit agreement this weekend, she invites you to hop on a conference call tomorrow morning at 11 a.m. Since you will be in the office anyhow, this is fine by you.

6:00 p.m.: You stop by both analysts' desks to see how they are doing. You divide up some minor tasks, so that everyone can get out of the office tonight, since it is a nice evening outside. With only a few hours of work on Saturday, you feel great about this weekend.

7:00 p.m.: You shut down the laptop, remind the analysts not to stay late since a lot of that work can be done tomorrow, and you head home. As for a 7 p.m. departure on a Friday, you have seen a lot worse!

Employer Directory

ABN AMRO
Gustav Mahlerlaan 10
1082 PP Amsterdam
Netherlands
Phone: +31-20-628-9393
Fax: +31-20-629-9111
www.abnamro.com

Bank of America Leveraged Finance
100 N. Tryon Street
Bank of America Corporate Center
Charlotte, NC 28255
Phone: (704) 386-5681
Fax: (704) 386-6699
www.bankofamerica.com

The Carlyle Group
1001 Pennsylvania Avenue NW
Washington, DC 20004-2505
Phone: (202) 729-5626
Fax: (202) 347-1818
www.thecarlylegroup.com

Citigroup
399 Park Avenue
New York, NY 10043
Phone: (212) 559-1000
Toll Free: (800) 285-3000
Fax: (212) 793-3946
www.citigroup.com

Credit Suisse
11 Madison Avenue
New York, NY 10010
Phone: (212) 325-2000
Fax: (212) 325-8057
www.csfb.com

Deutsche Bank
Taunusanlage 12
60262 Frankfurt
Germany
Phone: +49-69-910-00
Fax: +49-69-910-34-225
www.deutsche-bank.de

Goldman Sachs
85 Broad Street
New York, NY 10004
Phone: (212) 902-1000
Fax: (212) 902-3000
www.goldmansachs.com

Goodwin Procter LLP
Exchange Place, 53 State Street
Boston, MA 02109
Phone: (617) 570-1000
Fax: (617) 523-1231
www.goodwinprocter.com

Jefferies & Co
212 E 47th Street, Apartment 15F
New York, NY 10017-2124
Phone: (212) 284-2550

JPMorgan Chase
270 Park Avenue
New York, NY 10017
Phone: (212) 270-6000
Fax: (212) 270-1648
www.jpmorganchase.com

KeyBank
202 S Michigan Street
South Bend, IN 46601-2021
Phone: (574) 237-5200

Lehman Brothers
745 7th Avenue
New York, NY 10019
Phone: (212) 526-7000
Toll Free: (800) 666-2388
Fax: (212) 526-8766
www.lehman.com

Merrill Lynch
4 World Financial Center
250 Vesey Street
New York, NY 10080
Phone: (212) 449-1000
Toll Free: (800) 637-7455
Fax: (212) 449-9418
www.merrilllynch.com

National City
1900 E. 9th Street
Cleveland, OH 44114-3484
Phone: (216) 222-2000
Fax: (216) 222-9957
www.nationalcity.com

PNC
1 PNC Plaza, 249 5th Avenue
Pittsburgh, PA 15222-2707
Phone: (412) 762-2000
Toll Free: (888) 762-2265
Fax: (412) 762-7829
www.pnc.com

The Royal Bank of Scotland Group Leveraged Finance
36 St Andrew Square
Edinburgh, EH2 2YB
United Kingdom
Phone: +44-131-556-8555
Fax: +44-131-557-6140
www.rbs.com

SunTrust
303 Peachtree Street NE
Atlanta, GA 30308
Phone: (404) 588-7711
Toll Free: (800) 786-8787
Fax: (404) 332-3875
www.suntrust.com

UBS
101 Park Avenue
New York, NY 10178
www.ubs.com

Visit Vault at **www.vault.com** for insider company profiles, expert advice, career message boards, expert resume reviews, the Vault Job Board and more.

VAULT CAREER LIBRARY   **159**

Employer Directory, cont.

Wachovia

1 Wachovia Center

Charlotte, NC 28288-0013

Phone: (704) 374-6565

Toll Free: (800) 922-4684

Fax: (704) 374-3425

www.wachovia.com

Wells Fargo & Company

420 Montgomery Street

San Francisco, CA 94163

Phone: (866) 878-5865

Toll Free: (800) 869-3557

Fax: (626) 312-3015

www.wellsfargo.com

Managment Consulting

What is Consulting?

A giant industry, a moving target

Consulting, in the business context, means the giving of advice for pay. Consultants offer their advice and skill in solving problems, and are hired by companies who need the expertise and outside perspective that consultants possess. Some consulting firms specialize in giving advice on management and strategy, while others are known as technology specialists. Some concentrate on a specific industry area, like financial services or retail, and still others are more like gigantic one-stop shops with divisions that dispense advice on everything from top-level strategy to choosing training software, to saving money on paper clips.

But consulting firms have one thing in common: they run on the power of their people. The only product consulting firms ultimately have to offer is their ability to make problems go away. As a consultant, you are that problem-solver.

Not the kind of consulting we mean

As a standalone term, "consulting" lacks real meaning. In a sense, everyone's a consultant. Have you ever been asked by a friend, "Do I look good in orange?" Then you've been consulted about your color sense. There are thousands upon thousands of independent consultants who peddle their expertise and advice on everything from retrieving data from computers to cat astrology. There are also fashion consultants, image consultants and wedding consultants. For the purposes of this section, we are going to use the term "consulting" to refer specifically to management consulting.

Management consulting firms sell business advisory services to the leaders of corporations, governments, and nonprofit organizations. Typical concentrations in consulting include strategy, IT, HR, finance and operations. Types of problems in consulting include pricing, marketing, new product strategy, IT implementation or government policy. Finally, consulting firms sell services in virtually any industry, such as pharmaceuticals, consumer packaged goods or energy.

Firms can be organized or broken up according to topic, type of problem or industry. For example, a firm might focus on strategy problems only, but in virtually any industry. Bain & Company is an example of one such firm. Another firm might focus on a specific industry, but advise on nearly any type of issue. Oliver, Wyman and Company, which focuses on the financial services industry, is an example of this type of firm. Many of the larger firms have a "matrix" organization, with industry practice groups but also functional practice groups. And some firms are extremely specialized. For example, a firm might have only two employees, both focusing solely on competitive analysis in the telecommunications industry. All of these are examples of management consulting.

Caveats about consulting

All this might sound great, but before we go on, we should address some common misconceptions about consulting.

- **Implementation**—You might be thinking, "All consultants do is figure out problems at companies and explain them. Awesome. I'm going to be making great money for doing something really easy." Unfortunately, that's not true. Spotting a client's problems is a mere fraction of the battle. (Most people with a fair amount of common sense and an outsider's perspective can identify a client's problems. And in many cases, clients also understand where the problems lie.)

    The job of the consultant, therefore, isn't just about knowing what's wrong. It's about figuring out how to make it right. Even finding the solution isn't the end of the story. Consultants must make sure the solution isn't too expensive or impractical to implement. (Many consulting firms have what's called an 80 percent rule: it's better to put in place a solution

Visit Vault at **www.vault.com** for insider company profiles, expert advice, career message boards, expert resume reviews, the Vault Job Board and more.

VAULT CAREER LIBRARY   161

that takes care of 80 percent of the problem than to strive for a perfect solution that can't be put into place.) A corollary to this is the 80/20 rule: 80 percent of a problem can be solved in 20 percent of the time. Consultants must also get buy-in from the clients. Not only does bureaucracy often make implementation tough, but consultants must also convince individual client employees to help them make solutions work. It's tough to solve problems—and that's why clients hire consultants.

- **Glamour**—Consulting can indeed be exciting and high profile, but this is the exception, not the rule. Chances are, you won't be sitting across from the CEO at your next project kickoff, and you probably won't be staying in four-star hotels in the coolest cities in the world (though both are possible). Depending on the industry and location of your client's business, your environment might be a mid-range hotel in a small city, and you might be working with the senior vice president of one of the company's many business units.

- **Prestige**—Consulting is widely thought of as a prestigious career among business circles, particularly MBAs. But you should realize that in contrast to work in investment banking, your work in consulting will probably never get mentioned in *The Wall Street Journal*. Very few consulting firms are publicly recognized for the help they give.

As a result, few people outside of the industry really understand what consulting is. In fact, a running joke about consulting is that no one can explain it, no matter how hard or many times one tries. If you want a job you can explain to your grandmother, consulting isn't for you. Most "civilians" won't have heard of your firm—unless it has been involved in a scandal, that is.

- **Income**—The salary looks attractive on paper, but remember, it's not easy money. Divide your salary over the (large) number of hours, and the pay per hour isn't much better than other business careers.

So what does a consultant actually do, anyway?

Most "non-consultants" are mystified by the actual job and its day-to-day responsibilities. There are good reasons why this is so. While you're used to giving advice and solving problems, you may not understand how this translates into a career path. The problem is compounded because consultants tend to use a very distinctive vocabulary. You may not know what your skill set is, or how not to boil the ocean, or what the heck consultants mean when they talk about helicoptering. In addition, many consulting firms have their own specific philosophies and problem-attacking frameworks, which only raise the level of jargon.

The short answer is that you will be working on projects of varying lengths at varying sites for different clients. What you do will depend on your seniority, experience, phase of the project and your company. If you are a partner, you are selling work most of the time, whereas if you have a recent MBA degree, you are probably overseeing a couple of entry-level consultants doing research. For the most part, we'll describe the job that entry-level and midlevel (MBA or the equivalent) consultants do. Generally, projects follow the pitching/research/analysis/report writing cycle.

Depending where you are in the project lifecycle, here are some of the things you could be doing:

Pitching

- Helping to sell and market the firm (preparing documents and researching prospective clients in preparation for sales calls)
- Helping to write the proposal
- Presenting a sales pitch to a prospective client (usually with PowerPoint, Microsoft's presentation software)

Research

- Performing secondary research on the client and its industry using investment banking reports and other research sources (these include Bloomberg, OneSource, Hoover's Online, Yahoo! News and SEC filings)
- Interviewing the client's customers to gather viewpoints on the company
- Checking your firm's data banks for previous studies that it has done in the industry or with the client, and speaking to the project leads about their insights on the firm

- Facilitating a weekly client team discussion about the client company's business issues

Analysis

- Building Excel discounted cash flow (DCF) and/or other quantitative financial models
- Analyzing the gathered data and the model for insights
- Helping to generate recommendations

Reporting

- Preparing the final presentation (typically a "deck" of PowerPoint slides, though some firms write up longer reports in Microsoft Word format)
- Helping to present the findings and recommendations to the client

Implementation

- Acting as a project manager for the implementation of your strategy, if your firm is typically active during the implementation phase of a project
- Executing the coding, systems integration and testing of the recommended system, if you work for an IT consulting practice
- Documenting the team's work after the project is over

Administration

- Working on internal company research when your firm has no projects for you. (Being unstaffed is referred to as being "on the beach," a pleasant name for what is often a tedious time.)

- Filling out weekly time tracking and expense reports

Keep in mind that the analysis phase—usually the most interesting part—is probably the shortest part of any assignment. Consultants staffed on projects typically do a lot of research, financial analysis, Excel model building and presentation. You will attend lots of meetings in your quest to find the data, create the process and meet the people who will help you resolve the issues you've been hired to address. And, when you're not staffed, you will spend time "on the beach" doing research on prospective clients and helping with marketing efforts. (It's called "on the beach" because the time when you're not staffed on a paid engagement is usually less frenetic—though not always so!) Consulting firms spend a lot of time acquiring the work, and depending on how the firm is structured or how the economy is doing, you could spend significant amounts of time working on proposals. For you, this usually means lots of research, which is then elucidated on the omnipresent PowerPoint slides.

To some extent, though, the boundaries of the job are virtually limitless. Each project carries with it a new task, a new spreadsheet configuration, a new type of sales conference, or an entirely new way of thinking about business. To top it all off, you often must travel to your work assignment and work long hours in a pressurized environment. It's not easy.

Consulting Skill Sets

Consultants focus their energies in a wide variety of practice areas and industries. Their individual jobs, from a macro level, are as different as one could imagine. While a supply chain consultant advises a client about lead times in their production facility, another consultant is creating a training protocol for a new software package. What could be more different?

Despite the big picture differences, however, consultants' day-to-day skill sets are, by necessity, very similar. (Before we go any further: by skill set, we mean "your desirable attributes and skills that contribute value as a consultant." Skill set is a handy, abbreviated way to refer to same.)

Keep in mind that there is a big difference between the job now and the job six to eight years from now, if and when you are a partner. We are going to talk about whether you would like the job now, but you should think about whether this might be a good

Visit Vault at **www.vault.com** for insider company profiles, expert advice, career message boards, expert resume reviews, the Vault Job Board and more.

VAULT CAREER LIBRARY 163

long-term career for you. Is your goal to see it through to partner? If you would rather have an interesting job for six years, you just have to know you have the qualities to be a good consultant and manager. To be a partner, you have to be a persuasive salesperson. You will spend nearly 100 percent of your time selling expensive services to companies who don't think they need help. Your pay and job security will depend on your ability to make those sales.

Do you have the following characteristics in your skill set?

- **Do you work well in teams?** Consultants don't work alone. Not only do they frequently brainstorm with other consultants, but they also often work with employees at the client company, or even with consultants from other companies hired by the client. Consultants also frequently attend meetings and interview potential information sources. If you're the sort of person who prefers to work alone in quiet environments, you will not enjoy being a consultant.

- **Do you multitask well?** Not only can consulting assignments be frenetic, but consultants are often staffed on more than one assignment. Superior organizational skills and a good sense of prioritization are your friends. Would your friends describe you as a really busy person who's involved in a ton of activities, and still able to keep your personal life on track?

- **Speaking of friends, do you like talking to people?** Do you find yourself getting into interesting conversations over lunch and dinner? If you consider yourself a true introvert and find that speaking to people all day saps your energy, you will likely find consulting quite enervating. On the other hand, if you truly relish meetings, talking to experts, explaining your viewpoints, cajoling others to cooperate with you and making impromptu presentations, you've got some valuable talents in your consulting skill set.

- **Did you love school?** Did you really like going to class and doing your homework? There's a high correlation between academic curiosity and enjoyment of consulting.

- **Are you comfortable with math?** Consulting firms don't expect you to be a math professor, but you should be comfortable with figures, as well as commonly used programs like Excel, Access and PowerPoint. If you hate math, you will hate consulting. On a related note, you should also relish and be good at analysis and thinking creatively. Consultants have a term, now infiltrating popular culture, called "out of the box thinking." This means the ability to find solutions that are "outside of the box"—not constrained by commonly accepted facts.

- **Are you willing to work 70, even 80 hours a week?** Consultants must fulfill client expectations. If you must work 80 hours a week to meet client expectations, then that will be your fate. If you have commitments outside work, for example, you may find consulting hours difficult. Even if you have no major commitments outside work, understand what such a schedule means to you. Try working from 8 a.m. to 10 p.m. one day. Now imagine doing so five days a week for months on end.

- **Last, but certainly not least, are you willing to travel frequently?** Be truthful. If you can't answer most of these points with a resounding "yes," consulting is most likely not for you. The point is not just to get the job, but also to know what you're getting into—and to truly want to be a consultant.

The Traveling Salesman Problem

A lot of people go into the consulting field with the notion that travel is fun. "Traveling four days a week? No problem! My last vacation to Italy was a blast!" However, many soon find the traveling consultant's life to be a nightmare. Many consultants leave the field solely because of travel requirements.

Here's what we mean by consulting travel. Different consulting firms have different travel models, but there are two basic ones:

- A number of consulting firms (the larger ones) spend four days on the client site. This means traveling to the destination city Monday morning, spending three nights in a hotel near the client site, and flying home late Thursday night. (This will, of course, vary, depending on client preference and flight times.) The same firms often try to staff "regionally" to reduce flying time for consultants.

- The other popular travel model is to go to the client site "as needed." This generally means traveling at the beginning of the project for a few days, at the end of the project for the presentation, and a couple of times during the project. There is less regularity and predictability with this travel model, but there is also less overall time on the road.

Here are some variations of these travel modes that pop up frequently:

- International projects involve a longer-term stay on the client site. (Flying consultants to and from the home country every week can get expensive.) For example, the consultant might stay two or three weeks on or near the client site (the client might put you up in a corporate apartment instead of a hotel to save costs) and then go home for a week, repeating the process until the end of the project.

- Then, there is the "local" project that is really a long commute into a suburb, sometimes involving up to two hours in a car. Examples of this include consulting to Motorola (based in not-so-convenient Schaumburg, Ill.) while living in Chicago, or consulting to a Silicon Valley client while living in San Francisco. In these cases, you might opt to stay at a local hotel after working late, instead of taking the long drive home. This is not very different from nonlocal travel, and it can be more grueling, due to the car commute.

You need to ask yourself a number of questions to see if you are travel-phobic. For example, when you pack to go on vacation, do you stress about it? Do you always underpack or overpack? Do you hate flying? Do you hate to drive? Do you mind sleeping in hotel rooms for long periods of time? Are you comfortable with the idea of traveling to remote cities and staying there for three or four nights every week for 10 weeks? If you're married, do you mind being away from your spouse (and children if you have them) for up to three nights a week? Does your family mind? Will your spouse understand and not hold it against you if you have to cancel your anniversary dinner because the client wants you to stay a day later? If you and your spouse both travel for work, who will take care of the pets? Does the idea of managing your weekly finances and to-do lists from the road bother you?

If these questions make your stomach churn, look for consulting companies that promise a more stable work environment. For example, if you work in financial consulting and live in New York City, most of your clients may be local.   But because consulting firms don't always have the luxury of choosing their clients, they can't guarantee that you won't travel. Moreover, many large companies build their corporate campus where they can find cost-effective space, often in the suburbs or large corporate parks. (If you absolutely cannot travel, some of the largest consulting firms, such as Accenture, have certain business units that can guarantee a non-traveling schedule. Ask.)

Note that travel is common in the consulting field, but not all consultants travel. And not all clients expect you to be on site all the time. It absolutely depends on the firm's travel model, industry, your location, and most importantly, your project.

A Day in the Life: Associate Strategy Consultant

Greg Schneider is an associate at the Boston office of a top strategy consulting firm office. He kindly agreed to share a "typical" workday with Vault, noting that no day at any consulting firm can be called typical.

6:15 a.m.: Alarm goes off. I wake up asking myself why I put "run three times per week" into the team charter. I meet another member of the team, and we hobble out for a jog. At least it's warm out—another advantage of having a project in Miami.

7:15 a.m.: Check voicemail. Someone in London wants a copy of my knowledge building document on managing hypergrowth. A co-worker is looking for information about what the partner from my last team is like to work with.

Visit Vault at **www.vault.com** for insider company profiles, expert advice, career message boards, expert resume reviews, the Vault Job Board and more.

VAULT CAREER LIBRARY   **165**

7:30 a.m.: Breakfast with the team. We discuss sports, Letterman and a morning meeting we have with the client team (not necessarily in that order). We then head out to the client.

9:00 a.m.: Meet with the client team. We've got an important progress review with the CEO next week, so there's a lot going on. We're helping the client to assess the market potential of an emerging technology. Today's meeting concerns what kind of presentation would be most effective, although we have trouble staying off tangents about the various analyses that we've all been working on. The discussion is complicated by the fact that some key data is not yet available. We elect to go with a computer-based slide show and begin the debate on the content.

10:53 a.m.: Check voicemail. The office is looking for an interviewer for the Harvard Business School hell weekend. The partner will be arriving in time for dinner and wants to meet to discuss the progress review. A headhunter looking for a divisional VP. My wife reminding me to mail off the insurance forms.

11:00 a.m.: I depart with my teammate for an interview. We meet with an industry expert (a professor from a local university) to discuss industry trends and in particular what the prospects are for the type of technology we're looking at. As this is the last interview we plan to do, we are able to check many of our hypotheses. The woman is amazing—we luck out and get some data we need. The bad news is, now we have to figure out what it means.

12:28 p.m.: As I walk back in to the client, a division head I've been working with grabs me and we head to lunch. He wanted to discuss an analysis he'd given me some information for, and in the process I get some interesting perspectives about the difficulties in moving the technology into full production and how much it could cost.

1:30 p.m.: I jump on a quick conference call about an internal knowledge building project I'm working on for the marketing practice. I successfully avoid taking on any additional responsibility.

2:04 p.m.: Begin to work through new data. After discussing the plan of attack with the engagement manager, I dive in. It's a very busy afternoon, but the data is great. I get a couple "a-ha"s—always a good feeling.

3:00 p.m.: Short call with someone from legal to get an update on the patent search.

6:00 p.m.: Team meeting. The engagement manager pulls the team together to check progress on various fronts and debate some issues prior to heading to dinner with the partner. A quick poll determines that Italian food wins—we leave a voicemail with the details.

6:35 p.m.: Call home and check in with the family. Confirm plans for weekend trip to Vermont. Apologize for forgetting to mail the insurance forms.

7:15 p.m.: The team packs up and heads out to dinner. We meet the partner at the restaurant and have a productive (and calorific) meal working through our plans for the progress review, the new data, what's going on with the client team, and other areas of interest. She suggests some additional uses for the new data, adds her take on our debates and agrees to raise a couple issues with the CFO, whom she's known for years. She takes a copy of our draft presentation to read after dinner.

9:15 p.m.: Return to hotel. Plug in computer and check e-mail, since I hadn't had a chance all day. While I'm logged in, I download two documents I need from the company database, check the Red Sox score, and see how the client's stock did.

10:10 p.m.: Presleep voicemail check. A client from a previous study is looking for one of the appendices, since he lost his copy. The server will be down for an hour tomorrow night.

10:30 p.m.: Watch *SportsCenter* instead of going right to sleep, as I know I probably should.

Note: Had this been an in-town study, the following things would have been different: I wouldn't have run with another member of my team, and we'd have substituted a conference call for the dinner meeting, so we could go home instead. Also, I probably wouldn't have watched *SportsCenter*.

Q&A: Heather Eberle, Deutsche Post World Net Inhouse Consulting

Before attending Thunderbird, the Garvin School of International Management, Heather Eberle worked as an external consultant. Once at business school, she focused her job search on lesser known internal consulting opportunities. After graduating in February 2006, she joined the in-house consulting division of international shipping giant Deutsche Post World Net (DPWN). She spoke with Vault about her experience with internal consulting at DPWN, especially in light of her previous experience as an external consultant.

Vault: Tell me about your background prior to getting your MBA.

Eberle: I was in consulting for five years at a smaller HRIS/strategy implementation firm.

Vault: So when you went to get your MBA, were you specifically looking for internal consulting positions?

Eberle: Yes, consulting or operations. Internal consulting had always appealed to me because it seemed like the work/life balance was better than the external consulting opportunities.

With external consulting, the travel is difficult. Maybe you are home on a Thursday night, but then leave Sunday night—every week. You are lucky if you get 48 hours at your house every week.

Vault: How did you find the position at DPWN?

Eberle: Alumni recruiting at school. We also had alumni postings for other in-house consulting positions, which opened my eyes to the size and scope of this job market. In my experience, these in-house jobs were often referred to as "in-house consulting" or "strategic projects group" along with some other key phrases. PMOs—project management organizations—which plan and manage projects are also an option and can be similar to consulting organizations.

Vault: How large is the DPWN InHouse Consulting group?

Eberle: In total around 150 people with about 20 each in our Fort Lauderdale and Singapore offices and the remainder in Bonn, Germany.

There is quite a bit of movement between offices as projects change. The organization is large enough to accommodate those who choose not to travel, but offers the opportunity for those who would like to work in another office. In addition, because of the group's worldwide footprint, there are project opportunities in many different countries and regions.

The consulting practice started in 1999 in Germany and the U.S. group was incorporated a year ago. We just returned from the annual InHouse Consulting conference in Germany where one of the main goals was to build up the ties between the groups and networking.

Vault: Is it mostly MBAs or also undergrad analysts?

Eberle: Mostly MBAs.

Vault: How does the work at DPWN compare to your previous experience in consulting?

Eberle: I would say that it is pretty similar to what you would expect with respect to the typical consulting engagement—all projects differ based on client needs.

Within DPWN there are organizational strategy projects that last six to nine months, operations projects that last three months and incremental improvement projects that last a month or two such as sales force optimization. It all depends on the scope of the project.

Visit Vault at **www.vault.com** for insider company profiles, expert advice, career message boards, expert resume reviews, the Vault Job Board and more.

VAULT CAREER LIBRARY 167

Vault: How is staffing done?

Eberle: Staffing is based on availability and skill set. DPWN probably does a better job than some eternal consultancies, which have a tendency to move consultants around frequently. At DPWN you would not be pulled off your project and moved to a new project unless you have some very specific expertise that is needed and unavailable elsewhere within the group.

Vault: So who are your "clients" when you're working on an engagement?

Eberle: We only accept projects that are sponsored by a member of the management board. However, the client may be a director, SVP or EVP with P&L ownership. In these cases we add them into the discussion regarding the consulting approach in-house consulting will employ. If there is no agreement, we decline to take the project.

Vault: And how are the projects requested? Or is it that they're not requested but that the CEO or some other high-level manager wants your group to go in and work with a group?

Eberle: In many cases, the business is requesting assistance either because they lack the project expertise or need someone from outside their department who is better able to identify key issues or manage pressure from disparate stakeholders.

In other cases, we identify a business issue that appears to be similar to another project we have worked on. If we felt that the methodology and expertise of InHouse Consulting could help the business, we would prepare a proposal—however, this is less common.

Vault: And so it's not often that it's because of poor performance that you're there and they don't actually want you to be there?

Eberle: I think that it is less the case that the business does not want us to be there for two reasons. One, InHouse Consulting does not engage in projects that are unlikely to secure buy-in and therefore success. Two, as DPWN employees our goal is to increase the success of the group—not get paid a fat bonus for a solution that won't work, and I think others in the business recognize this.

This is reflected in the amount of information you can get regarding the problem and solutions. I have found that it is really fun to get into the nitty-gritty because it is much more challenging to say here's 10 general best-practice recommendations versus here's 10 extremely detailed recommendations you can begin implementing tomorrow.

Vault: Why are you able to get into more detail?

Eberle: Because we are part of the company, there is zero likelihood we, as a consulting group, would data mine information from one project and use it for a competitor's project. For example, the five-year strategic operations roadmap for a business is not going to be shared with other consulting groups due to security concerns. By having access to the roadmap we may find out about an acquisition target that would change our recommendations.

The other great thing about InHouse Consulting is all the specialized knowledge we have within the group. It is enormously helpful to have a network to rely on if you have a question about anything logistics related. If you worked at an outside consulting firm unless you had a large logistics practice, it could take you days to come up with answers to some of the specialized logistics questions.

At InHouse Consulting everyone is extremely supportive and friendly. The best part is that we all work together, working towards the same goal of increasing the organizational effectiveness of DPWN. I didn't always get that feeling as an external consultant.

Vault: What sort of projects have you worked on?

Eberle: I worked on a project investigating market opportunities, which was great fun. I have worked on project working on sales force optimization and I am currently on a project looking at finance and accounting. The projects are quite different but each has been very interesting.

Visit Vault at **www.vault.com** for insider company profiles, expert advice, career message boards, expert resume reviews, the Vault Job Board and more.

VAULT CAREER LIBRARY   **169**

Vault: Were all these projects in Florida?

Eberle: They were all based in Fort Lauderdale but have included components from all regions of the world. The great thing about DPWN is that every project has a high degree of internationalization to it.

Vault: What are your hours like?

Eberle: Usually, 9 to 7. The group generally does not work weekends, which has been nice. There may be some travel, but it is not the weekly grind and usually you get to come home to sleep in your own bed—which means you are pretty much guaranteed to get a good night's sleep.

Vault: What are some other advantages of in-house consulting versus external consulting?

Eberle: One of the key advantages is that many in-house consulting groups have strong ties within the management level of the organization, which often allows for movement directly from the consulting group into the management track.

In this respect in-house consulting is similar to project based management development programs, but in-house consulting groups typically have a higher degree of project diversity. Because you have worked on projects for a variety of functions within the organization, you can often follow an accelerated career path.

In-house consulting also allows you to build a really strong network due to the number of clients you work with. With external consulting, while there are opportunities to join the companies you're consulting with, you probably don't have experience working with a number of functions within the client organization.

Employer Directory

Deutsche Post World Net Inhouse Consulting

1200 S Pine Island Road
Suite 210
Plantation, FL 33324
Recruiting Contact Phone: (954) 888-7000
E-mail: www.ic.recruiting@dhl.com (Preferred)
www.ic.dpwn.com
www.dhl.com
www.dpwn.com

Inhouse Consulting is the internal top management consultancy of Deutsche Post World Net.

With a dynamic team of over 120 consultants and growing, we work at the heart of Deutsche Post World Net - globally: in international teams in projects worldwide. We develop high-impact strategies for the important business challenges of today and tomorrow, working for top executives of all business divisions. Inhouse Consulting is key in enhancing the value of Deutsche Post World Net and DHL.

We offer exceptional training and development as well as an MBA reimbursement program.

We thrive on global challenges, speed and change. We welcome you to join us.

DPWN Inhouse Consulting welcomes all qualified applicants to apply. Short list of current schools include but are not limited to: CHI- GSB; Duke; Emory (Goizuetta); Georgetown; HEC; McGill; IU (Kelley); Thunderbird; U Toronto (Rotman); York U (Schulich); ITESM (Tec de Monterrey)

Mitchell Madison Group

17 State Street, 22nd Fl
New York, NY 10004
Recruiting Contact: (646) 873-4100
www.mitchellmadison.com/careers.html
Email: MMGRecruiting@mitchellmadison.com

MITCHELL MADISON GROUP
Global Management Consultants

Mitchell Madison Group is a global management consulting firm that combines broad strategic capabilities, strong functional skills, economic insight and wide experience to serve our clients. We are highly diverse, both by way of background and in the breadth and depth of academic disciplines and career experience that we embrace.

Our on-campus hiring targets MBA candidates for associate positions. Associates work with managers and MMG's partners on engagements with new and continuing clients. We seek candidates in all disciplines who have the intellectual resources, relevant skills, and emotional maturity necessary to thrive in this particularly strenuous profession.

Business schools Mitchell Madison Group recruits from: Harvard Business School, Stanford Graduate School of Business, Columbia Business School, The Wharton School, Yale School of Management, INSEAD

Visit Vault at **www.vault.com** for insider company profiles, expert advice, career message boards, expert resume reviews, the Vault Job Board and more.

VAULT CAREER LIBRARY   171

Employer Directory, cont.

A.T. Kearney
222 West Adams Street
Chicago, IL 60606
Phone: (312) 648-0111
www.atkearney.com

Accenture
1345 Avenue of the Americas
New York, NY 10105
Phone: (917) 452-4400
Fax: (917) 527-5387
www.accenture.com

The Advisory Board Company
2445 M Street, NW
Washington, DC 20037
Phone: (202) 266-5600
Fax: (202) 266-5700
www.advisoryboardcompany.com

AlixPartners
2000 Town Center
Suite 2400
Southfield, MI 48075
Phone: (248) 358-4420
Fax: (248) 358-1969
www.alixpartners.com

Alvarez & Marsal
600 Lexington Avenue, 6th Floor
New York, NY 10022
Phone: (212) 759-4433
Fax: (212) 759-5532
www.alvarezandmarsal.com

Analysis Group, Inc.
111 Huntington Avenue, 10th Floor
Boston, MA 02199
Phone: (617) 425-8000
Fax: (617) 425-8001
www.analysisgroup.com

Aon Consulting Worldwide
Aon Center
200 East Randolph Street
Chicago, IL 60601
Phone: (312) 381-4844
Fax: (312) 381-0240
www.aon.com/hcc

Arthur D. Little
125 High Street
High Street Tower, 28th Floor
Boston, MA 02110
Phone: (617) 532-9550
Fax: (617) 261-6630
www.adlittle-us.com

Bain & Company
131 Dartmouth Street
Boston, MA 02116
Phone: (617) 572-2000
Fax: (617) 572-2427
www.bain.com

**BearingPoint Inc.
Management & Technology
Consultants**
1676 International Drive
McLean, VA 22102
Phone: (703) 747-3000
Fax: (703) 747-8500
www.bearingpoint.com

Booz Allen Hamilton
8283 Greensboro Drive
McLean, VA 22102
Phone: (703) 902-5000
Fax: (703) 902-3333
www.boozallen.com

The Boston Consulting Group
Exchange Place, 31st Floor
Boston, MA 02109
Phone: (617) 973-1200
Fax: (617) 973-1339
www.bcg.com

Cambridge Associates LLC
100 Summer Street
Boston, MA 02110
Phone: (617) 457-7500
Fax: (617) 457-7501
www.cambridgeassociates.com

Capgemini
750 Seventh Avenue
Suite 1800
New York, NY 10019
Phone: (212) 314-8000
Fax: (212) 314-8001
www.us.capgemini.com

CRA International, Inc.
John Hancock Tower
200 Clarendon Street, T-33
Boston, MA 02116
Phone: (617) 425-3000
Fax: (617) 425-3132
www.crai.com

Cornerstone Research
1000 El Camino Real
Suite 250
Menlo Park, CA 94025
Phone: (650) 853-1660
Fax: (650) 324-9204
www.cornerstone.com

Corporate Executive Board
2000 Pennsylvania Avenue NW
Suite 6000
Washington, DC 20006
Phone: (202) 777-5000
Fax: (202) 777-5100
www.executiveboard.com

Deloitte Consulting LLP
1633 Broadway, 35th Floor
New York, NY 10019
Phone: (212) 492-4500
Fax: (212) 492-4743
www.deloitte.com

Employer Directory, cont.

**Diamond Management &
Technology Consultants, Inc.**
John Hancock Center
875 North Michigan Avenue
Suite 3000
Chicago, IL 60611
Phone: (312) 255-5000
Fax: (312) 255-6000
www.diamondconsultants.com

**First Manhattan Consulting
Group**
90 Park Avenue
New York, NY 10016
Phone: (212) 557-0500
www.fmcg.com

FTI Consulting, Inc.
500 East Pratt Street
Suite 1400
Baltimore, MD 21202
Phone: (410) 951-4800
Fax: (410) 224-8378
www.fticonsulting.com

Gallup Consulting
The Gallup Building
901 F Street NW
Wasington, DC 20004
Phone: (202) 715-3030
Fax: (202) 715-3041
www.gallupconsulting.com

Gartner, Inc.
56 Top Gallant Road
Stamford, CT 06902
Phone: (203) 964-0096
www.gartner.com

Giuliani Partners LLC
5 Times Square
New York, NY 10036
Phone: (212) 931-7300
Fax: (212) 931-7310
www.giulianipartners.com

Hay Group
The Wanamaker Building
100 Penn Square East
Philadelphia, PA 19107
Phone: (215) 861-2000
Fax: (215) 861-2111
www.haygroup.com

Hewitt Associates
100 Half Day Road
Lincolnshire, IL 60069
Phone: (847) 295-5000
Fax: (847) 295-7634
www.hewitt.com

Huron Consulting Group
550 West Van Buren
Chicago, IL 60607
Phone: (312) 583-8700
Toll Free: (866) 229-8700
Fax: (312) 583-8701
www.huronconsultinggroup.com

IBM Global Services
New Orchard Road
Armonk, NY 10504
Phone: (914) 499-1900
Fax: (914) 765-7382
www.ibm.com/consulting/careers

Katzenbach Partners LLC
381 Park Avenue South
New York, NY 10016
Phone: (212) 213-5505
Fax: (212) 213-5024
www.katzenbach.com

Kurt Salmon Associates
1355 Peachtree Street NE
Suite 900
Atlanta, GA 30309
Phone: (404) 892-0321
Fax: (404) 898-9590
www.kurtsalmon.com

L.E.K. Consulting
28 State Street, 16th Floor
Boston, MA 02109
Phone: (617) 951-9500
Fax: (617) 951-9392
www.lek.com

LECG
2000 Powell Street
Suite 600
Emeryville, CA 94608
Phone: (510) 985-6700
www.lecg.com

Lippincott
499 Park Avenue
New York, NY 10022
Phone: (212) 521-0000
Fax: (212) 308-8952
www.lippincott.com

Mars & Co
124 Mason Street
Greenwich, CT 06830
Phone: (203) 629-9292
Fax: (203) 629-9432
www.marsandco.com

Marakon Associates
245 Park Avenue, 44th Floor
New York, NY 10167
Phone: (212) 377-5000
Fax: (212) 377-6000
www.marakon.com

McKinsey & Company
55 East 52nd Street
New York, NY 10022
Phone: (212) 446-7000
Fax: (212) 446-8575
www.mckinsey.com

**Mercer Delta Organizational
Consulting**
1166 Avenue of the Americas
New York, NY 10036
Phone: (212) 345-8000
www.oliverwyman.com

Visit Vault at **www.vault.com** for insider company profiles, expert advice,
career message boards, expert resume reviews, the Vault Job Board and more.

VAULT CAREER LIBRARY 173

Employer Directory, cont.

Mercer Human Resource Consulting
1166 Avenue of the Americas
New York, NY 10036
Phone: (212) 345-7000
Fax: (212) 345-7414
www.mercerhr.com

Mercer Management Consulting
1166 Avenue of the Americas
New York, NY 10036
Phone: (212) 345-8000
www.oliverwyman.com

Monitor Group
Two Canal Park
Cambridge, MA 02141
Phone: (617) 252-2000
Fax: (617) 252-2100
www.monitor.com

Navigant Consulting, Inc.
615 North Wabash Avenue
Chicago, IL 60611
Phone: (312) 573-5600
Fax: (312) 573-5678
www.navigantconsulting.com

NERA Economic Consulting
50 Main Street, 14th Floor
White Plains, NY 10606
Phone: (914) 448-4000
Fax: (914) 448-4040
www.nera.com

The Parthenon Group
200 State Street, 14th Floor
Boston, MA 02109
Phone: (617) 478-2550
Fax: (617) 478-2555
www.parthenon.com

PRTM
444 Castro Street
Suite 600
Mountain View, CA 94041
Phone: (650) 967-2900
Fax: (650) 967-6367
www.prtm.com

Putnam Associates
25 Burlington Mall Road
Burlington, MA 01803
Phone: (781) 273-5480
Fax: (781) 273-5484
www.putassoc.com

Putnam Associates
25 Burlington Mall Road
Burlington, MA 01803
Phone: (781) 273-5480
Fax: (781) 273-5484
www.putassoc.com

Roland Berger Strategy Consultants
230 Park Avenue
Suite 112
New York, NY 10022
Phone: (212) 651-9660
Fax: (212) 756-8750
www.rolandberger.com

Towers Perrin
One Stamford Plaza
263 Tresser Boulevard
Stamford, CT 06901
Phone: (203) 326-5400
www.towersperrin.com

Watson Wyatt Worldwide
901 North Glebe Road
Arlington, VA 22203
Phone: (703) 258-8000
Fax: (703) 258-8585
www.watsonwyatt.com

ZS Associates
1800 Sherman Avenue, 7th Floor
Evanston, IL 60201
Phone: (888) 972-4173
Fax: (888) 972-7329
www.zsassociates.com

Manufacturing

Industry Overview

Got the motor running ...

America's manufacturing industry is a powerful engine that drives the nation's economy, making up 11 percent of employment and 12 percent of the U.S. gross domestic product (GDP) in 2006. In the past decade, the industry contributed 22 percent of the country's economic growth, or 28 percent with the addition of software production. Through a phenomenon known as the multiplier effect, manufacturing actually creates economic output in other industries by using intermediate goods and services in its production process—so that, according to the National Association of Manufacturers (NAM), every $1 of a manufacturing product sold to a final user has created an additional $1.37 in intermediate economic output, more than from any other economic group. The U.S. continues to lead the world in many manufacturing areas, including automobiles, aerospace, steel, telecommunications and consumer goods. In addition, it's the No. 2 country in terms of exports of manufactured products, and its total manufacturing output in dollars (close to $1.5 trillion in 2006) surpasses the GDP of all but eight of the world's countries. The manufacturing and exporting of goods is critical to maintaining a strong currency and economy, so it's no wonder economists pay close attention to manufacturing stats and figures.

The manufacturing process is a part of a wide array of businesses, from mineral products, metals, chemicals, plastics, machinery, computers and electronics to motor vehicles, furniture, paper, textiles and clothing. Several of the more important sectors are discussed in the paragraphs below; the Vault profile of the consumer products industry contains information about the manufacturing and marketing of food.

Greener pastures

The current media focus on global warming and greenhouse gases has begun to trickle down to manufacturers' corporate officers, who (in some cases) look forward to devising environmentally-friendly policies and products. DuPont chief Chad Holliday has made no secret of his decade-long involvement with eco-positive projects, and estimates that $5 billion of DuPont's annual $29 billion revenue comes from items that either energy-efficient or non-harmful to the planet. His company's pet projects include biofuels and a miracle fiber called bio-PDO (made from genetically-adjusted corn sugar). DuPont, Alcoa, Caterpillar and other firms are part of the U.S. Climate Action Partnership (USCAP), which proposes a market system that would lower the cost of cutting greenhouse-gas emissions, giving companies an incentive to do so. And in April 2007, Ford CEO Alan Mullaly said that he clearly believed in the reality of global warming, and created an executive slot devoted to environmentally-friendly strategies, the first such staff position for an automaker.

Auto manufacturing for the people

Manufacturing has long been closely tied to automobile production, and big-ticket purchases like cars are closely tied to consumer confidence. Indeed, a Michigan assembly line may be what many people think of when they hear the word "manufacturing." The U.S. has been able to weather the competition from Japanese companies, but just barely. General Motors remains the world's largest auto manufacturer, but its share of the U.S. market hit an 80-year low (24.6 percent) in 2006. It also faces a big threat in Toyota, which overtook Ford Motors as the No. 2 manufacturer and seller for several months in 2007 by continuously, and thoughtfully, improving product quality. (Toyota is expected to maintain that ranking in the year-end tabulations.) The so-called "Big Three" automakers—General Motors, DaimlerChrysler and Ford—claim about 55 percent of the U.S. passenger car market, though American-made staples like the Ford Excursion and Chevy Tahoe have witnessed an ongoing decline in sales. The main culprits in the auto industry slump include the hike in gas prices to record-high levels per gallon and the rapidly increasing price of steel per ton, which more than doubled from $260 in midyear 2003

Visit Vault at **www.vault.com** for insider company profiles, expert advice, career message boards, expert resume reviews, the Vault Job Board and more.

V∧ULT CAREER LIBRARY 175

to $580 in 2006 (according to purchasingdata.com). In turn, the steel industry and other automotive-related sectors experience a negative ripple effect from manufacturing slowdowns.

As the auto industry has attempted to rebound in the face of crashing demand for trucks and sport utility vehicles—sales of Ford's F-series pickup trucks, reportedly the company's most important product, were down by more than 45 percent in June 2006 from the previous year—analysts warned that U.S. companies need to look to the east as Asian markets improve and manufacturers like Toyota and Honda pick up the pace. To pique public interest, automotive companies are increasingly combining with major electronics manufacturers to provide a variety of in-vehicle add-ons like satellite radio, crash avoidance systems and iPods; the percentage of electronic content in automobiles is expected to increase to 40 percent by 2010. At the same time, though, such developments also increase automotive warranty costs and the possibility of vehicle recalls. Furthermore, expected changes in regulation of emissions and fuel efficiency (and consumer leanings away from gas-guzzlers in these times of lofty gasoline prices) are forcing the larger U.S. automakers to more seriously consider their contributions to the global warming problem. GM is toying with a battery-powered car (the Chevrolet Volt) and Ford has created an executive position devoted to environmentally-friendly strategies.

Vehicle manufacturing is also coming from a new source: auto makers such as BMW, Honda, Hyundai and Toyota have moved manufacturing plants to the Southeast U.S. In the past 20 years, these companies have quietly cut down on imports and increased domestic production by seven times—in fact, 2005 was the first year that Japanese car makers made more cars in the U.S. than in Japan. The Association of International Automobile Manufacturers estimates that by 2009 these foreign auto makers will have invested $3.3 billion and have hired 10,000 additional workers.

Steely resolve

Steel, demand for which has been bolstered by the developing economies of India and China (which was responsible for 30 percent of the world's demand in 2005), is another U.S. manufacturing mainstay. In addition, the destruction caused by hurricanes Katrina and Rita destroyed many steel structures in the Southeast, such as bridges, barges and oil rigs, which needed to be replaced or extensively repaired. The steel market hasn't always been so strong, however. Prices in 2002 were low, with seven companies controlling nearly half of American steel production. Along with rising prices and increased efficiency, a spate of acquisitions revived the industry; in 2006 alone, 241 buyouts or mergers were announced, to the tune of $82.3 billion (with another 129 agreements signed in the first half of 2007) and the Standard and Poor's Supercomposite Steel Index soared 63 percent. The largest domestic manufacturer, U.S. Steel, purchased Lone Star Technologies for $2.1 billion in early 2007 to command the top spot as producer of pipes for gas and oil interests, and intrigued speculators by talking with Germany's ThyssenKrupp (the world's 10th-largest steel concern according to the International Iron and Steel Institute) in June 2007.

Chemically altered

Besides representing the largest single slice—4 percent—of the manufacturing pie, chemical production is perhaps the most important segment of the industry, since it produces the solvents, dyes and other compounds used in all manner of other manufacturing industries: automobile production, paper processing, pharmaceuticals, electronics and agricultural. (Over 55 percent of all manufacturers say that their production is significantly, directly dependent on chemicals.) In addition, it makes soaps, bleaches and cleaners purchased by consumers for use at home. The hurricanes of 2004 and 2005 in the Southeastern U.S. hurt this segment by destroying a number of factories. Also, high oil prices drove up the cost of many petrochemical-derived products, and rising prices for natural gas, used as part of many manufacturing processes, have added costs as well. This has resulted in decreased revenues along with an increased drive toward mergers and acquisitions—like the June 2006 BASF purchase of the Engelhard Corp., a maker of pigments and chemical catalysts, for $5 billion. Analysts see specialty chemicals such as these as perhaps the best avenue for growth; manufacturers can keep a competitive edge by producing agents used for highly specific purposes.

Despite estimates of higher production, the BLS expects employment within the chemical manufacturing segment of the manufacturing industry to decline by 14 percent by 2014, due to increased efficiency, production outsourcing and more stringent regulation, among other factors. Three sectors—basic chemicals, other chemical products and synthetics—are projected to be the hardest hit, losing a total of 80,000 workers.

All roads lead to tech

Electronics manufacturing covers companies engaged in manufacturing power distribution equipment, communications devices, semiconductors, industrial electronics and household appliances, among other things. Above all, the sector plays a vital role in a number of other industries, including telecommunications, medical and automotive. Electronics demand is thus inextricably tied to the rise and fall of dependent industries. Innovative new consumer products and advancing digital technology have opened up new markets and avenues of revenue. Despite this, the BLS expects that employment in this sector will decrease by 7 percent through 2014 due to increased efficiency and jobs being moved overseas.

Cruising the skies

Aerospace is another sector that contributes significantly to U.S. manufacturing. In the commercial sphere, airplane manufacturing is dominated by Boeing and European rival Airbus. These companies and others, like Lockheed Martin, Northrop Grumman and Raytheon, are also involved in the production of military aircraft, missiles and space equipment. The commercial airline sector saw a severe downturn following September 11, but the past several years have seen a rebound. During 2005 and 2006, aerospace sales, orders, exports and employment all increased significantly, across all sectors of the industry, according to the Aerospace Industries Association (AIA). The civil aircraft segment, with a 21 percent sales boom, was particularly robust. Total sales in 2006 of $184 billion represented an increase of 8 percent over the previous year, and the AIA's predictions for 2007 remain on the positive side, with another 6 percent surge.

Production grab-bag

Other manufacturing sectors include textiles, apparel, forestry products (furniture and paper), rubber and minerals; together these hold claim to roughly 22 percent of all U.S. manufacturing output. Here again, employment figures have plummeted in recent years due to a convergence of unfavorable economic conditions and changes in demand due to the new "paperless" business environment as well as manufacturing techniques for furniture and cabinetry that use less wood. For a while, the industry expected solid profits due to the increasing demand for lumber driven by a rise in housing and construction activity in the hurricane-damaged Southeast. But the good news didn't last long. A severe depression in the housing market settled in, demand for lumber declined, and predictions for new home construction in 2007 came in at a nine-year low.

Work hard for the money

Though the industry as a whole enjoys higher wages than private industry as a whole (by nearly 25 percent), its component sectors vary wildly. Nonsupervisory workers at apparel manufacturers have average weekly earnings considerably lower ($351) than the average for all manufacturing ($659)—and worse, the textile sector projects a loss of 46 percent of its staff due to imports and technological advancements in the coming years. Steel workers and manufacturers of autos and aerospace products have the highest salaries in the group.

Nonetheless, the industry finds a great deal of pricing pressure in the mid-2000s. The price of natural gas, used in many processes, has jumped, and a combination of higher costs (corporate taxes, insurance and legal costs, pollution abatement fees and employee benefit programs) has put the U.S. at a significant disadvantage. In a report, the NAM and AMR Research calculate that these "add 31.7 percent to the cost of doing business in the United States compared to our nine (-largest) trading

Visit Vault at www.vault.com for insider company profiles, expert advice, career message boards, expert resume reviews, the Vault Job Board and more.

VAULT CAREER LIBRARY 177

competitors." And as the proportion of goods exported has risen, passing these costs along to the consumer has become extremely difficult. These facts point to possible escalating encroachment on the manufacturing industry by foreign firms.

A shifting outlook

Following a boom that spanned most of the 20th century, manufacturing employment declined sharply during the 2001-2003 economic downturn. Despite the economy's general resurgence from 2003 to 2006, industry employment has, according to the Bureau of Labor Statistics (BLS), only begun to level off. A number of circumstances led to the slump, including increased oil and energy prices. And like many industries, manufacturing has seen a steady push toward technologies that promise greater efficiency and productivity while reducing the need for manpower. It's likely that many of the factory jobs lost since the beginning of the century will never return, signaling a fundamental shift in the industry as a whole. The BLS predicts total manufacturing employment will decrease by 0.6 percent through 2014. Statistics from the Labor Department released in June 2007 showed a decline in manufacturing jobs for the eleventh straight month, placing employment at just above 14 million—the lowest total since the 1950s. As of midyear 2007, the auto sector accounted for about one million jobs, according to seasonally-adjusted data from the BLS. However, this represents 80,000 less than at the prior year's midpoint, the latest evidence of years of major job cuts.

Despite the forecasts of general decline, however, the job market is remarkably vibrant. According to a 2005 survey done by Deloitte with NAM, 90 percent of employers in the industry reported a demand for skilled workers, and 65 percent needed scientists and engineers. In another finding from the same report, about 83 percent of manufacturers thought that shortages were affecting their service to customers.

On the other hand, those statistics are just where some insiders see an upcoming crisis. At a 2005 trade show, NAM President John Engler said, "The emerging problem in manufacturing is not a shortage of jobs, but rather a shortage of qualified applicants." Companies and trade groups are developing initiatives (manufacturing certification programs, school and community career information sessions) to address the gap before the problem becomes critical.

What is the Supply Chain?

Suppliers and vendors

A simple definition of supply chain is the network of vendors that provides materials for a company's products, but in reality, the supply chain is more complicated. There is a stream of flows from supplier to supplier until a product reaches an end user. For example, oil is rigged from the ground, sent to a refinery, plastic is made, an injection molding shop buys plastic pellets, makes plastics components, ships the components to a customer, the customer assembles the plastic parts into their machine, and then sells the machine to their customer. The farther away from the customer, the farther "upstream" a supplier is considered to be.

The network of vendors in a supply chain often includes tiered suppliers (meaning a company does not receive materials directly from the supplier, but is involved in getting materials or parts from an upstream supplier to a downstream supplier). The more complex a product, the more significant the upstream supplier's roles are. From a supply chain manager's perspective, his suppliers are primarily responsible for managing their own supply chain but he should have some involvement.

Oftentimes, a manufacturing facility acts as a supplier to a downstream manufacturing facility. For example, a company could have their manufacturing plant in the U.S. and their assembly plant in Mexico. The U.S. plant would be considered an internal supplier, since it's part of the same company. The transportation of materials throughout the supply chain is often called logistics. This includes air, land and sea shipping as well as customs processing to allow materials to cross borders. The supply chain does not end until the product reaches the consumer. For this reason, distribution centers, distributors and wholesalers are all part of the supply chain. It is not rare for a supply chain to involve a dozen parties.

The relationship between a supplier and a manufacturing company is not as simple as a supply chain manager ordering parts and the supplier shipping them. There are continuous flows between the supplier and the customer. The Supply Chain Flow Process (on the following page) shows these flows in chronological order from top to bottom. (Note that this figure is for an already established supplier and material.) In the case of a new supplier, a supplier audit (a verification that a supplier has the potential to meet the manufacturer's needs) should be conducted first to determine if the supplier is appropriate for the work.

In the case of new material, the customer must first supply the anticipated number of units required, along with all of the drawings and specifications, to the supplier to get a quotation of unit price and lead time. After the quotes are received and a supplier is chosen, a purchase order should be done for the setup costs and samples. Setup costs can be a few hundred to hundreds of thousands of dollars (mostly tooling costs). A supply chain manager should always present the setup costs along with the piece price quote when working with engineers (so manufacturing methods are not specified solely on unit cost). For example, making a simple part by thermoforming would cost about $50 each, whereas making it by injection molding would cost $5 each. However, injection molding requires a $10,000 mold. If you only need 20 pieces annually, you are better off using thermoforming.

Depending on whether prototypes or the component have already been made or not, the samples ordered may be just to verify the ability of the supplier to make the parts, or to verify the design of the finished product. In other words, the supplier may fabricate a part correctly, but a manufacturer's engineering department may determine that the part needs to be redesigned. This would start the process over. Once samples have been approved, the flow of The Supply Chain Flow Process can be followed.

A manufacturing company has to furnish a forecast (usually annually) so the supplier can then go through his supply chain and make sure that all the materials needed (i.e., material, lubricant, machine capacity, labor resources) for the component the supplier provides will be available. A manufacturer then issues a purchase order, which serves as a commitment to purchase a defined number of units. A purchase order must have terms and conditions accompanying it to protect your company. Usually, a customer will not want to receive the entire forecast amount at once. Instead, a manufacturer could issue multiple purchase orders throughout the year, or do what is called a blanket purchase order for a large amount and then make releases against that purchase order for small amounts when they actually want it.

For example, a company uses 1,000 rods of aluminum in a year. They may lock into a price for the entire year (the price of aluminum changes daily), but not take delivery of all 1,000 rods at once. Instead, the supply chain manager would request economic order quantity (EOQ) releases. An EOQ is the optimal balance between taking delivery for the entire 1,000 rods at once and paying for material that will not be used for months, and paying transportation, inspection and transaction costs for receiving frequent smaller shipments. The formula for EOQ is:

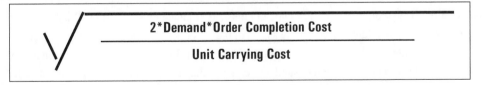

$$\sqrt{\frac{2*Demand*Order\ Completion\ Cost}{Unit\ Carrying\ Cost}}$$

Where the order completion cost is the total cost of placing the purchase order, paying for a setup at the vendor (if applicable), and paying the transportation and in-house handling to get the components to the production floor. The unit carrying cost is the cost of holding inventory (insurance, warehouse lease, shrinkage costs, security, cost of capital, etc.).

Customers can do releases to the supplier at specific time intervals or specific inventory intervals. With inventory intervals, when a customer gets to a certain number of rods left, they would issue a release for the next shipment of rods.

Visit Vault at **www.vault.com** for insider company profiles, expert advice, career message boards, expert resume reviews, the Vault Job Board and more.

VAULT CAREER LIBRARY 179

A supplier should send a confirmation to the customer acknowledging they have received the purchase order and agreed to the terms and conditions described therein. The supplier sends the material per the purchase order and then sends an invoice for the amount shipped. Once the goods have been accepted by the customer, a payment is sent to the supplier equal to the amount of the invoice.

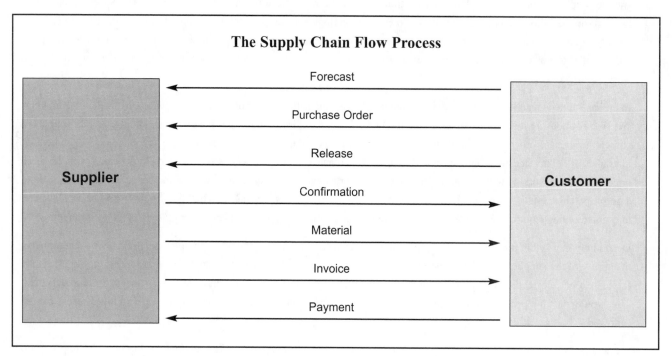

OEM suppliers

There are basically three types of suppliers. In the first, or most conventional scenario, a company provides a design for what they want the supplier to furnish and the supplier makes it to the company's specifications. The second is the original equipment manufacturer (OEM) supplier. In this case, the company does not specify the design for a custom product, but in fact buys a product that the supplier sells to many customers. These products are called off-the-shelf (a screw is an example of a component that is usually purchased as an off-the-shelf product rather than being custom designed).

Contract manufacturers

Contract manufacturers are the third type of suppliers, in which formal contracts between the supplier (the contract manufacturer) and your manufacturing company are relied upon. The contract manufacturer purchases or makes all of the components, assembles the product, tests it, and ships the finished product either directly to the customer or to a warehouse. Companies that want to get out of the manufacturing aspect of their products turn to contract manufacturers. The supply chain manager finds suitable contract manufacturers and manages the relationship after a contract has been signed. A company has to put a huge amount of trust into the contract manufacturer, since the customer does not have the same level of visibility or control over the manufacturing of the product as they do when they are making the product themselves. Contract manufacturing is an option in almost every industry from food processing to semiconductors.

Freight forwarders and transportation providers

Transportation providers and freight forwarders are also controlled by a supply chain management practitioner. Transportation providers pick up product from one location and deliver them to another. Obviously, it is very costly to pick up some cargo in Los Angeles and drive it all the way to New York for delivery. For this reason, these companies consolidate shipments from different places in a departing hub (whether it be a port, a warehouse or an airport), send them to an arriving hub, and then deliver them to their final destination. It is quite common for a transportation provider to hand off a shipment to another company to carry out some or all of the transportation. This is called subcontracting or third party carriers. Specialty transportation providers also exist (i.e., for transporting explosive materials, refrigerated cargo, etc.). Some manufacturing companies have traffic, transportation, or logistics departments that take care of most of this work so a supply chain manager can concentrate on suppliers only.

Freight forwarders specialize in transportation across borders. They coordinate the paperwork, book the space with a transportation provider, and track the goods from pickup to delivery. Because of the complexity of customs requirements, tariff codes and language barriers for different countries, it is better to have freight forwarders involved if a company is dealing with more than a few countries or commodities.

Supply Chain Careers

Supply chain management occupations

Below are brief summaries of the duties for supply chain management occupations. Not every organization will have all of these positions and the duties of the positions will not be limited to those described here.

Buyer: Buyers do purchasing just like supply chain managers. The difference is that supply chain managers buy parts and materials for the company's products, whereas buyers purchase everything else. Some examples of items that buyers procure are desktop computers, office supplies and hand tools.

Planner: A planner takes the forecast from marketing/sales and breaks that into a build schedule of what products should be built and when they should be built to meet inventory goals. Planners also work with supply chain managers to control inventory of parts and materials.

Purchasing administrative assistant: A purchasing administrative assistant takes care of the filing of paperwork for the purchasing department. He/she will also coordinate travel arrangements.

Logistics manager: A logistics manager is responsible for the traffic of goods coming to and going from the factory. This encompasses air, land, and ocean traffic, both domestic and international.

Supply chain engineer: A supply chain engineer works on technical issues with the supplier. This involves working with suppliers to improve their quality, helping them to analyze failures, and developing new products.

Commodity manager: A commodity manager is similar to a supply chain manager. Some companies separate the ownership of parts and materials for the supply chain managers by product line. For example, if a company makes binoculars, telescopes, cameras and microscopes, and they have four supply chain managers, they might assign one supply chain manager for each product family. Another approach is to distribute the work by commodity. One supply chain manager would be responsible for the optics on all of the product families and one supply chain manager would be responsible for the plastic parts on all of the product families. When this is the case, the supply chain managers can be called commodity managers.

Receiving inspector: A receiving inspector is responsible for checking the quality of the parts and materials that come from the vendor before they get moved to the production floor for consumption and before the supplier gets paid. There are statistics charts that define the number of samples from a shipment that need to be checked to meet the desired confidence level that the entire lot received is acceptable, so a receiving inspector does not check 100 percent of the incoming items.

Visit Vault at **www.vault.com** for insider company profiles, expert advice, career message boards, expert resume reviews, the Vault Job Board and more.

VAULT CAREER LIBRARY   **181**

Procurement manager: A procurement manager is in charge of the buyers and supply chain managers. The procurement manager sets the goals for the department and provides a level of escalation when a supply chain manager is having trouble managing a supplier.

Receiving coordinator: The receiving coordinator processes the parts and materials delivered. This includes doing a receiving transaction in ERP, moving the parts to their location, and making sure the paperwork the supplier sends matches what was received.

Receiving supervisor: The receiving supervisor is responsible for the receiving department. Besides supervising receiving department workers, the receiving supervisor is in charge of creating and improving department processes.

Accounts payable coordinator: The accounts payable coordinator works in the accounting department and processes the invoices from the suppliers. After verifying the invoices match what was actually received, the accounts payable coordinator sends a payment to the supplier.

The MBA in Supply Chain Management

MBA graduates seeking opportunities in supply chain management usually pursue either a project manager or director of materials position. Both of these vocations require previous experience in supply chain management, so the likelihood of a new graduate landing one of these positions is low.

A project manager is responsible for large transitions related to supply chain management. One example of these transitions is a plant shutdown. A company may decide that it is more cost-effective to stop manufacturing their products themselves, and instead have a vendor do it for them. The management of a plant shutdown project requires cross-functional teamwork between accounting (working out the costs), engineering (helping the vendors get up and running), human resources (laying off the production workers), and manufacturing (managing the inventory to make a seamless transition). Another example of a transition is a large scale vendor change. A company may have a contract manufacturer in Mexico making its products. In an effort to reduce costs, the company may want to partner with a contract manufacturer in Vietnam instead. Making this transition can be even harder than a plant shutdown, because the existing supplier may become bitter and refuse to cooperate. Most often, these transitions are done without notifying the existing supplier until the new supplier is running at the required capacity.

A director of materials is responsible for the strategy of the purchasing group. He does not get involved in the details of the day-to-day operations of the supply chain management department, but will assume the reins when issues get out of control or need upper-management attention. A director of materials also sets the practices of his departments and approves large dollar item purchases. Similarly, the director of materials participates in vendor relationship management for the suppliers with whom the company spends the most money. In addition to providing strategic direction to the purchasing group, the director of materials spends significant time meeting with the other executives in the company, sharing expertise, championing causes, and staying abreast of issues facing the company. A director of materials also spends a lot of time networking with people outside of the company (i.e., industry experts, competitors and prospective vendors).

Employer Directory

AAR Corporation
1 AAR Place
1100 N. Wood Dale Road
Wood Dale, IL 60191
Phone: (630) 227-2000
Fax: (630) 227-2019
www.aacorp.com

ABB Limited
Affolternstrasse 44
CH-8050 Zürich
Switzerland
Phone: +41-43-317-7111
Fax: +41-43-317-4420
www.abb.com

Airbus
1, Rond point Maurice Bellonte
31707 Blagnac Cedex
France
Phone: +33-5-6193-3333
Fax: +33-5-6193-4955
www.airbus.com

Alcoa Incorporated
201 Isabella Street
Pittsburgh, PA 15212
Phone: (412) 553-4545
Fax: (412) 553-4498
www.alcoa.com

Amcor Limited
679 Victoria Street
Abbotsford, VIC 3067
Australia
Phone: +61-3-9226-9000
Fax: +61-3-9226-9050
www.amcor.com

Amphenol Corporation
358 Hall Avenue
Wallingford, CT 06492
Phone: (203) 265-8900
Fax: (203) 265-8516
www.amphenol.com

APC Corporation
132 Fairgrounds Road
West Kingston, RI 02892
Phone: (401) 789-5735
Fax: (401) 789-3710
www.apc.com

Apogee Enterprises Incorporated
7900 Xerxes Avenue South
Suite 1800
Minneapolis, MN 55431
Phone: (952) 835-1874
Fax: (952) 835-3196
www.apog.com

Armstrong World Industries
2500 Columbia Avenue
Lancaster, PA 17603
Phone: (717) 397-0611
www.armstrong.com

BAE Systems plc
6 Carlton Gardens
London, SW1Y 5AD
United Kingdom
Phone: +44-12-5237-3232
Fax: +44-12-5238 3000
www.baesystems.com

BASF AG
Carl-Bosch-Straße 38
67056 Ludwigshafen
Germany
Phone: +49-621-600
Fax: +49-621-604-2525
www.basf.com

BE&K
2000 International Park Drive
Birmingham, AL 35243
Phone: (205) 972-6000
Fax: (205) 972-6651
www.bek.com

Bell Microproducts
1941 Ringwood Avenue
San Jose, CA 95131
Phone: (408) 451-9400
Fax: (408) 451-1600
www.bellmicro.com

BHP Billiton
180 Lonsdale Street
Melbourne 3000
Australia
Phone: +61-1300-554-757
Fax: +61-39-609-3015
www.bhpbilliton.com

The Black & Decker Corporation
701 E. Joppa Road
Towson, MD 21286
Phone: (410) 716-3900
Fax: (410) 716-2933
www.bdk.com

BMW Group
Petuelring 130
Munich D-80788
Germany
Phone: +49-89-382-0
Fax: +49-89-3822-4418
www.bmwgroup.com

Boeing
100 N. Riverside Plaza
Chicago, IL 60606-1596
Phone: (312) 544-2000
Fax: (312) 544-2082
www.boeing.com

Boise Cascade Holdings LLC
1111 W. Jefferson Street
Boise, ID 83702
Phone: (208) 384-6161
Fax: (208) 384-7189
www.bc.com

Visit Vault at **www.vault.com** for insider company profiles, expert advice,
career message boards, expert resume reviews, the Vault Job Board and more.

V∆ULT CAREER LIBRARY **183**

Employer Directory, cont.

Caterpillar Incorporated
100 NE Adams Street
Peoria, IL 61629
Phone: (309) 675-1000
Fax: (309) 675-1182
www.cat.com

Chevron Phillips Chemical Company LLC
10001 Six Pines Drive
The Woodlands, TX 77380
Phone: (800) 231-1212
Fax: (800) 231-3890
www.cpchem.com

Cintas Corporation
6800 Cintas Boulevard
Cincinnati, OH 45262
Phone: (513) 459-1200
Fax: (513) 573-4130
www.cintas.com

Commercial Metals Company
6565 N. MacArthur Boulevard
Suite 800
Irving, TX 75039
Phone: (214) 689-4300
Fax: (214) 689-5886
www.cmc.com

Cooper Tire & Rubber Company
701 Lima Avenue
Findlay, OH 45840
Phone: (419) 423-1321
Fax: (419) 424-4108
www.coopertire.com

Crown Holdings
One Crown Way
Philadelphia, PA 19154-4599
Phone: (215) 698-5100
Fax: (215) 676-7245
www.crowncork.com

Cummins Incorporated
500 Jackson Street
Columbus, IN 47202
Phone: (812) 377-5000
Fax: (812) 377-3334
www.cummins.com

DaimlerChrysler AG
Epplestraße 225
70546 Stuttgart
Germany
Phone: +49-711-17-0
Fax: +49-711-17-22244
www.daimlerchrysler.com

Dana Corporation
4500 Dorr Street
Toledo, OH 43615
Phone: (419) 535-4500
Fax: (419) 535-4643
www.dana.com

Delphi Corporation
5725 Delphi Drive
Troy, MI 48098
Phone: (248) 813-2000
Fax: (248) 813-2670
www.delphi.com

Donaldson Company
1400 West 94th Street
Minneapolis, MN 55431
Phone: (952) 887-3131
Fax: (952) 887-3155
www.donaldson.com

The Dow Chemical Company
2030 Dow Center
Midland, MI 48674
Phone: (989) 636-1000
Fax: (989) 636-3518
www.dow.com

Dril-Quip Incorporated
13550 Hempstead Highway
Houston, TX 77040
Phone: (713) 939-7711
Fax: (713) 939-8063
www.dril-quip.com

DuPont
1007 Market Street
Wilmington, DE 19898
Phone: (302) 774-1000
Fax: (302) 999-4399
www.dupont.com

Eaton Corporation
Eaton Center
1111 Superior Avenue
Cleveland, OH 44114-2584
Phone: (216) 523-5000
Fax: (216) 523-3787
www.eaton.com

Ecolab
370 N. Wabasha Street
St. Paul, MN 55012
Phone: (651) 293-2233
Fax: (651) 293-2092
www.ecolab.com

Emerson
8000 W. Florissant Avenue
St. Louis, MO 63136
Phone: (314) 553-2000
Fax: (314) 553-3527
www.gotoemerson.com

Federal-Mogul Corporation
26555 Northwestern Highway
Southfield, MI 48034
Phone: (248) 354-7700
Fax: (248) 354-8950
www.federal-mogul.com

Employer Directory, cont.

Foamex
1000 Columbia Avenue
Linwood, PA 19061-3997
Phone: (610) 859-3000
Fax: (610) 859-3035
www.foamex.com

Ford Motor Company
1 American Road
Dearborn, MI 48126-2798
Phone: (313) 322-3000
Fax: (313) 845-6073
www.ford.com

General Dynamics Corporation
2941 Fairview Park Drive
Suite 100
Falls Church, VA 22042-4513
Phone: (703) 876-3000
Fax: (703) 876-3125
www.gd.com

General Motors Corporation
300 Renaissance Center
Detroit, MI 48265-3000
Phone: (313) 556-5000
Fax: (313) 556-5108
www.gm.com

Georgia Gulf Corporation
115 Perimeter Center Place
Suite 460
Atlanta, GA 30346
Phone: (770) 395-4500
Fax: (770) 395-4529
www.ggc.com

Georgia-Pacific
133 Peachtree Street, Northeast
Atlanta, GA 30303
Phone: (404) 652-4000
Fax: (404) 230-1674
www.gp.com

Goodrich Corporation
Four Coliseum Centre
2730 West Tyvola Road
Charlotte, NC 28217-4578
Phone: (704) 423-7000
Fax: (704) 423-7002
www.goodrich.com

Goodyear
1144 East Market Street
Akron, OH 44316-0001
Phone: (330) 796-2121
Fax: (330) 796-2222
www.goodyear.com

Hamilton Sundstrand
1 Hamilton Road
Windsor Locks, CT 06096-1010
Phone: (860) 654-6000
Fax: (860) 654-2399
www.hamiltonsundstrandcorp.com

Handy & Harman
International Corporate Center
555 Theodore Fremd Avenue
Rye, NY 10580
Phone: (914) 921-5200
Fax: (914) 925-4496
www.handyharman.com

Harley-Davidson
3700 West Juneau Avenue
Milwaukee, WI 53208
Phone: (414) 342-4680
Fax: (414) 343-8230
www.harley-davidson.com

Herman Miller Incorporated
855 East Main Avenue
Zeeland, MI 49464-0302
Phone: (616) 654-3000
Fax: (616) 654-5234
hermanmiller.com

HNI Corporation
414 E. 3rd Street
Muscatine, IA 52761-0071
Phone: (563) 264-7400
Fax: (563) 264-7217
www.hnicorp.com

Honda Motor Company Limited
2-1-1 Minami-Aoyama, Minato-ku
Tokyo 107-8556
Japan
Phone: +81-3-3423-1111
Fax: +81-3-5412-1515
www.world.honda.com

Honeywell International
101 Columbia Road
Morristown, NJ 07962-1219
Phone: (973) 455-2000
Fax: (973) 455-4807
www.honeywell.com

Hyundai Motor America
10550 Talbert Avenue
Fountain Valley, CA 92728-0850
Phone: (714) 965-3000
Fax: (714) 965-3149
www.hyundaiusa.com

IKEA
496 W. Germantown Pike
Plymouth Meeting, PA 19462
Phone: (610) 834-0180
Fax: (610) 834-0872
www.ikea.com

Imperial Chemical Industries
20 Manchester Square
London, W1U 3AN
United Kingdom
Phone: +44-20-7009-5000
Fax: +44-20-7009-5001
www.ici.com

Visit Vault at **www.vault.com** for insider company profiles, expert advice, career message boards, expert resume reviews, the Vault Job Board and more.

VAULT CAREER LIBRARY 185

Employer Directory, cont.

Ingersoll Rand Company Limited
Clarendon House
2 Church Street
Hamilton HM 11
Bermuda
Phone: (441) 295-2838
www.irco.com

International Paper Company
6400 Poplar Avenue
Memphis, TN 38197
Phone: (901) 419-9000
www.ipaper.com

ITT Corporation
4 W. Red Oak Lane
White Plains, NY 10604
Phone: (914) 641-2000
Fax: (914) 696-2950
www.itt.com

Jaguar Cars Limited
Browns Lane, Allesley
Coventry
West Midlands, CV5 9DR
United Kingdom
Phone: +44-24-7640-2121
Fax: +44-24-7620-2101
www.jaguarvehicles.com

John Deere
1 John Deere Place
Moline, IL 61265
Phone: (309) 765-8000
Fax: (309) 765-5671
www.deere.com

Johnson Controls Incorporated
5757 North Greenbay Avenue
Milwaukee, WI 53201
Phone: (414) 524-1200
Fax: (414) 524-2077
www.johnsoncontrols.com

Land Rover
Banbury Road, Gaydon
Warwick, CV35 0RR
United Kingdom
Phone: +44-1962-641-111
Fax: +44-1962-641-597
www.landrover.com

Land Rover North America
1 Premier Place
Irvine, CA 92618
Phone: (949) 341-6100
Toll Free: (800) 346-3493
www.landroverusa.com

Lockheed Martin Corporation
6801 Rockledge Drive
Bethesda, MD 20817-1877
Phone: (301) 897-6000
Fax: (301) 897-6704
www.lockheedmartin.com

Lone Star Technologies
15660 N. Dallas Parkway
Suite 500
Dallas, TX 75248
Phone: (972) 770-6401
Fax: (972) 770-6411
www.lonestartech.com

MeadWestvaco Corporation
11013 West Broad Street
Glen Allen, VA 23060
Phone: (804) 327-5200
Fax: (804) 327-6363
www.meadwestvaco.com

Monsanto Company
800 North Lindbergh Boulevard
St. Louis, MO 63167
Phone: (314) 694-1000
Fax: (314) 694-8394
www.monsanto.com

Moog Incorporated
Jamison Road
East Aurora, NY 14052
Phone: (716) 652-2000
Fax: (716) 687-4457
www.moog.com

National Oilwell Varco
10000 Richmond Avenue
Houston, TX 77042
Phone: (713) 346-7500
Fax: (713) 458-2175
www.natoil.com

Nissan Motor Company Limited
17-1, Ginza 6-chome, Chuo-ku
Tokyo 104-8023
Japan
Phone: +81-3-3543-5523
Fax: +81-3-5565-22287
www.nissan-global.com

Northrop Grumman Corporation
1840 Century Park East
Los Angeles, CA 90067-2199
Phone: (310) 553-6262
Fax: (310) 553-2076
www.northropgrumman.com

Nucor Corporation
2100 Rexford Road
Charlotte, NC 28211
Phone: (704) 366-7000
Fax: (704) 362-4208
www.nucor.com

Owens Corning
1 Owens Corning Parkway
Toledo, OH 43659
Phone: (419) 248-8000
Fax: (419) 248-5337
www.owenscorning.com

Employer Directory, cont.

PACCAR Incorporated
777 106th Avenue NE
Bellevue, WA 98004
Phone: (425) 468-7400
Fax: (425) 468-8216
www.paccar.com

Parker Hannifin Corporation
6035 Parkland Boulevard
Cleveland, OH 44124
Phone: (216) 896-3000
Fax: (216) 896-4000
www.parker.com

Pitney Bowes Incorporated
1 Elmcroft Road
Stamford, CT 06926-0700
Phone: (203) 356-5000
Fax: (203) 351-7336
www.pb.com

Plum Creek Timber Company
999 Third Avenue, Suite 4300
Seattle, WA 98104-4096
Phone: (206) 467-3600
Fax: (206) 467-3795
www.plumcreek.com

PolyOne Corporation
33587 Walker Road
Avon Lake, OH 44012
Phone: (440) 930-1000
Fax: (440) 930-1750
www.polyone.com

PPG Industries
One PPG Plaza
Pittsburgh, PA 15272
Phone: (412) 434-3131
www.ppg.com

Quanex Corporation
1900 West Loop South
Suite 1500
Houston, TX 77027
Phone: (713) 961-4600
Fax: (713) 439-1016
www.quanex.com

Rayonier Incorporated
50 North Laura Street
Jacksonville, FL 32202
Phone: (904) 357-9100
Fax: (904) 357-9101
www.rayonier.com

Raytheon Company
870 Winter Street
Waltham, MA 02451-1449
Phone: (781) 522-3000
Fax: (781) 522-3001
www.raytheon.com

Rockwell Automation
1201 South Second Street
Milwaukee, WI 53204
Phone: (414) 382-2000
Fax: (414) 382-4000
www.rockwellautomation.com

Rolls-Royce plc
65 Buckingham Gate
London SW1E 6AT
United Kingdom
Phone: +44-20-7222-9020
Fax: +44-20-7227 9178
www.rolls-royce.com

Sanmina-SCI Corporation
2700 N. 1st Street
San Jose, CA 95134
Phone: (408) 964-3500
Fax: (408) 964-3636
www.sanmina-sci.com

Shanghai Automotive Industry Corporation
489 Wei Hai Road
Shanghai, 200041
China
Phone: +86-21-2201-1888
Fax: +86-21-2201-1777
www.saicmotor.com

Shaw Industries Incorporated
616 E. Walnut Avenue
Dalton, GA 30722
Phone: (706) 278-3812
www.shawfloors.com

Sherwin-Williams
101 Prospect Avenue NW
Cleveland, OH 44115-1075
Phone: (216) 566-2000
Fax: (216) 566-2947
www.sherwin-williams.com

The Stanley Works
1000 Stanley Drive
New Britain, CT 06053
Phone: (860) 225-5111
Fax: (860) 827-3895
www.stanleyworks.com

Tenneco Incorporated
500 N. Field Drive
Lake Forest, Il 60045
Phone: (847) 482-5000
Fax: (847) 482-5940
www.tenneco.com

Textron Incorporated
40 Westminster Street
Providence, RI 02903
Phone: (401) 421-2800
www.textron.com

Toyota Motor Corporation
1, Toyota-cho, Toyota City
Aichi Prefecture 471-8571
Japan
Phone: +81-565-28-2121
Fax: +81-565-23-5800
www.toyota.co.jp
www.toyota.com

TRW Automotive
12025 Tech Center Drive
Livonia, MI 48150
Phone: (734) 855-2600
www.trw.com

Tyco International Limited
9 Roszel Road
Princeton, NJ 08540
Phone: (609) 720-4200
Fax: (609) 720-4208
www.tyco.com

Visit Vault at **www.vault.com** for insider company profiles, expert advice, career message boards, expert resume reviews, the Vault Job Board and more.

VAULT CAREER LIBRARY   187

Employer Directory, cont.

United States Steel Corporation
600 Grant Street
Pittsburgh, PA 15219-2800
Phone: (412) 433-1121
Fax: (412) 433-5733
www.ussteel.com

United Technologies Corporation
One Financial Plaza
Hartford, CT 06103
Phone: (860) 728-7000
Fax: (860) 728-7979
www.utc.com

Universal Forest Products Incorporated
2801 East Beltline Avenue NE
Grand Rapids, MI 49525
Phone: (800) 598-9663
Fax: (616) 364-1930
www.ufpi.com

Valspar Corporation
1101 S. Third Street
Minneapolis, MN 55415
Phone: (612) 332-7371
Fax: (612) 375-7723

Vitro America
965 Ridge Lake Boulevard
P.O. Box 171173
Memphis, TN 38187
Phone: (800) 767-7111
Fax: (901) 683-9351
www.vitroamerica.com

Volkswagen AG
Brieffach 1848-2
Wolfsburg 38436
Germany
Phone: +49-53-61-90
Fax: +49-53-61-92-82-82
www.vw.com

Vulcan Materials
1200 Urban Center Drive
Birmingham, AL 35242
Phone: (205) 298-3000
Fax: (205) 298-2960
www.vulcanmaterials.com

Walter Industries Incorporated
4211 W. Boy Scout Boulevard
Tampa, FL 33607
Phone: (813) 871-4811
Fax: (813) 871-4399
www.walterind.com

Weyerhaeuser Company
33663 Weyerhaeuser Way South
Federal Way, WA 98003
Phone: (253) 924-2345
Fax: (253) 924-5921
www.weyerhaeuser.com

Worthington Industries
200 Old Wilson Bridge Road
Columbus, OH 43085
Phone: (614) 438-3210
Fax: (614) 438-7948
www.worthingtonindustries.com

Media and Entertainment

Media and Entertainment MBAs

Not long ago, the creative types in media kept a wary eye on the suits or the bean counters, as the business side of media is known. For years, Wall Street paid little attention to the media biz, an industry it didn't take that seriously. Now, with the rise of the global conglomerates and the aftermath of dot-com meltdown, many media professionals, both on the creative and business sides, are finding it necessary to pursue an MBA.

A new order

"When we started, I had two courses and we had about 40 people in each. Today, in any given semester we have about 400 to 500 students taking one or more classes," says Al Lieberman, executive director of NYU Stern's Entertainment, Media and Technology Initiative. Started in 1996, Stern's EMT program awards a certificate to those students who complete at least nine credits in courses like Entertainment Finance and The Business of Sports Marketing. Over at Fordham Business School, Dr. Everette Dennis, chair of the communications and media management program has also seen an increased interest over the last couple of years, "We have a relatively small program, but we've had probably a 20 to 25 percent increase in applications." Fordham's program, believed to be one of the first in the country, began in the mid-1980s when Arthur Taylor, a former president of CBS, arrived as the business school's new dean and brought in William Small, another CBS executive, to head up the program.

So why are more and more media professionals interested in an MBA? Of course, many can argue that a wave of dot-com dropouts have decided to hide out in business school in the wake of the collapse of the dot-coms and the weak ad market. Lieberman argues that this is no trend. "It's a fundamental change because the competitive factors that are driving this are not going away. They are intensifying." He is talking about the shakeup of the media landscape. Deregulation and mergers have given rise to media behemoths.

Technology, without a doubt, has wrought havoc in the industry, forcing firms to rethink their business strategies. That's one reason why Jason Oberlander, a first-year student at Columbia Business School, finds the business side of media so attractive. "The technology that comes out, it's coming out so quickly that it requires people who are able to adapt and think on their feet and are able to pursue new opportunities in order to be successful and compete effectively."

Consumers today have a rainbow of media products to choose from. Dennis says the media industry has become an important economic engine and Wall Street has taken notice. "All of the sudden this was an industry to be reckoned with." Lieberman points to a shift towards cooperation and the building of alliances as well, in an industry that has been notoriously competitive. The current negotiations between CNN and *ABC News* would have been unheard of just 10 years ago. Not only has media seen enormous domestic growth, but abroad as well; says Lieberman, "For every dollar that is generated in the United States, 15 years ago the most they could look for was maybe 25 cents outside, as an export. Now it is dollar for dollar."

What does an MBA really offer?

"A few years ago, I would have said, 'An MBA—that would be nice, but it really isn't necessary.' Now, I think an MBA, or at least some exposure to business practices, is probably essential," says Dennis. He cites a growing need for better understanding of market research, audiences, how to manage change and the cash position of a company. In the mid 1980s, Lieberman started a marketing firm focused on entertainment and media. At the time, he couldn't find enough qualified candidates to keep pace with the growth of the firm. He ended up recruiting people right out of one of the courses he was teaching at NYU. "I taught this course that I created, called The Marketing of Entertainment Industries at the NYU School of Continuing Education. Out of the 40 or 45 adults that would come in from all kinds of industries to learn about this, I'd pick one or two that were the best and offer them jobs."

Visit Vault at **www.vault.com** for insider company profiles, expert advice, career message boards, expert resume reviews, the Vault Job Board and more.

VAULT CAREER LIBRARY 189

Oberland left Showtime as a communications manager in sports and event programming, but felt an MBA was the only way to increase his chances for advancement. "I felt that doing the transition within the company would have been difficult. I certainly would have had to take a significant step down in title and in compensation." Dennis concurs that an MBA is increasingly becoming a requirement for management in media companies. "I think people on the creative side are not going to move into major management and executive roles unless they either get this kind of background and experience on their own in some way, or they go to a business school and get it where it is taught systematically."

Bridging the gap

"One of the biggest problems was the business people who stepped into this world of creativity, didn't understand the creative product, didn't understand how it made money, didn't understand how to apply the basic strategic thinking, therefore there was a huge disconnect," says Lieberman. It takes two to tango, and the creative side has also contributed to the disconnect. Fordham, recognizing the interest by some creative folks to bridge this gap, will be launching a new MS program soon, "It's really tailored to the people from the creative side who do need to know and understand more about business." Stern is also helping the business types better understand the creative process by encouraging Stern students to take courses in filmmaking at the Tisch School of the Arts. "They're not going to make films, but at least they understand the skills, so they don't come on a set and make complete idiots of themselves." At the end of the day, Oberland argues that you need the overall package to get ahead. "I think someone who balances the creative skills with business skills is the most suitable person to run a business from a general management standpoint."

Media Business Positions

Strategic planning

Strategic planning groups are small groups of about five to 40 professionals that serve as in-house consulting and investment banking arms. Not coincidentally, most employees are ex-consultants and bankers. Strategists are involved in valuation and negotiation decisions for acquisitions, business plans for new ventures, the expansion of the current business lines (and sometimes creating new ones), forward-looking financial plans to provide budgeting and overall prognosis for the health of all divisions of the company, and any other high-level issues that the company as a whole may be facing.

Because these projects affect the overall health of the company, meetings are often power sessions in the corporate dining room or top-floor board rooms with the company's senior executives, including the CEO, COO and CFO. While exposure to these individuals is one of the perks of this position, the jobs also tend to be incredibly challenging and taxing, as inordinate amounts of background data, research and information are synthesized and spun into a story prior to the presentation of findings. This group's job is all the more challenging, given that the recommendations that strategic planning groups deliver must necessarily be at odds with decisions that have already been made. Strategic planners, after all, are constantly trying to maximize the returns on the company's capital, which means analyzing and dismissing many current projects.

This function is also sometimes called corporate development, business development or in-house consulting. Because of the frequent exposure to high-level executives, the overall clout of the group and its impact in the major decisions of media conglomerates, these tend to be highly sought-after jobs, mostly filled by top-notch MBAs.

Corporate finance

Corporate finance is a sister group to strategic planning. Corporate financiers are the people who work in concert with investment bankers (or in lieu of them) to price deals, investigate options and plot the course of the company's growth through acquisitions of other companies.

Nearly all the major entertainment companies have grown through major acquisitions in the past two decades, increasing the importance of their corporate financiers. Corporate finance professionals investigate acquisition opportunities, gather competitive intelligence on other companies, determine synergies and negotiate deals. Likewise, they also divest businesses that may be undesirable in exchange for cash.

Most individuals in the corporate finance function are former investment bankers, accounting wizards and CFOs-to-be who bring their expertise in finance and public company performance to the entertainment industry.

Corporate marketing

Corporate marketing assesses consumer reaction to new projects, initiatives and endeavors. Often these groups are direct reports of business units (where each division has its own marketing group), but there are also many cases in which these groups are centralized under corporate and provide their services on an as-needed basis. The benefit of centralized marketing is that it enables the sharing of data across the company since the information is compiled by one group that can then spread the information. It also provides leverage with outside vendors (advertising agencies, media placement agencies, market research firms) when negotiating fees: the more money a company plans on spending with one deal, the better its negotiating position when choosing among competing agencies.

Corporate marketing encompasses many objectives:

- Market research and the execution of both quantitative and qualitative research
- The management of outside vendors who oversee new software, focus groups or large research studies
- Determining revenue projections for new products
- Soliciting consumer feedback on new and existing products
- Creating pricing models
- Estimating market penetration and rollout strategies
- Authoring marketing plans
- Supervising advertising and direct mail
- Overseeing overall brand equity and elements of brand differentiation like logo and identity
- Overseeing product-specific public relations efforts that drive coverage in the media

Corporate marketers often have an extensive background with advertising agencies or marketing consultancy firms.

Corporate public relations

For years, corporate PR was considered to be exclusively for damage control during events like the Exxon Valdez or the Tylenol cyanide scare. Whenever a CEO had problems with the press, the white knights of corporate PR came to the rescue to help avert a worse catastrophe. Corporate PR groups still perform this function. However, the work of corporate PR groups is much broader than just handling crisis management. Corporate PR groups now manage corporate spokespersons, serve as experts on media training and public appearances and coach CEOs as they prepare for media appearances and event marketing.

The corporate PR group is also known for initiating major press coverage in industry and business trade publications, as well as corporate-focused articles in general interest magazines like *Time*, *Newsweek* or *Vanity Fair*. PR professionals also develop relationships with government officials and lobbying groups that may have influence over legislation affecting the company's growth and development. Often, this group works with outside public relations agencies like Edelman Worldwide, Bozell or Hill & Knowlton.

Visit Vault at **www.vault.com** for insider company profiles, expert advice, career message boards, expert resume reviews, the Vault Job Board and more.

VAULT CAREER LIBRARY   191

Internet strategy

As content becomes increasingly commoditized due to the fact that so much on the Internet is free, there are challenges in protecting the hallowed material that entertainment companies create. While studios would love to use the Internet to hoard their content and prevent anyone else from distributing and profiting from it (sort of a preemptive strike against companies like Napster), the Internet is also an incredibly seductive resource for marketing, mainly because information can be communicated broadly and cheaply—much more inexpensively than TV commercials, billboards and bus shelters. The popularity of *The Blair Witch Project*, a surprise hit, was partially attributed to a very effective web site.

This tension (to promote our properties or protect them?) feeds the very complex and critical role that Internet strategy plays in the growth of media and entertainment companies. Because of the constantly evolving and still uncertain nature of the business, there are hundreds of individuals at nearly all major entertainment companies, tracking evolving technologies, coding pages, maintaining fresh web site content and otherwise marketing via the Web. Media companies with Internet strategy groups include Walt Disney/ABC and AOL Time Warner.

Real estate development

Real estate development within an entertainment company involves not only theme parks, but also extensions of an entertainment empire's brands, including themed restaurants (Hard Rock Café), sports stadiums, entertainment complexes (Sony Metreon) and other destinations that involve large tracts of land that can both provide steady revenue streams and impress an entertainment-seeking audience. The major entertainment companies often have proprietary lots of their own land that were either part of the company's origin (as Disney does with its land in Florida and Southern California, now managed under the aegis of the Disney Development Corporation), were results of acquisitions or were acquired over time.

As real estate development is its own unique business with special financing rules and its own intrinsic rewards, the field generally attracts individuals from outside the entertainment industry. The most successful individuals in these divisions are those with substantial experience managing vendors, contractors and landscape architects, working with community development offices, leveraging tax benefits and executing visionary blueprints. Real estate development is a particularly exciting division for individuals wishing to combine interests in the hospitality industry, finance and real estate.

Our Survey Says: Lifestyle and Pay

Hours

Like so many industries, there is a work/life trade-off that comes in the entertainment industry. "There are tons of trade-offs," says one longtime employee in the strategic planning group of a studio. "The entertainment industry definitely doesn't come to mind when I think about a balanced lifestyle. It's a rare day I don't put in 12 hours."

But that's not always the case. There are many individuals that report (mostly outside of strategic planning and other corporate groups) consistently being home by 6 p.m. While the career trajectory is slower and the compensation is lower in the "business units" (versus the "corporate side"), the hours and the requirements are less demanding. There are always exceptions. Says one theme park executive: "Hours are usually 9 to 6, but every year for a few weeks in the spring during our five-year planning process, it's not uncommon for us to put in 12 hours a day, seven days a week."

One rule of thumb: Corporate jobs that report to the CEO typically face "fire drills" (i.e., urgent deadlines imposed at the last minute) on a regular basis. Jobs that are more predictable (i.e., positions with business units rather than corporate-level positions) generally have more predictable hours.

Pay

"The pay in corporate jobs is usually up there with investment banking and management consulting," reports one former consultant-turned-analyst at a publishing house. The business units, however, are typically known for paying less, both because they are responsible for profit and loss (high salaries come straight out of the topline) and because of the less grueling hours.

At the corporate level, beginning-level analysts out of college typically start at around $40,000, with several thousand dollars in bonuses and a 15 percent raise after a year. Managers make at least $80,000 and directors usually crack six figures. VPs earn in the low $100K range.

In business units, the pay can be anywhere from 10 to 30 percent lower.

Other perks

Entertainment is attractive partly because of its perks. "Let's face it, I got into the industry hoping to hang out with rock stars," confesses one record industry insider. Employees get discounts on products, invitations to advance screenings of movies and tickets to movie premieres and gala parties. That said, the perks are not nearly as lavish as the expense accounts and freebies that come on the creative side of the business. There are the stories of the business folks who occasionally get free lunches, tickets to movie premieres and celebrity wedding invitations, but these are mostly the result of a person's personal connections.

Another practice, widely considered a perk, is that many within the industry itemize taxes and deduct all their entertainment expenses in the name of the job. "I itemized everything from my stereo to my movie tickets," boasts one corporate finance manager.

Promotions and competition

There is indeed jockeying for certain roles and positions, as there is in any industry, but the business side is not as ugly as the creative side when it comes to competition. Promotion decisions are not based on whether people like you, or on how your last film did, but rather on the body of your professional work. Even though there is an oversupply of people vying for the available jobs, it is a largely meritocratic industry.

Visit Vault at **www.vault.com** for insider company profiles, expert advice, career message boards, expert resume reviews, the Vault Job Board and more.

VAULT CAREER LIBRARY   193

A Day in the Life: Strat Planning Executive

While there's no "typical" day in strat planning at a media company, below are some of the most common day-to-day tasks:

• Interfacing with other business units, domestically and abroad, either in calls or in meetings (25 percent)

• Presentations to the senior executive team on key decisions (25 percent)

• Presentations from the business units on growth initiatives within other groups (10 percent)

• Responding to requests from senior management (25 percent)

• Managing junior team members (15 percent)

If this sounds murky or unclear, read on for an illustration of the specifics. Overall, the hours are long. There are often stories of many executives who do not have families or children, or often forsake them for their careers.

7:00 a.m.: Arrive at work, make conference calls to Europe to discuss progress on a major new initiative to expand in Europe.

8:00 a.m.: Breakfast meeting with a manager in another business unit to update one another on work and "keep both ears close to the ground."

9:00 a.m.: Review a subordinate's presentation, assigned last night. The presentation is due early tomorrow for the CEO—revisions must be made with haste.

10:00 a.m.: Return some morning phone calls. Glance at e-mail for anything urgent.

10:30 a.m.: Leave for an off-site meeting to discuss what to do with a waning division in which the top chief just left.

10:45 a.m.: Call my assistant. Have her type up e-mail responses to some new e-mails and send them off on my behalf.

10:55 a.m.: Arrive at off-site meeting. Listen to presentations from key leaders on what to do next.

12:00 p.m.: Depart for lunch meeting with a senior VP at another small entertainment company to propose an acquisition.

1:30 p.m.: Return to office to debrief with CFO on the numbers needed for a five-year plan.

3:00 p.m.: Answer e-mails, review daily trade publications, *The Hollywood Reporter* and *Daily Variety*.

3:45 p.m.: For fun and to build team morale, respond to office pool on what the weekend's box office will be.

3:47 p.m.: Spontaneous meeting with CEO in the hallway—turns out the presentation originally due tomorrow is not that urgent.

4:00 p.m.: Tell junior manager to call off work and go home since she's been pulling all-nighters for a couple of days.

4:10 p.m.: Start reviewing budget requests and expense reports of department employees.

5:00 p.m.: Peruse the proposals from three top management consulting firms, all vying for a piece of a major project.

6:30 p.m.: Make a conference call to Asia executives to discuss progress on their latest initiative.

7:30 p.m.: Answer all outstanding e-mails.

8:30 p.m.: Leave the office.

Employer Directory

ABC, Inc.
77 W. 66th Street
New York, NY 10023-6298
Phone: (212) 456-7777
Fax: (212) 456-1424
www.abc.go.com

Activision
3100 Ocean Park Boulevard
Santa Monica, CA 90405
Phone: (310) 255-2000
Fax: (310) 255-2100
www.activision.com

AMC Entertainment, Inc.
920 Main Street
Kansas City, MO 64105
Phone: (816) 221-4000
Fax: (816) 480-4617
www.amctheatres.com

Bad Boy Entertainment
1710 Broadway
New York, NY 10019
Phone: (212) 381-1540
Fax: (212) 381-1599
www.badboyonline.com

Bertelsmann AG
Carl-Bertelsmann-Strasse 270
D-33311 Gütersloh
Germany
Phone: +49-5241-80-0
Fax: +49-5241-80-9662
www.bertelsmann.com

Black Entertainment Television
One BET Plaza
1235 W. Street NE
Washington, DC 20018
Phone: (202) 608-2000
Fax: (202) 608-2589
www.bet.com

Bloomberg L.P.
731 Lexington Avenue
New York, NY 10022
Phone: (212) 318-2000
Fax: (917) 369-5000
www.bloomberg.com

British Broadcasting Corporation
Broadcasting House, Portland Place
London, W1A 1AA
United Kingdom
Phone: +44-20-7580-4468
Fax: +44-20-7637-1630
www.bbc.co.uk

Creative Artists Agency
2000 Avenue of the Stars
Los Angeles, CA 90067
Phone: (424) 288-2000
Fax: (424) 288-2900
www.caa.com

CBS, Inc.
51 W. 52nd Street
New York, NY 10019
Phone: (212) 975-4321
Fax: (212) 975-4516
www.cbs.com

Clear Channel Communications
200 E. Basse Road
San Antonio, TX 78209
Phone: (210) 822-2828
Fax: (210) 822-2299
www.clearchannel.com

CNN News Group
1 CNN Center
Atlanta, GA 30303
Phone: (404) 827-1700
Fax: (404) 827-1099
www.cnn.com

Comcast Corporation
1500 Market Street
Philadelphia, PA 19102-2148
Phone: (215) 665-1700
Fax: (215) 981-7790
www.comcast.com

Cox Communications, Inc.
1400 Lake Hearn Drive
Atlanta, GA 30319
Phone: (404) 843-5000
Fax: (404) 843-5975
www.cox.com

DIRECTV
2230 E. Imperial Highway
El Segundo, CA 90245
Phone: (310) 964-5000
Fax: (310) 535-5225
www.directv.com

Discovery Communications, Inc.
1 Discovery Place
Silver Spring, MD 20910
Phone: (240) 662-2000
Fax: (240) 662-1868
www.discovery.com

Dow Jones & Company, Inc.
1 World Financial Center
200 Liberty Street
New York, NY 10281
Phone: (212) 416-2000
Fax: (212) 416-4348
www.dj.com

DreamWorks SKG L.L.C.
1000 Flower Street
Glendale, CA 91201
Phone: (818) 733-7000
Fax: (818) 695-7574
www.dreamworks.com

Visit Vault at **www.vault.com** for insider company profiles, expert advice, career message boards, expert resume reviews, the Vault Job Board and more.

VAULT CAREER LIBRARY 195

Employer Directory, cont.

The E. W. Scripps Company
312 Walnut Street
Cincinnati, OH 45202
Phone: (513) 977-3000
Fax: (513) 977-3721
www.scripps.com

Electronic Arts
209 Redwood Shores Parkway
Redwood City, CA 94065
Phone: (650) 628-1500
Fax: (650) 628-1422
www.ea.com

EMI Group plc
27 Wrights Lane
London, W8 5SW
United Kingdom
Phone: +44-20-7795-7000
Fax: +44-20-7795-7296
www.emigroup.com

Fox Entertainment Group
10201 W. Pico Boulevard
Los Angeles, CA 90035
Phone: (310) 369-1000
www.fox.com

Gannett Company, Inc.
7950 Jones Branch Drive
McLean, VA 22107-0910
Phone: (703) 854-6000
Fax: (703) 854-2046
www.gannett.com

Home Box Office (HBO)
1100 Avenue of the Americas
New York, NY 10036
Phone: (212) 512-1000
Fax: (212) 512-1182
www.hbo.com

International Data Group
1 Exeter Plaza, 15th Floor
Boston, MA 02116-2851
Phone: (617) 534-1200
Fax: (617) 423-0240
www.idg.com

Liberty Media
12300 Liberty Boulevard
Englewood, CO 80112
Phone: (720) 875-5400
Fax: (720) 875-7469
www.libertymedia.com

Lucasfilm Limited
1110 Gorgas Avenue
San Francisco, CA 94129
Phone: (415) 662-1800
www.lucasfilm.com

Martha Stewart Living Omnimedia, Inc.
11 W. 42nd Street
New York, NY 10036
Phone: (212) 827-8000
Fax: (212) 827-8204
www.marthastewart.com

The McGraw-Hill Companies, Inc.
1221 Avenue of the Americas
New York, NY 10020
Phone: (212) 512-2000
Fax: (212) 512-3840
www.mcgraw-hill.com

Metro-Goldwyn-Mayer Inc.
10250 Constellation Boulevard
Los Angeles, CA 90067
Phone: (310) 449-3000
Fax: (310) 449-8857
www.mgm.com

MTV Networks
1515 Broadway
New York, NY 10036
Phone: (212) 258-8000
Fax: (212) 258-6175
www.mtv.com

National Cable Satellite Corporation (C-SPAN)
400 N. Capitol Street NW, Suite 650
Washington, DC 20001-1550
Phone: (202) 737-3220
Fax: (202) 737-6226
www.c-span.org

National Public Radio, Inc.
635 Massachusetts Avenue NW
Washington, DC 20001-3753
Phone: (202) 513-2000
Fax: (202) 513-3329
www.npr.org

NBC Universal
30 Rockefeller Plaza
New York, NY 10112
Phone: (212) 664-4444
Fax: (212) 664-4085
www.nbcuni.com

News Corporation
1211 Avenue of the Americas
8th Floor
New York, NY 10036
Phone: (212) 852-7017
Fax: (212) 852-7145
www.newscorp.com

Nintendo of America
4820 150th Avenue Northeast
Redmond, WA 98052
Phone: (425) 882-2040
Fax: (425) 882-3585
www.nintendo.com

Paramount Pictures
5555 Melrose Avenue
Hollywood, CA 90038
Phone: (323) 956-5000
Fax: (323) 862-1204
www.paramount.com

Pixar Animation Studios
1200 Park Avenue
Emeryville, CA 94608
Phone: (510) 752-3000
Fax: (510) 752-3151
www.pixar.com

Primedia
745 Fifth Avenue
New York, NY 10151
Phone: (212) 745-0100
Fax: (212) 745-0121
www.primedia.com

Employer Directory, cont.

Public Broadcasting Service
2100 Crystal Drive
Arlington, VA 22202-3785
Phone: (703) 739-5000
Fax: (703) 739-8495
www.pbs.org

Reed Elsevier PLC
1-3 Strand
London, WC2N 5JR
United Kingdom
Phone: +44-20-7930-7077
Fax: +44-20-7166-5799
www.reedelsevier.com

Reed Elsevier NV
Raderweg 29
1043 NX Amsterdam
The Netherlands
Phone: +31-20-485-2222
Fax: +31-20-618-0325

Reuters Group PLC
85 Fleet Street
London, EC4P 4AJ
United Kingdom
Phone: +44-20-7250-1122
Fax: +44-20-7542-4064
www.reuters.com

Regal Entertainment Group
7132 Regal Lane
Knoxville, TN 37918
Phone: (865) 922-1123
Fax: (865) 922-3188
www.regalcinemas.com

Sirius Satellite Radio Inc.
1221 Avenue of the Americas
36th Floor
New York, NY 10020
Phone: (212) 584-5100
Fax: (212) 584-5200
www.sirius.com

Sony/BMG Music
550 Madison Avenue
New York, NY 10022-3211
Phone: (212) 833-7100
Fax: (212) 833-7416
www.sonybmg.com

Sony Corporation of America
550 Madison Avenue
New York, NY 10022
Phone: (212) 833-6800
Toll Free: (800) 556-3411
Fax: (212) 833-6938
www.sony.com

SourceMedia
One State Street Plaza
27th Floor
New York, NY 10004
Phone: (212) 803.8200
www.sourcemedia.com

Time Warner
1 Time Warner Center
New York, NY 10019
Phone: (212) 484-8000
Fax: (212) 489-6183
www.timewarner.com

USA Network, Inc.
30 Rockefeller Plaza
New York, NY 10112
Phone: (212) 664-4444
Fax: (212) 664-6365
www.usanetwork.com

Viacom Inc.
1515 Broadway
New York, NY 10036
Phone: (212) 258-6000
Fax: (212) 258-6464
www.viacom.com

Vivendi
42 avenue de Friedland
75380 Paris Cedex 08
France
Phone: +33-1-71-71-10-00
Fax: +33-1-71-71-10-01
www.vivendiuniversal.com

The Walt Disney Company
500 S. Buena Vista Street
Burbank, CA 91521-9722
Phone: (818) 560-1000
Fax: (818) 560-1930
disney.go.com

William Morris Agency
1 William Morris Place
Beverly Hills, CA 90212
Phone: (310) 859-4000
Fax: (310) 859-4462
www.wma.com

Visit Vault at **www.vault.com** for insider company profiles, expert advice,
career message boards, expert resume reviews, the Vault Job Board and more.

VAULT CAREER LIBRARY   **197**

Life.
Enhanced.

New Breakthroughs, New Opportunities.

If you're looking for an exciting place to work with a future full of opportunities, consider Bristol-Myers Squibb.

In just over three years, we have introduced several major medicines to treat serious diseases. And we have a robust pipeline of investigational medicines in full development.

Help us fulfill our mission **to extend and enhance human life**. You'll not only help enrich the lives of others, but also have the opportunity for a rewarding career with personal and professional advancement in a high-caliber, team-oriented environment.

Please see our website at
www.bms.com/career
for a complete listing of opportunities

BMS offers opportunities for MBA students and graduates to join Summer and Full-Time Associate Programs in the following areas: Marketing, Finance, Information Management, and Technical Operations.

Undergraduate-level students and other advanced-degree graduates may also pursue internship, co-op and permanent job opportunities in many business divisions and functions across BMS and its family of companies.

Bristol-Myers Squibb

Bristol-Myers Squibb
P.O. Box 4000, Princeton, NJ 08543-4000

Bristol-Myers Squibb is an equal opportunity employer.

© 2007 Bristol-Myers Squibb Company   ZN-K0112 11/07

Pharmaceuticals and Biotech

What's in a Name: Big Pharma, Big Biotech and Biopharma

Small molecules and large companies

Strictly speaking, the term "pharmaceuticals" refers to medicines composed of small, synthetically produced molecules, which are sold by large, fully integrated drug manufacturers. The largest of these players—companies like Pfizer, GlaxoSmithKline and Merck—as well as a handful of others are known as "Big Pharma" because they are huge research, development and manufacturing concerns with subsidiaries around the globe. Indeed, Big Pharma is where most of the industry's sales are generated. During 2006, the industry boasted about $643 billion in global sales, and prescription revenue increased about 8 percent in the United States.

A profitable business

According to the Kaiser Family Foundation, from 1995 to 2002, the pharmaceutical business was the most lucrative industry in America. Pharmaceutical manufacturers didn't fare as well in later years, however. In 2003, the pharmaceutical industry ranked third, and in 2005 it ranked fifth. However, in 2006, the pharmaceutical industry ranked second in the country.

From aspirin to Herceptin: a brief history of the industry

Many of today's big pharmaceutical firms have roots that go back to the late 19th or early 20th century. Not all of these companies started out as drug manufacturers. For instance, Frederich Bayer founded Bayer in Germany in 1863 to make synthetic dyes. In the 1920s and 1930s, scientists discovered miracle drugs such as insulin and penicillin, and pharmaceutical companies began to market researchers' life-saving inventions. During the 1950s and 1960s, companies started to mass produce and market new drugs such as blood-pressure medications, birth control pills and Valium. Pharmaceutical companies researched and developed new cancer treatments, including chemotherapy, in the 1970s. The modern biotech business was born when Herbert Boyer and Robert Swanson founded Genentech, which would eventually make breast cancer biologic Herceptin. In the 1980s, drug companies faced new environmental and safety regulations and mounting economic pressures. For Big Pharma, the 1990s was a time of turmoil. There were lots of mergers and acquisitions in the industry during that decade, and pharmaceutical companies also began to use contract research organizations for more of their R&D efforts.

Big Pharma

In 2006, large pharmaceutical companies launched several high-profile products including HVP vaccine Gardasil, oral diabetes drug Januvia, and cancer treatment Sutent.

Big Pharma is responsible for all those television commercials urging us to contact our doctors if we suspect we suffer from restless leg syndrome or social anxiety disorder. Yet despite life-saving, cancer-fighting drugs and significant corporate philanthropy, Big Pharma's recent product recalls and concerns over drug safety have made it the industry many people love to hate. In 2007, diabetes medication Avandia made the headlines after researchers found it increased patients' risk of heart attack.

Before we help you chart a career in the industry, we should point out that both the scope of players and the types of products the industry produces are moving targets. This is because the pharmaceutical and biotech industries are gradually integrating into one industry.

Visit Vault at **www.vault.com** for insider company profiles, expert advice, career message boards, expert resume reviews, the Vault Job Board and more.

VAULT CAREER LIBRARY   199

Most of the largest Big Pharma players are either gobbling up small biotechs through outright acquisitions or, alternatively, are entering licensing agreements. For example, in 2006, AstraZeneca acquired small biotech firm Cambridge Antibody Technology Group and Merck purchased GlycoFi and Abmaxis. This trend is likely to continue throughout the rest of this decade, since it's increasingly difficult to find innovative new drugs through traditional science.

In fact, innovation is the industry's biggest current challenge. Companies are using acquisitions and alliances to round out their product pipelines and meet investor expectations. Big drug manufacturers can now claim to research, manufacture and sell both types of drugs: synthetic small molecules (or old chemistry) and injectable large molecules (or biologics).

Organizational structures

Pharmaceutical companies are generally organized around the "blockbuster" model, i.e., they derive most of their sales and profits from a handful of broadly acting drugs. By industry consensus, a "blockbuster" is a drug whose annual revenue reach or exceed $1 billion. An example of a Big Pharma blockbuster is AstraZeneca's cholesterol-lowering Crestor, which had more than $2 billion in sales in 2006 and has been prescribed to more than six million people.

The biotech firms, on the other hand, tend to be organized around smaller franchises, i.e., their products are targeted to small patient populations with rare genetic diseases. Their biologics are sold by specialty sales representatives, who often have a relatively high degree of scientific knowledge. Because of this focus, biotech products are often referred to as specialty pharmaceuticals. To complicate matters, some biologics reach blockbuster status with respect to their revenues, since they are usually much more expensive than synthetics. Considering that some biologics cost $10,000 per patient per year, you would need a mere 100,000 patients to reach $1 billion in revenues.

Introducing "biopharma"

The dividing line between the pharma and biotech industries will continue to blur. That leaves us with the problem of how to refer to the emerging industry. We'll be using the term "biopharma" to include both types of products.

One final comment about the industry's products: Both synthetic and biologic drugs are directed toward the treatment of disease. The industry refers to this broad category as "therapeutics," since these drugs have a therapeutic effect on the disease condition. But the biopharma industry also has another category of products focused on helping medical scientists more accurately determine (or diagnose) a disease condition from a patient presenting multiple, often difficult-to-interpret symptoms. These products are called "diagnostics" and may come from biologic sources. Often, diagnostic agents (they are NOT called drugs) are used in conjunction with a medical device or instrument. A good example is the diagnostic imaging agent technetium 99m, which helps MRI machines create clearer cross-sections of the human body.

The Global Pharmaceutical Industry

Three major market segments dominate the global industry. North America is the largest and comprises more than 47 percent of the total market, Europe is second with some 30 percent. Japan comes in third at about 9 percent in 2006 sales. Although these combined markets account for nearly 87 percent of global sales, the remaining emerging market segments—other Asian countries, Africa, Australia and Latin America—are growing rapidly. According to IMS Health, Inc., a health care research and information company, in 2006 sales in Asia, Africa and Australia were $52 billion, a 9.8 percent increase from 2005. Global pharmaceutical sales in Latin America in 2006 were $27.5 billion, a 12.9 percent increase from the previous year.

Although a handful of super-large companies rake in most of the pharmaceutical industry's revenue, the global industry is actually highly fragmented. Over 2,000 pharmaceutical and biotech companies exist worldwide. In the top tier are the large, multinational companies that dominate the market, or Big Pharma. In the middle tier are the specialty companies. Many large companies have tended to absorb second-tier companies before they can grow enough to pose a competitive threat. That trend has a contracting effect on the number of firms. The opposite happens on the third and lowest tier, which is composed of an ever-increasing group of startups mostly focused on discovery research.

According to IMS Health, Inc., as recently as 1999, the global pharmaceutical market was valued at $334 billion. By 2006, total global sales had nearly doubled to $643 billion, or more than half a trillion dollars! (IMS derived this figure from retail sales in major global markets.) This astonishing growth reflects the increasing role of pharmaceuticals as a first-line treatment option for many disease conditions in the developed world. The term "first-line" means that physicians opt to prescribe a pharmaceutical first in lieu of a more invasive procedure, such as surgery. In some cancers, physicians now have the option of recommending a tumor-shrinking drug, for example, before surgery to minimize the level of invasiveness to the body.

In the U.S.

The U.S. pharmaceutical industry is comprised of approximately 100 companies, according to the Pharmaceutical Research and Manufacturers of America (PhRMA), a leading industry trade and lobbying organization, with the top-10 companies referred to as Big Pharma. According to the Biotechnology Industry Organization (BIO), there were also 1,415 biotech companies in the United States at the end of 2005.

The U.S. has not only the largest pharmaceutical market in the world but also the only one without government price controls. This is a consequence of the privately owned system prevalent in the U.S. and a strong industry lobby, which has resisted government incursions into its market-based pricing. On the other hand, developed economies with universal health care access (European Union, U.K., Japan) exert stringent controls on the prices companies can charge. A big consequence is that, with thin profit margins, the incentive for innovation is curbed, and former leaders, especially in the EU (German and French companies, in particular) lost the lead in innovation in the 1990s. Standard & Poor's expects the U.S. to continue to be the largest of the top-10 pharmaceutical markets for the foreseeable future, as well as the fastest growing.

Although pharmaceutical companies are scattered throughout the continental United States, the industry is geographically concentrated in the Mid-Atlantic states (New York, New Jersey and Pennsylvania) and on the West Coast in California. A handful of companies can also be found in Massachusetts, Illinois and North Carolina. New Jersey is the heart of the industry and has by far the largest number of companies within a single state. According to the California Healthcare Institute, roughly a quarter of U.S. biotech jobs are in sunny California.

Medicare change boosts drugs sales

Before January 1, 2006, Medicare, the federal health program for the disabled and elderly, didn't pay for outpatient prescription drugs. The Medicare Prescription Drug, Improvement and Modernization Act—known as Part D—gave Medicare beneficiaries the option to enroll in private drug plans. Due to the changes, Medicare became the country's largest public customer of prescription medications in 2006. The change to Medicare helped boost prescription sales in the United States in 2006, but the U.S. Department of Health and Human Services doesn't think it will have a huge impact on drug spending in the future.

Growth in generics

In 1984, the passage of the Drug Price Competition and Patent Term Restoration Act, also called the Hatch-Waxman Act, increased generic drug manufacturers' access to the marketplace. One recent trend in the industry has been a boom in generic drug sales. The biggest generic drug manufacturers, such as Israeli firm Teva and U.S.-based companies Mylan and Barr, have thousands of employees and boasted more than a billion dollars in revenue in 2006. According to the Kaiser Family

Visit Vault at **www.vault.com** for insider company profiles, expert advice, career message boards, expert resume reviews, the Vault Job Board and more.

V∧ULT CAREER LIBRARY **201**

Foundation, in 2006 more than 60 percent of prescriptions dispensed and 20 percent of prescription drug sales were generics, and sales of generic drugs grew 22 percent from 2005 to 2006.

In the United States, managed health care has contributed to the rise in generic drugs. Managed care programs, such as HMOs, often ask their doctors to prescribe generic drugs in place of more expensive brand-name products. Recent changes to the Medicare program in the United States are also likely to lead to an increase in generic drug sales. Under Medicare Part D, through "multitiered pricing," plans can charge patients more for brand-name drugs than generics. In addition, plans can ask doctors to fill out prior authorization forms in order for patients to obtain branded drugs.

The expiration of patents on branded pharmaceuticals has also increased generic drug companies' revenue. As more brand-name drugs go off patents in coming years, generic drug manufacturers' profits are likely to increase. Big pharmaceutical companies that make brand-name drugs usually attempt to extend their drugs' exclusivity and prevent generic competition. They do this in various ways, including litigation. Some big pharmaceutical companies have responded to generic competition by entering into licensing agreements with generic drug manufacturers.

To complicate things further, not all pharmaceutical companies make just generics or only branded drugs. For example, Novartis has a generics division called Sandoz. Due to strong growth and two major acquisitions in 2005, Sandoz is currently the second-largest generics company in the world based on sales after Teva. Some generic companies also sell branded pharmaceuticals. For instance, generic drug manufacturer Barr's subsidiary Duramed Pharmaceuticals develops, makes and sells the firm's proprietary pharmaceuticals, mostly female health care products such as Seasonale and Seasonique oral contraceptives.

Generic drug companies are also branching out into generic versions of biologic drugs. In 2005, Barr Pharmaceuticals announced a deal to license Croatian pharmaceutical company Pliva's version of Neupogen, a white-blood-cell booster made by Amgen. In 2006, Barr and Iceland's Actavis Group battled for Pliva. Barr outbid Actavis, and—in a deal worth $2.5 billion—the company acquired Pliva. The Croatian company is working on a copycat version of Amgen's Epogen, a protein that boosts red blood cells. Barr has also broken ground on a $25 million biotech factory in Croatia.

A rise in CROs

Increasingly, pharmaceutical companies have been outsourcing drug research and development. As a result, contract research organizations (or CROs) have been on the rise. In 2005, a survey by Cambridge Healthtech Advisors found that 45 percent of pharmaceutical companies expected to outsource at least 60 percent of their clinical development work by 2008. Examples of CROs include New Jersey-based Covance and North Carolina's Quintiles Transnational Corporation. In 2006, Covance worked with more than 300 biopharmaceutical companies, ranging from small and startup organizations to the world's largest pharmaceutical companies. Quintiles has helped develop or commercialize the world's 30 best-selling drugs.

MBA Level Sales and Marketing Jobs

Most companies consider sales and marketing to be one function, but with two basic areas of activity. Within the sales function, you can typically find three career tracks: field sales, sales management and managed markets. A fourth track, sales training is closely associated with sales and is distinct from the broader training and development function, which is usually associated with human resource departments. Sales training groups bridge the sales and marketing function: in some companies, they are considered part of marketing support, and hence part of the marketing function. The main point, however, is that all companies that have field sales forces have rigorous sales training departments.

Within the marketing function are two main areas of activity: marketing management and marketing support. The latter is actually composed of several distinct groups, some of which are quite large, but all of which serve essentially the same purpose: to provide support services for marketing managers. Depending on the size of the company, the distinction between the two areas may be either blurred or nonexistent. Typical groups include training and development, advertising and promotion, market analysis, customer call center, e-business, and commercialization and strategic planning.

Fully integrated Big Biotech companies have their own sales and marketing infrastructure and essentially the same job classifications. The main difference from their Big Pharma cousins is that biotech sales reps are specialty reps, who market products to specific and highly defined patient groups. On an experiential level, the big difference is that that very focus prevents the overreaching to the mass market that is now plaguing the marketers of broadly acting agents.

The good thing about the sales and marketing function in the biopharmaceutical industry is that, once you get hired in a particular work area, it is possible, and even encouraged, to gain experience in other areas.

Sales management

Managing a sales force can be one of the most lucrative tracks in the pharmaceutical industry. District sales manager is the first rung on the management ladder, followed by regional sales manager, area sales director and vice president of sales. Each level has increasing responsibility for the sales of a broader geographic area. This is not an entry-level job and usually requires several years of direct sales experience plus evidence of leadership potential. In particular, the first level, district sales manager, is a position people from several areas of activity can move in and out of to get perspective on sales activity.

Like field reps, the responsibilities of a sales manager fall into three distinct categories. Management responsibilities require a sales manager to lead assigned sales district in meeting upper management goals; recruit, hire and train sales reps; ensure efficient coverage of their assigned geographic area; plan and lead meetings to review sales achievements; and manage reps' activities when coordinating educational events (e.g., symposia, speakers bureaus, seminars, etc.). Administrative responsibilities require sales managers to develop business plans and plans of action (POAs), implement market strategies, monitor progress of ongoing sales activity, stay current on industry and company issues that impact the sales force, ensure optimal distribution and consistent stocking of product samples, monitor the district's budget, and control its expenses. Professional development responsibilities require the sales manager to maintain a work environment that maximizes motivation, act as a coach and mentor to the sales reps, and create individualized development plans for each direct report.

Marketing management

Marketing management is the core work of the marketing function and is where strategy is formulated and implemented. Many companies organize marketing management according to therapeutic areas (i.e., oncology drugs, cardiovascular drugs, anti-hypertensives, etc.). Until recent years, marketing had a single upward path to senior positions. With large companies merging into mega-companies (e.g., Pfizer acquired both Warner-Lambert and Pharmacia to become the largest company in the industry), some companies have opted to organize therapeutic areas and their associated products into separate business units, so that marketing management decisions get made with fewer layers of oversight and with closer contact with customer physicians and targeted patient groups.

The main job title in marketing management is product manager and is consistent throughout the industry. From there, titles like product director, group product manager, and vice president of marketing represent higher level marketing management jobs. None of these are entry-level positions at the BS level, although MBAs with previous marketing experience can work in product management groups, as assistant or associate product managers.

Visit Vault at **www.vault.com** for insider company profiles, expert advice, career message boards, expert resume reviews, the Vault Job Board and more.

VAULT CAREER LIBRARY   **203**

A product manager's responsibilities fall into two main categories. Product management responsibilities require the product manager to develop and manage the short-term product strategy and marketing plans for assigned products, oversee development of business plans, specify the positioning of a product among its competitors, monitor those competitor products, acquire both a quantitative and intuitive feel for customer needs, and act as an in-house champion for a product or brand. From an administrative perspective, a product manager must develop budgets, maintain records of expenses, and manage and develop entry-level support staff.

In companies organized as business units, product managers effectively become mini-CEOs and are involved in virtually every aspect of getting a product to market. Most product managers also have substantial communication and negotiation skills, as they are required to interact with professionals from every part of the organization.

Marketing support: market analysis

Market analysis groups are responsible for gathering and analyzing business information in specific geographic areas to understand the economic profile of specific disease conditions in which the company specializes, the associated targeted patient populations—including demographic trends and shifts and progression of disease conditions—and the competitive landscape for the products under development. Jobs have titles like market analyst or regional analyst. Although these jobs are usually not entry-level with only a bachelor's degree, many MBAs target market analyst jobs after graduation and can land them if they have basic science education and can demonstrate evidence of some understanding of the industry's marketing issues.

A market analyst has primarily analytical responsibilities, which are consistent throughout the industry. Typical tasks are to perform local health care marketplace assessments, provide analysis and consulting support to sales and marketing management, develop and implement tools and processes for standard sales performance measurement, identify opportunities and assess threats for the company's products, measure financial ratios (e.g., return on investment or ROI, market share, etc.), and analyze tactical plans based on historic performance.

Business Development in Biotech

On the business development side, research analysts provide the extensive research and analysis needed to determine how and with whom a biotech company should partner with. Analysts generate the assessments that help business development management determine how to meet its goals. Analysts answer such questions as, "Should we expand organically or acquire other companies to grow?" and "Who should we partner with to become more competitive?" Research analysts work with attorneys to assess intellectual property and licensing issues, help develop and enforce agreements, and secure licenses for ongoing operations. Many companies have senior analyst positions with the same responsibilities, but operating more autonomously. Analysts can bring home salaries ranging from $90,000 to $110,000.

It's a significant step up to manager of corporate planning, a job that generally appears at the larger companies. They prepare long-range and strategic plans (usually several years out) and short-range/tactical plans (up to a year out). Other activities include designing and executing financial planning processes, setting targets and planning guidelines. The manager of corporate planning works closely with the CFO to develop the company's financial plans for senior management, industry analysts and investors. They complete competitive analysis and continually assess the prospects for the company. This senior position usually has salaries ranging from $110,000 to $120,000.

At the head of the group is the vice president of business development, a very important position in most biotech companies. The VP of biz dev oversees all efforts to identify, evaluate and pursue potential strategic partners, joint ventures and alliances. This person also directs the assessment of the licensing potential of targets, leads and drug candidates as well as the managing of all collaborations. They maintain partnership agreements and address the inevitable issues that arise in any relationship.

Most companies ask for impressive credentials to reach this level: an MBA, a science degree and nearly a decade of experience that includes knowledge of due diligence, asset valuation, alliance integration, and portfolio management. As an executive, the VP can expect to earn a salary ranging from $160,000 to $190,000 and also receive additional incentive compensation.

Visit Vault at **www.vault.com** for insider company profiles, expert advice, career message boards, expert resume reviews, the Vault Job Board and more.

VAULT CAREER LIBRARY

205

Employer Directory

Bristol-Myers Squibb Co

Bristol-Myers Squibb
P.O. Box 4000
Princeton, NJ 08543-4000
USA
Phone: (609) 252-4000
www.bms.com/career

BMS offers opportunities for MBA students and graduates to join summer and full-time associate programs in the following areas: marketing, finance, information management and technical operations.

Business Schools Firm Recruits From: Columbia, Cornell, Dartmouth, Duke, NYU, U. Michigan, North Carolina, Thunderbird

Abbott
100 Abbott Park Road
Abbott Park, IL 60064
Phone: (847) 937-6100
Fax: (847) 937-1511
www.abbott.com

Advanced Cell Technology, Inc.
1201 Harbor Bay Parkway
Suite 120
Alameda, CA 94502
Phone: (510) 748-4900
Fax: (510) 748-4950
www.advancedcell.com

Allergan, Inc.
2525 Dupont Drive
Irvine, CA 92612
Phone: (714) 246-4500
Fax: (714) 246-4971
www.allergan.com

Amgen, Inc.
One Amgen Center Drive
Thousand Oaks, CA 91320-1799
Phone: (805) 447-1000
Fax: (805) 447-1010
www.amgen.com

Applera Corporation
301 Merritt 7
Norwalk, CT 06856-5435
Phone: (203) 840-2000
Fax: (203) 840-2312
www.applera.com

AstraZeneca PLC
15 Stanhope Gate
London, W1K 1LN
United Kingdom
Phone: +44-20-7304-5000
Fax: +44-20-7304-5183
www.astrazeneca.com

Baxter International Laboratory
1 Baxter Parkway
Deerfield, IL 60015-4625
Phone: (847) 948-2000
Fax: (847) 948-2016
www.baxter.com

Bayer AG
Bayerwerk, Gebäude W11, Kaiser-Wilhelm-Allee
51368 Leverkusen
Germany
Phone: +49-214-30-1
Fax: +49-214-30-66328
www.bayer.de

Becton, Dickinson and Company
One Becton Drive
Franklin Lakes, NJ 07147-1880
Phone: (201) 847-6800
www.bd.com

Biogen Idec Inc.
14 Cambridge Center
Cambridge, MA 02142
Phone: (617) 679-2000
Fax: (617) 679-2617
www.biogenidec.com

Celgene Corporation
86 Morris Avenue
Summit, NJ 07901
Phone: (908) 673-9000
www.celgene.com

Cephalon, Inc.
41 Moo0res Road
Frazer, PA 19355
Phone: (610) 344-0200
Fax: (610) 738-6590
www.cephalon.com

Charles River Laboratories International, Inc.
251 Ballardvale Street
Wilmington, MA 01887-1000
Phone: (978) 658-6000
Fax: (978) 658-7132
www.criver.com

Employer Directory, cont

Covance
210 Carnegie Center
Princeton, NJ 08540
Phone: (609) 452-4440
Toll Free: (888) 268-2623
Fax: (609) 452-9375
www.covance.com

CSL Behring L.L.C.
1020 First Avenue
P.O. Box 61501
King of Prussia, PA 19406
Phone: (610) 878-4000
Fax: (610) 878-4009
www.zlbbehring.com

Eli Lilly and Company
Lilly Corporate Center
893 S. Delaware
Indianapolis, IN 46285
Phone: (317) 276-2000
Fax: (317) 277-6579
www.lilly.com

Forest Laboratories
909 3rd Avenue
New York, NY 10022
Phone: (212) 421-7850
Fax: (212) 750-9152
www.frx.com

Genentech, Inc.
1 DNA Way
South San Francisco, CA 94080
Phone: (650) 225-1000
Fax: (650) 225-6000
www.gene.com

Genzyme Corporation
500 Kendall Street
Cambridge, MA 02142
Phone: (617) 252-7570
Fax: (617) 252-7600
www.genzyme.com

Gilead Sciences, Inc.
333 Lakeside Drive
Foster City, CA 94404
Phone: (650) 574-3000
Toll Free: (800) 445-3235
Fax: (650) 578-9264
www.gilead.com

GlaxoSmithKline
980 Great West Road, Brentford
London, TW8 9GS
United Kingdom
Phone: +44-20-8047-5000
Fax: +44-20-8047-7807
www.gsk.com

Hospira, Inc.
275 N. Field Drive
Lake Forest, IL 60045
Phone: (224) 212-2000
Toll Free: (877) 946-7747
Fax: (224) 212-3350
www.hospira.com

**ImClone Systems
Incorporated**
180 Varick Street
New York, NY 10014
Phone: (212) 645-1405
Fax: (212) 645-2054
www.imclone.com

ImmunoGen, Inc.
128 Sidney Street
Cambridge, MA 02139
Phone: (617) 995-2500
Fax: (617) 995-2510
www.immunogen.com

Incyte Corporation
Experimental Station
Route 141 & Henry Clay Road
Building E336
Wilmington, DE 19880
Phone: (302) 498-6700
Fax: (302) 425-2750
www.incyte.com

Invitrogen Corporation
1600 Faraday Avenue
Carlsbad, CA 92008
Phone: (760) 603-7200
Fax: (760) 602-6500
www.invitrogen.com

Johnson & Johnson Inc.
1 Johnson & Johnson Plaza
New Brunswick, NJ 08933
Phone: (732) 524-0400
Fax: (732) 524-3300
www.jnj.com

**Laboratory Corporation of
America Holdings**
358 S. Main Street
Burlington, NC 27215
Phone: (336) 229-1127
Fax: (336) 436-1205
www.labcorp.com

McKesson Corporation
1 Post Street
San Francisco, CA 94104
Phone: (415) 983-8300
Fax: (415) 983-7160
www.mckesson.com

Merck & Co., Inc.
One Merck Drive
Whitehouse Station, NJ 08889
Phone: (908) 423-1000
www.merck.com

**Millennium Pharmaceuticals,
Inc.**
40 Landsdowne Street
Cambridge, MA 02139
Phone: (617) 679-7000
Toll Free: (800) 390-5663
Fax: (617) 374-7788
www.mlnm.com

Visit Vault at **www.vault.com** for insider company profiles, expert advice,
career message boards, expert resume reviews, the Vault Job Board and more.

V▲ULT CAREER LIBRARY   207

Employer Directory, cont.

Monsanto Company
800 N. Lindbergh Boulevard
St. Louis, MO 63137
Phone: (314) 694-1000
Fax: (314) 694-8394
www.monsanto.com

Novartis AG
Lichtstrasse 35
CH-4056 Basel
Switzerland
Phone: +41-61-324-1111
Fax: +41-61-324-8001
www.novartis.com

Pfizer Inc.
235 E. 42nd Street
New York, NY 10017
Phone: (212) 573-2323
Fax: (212) 573-7851
www.pfizer.com

Promega Corporation
2800 Woods Hollow Road
Madison, WI 53711-5300
Phone: (608) 274-4330
Toll Free: (800) 356-9526
Fax: (608) 277-2601
www.promega.com

Roche Holding Ltd
Grenzacherstrasse 124
CH-4070 Basel
Switzerland
Phone: +41-61-688-1111
Fax: +41-61-691-9391
www.roche.com

Sanofi-Aventis
174 Avenue de France
Paris 75013
France
Phone: +33-1-53-77-40-00
Fax: +33-1-53-77-42-96
www.sanofi-aventis.com

Schering-Plough Corporation
2000 Galloping Hill Road
Kenilworth, NJ 07033
Phone: (908) 298-4000
Fax: (908) 298-7653
www.sch-plough.com

Siemens Medical Solutions
Henkestraße 127
91052 Erlangen
Germany
Phone: +49-91-31-84-0
Fax: +49-91-31-84-29-24
www.medical.siemens.com

Teva Pharmaceutical Industries Limited
5 Basel Street
Petach Tikva, 49131
Israel
Phone: +972-3-926-7267
Fax: +972-3-923-4050
www.tevapharm.com

Wyeth Pharmaceuticals
500 Arcola Road
Collegeville, PA 19426-3982
Phone: (610) 902-1200
www.wyeth.com

Private Wealth Management

What do Private Wealth Managers Do?

The private wealth management industry integrates the varied and complex business of managing wealth by accounting for income needs, taxes, estate preservation and asset protection for the wealthy. Typically, private wealth management is a smaller division of a much larger investment firm or bank. The private wealth manager leverages the expertise of the various departments inside the firm (such as the trust department) to present clients with solutions to wealth management issues. Though not required to be expert in one particular area of wealth management, private wealth managers must know enough about each area to expertly represent their clients' best interests and, where appropriate, offer advice.

Creating income

It is the first job of private wealth managers to help create, from among various investment strategies, income or growth sufficient for the everyday needs of their clients. In addition, they must provide enough excess growth to account for inflation in order that their client's purchasing power does become eroded over time. Let's face it, $1 doesn't buy as much as it used to for Jed and Granny. In addition, hopefully the wealth manager will continue to grow the clients' assets so that they become richer.

Because the rich wealthy often need to live solely off of their investments, today's private wealth managers must use a variety of investment techniques to help clients create enough income every year to live off of. Sounds easy enough right? Not really. When you consider that someone who invests $1 million in a conservative corporate bond returning 5 percent creates a modest $50,000 a year in income, it becomes obvious that having a million dollars or so just isn't as a big a deal as it used to be. Sure $50,000 is a lot of money for doing nothing. But living on champagne and caviar is out of the question. With average wages in the U.S. at a little over $35,000 per year as of 2004, according to the Social Security Administration, the average typical family with two income-earners can earn more than someone with $1 million in the bank who lives off of his or her investments. Indeed, because of inflation, the portfolio with a $1 million must return in excess of 7.5 percent just to keep up with the two-worker household that can possibly expect to get raises every year. With rates of return in the stock market sometimes as high 20 percent or more, 7.5 percent may not seem a very high return, but when you consider that the S&P 500 over the last six years has returned less than 1 percent annually, you'll see that the job of private wealth managers in creating income for their clients isn't always easy.

Paying taxes

Another problem wealthy clients often encounter is taxes. None of us like paying taxes. For most of us, however, we would willingly pay additional taxes if it meant that we were making additional income. For the wealthy, it isn't quite as simple. When managing large pools of assets, small differences in tax rates can translate into big changes in after-tax returns. Various types of investments used by the wealthy are treated and taxed differently by the IRS. For example, income derived from the interest rates of bonds is taxed differently than long-term capital gains derived from selling stock. It is the private wealth manager's job to balance assorted types of investments to create the most tax efficient combination for the client.

Asset protection

In today's society, people with money are sometimes targeted with lawsuits just because they happen to have money. So, an increasingly popular area of practice for private wealth managers is called "asset protection," which helps the wealthy guard against losing their money in civil lawsuits. There are several techniques used to protect assets, including U.S. trusts laws and foreign, offshore banks. Advocates of asset protection methods contend that making their clients impervious to lawsuits doesn't just protect assets, but also prevents lawsuits from even happening.

Visit Vault at **www.vault.com** for insider company profiles, expert advice, career message boards, expert resume reviews, the Vault Job Board and more.

VAULT CAREER LIBRARY   209

Career Paths

The primary role in private wealth management is the private banker, also called the investment or financial advisor. This is the person who evaluates a client's financial position, recommends solid investments, helps with the fiduciary aspects of their client's accounts (regularly consulting tax and accounting experts within the firm), and even sets up a family office for wealthier clients to pay bills, staff and make sure family members are appropriately taken care of, or "given their allowances" as one banker put it.

Analysts

The career track for the private banker is fairly cut and dry at the major corporate banks and Wall Street brokerage firms. Undergrads coming in are called analysts, just as they are in the sales and trading division and the investment banking arm and everywhere else within the corporation. They're the ones who do all the researching, number crunching, report writing, and yes, coffee fetching on occasion, for the higher ups who are actually working for the clients.

Being an analyst at a private bank is very much akin to similar roles in trading and investment banking. If a private banker needs an analysis done on a client's tax status, you'll tap the appropriate expertise within the firm to draw up the report. If a client is looking for a hedge fund investment with a specific strategy, you'll provide the banker or relationship manager with the best options. And while the banker can be called at any time to address a client's needs, you'll be called by the banker to assist and probably will keep longer hours on top of that as well.

The rewards can be fairly standard for the financial industry, with starting salaries ranging around $45,000 to $60,000 annually. Bonuses can be lighter than those given to investment bankers, however, anywhere from the $15,000 to $30,000 range. At smaller firms, that bonus range can vary from analyst to analyst, depending on how useful they were in addressing client needs. The same goes for larger firms, of course, but the range is smaller, especially if there's an entire analyst class to consider.

Associates

The next rank up is associate, or just plain old private banker at the smaller firms. These are the guys who work with the clients and attract new business, the real face of the private bank for most clients. This is considered a very entrepreneurial job, in that you'll be expected to not only serve clients, but attract new clients as well. At many firms, you'll also be expected to attempt to sell your clients on the company's proprietary financial products, though the practice is starting to be curtailed at some firms.

Associates will work closely with clients to create an overall financial strategy that encompasses not only investment, but also income management, budget, real estate holdings, taxes, small business partnerships, estate planning and even paying the day-to-day bills of the household, all depending on the level of service the client wants (and the fees he or she is willing to pay, but at this level, fees are a secondary consideration to impeccable service and peace of mind).

Associate pay generally mirrors other Wall Street positions, with a newly minted associate making about $75,000 to $85,000 per year. Bonuses can vary, however, depending on how the firm structures compensation. Some private bankers receive bonuses solely on selling the client new services and the company's investment products, getting a percentage of the business the private bank brings in from that client. Others have more complex metrics, measuring performance against the client's stated goals. For example, some private wealth management clients may not want anything more complex than safe fixed-income investments that generate income with little or no risk, with a stated goal of five percent yield each year. If the private banker reached that goal, he would get a larger bonus than he would have if the investment only yielded 4.85 percent. Or if the banker managed to get 5.35 percent—without altering the client's risk profile or otherwise deviating from the state goals—the bonus would be higher.

Some private wealth managements eschew commission bonuses altogether, preferring to grant bonuses that do not give clients the appearance that their banker is simply interested in selling them on products. These firms' bonus metrics are primarily based on fulfilling the clients' goals—a few firms even ask clients to review their bankers each year. Of course, firms will always appreciate it when associates convince their clients to use the private bank's estate planning services instead of someone else's, and in that sense, selling a non-investment service is seen as very bonus-worthy.

Likewise, associates are expected to drum up new business, and bonuses can come if you manage to gain new clients. Sometimes this will come from word-of-mouth, as current clients recommend the associate to their high-net-worth peers. It also comes from good old-fashioned networking, which means an investment on the associate's part in both time and, at times, money—especially when belonging to the right club or attending the right charitable event can mean a room full of potential clients. Some private banking firms organize cultural events or sports outings for their clients as well, with the hopes that they'll bring well-moneyed colleagues or friends for associates to network with.

Vice presidents

In time, salaries and bonus money for motivated, skilled and trusted associates can top $500,000, usually anywhere from five to eight years, depending on the firm and opportunities that have presented themselves, and up to $1 million within 10 to 13 years of private banking. At that level, however, an associate has often already been promoted to the level of vice president. As such, he or she can be placed in a position overseeing a number of associates, or even a regional office. Alternatively, an associate that has specialized in spotting unique investment opportunities or has helped come up with new products can branch off from the client business and into an investment specialty. They may end up as market strategist or in-house portfolio consultants, gaining a smaller piece of individual clients' business, but making up for it by consulting with larger numbers of clients.

Managing directors

Finally, after years of service-and income that can top $2 million or more for the best performing vice presidents—a successful, entrepreneurial, client-driven VP can be named a managing director. In these positions, an MD can expect to be in charge of associates in a major branch office, or even in the headquarters city. They can be given the highest-net-worth clients, or the problem clients whose money is just too valuable for the firm to lose. In specialty positions, they may end up as the private bank's chief investment officer, chief fiduciary officer or general counsel. There are generally only a handful of MDs within any private wealth management firm, and they are often on the executive committees of the firm. At this level, salaries enter a realm in which the MD may want to find a private banker of his own—and are generally high enough that firms don't discuss them, though still nowhere near the level where they have to be reported to the Securities and Exchange Commission!

Job Responsibilities

Do wealth managers need to be good at Sales? Marketing? Investing? Schmoozing?

The answer to all of these questions is yes. A private wealth manager must be good at many things—he or she must be as skilled at developing relationships as investing.

Sales

Among the responsibilities of a private wealth manager are sales and prospecting for sales. If your heart fell a little when you read that you'd have to, gasp, gulp … s … s … sell, then hold on for just a minute. The first stop on the road to success for

Visit Vault at **www.vault.com** for insider company profiles, expert advice, career message boards, expert resume reviews, the Vault Job Board and more.

VAULT CAREER LIBRARY 211

any private wealth manager (or any other salesperson or manager for that matter) is to improve his or her listening skills. A good private wealth manager will be able to draw out a client's needs by asking the right questions then actively listening to the answers for cues and clues as to what the client might be thinking.

Money can be a very uncomfortable subject for people. Studies have shown that many people are more uncomfortable talking about money then they are about being naked in front of a strange doctor. Like a doctor, a private wealth manager's bedside manner, so to speak, will go a long way to identifying a client's needs.

When you improve your listening skills, you will find that you become a true professional salesperson. Such a professional salesperson is not someone who can simply talk another person into anything. A professional salesperson, rather, is an expert at listening to what clients need and filling that need by identifying a product or service appropriate for them. This means that often you are not selling anyone anything at all. Rather, you are listening to clients, building relationships with them, and understanding what their goals are. That's what sales is really all about. If you let it, it can be one of the best parts of your job.

Marketing

Marketing is the art of telling people who you are—whether you're a product or service—and why people should want to do business with you. This last part (why people should want to do business with you) is the most important aspect of promoting your business. And since private wealth management is a highly regulated industry, there are some notable challenges to marketing.

When it comes to marketing itself, the private wealth management industry has more restrictions on what it can lawfully claim than some other industries. For example, if you had owned an oil company and sold gasoline, like Jed Clampett, you could say that your gasoline made cars more fun to drive to promote your particular brand of gasoline. In the private wealth management business, though, it's a little more difficult to make claims of being "the best," or being "better than" something or someone else. Generally, the marketing is pretty standard, with some notable exceptions. Private wealth management companies might say they offer some sort of superior service quality or a degree of caring that may be missing from a competing firm. For instance, Raymond James and Associates offers BIO (by invitation only) visits to clients meeting certain liquid net-worth thresholds. These potential clients are flown down to Raymond James corporate headquarters and given a tour of the firm's four-acre campus in St. Petersburg, Florida. Clients then can meet with various departments of the firm, including the senior management, right up to the CEO.

What some firms lack in old-fashioned marketing, they allow (and expect) you to make up. Some wealth managers may use newsletters to promote themselves, others network in their community. How you market yourself will be a decision to make after thoroughly evaluating what strengths you can bring to your clients.

Many managers spend time on the golf course to meet prospective clients. But golfing isn't a marketing strategy that can replace the hard work of meeting or calling prospects. It might be one component of a networking plan, which may also include volunteering on community boards, doing charity work and getting involved in other activities that allow a wealth manager to have more contact with wealthy individuals.

Investing

Private management firms provide their wealth managers with professionals to help them handle their clients' day-to-day investment decisions. This does not mean that wealth managers won't have a lot of input about those decisions or that they could not make those types of decisions themselves given the time. But think for a moment about how their time should be best spent? Talking to clients? Prospecting for new clients? Meeting new contacts? Learning about new estate planning techniques? Or keeping a close eye on the market?

Certainly they need to develop well-informed opinions about investing and various investment strategies. And the most important function of a wealth manager in the investment process will be explaining the implications of the various strategies presented, thereby helping his or her clients select the most appropriate strategy.

Uppers and Downers

Like any job, there are pros and cons to a career in private wealth management. The vast majority of private bankers are quite content in their jobs—but then again, they wouldn't be there if they weren't. Here are some uppers and downers that private bankers experience every day.

Uppers

• **Clients.** You'll be helping people realize their hopes and dreams, manage the results of a lifetime of hard work and plan for their futures. They're generally interesting people with fascinating life experiences, and you may end up becoming very close to them.

• **Entrepreneurship.** Once you're an associate or higher, you'll be ultimately responsible for your clients' performance, and you'll have the opportunity to build your own client base. You'll have quite a bit of input into how much money you make, based on your drive and your investment savvy.

• **On-the-job knowledge.** It's not just stocks and bonds. While you'll have backing from experts or consultants made available to you by your firm, you'll end up learning quite a bit about a variety of investments and financial planning tools. From real estate to hedge funds, from prenups to estate planning, you'll only get smarter as time goes on.

• **Philanthropy.** Many private bankers find particular joy from helping their clients give their money away. While it's not a high-commission activity by any stretch, it's certainly good for the soul. And as one banker pointed out, it can lead to more business contacts and potential clients!

• **Lifestyle.** For the most part, you can actually have a life outside of work if you manage your time and client accounts properly. You won't have many eight-hour days, but you can reasonably expect to have weekends free, and you'll be able to take vacations like the rest of humanity.

• **Money.** While you'll never receive multimillion-dollar checks for leading a merger deal, you'll certainly be making plenty of money, enough to easily become a high-net-worth individual in your own right.

Downers

• **Clients.** While the majority of your clients will fall into the "uppers" category, a few will most certainly drive you nuts. They'll ignore your advice, do stupid things with their money, and then blame you for it. A few will call constantly with each tick of the market, and many will need hand-holding or supremely well-thought-out arguments for each move you think they should make. Even your best clients will make you want to pull your hair out every now and again.

• **Conservatism.** Many of your clients will be risk adverse, and investments that could make them (and you) a pretty penny could be summarily rejected despite your best arguments.

• **Income fluctuations**. Feeding into the above, you may end up having a run of low bonuses or commissions due to uncertainty in the markets or a conservative investing trend. Just as your clients can fall prey to the vagaries of the market, your own income will as well.

• **Always on.** While the majority of your clients will leave you alone on weekends, holidays and vacations, you'll constantly have to be ready to spring into action at a moment's notice. Don't think of even heading to the grocery store without your

Visit Vault at **www.vault.com** for insider company profiles, expert advice, career message boards, expert resume reviews, the Vault Job Board and more.

VAULT CAREER LIBRARY **213**

BlackBerry on, and if you're going on vacation, a laptop with a reliable wireless connection is essential. An understanding domestic partner is also important should a client call in the middle of a honeymoon or family holiday.

- **Limited geographic potential**. You're going to have to live where high-net-worth individuals live, which means a major U.S. or world city, with all the expense and headaches that comes along with it. You can certainly live in the suburbs, but if you're hankering for a small town lifestyle, you won't get it—at least not without a major commute.

A Day in the life: Analyst at a Wall Street Firm

Analyst with a large Wall Street firm's private wealth management arm

8:00 a.m.: I like to get in early, so if I'm not stuck on the subway, I'm already in the office. There's always something that someone laid on me the night before, so I want to check it over or, more likely, finish it up.

8:30 a.m.: Our section of the building is usually completely up and running by 8:30 a.m. I'm usually fielding e-mails from an associate or vice president on the work I've been doing for them. Recently, I've become the supposed fixed-income expert, so I've been pulling up historicals on the performance of short- and long-term corporates, investment (grade) and junk (grade), whenever the Treasury yield curve has inverted, like it's done a few times already this year.

9:00 a.m.: We all listen in to the conference call on the morning's trades. I like hearing what the experts think and comparing it to what I think is going to happen. Most of the time, I agree with the experts. When I don't, it's about 50-50, me winning half the time. Nobody says it's an exact science, and even the top guys on Wall Street can be wrong.

9:30 a.m.: This is generally a pretty big deadline on any given day for the research we do because the associates will want the research for their calls and meetings later in the day, once the market starts. Usually it's a rush to get things done. You can tell who's done the all-nighters and who hasn't.

10:00 a.m.: I settle in and get some more research done. One associate wants some portfolio projections, another wants some comparisons of different hedge funds, and somebody else is still hoping for that inverted yield curve study.

11:05 a.m.: One of the associates e-mails me with a question about a piece of research I did a few days ago. He's on a call with a client, but it appears he's glossed things over at the moment, but now I have to rush to find the answer. Thank God, it turns out he missed a footnote in what I wrote, and it's nothing I did. I e-mail him back, and he's kind enough to acknowledge that he missed it. Not all of them are that nice.

12:30 p.m.: Lunch. The analysts usually head out together, more or less, unless someone's crunching on something. Occasionally, an associate or VP who liked something we did will take us out. That's always nice, because it's a pretty good meal, but it also means that they'll probably hit you with something even more difficult to do down the road. Or before dessert.

1:30 p.m.: Back from lunch. More research.

2:00 p.m.: Class time. The firm wants us to learn as much as possible about a variety of investments, which makes sense to me, since we're going to be advising clients eventually on everything from hedge funds to real estate, to Asian equities. Today it's the latest thinking in estate planning, and how to best use the new tax laws to preserve as much as possible. The resident associate expert starts in, and then one of the analysts gives a PowerPoint talk, after which he's grilled by everyone from the analysts to the VPs and even an MD or two. We're usually doing one of these once every quarter or so, and it's a month of hell beforehand. You have to know your topic cold and be ready for anything.

3:30 p.m.: An associate for whom I did some last-minute work agreed to let me sit in on the client meeting—my little reward. I'm the dutiful assistant, getting coffee for everyone, taking notes. The associate let's me explain the work I did—I didn't expect that—and the client says "nice job" when I'm done. The client is old-school Wall Street, so I'm pretty sure he knows what that can mean to an analyst. Even when I try to be cynical, it's still nice to hear.

4:30 p.m.: The closing bell. I stop what I'm doing to see how the day went and if it's going to affect anything that I'm working on. Some of the newer analysts have to drop everything to do some technical analysis work on the day's trading in just about everything—stocks, bonds, commodities, you name it. The rest of us use it as a good excuse to grab coffee, usually with a shopping list in hand for the associates and VPs. Then, it's back to work.

6:30 p.m.: Decision time. If I'm ahead of the game and there's nothing pressing, I usually try to take off around this time. If I'm crunching on something, I'll order dinner and keep plugging away. I really like to get out most nights, even if it means I procrastinate—which usually means that when I do stay, I'm there until midnight or later.

Visit Vault at **www.vault.com** for insider company profiles, expert advice, career message boards, expert resume reviews, the Vault Job Board and more.

VAULT CAREER LIBRARY   215

Employer Directory

Bank of America, The Private Bank
One Federal Street
Boston, MA 02110
Phone: (617) 346-4477
Fax: (617) 346-4520
www.bankofamerica.com

The Bank of New York, The Private Bank
1 Wall Street
New York, NY 10286
Phone: (212) 495-1784
Fax: (212) 809-9528
E-mail: info@bankofny.com
www.bankofny.com

Barclays Private Bank
200 Park Avenue
New York, NY 10166
Phone: (212) 412-4000
E-mail: info@barclays.com
www.barclays.com

Bear Stearns Private Client Services
383 Madison Avenue
New York, NY 10179
Phone: (212) 272-2000
Fax: (212) 272-7038
www.bearstearns.com

Brown Brothers Harriman Private Wealth Management
140 Broadway
New York, NY 10005-1101
Phone: (212) 483-1818
Fax: (212) 493-7287
www.bbh.com

Citigroup Private Bank
399 Park Avenue
New York, NY 10043
Phone: (212) 559-1000
Fax: (212) 793-3946
www.citigroup.com

Commerce Bank Private Banking
Commerce Atrium
1701 Route 70 East
Cherry Hill, NJ 08034-5400
Phone: (856) 751-9000
Fax: (856) 751-9260
www.commerceonline.com

Credit Suisse Private Banking
11 Madison Avenue
New York, NY 10010
Phone: (212) 325-2000
www.credit-suisse.com

Deutsche Bank Private Wealth Management
Deutsche Bank AG
Taunusanlage 12
60325 Frankfurt am Main
Germany
Phone: +49-69-910-00
Fax: +49-69-910-34-225
E-mail: Deutsche.bank@db.com
www.db.com

Fifth Third Asset Management
Fifth Third Bancorp
Fifth Third Center
Cincinnati, OH 45263
Phone: (513) 534-5300
Fax: (513) 579-6246
www.53.com

Friedman Billings Ramsey Investment Management
1001 Nineteenth Street
North Arlington, VA 22209
Phone: (703) 312-9500
Fax: (703) 312-9501
www.fbr.com

Goldman Sachs Private Wealth Management
85 Broad Street
New York, NY 10004
Phone: (212) 902-1000
Fax: (212) 902-3000
www.gs.com

HSBC Private Bank
World Headquarters
8 Canada Square
London, E14 5HQ
United Kingdom
Phone: +44-020-7991-8888
Fax: +44-020-7992-4880

HSBC Bank USA
452 Fifth Avenue
New York, NY 10018
Phone: (212) 525-5000
www.us.hsbc.com

Jefferies Private Client Services
520 Madison Avenue
12th Floor
New York, NY 10022
Phone: (212) 284-2300
Fax: (212) 284-2111
www.jefferies.com

JPMorgan Private Bank
270 Park Avenue
New York, NY 10017
Phone: (212) 270-6000
Fax: (212) 270-1648
www.jpmorganchase.com

Lazard Private Client Group
30 Rockefeller Plaza
New York, NY 10020
Phone: (212) 632-6000
www.lazardnet.com

Legg Mason Wealth Management
100 Light Street
Baltimore, MD 21202-1099
Phone: (877) 534-4627
www.leggmason.com

Lehman Private Investment Management
745 Seventh Avenue
30th Floor
New York, NY 10019
Phone: (212) 526-7000
Fax: (212) 526-8766
www.lehman.com

Employer Directory, cont.

Lydian Wealth Management
2600 Tower Oaks Boulevard, Suite 300
Rockville, MD 20852
Phone: (301) 770-6300
Toll Free: (800) 251-9531
Fax: (301) 770-1408
www.lydianwealth.com

Mellon Private Wealth Management
One Mellon Center
Pittsburgh, PA 15258
Phone: (412) 234-5000
Fax: (412) 234-9495
www.mellon.com

Merrill Lynch Global Private Client
4 World Financial Center
250 Vesey Street
New York, NY 10080
Phone: (212) 449-1000
Fax: (212) 449-9418
www.ml.com

Morgan Keegan Private Client Group
Morgan Keegan Tower
Memphis, TN 38103
Phone: (901) 524-4100
www.morgankeegan.com

Morgan Stanley Private Wealth Management
1585 Broadway
New York, NY 10036
Phone: (212) 761-4000
www.morganstanley.com

Northern Trust Private Banking
50 South La Salle Street
Chicago, IL 60603
Phone: (312) 630-6000
www.ntrs.com

Raymond James Financial Private Client Group
880 Carillon Parkway
St Petersburg, FL 33702
Phone: (727) 567-1000
Fax: (727) 573-8365
www.raymondjames.com

Royal Bank of Canada Global Private Banking
200 Bay Street
Toronto, Ontario
Canada
Phone: (416) 974-5151
Fax: (416) 955-7800
www.rbcprivatebanking.com

Smith Barney
787 Seventh Avenue
New York, NY 10019
Phone: (212) 492-6900
www.smithbarney.com

Thomas Weisel Partners Private Client Services
One Montgomery Tower
One Montgomery Street
San Francisco, CA 94104
Phone: (415) 364-2500
Fax: (415) 364-6295
E-mail: TWPInfo@tweisel.com
www.tweisel.com

UBS Wealth Management
101 Park Avenue
New York, NY 10178
www.ubs.com

U.S. Bank Private Client Group
U.S. Bancorp Center
800 Nicollet Mall
Minneapolis, MN 55402
Phone: (651) 466-3000
www.usbank.com

U.S. Trust Wealth Management
11 West 54th Street
New York, NY 10019
Phone: (212) 852-1000
E-mail: info@ustrust.com
www.ustrust.com

Wachovia Wealth Management
301 South College Street
Suite 4000
One Wachovia Center
Charlotte, NC 28288-0013
Phone: (704) 374-6161
www.wachovia.com/wealth

Wells Fargo Private Client Services/Private Banking
420 Montgomery Street
San Francisco, CA 94104
Phone: (866) 249-3302
www.wellsfargo.com

William Blair Wealth Management
222 West Adams Street
Chicago, IL 60606
Phone: (312) 236-1600
www.wmblair.com

Visit Vault at **www.vault.com** for insider company profiles, expert advice, career message boards, expert resume reviews, the Vault Job Board and more.

VAULT CAREER LIBRARY

217

Real Estate

Industry Overview

A concrete business

Real estate is tangible. It's a piece of land and any building or structures on it, as well as the air above and the ground below. Everyone comes into direct contact with real estate; the places we live, work, vacation, shop and exercise are all assets to be bought, sold and rented. And it's always been an important element of the economy. The real estate industry is usually considered one of the most dynamic sectors in the American economy—people may divest their stocks, but they always need a place to buy groceries and lay their head at night.

Yes, it's for real

The real estate sector is largely dependent on a number of economic factors; small shifts can turn trends significantly. For example, the technology industry boom certainly helped the real estate industry in Silicon Valley in the 1990s. There was more demand for space—both commercial and residential—and as such asset values skyrocketed. The subsequent technology bust had a dramatic effect on some parts of the sector, too. Commercial real estate firms that deal with office and retail development projects found the market glutted with available space, driving prices down. Residential is affected by economic swings as well, in addition to changes in the federal interest rate (which affects mortgage interest rates) and the unemployment rate (which affects both consumer confidence and buying power). In turn, these have effects on mortgage lenders and housing construction companies (such as Lennar, Pulte Homes, Beazer Homes and KB Homes).

Most real estate offices are small and focus on properties in their immediate location. But their brand names come from just a few industry leaders. Realogy, a 2006 spin-off of Cendant, has several big names in its stable, including Sotheby's International, Corcoran Group, ERA, Century 21 and Coldwell Banker. The company claims it was involved in one in four real estate transactions in 2006. Realogy's competition includes RE/MAX and HomeServices of America. Firms that only handle commercial real estate are frequently larger and employ more brokers and salespeople than residential firms; they may also manage properties or administer real estate investment trusts (REITs). Most of the residential companies also deal in commercial sales.

Real estate rollercoaster

In the early part of the decade, the topic of real estate frequently popped up in the news media, as housing prices on both coasts and in urban areas skyrocketed. The reasons for this are numerous: following the market crash of 2000, the Federal Reserve rolled back interest rates from 6.5 percent to 1 percent over a three-year period, and a loosening of lending regulations made getting money to buy a house easier than ever. The influx of cheaper money fueled the boom: housing prices on the coasts shot up 55 to 100 percent, accounting for inflation, in five years. According to an article in *BusinessWeek*, in the first half of 2005, real estate accounted for 50 percent of the growth of the GDP; in less overheated markets it usually accounts for a tenth of that amount.

Since then, the sales market fell hard—and fast. Newly constructed properties, which had been built up rather optimistically over those five years, began to be offered at a discount to fill up empty units. By June 2006 the National Association of Realtors said the annual rate of residential sales was down nearly 9 percent compared to a year before. One year later, that figure was down another 10 percent to just under six million, the lowest seasonally-adjusted total in four years. The number of homes listed for sale at that point (4.4 million, the largest amount since 1992) was enough to last almost nine months at current sales rates. The situation in Florida was especially bad, compounded by huge property taxes, the hurricanes of 2004 and 2005 and the resultant spiral in insurance costs.

Visit Vault at **www.vault.com** for insider company profiles, expert advice, career message boards, expert resume reviews, the Vault Job Board and more.

VAULT CAREER LIBRARY 219

Even worse, prices plateaued, and then inched down for 10 straight months, dropping a total of 4 percent since October 2005. In a June 2007 article in *The New York Times*, Mark Zandi (chief economist at Moody's Economy.com) indicated that price declines were occurring in over 40 percent of metro areas in the U.S., some by 8 to 12 percent. If the downturn continues for an extended time, the results would be horrendous; bringing to mind the last time housing prices took a large fall: the Great Depression of the 1930s.

How to be real

As of 2006, the real estate business employed over nine million people. Those who work in this sector often enjoy greater flexibility in job responsibilities than in other industries. Drawbacks include low-paying, entry-level positions, competitive co-workers and long hours when starting out. Furthermore, once established in an area, relocation can be detrimental to your career—success in a new place requires a solid base of geographically-specific knowledge (i.e., the quality of local schools, business zoning issues, community concerns, etc.).

In order to sell real estate services, you must be a licensed professional in the state where you do business. To become a realtor, all states require a person to pass a written exam focused on real estate law and transactions and be affiliated with a broker. Most states require you to be at least 18 years old and a high school graduate, and to have completed a minimum number of classroom hours. Some states waive the classroom requirements for active attorneys or offer correspondence course credit options in lieu of the classroom hour requirement. The license fee varies, but runs around $100 for the exam and $400 for the classes. In addition, realtors must pay for their own errors and omissions insurance (around $500 a year) and annual dues to Realsource, an organization that manages the MLS (multiple listing service) that contains the details of all properties for sale in a given market.

Look both ways

The BLS predicts that over the next 10 years the demand for brokers and sales agents will increase between 9 and 17 percent. A growing population will also result in a steadily increasing demand for housing. There is relatively high turnover in the industry, which results in a fairly constant demand for new entrants. Impediments to growth include the increased use of the Internet, which allows people to search for properties that suit their criteria without consulting a professional (much like how the regular consumer has bypassed travel agents in the tourism industry). The industry is very sensitive to fluctuations in interest rates and to the overall health of the economy, and demand for employees can drop precipitously in the face of a sluggish economy or high interest rates.

But this may not be the best time to enter a field that could be, in polite economic terms, experiencing a "correction." Property sellers (reluctant to unload at a loss) and buyers (looking for a deal in the current environment) are finding little common ground, and realtors have time, but little commission, on their hands.

Valuing Real Estate

There are three generally accepted approaches to valuing real estate: the sales approach, the cost approach and the income approach. Professional appraisers will reach a valuation after carefully considering each approach. You should make sure to review all three approaches before any real estate interview.

The sales approach

The sales approach arrives at a value for a property based on recent sales of similar properties. This approach can be used for both residential and commercial properties. There are proprietary databases that track home and commercial building sales, which make it easier for real estate professionals to access market information used in valuing properties. One of the most popular databases is the Multilisting Service (MLS), which is used to track residential properties. The MLS contains useful information about homes, such as the sales history, tax records and property amenities that can be accessed for an annual fee. In the sales approach, appraisers will use databases, such as the MLS, to look for homes with similar characteristics (e.g., location and house specifics), as the subject property. For example, when valuing a four-bedroom, two-bathroom house in the Pacific Heights section of San Francisco, it is logical to value that property based on the most recent sales information for properties in the same area with similar characteristics. Bear in mind that no two properties are alike, so when valuing a property using the sales approach you must adjust for differences between the properties.

The cost approach

In markets where it is difficult to find similar properties, an appraiser can value a property based on the cost approach. This approach focuses on a few steps. First, you must determine the cost of replacing or reconstructing the improvements or building. Next, the age of the improvements must be considered and an appropriate amount of depreciation is subtracted from the value of improvements. Finally, the value of the land must be taken into consideration. The land value is added to the improvements minus the estimated property depreciation. The cost approach is used for truly unique properties like churches, which cannot use either the sales or income approach to arrive at a valuation.

The income approach

The income approach is the most quantitative of the three approaches. The income approach involves the use of net operating income (NOI) in calculating the value of the property. Think of NOI as the reason most investors buy a building. The investment community talks about NOI incessantly, so make sure to understand this concept if you plan on being involved with real estate investing.

There are two forms of the income approach. One form involves isolating NOI for one year, while the other form involves a longer time horizon. Both forms use a capitalization (cap) rate to calculate a value. The cap rate is a market mechanism, so don't worry about what goes in the calculation. Just be concerned with how it is used. In practice the cap rate is generally used in a formula with the NOI to arrive at a property value. For example, suppose you were buying an industrial facility whose net operating income in the following year was projected to be $500,000. If you knew the market cap rate for similar properties, you could arrive an estimated value of the property. Assume the market cap rate for industrial facilities was 10 percent. To arrive at the value of the building, divide NOI by the cap rate. In our example, the value of the building would be:

$$\text{Value} = \frac{\text{NOI}}{\text{Cap Rate}} = \frac{\$500,000}{.10} = \$5,000,000$$

The yield capitalization form uses a longer time horizon. It involves calculating a discounted cash flow to arrive a property value.

$$\text{Value} = \frac{\text{NOI year n}}{(1+\text{discount rate})^n} + \frac{\text{NOI year n}+1}{(1+\text{discount rate})^{n+1}} + \frac{\text{residual value}}{(1+\text{discount rate})^{n+1}}$$

In the example above, the numerator represents the cash flows that the building generates today and in the coming years, which theoretically provides a value for the asset. Note, that there is also a future residual value listed in

Visit Vault at **www.vault.com** for insider company profiles, expert advice, career message boards, expert resume reviews, the Vault Job Board and more.

VAULT CAREER LIBRARY 221

the formula. The discount rate reflects the cost of capital. Your client may provide this cost, or you may have to estimate the discount rate based on similar transactions and knowledge of the market. The discount rate is necessary because it allows you to bring all the future cash flows back to today's dollars or present value (PV). The discount rate factors in the opportunity cost of money or the return that you could expect elsewhere with the cash flows. The exponent "n" in the denominator represents the period or number of years in the future that you would receive that cash flow. The DCF is calculated based on a stated number of years and adds up the PVs. At some point in the future cash flows you have a residual value because it is assumed the property is eventually sold. The residual value is calculated by taking the NOI of the year after the assumed time horizon and then dividing that year's NOI by an assumed cap rate. Some investors use different time periods when calculating the DCF but 10 years is the generally accepted period to value an asset. The DCF is normally used for income-producing property, while a single-family house is typically valued by the sales comparison approach.

Although there are different ways to value real estate, there are a few common variables such as location, the property's condition and market demand that make real estate valuable regardless of the asset type. There is a popular industry saying, "The three most important things in real estate are location, location, location." You simply cannot underestimate the importance of location. While you can restore and upgrade a property as much as you want, there is no substitute for being located close to: transportation, good schools, attractive retail and an aesthetically pleasing area. While location is important, keeping the property in good working order also creates value because it lessens the need to make improvements or contribute capital to the property. In addition, fundamental macroeconomics plays a major role in real estate values. For example, when interest rates offered by lenders are low, people will rush to buy a house to take advantage of the low financing costs. If this new market demand is greater than the market supply, property prices will increase.

The Real Estate MBA

One possible educational route into real estate is to get an MBA at an inttution with a specific real estate program. Some of the best programs, based on *U.S. News & World Report* rankings, are Wharton, University of California-Berkeley's Haas Business School, MIT's Sloan School of Management, University of Wisconsin-Madison and Ohio State University's Fisher School of Business. These schools also have strong real estate clubs that produce annual conferences and other activities.

Job Seeking Advice for Real Estate MBAs

Joseph Pagliari, a clinical assistant professor and director of the Real Estate Center at the Kellogg School of Management, says, "There are host of opportunities in real estate for MBAs. The issue is identifying the best fit for the candidate. Positions that are good fits for MBAs are with firms that supply capital to the industry. Typically these are large, sophisticated, financially-oriented firms. MBAs should identify these institutions and aggressively pursue them for employment. In today's marketplace, this means looking at REITs, mezzanine funds (funds built around mezzanine financing, which combines equity and fixed income investments) and private equity firms.

"In general, the high-profile real estate positions and financially rewarding jobs are on the capital side," adds Pagliari, who is also a principal of a real estate investment firm. "These jobs are almost self-selecting because they are tough to get and you have to be smart and aggressive to succeed. Given that positions in the capital side of the business are reserved for the elite, MBAs should pursue these positions because many of them possess the necessary qualities for these roles."

Employers look for a variety of skill sets. "It is difficult to narrow it to just a few things," he says. "Some positions are very quantitative while others emphasize strong interpersonal skills. Having a combination of both is a competitive advantage. In general, I tell all my students to look for roles that speak to their skill sets. It is going to be hard enough to get the interview, so don't blow it by going after a job that probably doesn't fit your background. MBAs should do their homework on the types of roles out there and match their background and interest with the best fit. However, you still want to shoot for the sky and leverage your MBA."

Job seekers shouldn't be shy about using their contacts "This industry is very tough for outsiders or newcomers to break into and students should be ready to accept that," he advises. "Get in the hunt as soon as possible and network, network, network. Using alums or anyone else you know in the industry is something I always recommend." When you have the interview, be prepared to talk about the local market—or any other in which the company operates. If it's a public firm, check *The Wall Street Journal* for the scuttlebutt. Also, be certain they'll welcome your MBA.

"In the interview you will most likely be asked about why you are interested in real estate and a few technical questions," Pagliari warns. "Be ready to describe a cap rate and market specifics like rental rates and general economic conditions."

To MBA students just starting a real estate program who know they want to enter the industry, he stresses, "Don't rely on simply taking real estate classes, especially if you have no prior real estate experience." You need to demonstrate passion by joining a real estate club or getting active in real estate-related activities at school. "Do whatever it takes to be able to demonstrate your enthusiasm for the industry," he adds. "If it takes starting a real estate club or being the driving force behind an event, then so be it."

The professor also advises individuals who are evaluating MBA programs that offer real estate curriculums to: make sure the professors have some practical experience and the curriculum will give you a skill set that will meet your end goal. Don't sacrifice the overall MBA experience for a school that simply offers a strong real estate curriculum and is lacking in other areas.

For MBA students who are interested in real estate but whose programs do not offer real estate classes, Pagliari offers a solution. "Classes related to finance and economic principles that help you price risks are very useful," he says, noting that the ability to price risk is a strong differentiating factor. Pagliari also recommends taking business law classes because there are many legal issues involved in the industry. "Which is why you should not be surprised to find so many attorneys in the business," he says.

"I was a career switcher and was repeatedly asked in interviews about why I was interested in real estate," says Rich Monopoli, a recent graduate from business school. "Many of the interviewers wanted an explanation of how my background tied to my interest in real estate. I can't emphasize enough how important it is to be prepared to answer the question of why you are interested in real estate."

Visit Vault at **www.vault.com** for insider company profiles, expert advice, career message boards, expert resume reviews, the Vault Job Board and more.

VAULT CAREER LIBRARY   223

Employer Directory

AMB Property Corporation
Pier 1, Bay 1
San Francisco, CA 94111
Phone: (415) 394-9000
Fax: (415) 394-9001
www.amb.com

**Apartment Investment and
Management Company**
4582 S. Ulster Street Parkway
Suite 1100
Denver, CO 80237
Phone: (303) 757-8101
Fax: (303) 759-3226
www.aimco.com

Archstone-Smith
9200 E. Panorama Circle, Suite 400
Englewood, CO 80112
Phone: (303) 708-5959
Fax: (303) 708-5999
www.archstonesmith.com

AvalonBay Communities, Inc.
2900 Eisenhower Avenue, Suite 300
Alexandria, VA 22314
Phone: (703) 329-6300
Fax: (703) 329-1459
www.avalonbay.com

Beazer Homes
1000 Abernathy Road
Suite 1200
Atlanta, GA 30328
Phone: (770) 829-3700
Fax: (770) 481-2808
www.beazer.com

Boston Capital Corporation
1 Boston Place
Boston, MA 02108-4406
Phone: (617) 624-8900
Fax: (617) 624-8999
www.bostoncapital.com

Boston Properties, Inc.
111 Huntington Avenue
Boston, MA 02199-7610
Phone: (617) 236-3300
Fax: (617) 536-5087
www.bostonproperties.com

Brookfield Properties
BCE Place
181 Bay Street, Suite 330
Toronto, Ontario M5J 2T3
Canada
Phone: (416) 369-2300
Fax: (416) 369-2301
www.brookfieldproperties.com

**CarrAmerica Realty
Corporation**
1850 K Street NW
Washington, DC 20006
Phone: (202) 729-1700
Fax: (202) 729-1150
www.carramerica.com

Catellus—A ProLogis Company
4545 Airport Way
Denver, Colorado 80239
Phone: (303) 567-5700
www.catellus.com

CB Richard Ellis Group, Inc.
100 North Sepulveda Boulevard
Suite 1050
El Segundo, CA 90245
Phone: (310) 606-4700
Fax: (310) 606-4701
www.cbre.com

CBL & Associates Properties
2030 Hamilton Place Boulevard
Suite 500
Chattanooga, TN 37421-6000
Phone: (423) 855-0001
Fax: (423) 490-8390
www.cblproperties.com

Centex Corporation
2728 North Harwood Street
Dallas, TX 75201-1516
Phone: (214) 981-5000
Fax: (214) 981-6859
www.centex.com

Century 21 Real Estate LLC
1 Campus Drive
Parsippany, NJ 07054
Phone: (877) 221-2765
Fax: (973) 496-7564
www.century21.com

CNL Hotels & Resorts, Inc.
450 S. Orange Avenue
Orlando, FL 32801-3336
Phone: (407) 650-1000
Fax: (407) 650-1085
www.cnlhotels.com

**Coldwell Banker Real Estate
Corporation**
1 Campus Drive
Parsippany, NJ 07054
Phone: (973) 407-2000
Toll Free: (877) 373-3829
Fax: (973) 496-7217
www.coldwellbanker.com

Day & Zimmermann Group
1818 Market Street, Floor 22
Philadelphia, PA 19103-3672
Phone: (215) 299-8000
Fax: (215) 299-8030
www.dayzim.com

Developers Diversified Realty
3300 Enterprise Parkway
Beachwood, OH 44122
Phone: (216) 755-5500
Fax: (216) 755-1500
www.ddrc.com

Employer Directory, cont.

Duke Realty Corporation
600 E. 96th Street, Suite 100
Indianapolis, IN 46240
Phone: (317) 808-6000
Fax: (317) 808-6794
www.dukerealty.com

Equity Office Properties Trust
2 N. Riverside Plaza, Suite 2100
Chicago, IL 60606
Phone: (312) 466-3300
Fax: (312) 454-0332
www.equityoffice.com

Equity Residential
2 N. Riverside Plaza, Suite 450
Chicago, IL 60606
Phone: (312) 474-1300
Fax: (312) 454-8703
www.equityresidential.com

FelCor Lodging Trust Incorporated
545 E. John Carpenter Freeway
Suite 1300
Irving, TX 75062
Phone: (972) 444-4900
Fax: (972) 444-4949
www.felcor.com

Forest City Enterprises, Inc.
50 Public Square, Suite 1100
Cleveland, OH 44113-2203
Phone: (216) 621-6060
Fax: (216) 263-4808
www.forestcity.net

General Growth Properties, Inc.
110 N. Wacker Drive
Chicago, IL 60606
Phone: (312) 960-5000
Fax: (312) 960-5475
www.generalgrowth.com

Heitman LLC
191 N. Wacker Drive, Suite 2500
Chicago, IL 60606
Phone: (312) 855-5700
www.heitman.com

Hilton Hotels Corporation
9336 Civic Center Drive
Beverly Hills, CA 90210
Phone: (310) 278-4321
Fax: (310) 205-7678
www.hiltonworldwide.com

Hines
Williams Tower
2800 Post Oak Boulevard
Houston, TX 77056-6118
Phone: (713) 621-8000
Fax: (713) 966-2053
www.hines.com

Hospitality Properties Trust
00 Centre Steet
Newton, MA 02458
Phone: (617) 964-8389
Fax: (617) 969-5730
www.hptreit.com

Host Hotels & Resorts, Inc.
6903 Rockledge Drive, Suite 1500
Bethesda, MD 20817
Phone: (240) 744-1000
Fax: (240) 744-5125
www.hostmarriott.com

Hovnanian Enterprises, Inc.
110 W. Front Street
Red Bank, NJ 07701
Phone: (732) 747-7800
Fax: (732) 747-7159
www.khov.com

HRPT Properties Trust
400 Centre Street
Newton, MA 02458-2076
Phone: (617) 332-3990
Fax: (617) 332-2261
www.hrpreit.com

Jones Lang LaSalle
200 E. Randolph Drive
Chicago, IL 60601
Phone: (312) 782-5800
Fax: (312) 782-4339
www.joneslanglasalle.com

KB Home
10990 Wilshire Boulevard, 7th Floor
Los Angeles, CA 90024
Phone: (310) 231-4000
Fax: (310) 231-4222
www.kbhome.com

Kimco Realty Corporation
3333 New Hyde Park Road
New Hyde Park, NY 11042-0020
Phone: (516) 869-9000
Fax: (516) 869-9001
www.kimcorealty.com

Lend Lease Corporation Limited
Level 4, 30 The Bond
30 Hickson Road
Millers Point, New South Wales 2000
Australia
Phone: +61-2-9236-6111
Fax: +61-2-9252-2192
www.lendlease.com.au

The McCormick Group
1440 Central Park Boulevard
Suite 207
Fredericksburg, VA 22401
Phone: (540) 786-9777
Fax: (540) 786-9355
www.mccormickgroup.com

MetroList, Inc.
7100 E. Belleview Avenue
Englewood, CO 80111-1632
Phone: (303) 850-9576
www.metrolistmls.com

Morgan Stanley Real Estate
1585 Broadway
New York, NY 10036
Phone: (212) 761-4000
www.morganstanley.com/realestate

Visit Vault at **www.vault.com** for insider company profiles, expert advice, career message boards, expert resume reviews, the Vault Job Board and more.

VAULT CAREER LIBRARY 225

Employer Directory, cont.

Parkway Properties, Inc.
1 Jackson Place
188 E. Capitol Street, Suite 1000
Jackson, MS 39201-2195
Phone: (601) 948-4091
Fax: (601) 949-4077
www.pky.com

ProLogis
4545 Airport Way
Denver, CO 80239
Phone: (303) 567-5000
Toll Free: (800) 566-2706
Fax: (303) 567-5605
www.prologis.com

Public Storage, Inc.
701 Western Avenue
Glendale, CA 91201-2349
Phone: (818) 244-8080
Fax: (818) 553-2376
www.publicstorage.com

Rayonier Inc.
50 North Laura Street
Jacksonville, FL 32202
Phone: (904) 357-9100
Fax: (904) 357-9101
www.rayonier.com

RE/MAX International, Inc.
5075 S. Syracuse Street
Denver, CO 80237-2712
Phone: (303) 770-5531
Toll Free: (800) 525-7452
Fax: (303) 796-3599
www.remax.com

RREEF America L.L.C.
875 N Michigan Avenue
Chicago, IL 60611-1803
Phone: (312) 266-9300
www.dbrealestate.com/rreef

Tishman Speyer Properties
45 Rockefeller Plaza
New York, NY 10111
Phone: (212) 715-0300
Fax: (212) 895-0326
www.tishmanspeyer.com

Trammell Crow Residential
2 Buckhead Plaza
3050 Peachtree Road NW, Suite 500
Atlanta, GA 30305
Phone: (770) 801-1600
Fax: (770) 801-1256
www.tcresidential.com

URS Corporation
600 Montgomery Street, 26th Floor
San Francisco, CA 94111
Phone: (415) 774-2700
Fax: (415) 398-1905
www.urscorp.com

USG Corporation
550 W. Adams Street
Chicago, IL 60661-3676
Phone: (312) 436-4000
Fax: (312) 436-4093
www.usg.com

Vornado Realty Trust
888 7th Avenue
New York, NY 10019
Phone: (212) 894-7000
Fax: (212) 894-7070
www.vno.com

Walton Street Capital L.L.C.
900 North Michigan Avenue
Suite 1900
Chicago, IL 60611
Phone: (312) 915-2800
Fax: (312) 915-2881
www.waltonst.com

Sales and Trading

The War Zone

If you've ever been to an investment banking trading floor, you've witnessed the chaos. It's usually a lot of swearing, yelling and flashing computer screens: a pressure cooker of stress. Sometimes the floor is a quiet rumble of activity, but when the market takes a nosedive, panic ensues and the volume kicks up a notch. Traders must rely on their market instincts, and salespeople yell for bids when the market tumbles. Deciding what to buy or sell, and at what price to buy and sell, is difficult when millions of dollars are at stake.

However, salespeople and traders work much more reasonable hours than research analysts or corporate finance bankers. Rarely does a salesperson or trader venture into the office on a Saturday or Sunday; the trading floor is completely devoid of life on weekends. Any corporate finance analyst who has crossed a trading floor on a Saturday will tell you that the only noise to be heard on the floor is the clocks ticking every minute and the whir of the air conditioner.

Shop Talk

Here's a quick example of how a salesperson and a trader interact on an emerging market bond trade.

Salesperson: Receives a call from a buy-side firm (say, a large mutual fund). The buy-side firm wishes to sell $10 million of a particular Mexican Par government-issued bond (denominated in U.S. dollars). The emerging markets bond salesperson, seated next to the emerging markets traders, stands up in his chair and yells to the relevant trader, "Give me a bid on $10 million Mex Par, six and a quarter, nineteens."

Trader: "I got 'em at 73 and an eighth."

Translation: I am willing to buy them at a price of $73.125 per $100 of face value. As mentioned, the $10 million represents amount of par value the client wanted to sell, meaning the trader will buy the bonds, paying 73.125 percent of $10 million plus accrued interest (to factor in interest earned between interest payments).

Salesperson: "Can't you do any better than that?"

Translation: Please buy at a higher price, as I will get a higher commission.

Trader: "That's the best I can do. The market is falling right now. You want to sell?"

Salesperson: "Done. $10 million."

S&T: A Symbiotic Relationship?

Institutional sales and trading are highly dependent on one another. The propaganda that you read in glossy firm brochures portrays those in sales and trading as a shiny, happy integrated team environment of professionals working for the client's interests. While often that is true, salespeople and traders frequently clash, disagree and bicker.

Simply put, salespeople provide the clients for traders, and traders provide the products for sales. Traders would have nobody to trade for without sales, but sales would have nothing to sell without traders. Understanding how a trader makes money and how a salesperson makes money should explain how conflicts can arise.

Traders make money by selling high and buying low (this difference is called the spread). They are buying stocks or bonds for clients, and these clients filter in through sales. A trader faced with a buy order for a buy-side firm couldn't care less about

Visit Vault at **www.vault.com** for insider company profiles, expert advice, career message boards, expert resume reviews, the Vault Job Board and more.

VAULT CAREER LIBRARY 227

the performance of the securities once they are sold. He or she just cares about making the spread. In a sell trade, this means selling at the highest price possible. In a buy trade, this means buying at the lowest price possible.

The salesperson, however, has a different incentive. The total return on the trade often determines the money a salesperson makes, so he wants the trader to sell at a low price. The salesperson also wants to be able to offer the client a better price than competing firms in order to get the trade and earn a commission. This of course leads to many interesting situations, and at the extreme, salespeople and traders who eye one another suspiciously.

The personalities

Salespeople possess remarkable communication skills, including outgoing personalities and a smoothness not often seen in traders. Traders sometimes call them bullshit artists while salespeople counter by calling traders quant guys with no personality. Traders are tough, quick and often consider themselves smarter than salespeople. The salespeople probably know better how to have fun, but the traders win the prize for mental sharpness and the ability to handle stress.

The MBA in S&T

Do I need an MBA to be promoted on a sales and trading desk?

Generally, sales and trading is a much less hierarchical work environment than investment banking. For this reason, it is widely believed that you don't need an MBA to get promoted on sales and trading desks. This view is often perpetuated be people who work on trading desks, but just because you hear this once or twice, don't accept it as truth. Whether you need an MBA or not is really a function of the firm you work for and the desk you're on. If the firm you're considering hires both associates and analysts, but you notice that associates are offered twice as much pay as analysts, then this is certainly an indication that MBAs are better paid. This doesn't mean that you can't be promoted without an MBA; you'll just have to work much harder to get recognized. When it's time for a promotion, you may also be somewhat behind in the pecking order. Some firms, on the other hand, don't want MBAs. This may result from budgetary constraints, or explicit firm policy. Some firms also hold the view that it's hard to teach an old dog new tricks, so they will hire exclusively out of undergraduate programs.

A more subtle point to discern are the desk dynamics. A lot about being on a trading desk is about fitting in, and if everyone else, including the boss, doesn't have an MBA, then chances are that having an MBA won't add too much value in this environment. In fact, an MBA degree may even hurt your career prospects if there's a downright disdain for MBA-types. Alternatively, if the desk you're on is populated with MBAs, then not having an MBA could potentially limit your career advancement. Alternatively, you can be in a situation where you're the only MBA and everyone thinks that you're the brain, which can work to your advantage even if the boss has no personal biases about the value of the degree.

The bottom line is that there are no hard and fast rules. Depending on the particular firm and desk, an MBA may not advance your career. Be aware of the aforementioned issues, and ask some good questions to get a better feel for whether an extra degree is a benefit.

What are some of the tangible benefits of an MBA?

The pay is better and you will generally have a faster track for promotion to salesperson or trader. The MBA associate will typically have to do the same demeaning things that an undergraduate analyst does, but mercifully for a shorter period of time. In some cases, MBAs are also more likely to be assigned the desk that they'd like to work for. Undergraduate sales and trading recruiting programs, on the other hand, may hire you as part of a generalist pool and place you on a desk that isn't your top choice.

Another tangible benefit for the MBA candidate is the availability of more exit options.

A Day in the Life: Sales-Trader

Here's a look at a day in the life of a sales-trader, given to us by an associate in the equities division at Lehman Brothers.

6:30 a.m.: Get into work. Check voicemail and e-mail. Chat with some people at your desk about the headlines in the Journal.

7:15 a.m.: Equities morning call. You find out what's up to sell. ("I'm sort of a liaison between the accounts [clients] and the block traders. What I do is help traders execute their trading strategies, give them market color. If they want something I try to find the other side of the trade. Or if I have stuff available, I get info out, without exposing what we have.")

9:30 a.m.: Markets open. You hit the phones. ("You want to make outgoing calls, you don't really want people to call you. I'm calling my clients, telling them what research is relevant to them, and what merchandise I have, if there's any news on any of their positions.")

10:00 a.m.: More calls. ("I usually have about 35 different clients. It's always listed equities, but it's a huge range of equities. The client can be a buyer or seller—there's one sales-trader representing a buyer, another representing the seller.")

10:30 a.m.: On the phone with another Lehman trader, trying to satisfy a client. ("If they have questions in another product, I'll try to help them out.")

11:00 a.m.: Calling another client. ("It's a trader at the other end, receiving discussions from portfolio manager; their discretion varies from client to client.")

12:00 p.m.: You hear a call for the sale for a stock that several of your clients are keen on acquiring. ("It's usually a block trader, although sometimes it's another sales-trader. The announcement comes 'over the top,'—over the speaker. It also comes on my computer.")

12:30 p.m.: Food from the deli comes in. ("You can't go to the bathroom sometimes, say you're working 10 orders, you want to see every stock. We don't leave to get our lunch, we order lunch in.")

1:00 p.m.: Watching your terminal ("There's a lot of action. If there's 200,000 shares trade in your name [a stock that a client has a position in or wants] and it's not you, you want to go back to your client and say who it was.)

2:00 p.m.: Taking a call from a client. ("You can't miss a beat, you are literally in your seat all day.")

2:05 p.m.: You tell the client that you have some stock he had indicated interest in previously, but you don't let him know how much you can unload. ("It's a lot of how to get a trade done without disclosing anything that's going to hurt the account. If you have one stock up you don't want the whole Street to know, or it'll drive down the price.")

4:30 p.m.: Head home to rest a bit before going out. ("I leave at 4:30 or sometimes 5:00. It depends.")

7:00 p.m.: Meet a buy-side trader, one of your clients, at a bar. ("We entertain a lot of buy-side traders—dinner, we go to baseball games, we go to bars. Maybe this happens once or twice a week.")

MBA Career Path

First-year MBA students and recent MBA graduates are eligible for summer associate and full-time associate positions respectively. Associates start with similar responsibilities as analysts, but add more responsibility quickly and are typically on a faster track for promotion.

MBAs are also more likely to have the opportunity to get staffed abroad. For example, Goldman Sachs, Morgan Stanley and Lehman Brothers have recently hired MBAs from American business schools directly into their European trading desks. MBAs

Visit Vault at **www.vault.com** for insider company profiles, expert advice, career message boards, expert resume reviews, the Vault Job Board and more.

VAULT CAREER LIBRARY   **229**

interested in pursuing sales and trading opportunities abroad must be able to demonstrate local language proficiency, and a strong desire to make a long-term commitment to the region. Each of these firms has recently also offered summer internship opportunities, but these programs are less established than the New York-based opportunities, and therefore shouldn't be counted on as a stable source of MBA hiring demand.

Associate pay: to infinity and beyond

Sales and trading associates will start at about the same base pay as their investment banking counterparts. The going rate has held up around $80,000 to $85,000 per year plus an end of year bonus of $20,000 to $30,000. While signing bonuses were the norm during the bull market of the late 1990s, they are now rare. Salaries increase primarily through performance bonuses, especially if you've become a position trader for the firm. Bonuses are normally computed as a percentage of the trading revenue you generate (or commission dollars that you generate if you're a salesperson), so depending on how cheap or generous your firm is, this number can be normally expected to fluctuate between 0 percent and 10 percent in any given year.

If you make $10 million for the firm, however, don't expect to receive a cool million for your efforts. Wall Street firms are highly conscious of expense control, and the largest expense item is compensation. To keep compensation expense at or below 50 percent of revenue, investment banks hand out compensation packages that include among other things, cash, stock options and restricted stock. Generous stock option grants are a non-cash form of compensation that doesn't hit the income statement, but aren't quite as motivating as cash. Another game in the compensation is the granting of restricted stock. This is a major component of pay as you move up the ladder, and you can only convert this compensation into cash according to a vesting schedule that stretches out for years.

Finally, keep in mind that investment banks are operating across all markets and products sectors. In a simplified world, the investment bank operates a bond desk and an equity desk. The bond traders make more money and the salespeople sell more bonds when the economy is in recession. On the other hand, the stock traders make more money and the sales-traders sell more stock when the economy is robust. What happens at the end of the year when the compensation committee is determining how big the bond bonus pool and the equity bonus pool should be? Most firms tend to cross-subsidize the equity desk with the bond desk's revenue when the stock market falls on hard times, and to return the favor to the bond desk when the bond market falls on hard times. This makes sense at the corporate level (preventing mass defections, for example), but the immediate consequence to the stock trader that generated $10 million in revenue and is expecting a $1 million check is that he'll see a lot less than $1 million. The small consolation to the expectant stock trader is that when he makes substantially less than his budget, maybe the bond desk will stuff his stocking.

The winding promotion road in S&T

The path to promotion on a sales and trading desk is less standard than it is in investment banking. Investment banking analysts really don't have much too look forward to except perhaps a third year and then back to business school or some other career. By contrast, undergraduate analysts who have a demonstrated ability to add value to a desk have the potential to move up without an MBA.

One common scenario that unfolds is that after several years, the restless undergraduate analyst decides to apply to business school and gets accepted. If this analyst is a prized employee, then the boss might offer the analyst a promotion to associate in order to keep the analyst on the desk.

Promotions on trading desks are generally not much to celebrate, except that it leads to potentially higher pay. Investment banking associates can look forward to moving out of the bullpen and into a real office with a secretary. Salespeople and traders settle for better accounts and more trading responsibility. The focus of promotions shouldn't be to achieve a particular title (vice president, director, managing director, etc.), but rather, to earn real sales and trading responsibility. Of course, if you do your job well, you'll be duly compensated and promoted, but after reaching a level of significant responsibility, you shouldn't be expecting to get promoted every couple of years.

Employer Directory

A.G. Edwards & Sons
1 N. Jefferson Avenue
St. Louis, MO 63103-2205
Phone: (314) 955-3000
Toll Free: (877) 835-7877
Fax: (314) 955-2890
www.agedwards.com

Arnhold S. Bleichroeder
1345 Avenue of the Americas
44th Floor
New York, NY 10105-4300
Phone: (212) 698-3000
Toll Free: (800) 800-9006
Fax: (212) 299-4360
www.asbai.com

Banc of America Investment Services, Inc.
Gateway Village, Building 900
900 W. Trade Street
Charlotte, NC 28255
Phone: (800) 926-1111
www.baisidirect.com

Barclays Capital
The North Colonnade
Canary Wharf
London, E14 4BB
United Kingdom
Phone: +44-20-7623-2323
www.barcap.com

Bear Stearns
383 Madison Avenue
New York, NY 10179
Phone: (212) 272-2000
Fax: (212) 272-4785
www.bearstearns.com

Bernard L. Madoff Securities
885 3rd Avenue
New York, NY 10022
Phone: (212) 230-2424
Fax: (212) 486-8178
www.madoff.com

BMO Capital Markets
100 King Street W
1 First Canadian Place
Toronto, Ontario M5X 1H3
Canada
Phone: (416) 359-4000
www.bmocm.com

Cantor Fitzgerald
499 Park Avenue
New York, NY 10022
Phone: (212) 938-5000
Fax: (212) 829-5280
www.cantor.com

Charles Schwab Corporation
101 Montgomery Street
San Francisco, CA 94104
Phone: (415) 636-7000
Toll Free: (800) 648-5300
Fax: (415) 636-9820
www.schwab.com

CIBC World Markets
161 Bay Street, BCE Place
Toronto, Ontario M5J 2S8
Canada
Phone: (416) 594-7000
Fax: (416) 956-6958
ww.cibcwm.com

Citigroup's Global Corporate and Investment Bank (formerly Salomon Smith Barney)
388 Greenwich Street
New York, NY 10013
Phone: (212) 816-6000
www.citigroupcib.com

Collins Stewart LLC
350 Madison Avenue
New York, NY 10017
Phone: (212) 389-8000
Fax: (212) 389-8810
www.unterberg.com

Crédit Agricole S.A.
91-93 Boulevard Pasteur
75015 Paris
France
Phone: +33-1-43-23-52-02
Fax: +33-1-43-23-34-48
www.credit-agricole-sa.fr

Credit Suisse
11 Madison Avenue
New York, NY 10010-3629
Phone: (212) 325-2000
Fax: (212) 325-6665
www.credit-suisse.com/us/en

Daiwa Securities Group Inc.
6-4, Otemachi 2-chome, Chiyoda-ku
Tokyo, 100-8101
Japan
Phone: +81-3-3243-2100
Fax: +81-3-3242-0955
www.daiwa.jp

Deutsche Bank
Taunusanlage 12
60262 Frankfurt
Germany
Phone: +49-69-910-00
Fax: +49-69-910-34-225
www.deutsche-bank.de

Dresdner Bank AG
Jürgen-Ponto-Platz 1
D-60329 Frankfurt
Germany
Phone: +49-69-263-0
Fax: +49-69-263-15839
www.dresdner-bank.com

Ferris Baker Watts
100 Light Street
Baltimore, MD 21202
Phone: (410) 685-2600
Toll Free: (800) 436-2000
Fax: (410) 468-2746
www.fbw.com

Visit Vault at **www.vault.com** for insider company profiles, expert advice,
career message boards, expert resume reviews, the Vault Job Board and more.

VAULT CAREER LIBRARY   231

Employer Directory, cont.

Fox-Pitt Kelton
420 Fifth Avenue, 5th Floor
New York, NY 10018
Phone: (212) 687-1105
Fax: (212) 599-2723
www.fpk.com

Friedman Billings Ramsey
1001 19th Street North
Arlington, VA 22209
Phone: (703) 312-9500
Toll Free: (800) 846-5050
Fax: (703) 312-9501
www.fbr.com

Goldman Sachs
85 Broad Street
New York, NY 10004
Phone: (212) 902-1000
Fax: (212) 902-3000
www.goldmansachs.com

Group One Trading
220 Bush Street, Suite 360
San Francisco, CA 94104-3533
Phone: (415) 283-3410

J.P. Morgan Chase
270 Park Avenue
New York, NY 10017
Phone: (212) 270-6000
Fax: (212) 270-2613
www.jpmorganchase.com

Janney Montgomery Scott
1801 Market Street
Philadelphia, PA 19103-1675
Phone: (215) 665-6000
Toll Free: (800) 526-6397
Fax: (215) 564-9597
www.janneys.com

Jefferies & Co.
212 E 47th Street, Apartment 15F
New York, NY 10017-2124
Phone: (212) 284-2550
www.jefco.com

Johnson Rice & Co
639 Loyola Avenue, Suite 2775
New Orleans, LA 70113-7115
Phone: (504) 525-3767

Kaufman Bros., L.P.
800 Third Avenue, 30th Floor
New York, NY 10022
Phone: (212) 292-8100
Fax: (212) 292-8101
www.kbro.com

Ladenburg Thalmann
4400 Biscayne Boulevard, 12th Floor
Miami, FL 33137
Phone: (305) 572-4100
Toll Free: (800) 523-8425
Fax: (305) 572-4199
www.ladenburg.com

Legg Mason
100 Light Street
Baltimore, MD 21202
Phone: (877) 534-4627
www.leggmason.com

Lehman Brothers
745 Seventh Avenue
New York, NY 10019-6801
Phone: (212) 526-7000
www.lehman.com

Merrill Lynch
4 World Financial Center
250 Vesey Street
New York, NY 10080
Phone: (212) 449-1000
www.ml.com

Miller Tabak & Co
331 Madison Avenue, Floor 12
New York, NY 10017-5107
Phone: (212) 370-0040

Morgan Stanley
1585 Broadway
New York, NY 10036
Phone: (212) 761-4000
www.morganstanley.com

Neuberger Berman
605 3rd Avenue
New York, NY 10158
Phone: (212) 476-8800
Toll Free: (800) 877-9700
Fax: (212) 476-9090
www.nb.com

Oscar Gruss & Son
74 Broad Street, Floor 5
New York, NY 10004-2210
Phone: (212) 952-1100

Piper Jaffray & Co.
800 Nicollet Mall, Suite 800
Minneapolis, MN 55402-7020
Phone: (800) 333-6000
www.piperjaffray.com

Prudential Securities
751 Broad Street
Newark, NJ 07102-3777
Phone: (973) 802-6000
Toll Free: (800) 346-3778
Fax: (973) 802-4479
www.prudential.com

RBC Capital Markets
1 Liberty Plaza, Room 300
New York, NY 10006-1404
Phone: (212) 858-7000
www.rbccm.com

Robert W. Baird
777 E. Wisconsin Avenue
Milwaukee, WI 53201
Phone: (414) 765-3500
Toll Free: (800) 792-2473
www.rwbaird.com

Sanders Morris Harris
600 Travis, Suite 3100
Houston, TX 77002
Phone: (713) 993-4610
Toll Free: (800) 900-4611
Fax: (713) 224-1101
www.smhgroup.com

Employer Directory, cont.

Sanford C. Bernstein
1345 Avenue of the Americas
New York, NY 10105
Phone: (212) 486-5800
Fax: (212) 969-6189
www.bernstein.com

SunTrust Banks, Inc
303 Peachtree Street NE
Atlanta, GA 30308
Phone: (404) 588-7711
Toll Free: (800) 786-8787
 Fax: (404) 332-3875
www.suntrust.com

Susquehanna International Group, LLP
401 City Avenue, Suite 220
Bala Cynwyd, PA 19004
Phone: (610) 617-2600
Fax: (610) 617-2689
www.sig.com

Thomas Weisel Partners
1 Montgomery Tower
1 Montgomery Street
San Francisco, CA 94104
Phone: (415) 364-2500
Fax: (415) 364-2695
www.tweisel.com

UBS
Bahnhofstrasse 45
CH-8098 Zurich
Switzerland
Phone: +41-44-234-11-11
Fax: +41-44-239- 91-11
www.ubs.com

Van der Moolen Holding N.V.
Keizersgracht 307
1016 ED Amsterdam
Netherlands
Phone: +31-20-535-6789
Fax: +31-20-535-6788
www.vandermoolen.com

Wachovia
1 Wachovia Center
Charlotte, NC 28288-0013
Phone: (704) 374-6565
Toll Free: (800) 922-4684
Fax: (704) 374-3425
www.wachovia.com

Wedbush Morgan Securities
1000 Wilshire Boulevard
Los Angeles, CA 90017
Phone: (213) 688-8000
Fax: (213) 688-6652
www.wedbush.com

William Blair & Co.
222 W. Adams Street
Chicago, IL 60606
Phone: (312) 236-1600
Toll Free: (800) 621-0687
Fax: (312) 368-9418
www.williamblair.com

Visit Vault at **www.vault.com** for insider company profiles, expert advice,
career message boards, expert resume reviews, the Vault Job Board and more.

V∧ULT CAREER LIBRARY   **233**

Technology Consulting

The State of Technology Consulting

Slow and steady

In 2006, the technology consulting industry thrived, as corporate spending was in full swing and businesses sought ways to use technology to boost profits. After the stock market downturn of 2000-2001 and the tech-bubble burst, IT consulting languished when businesses were forced to curb budgets for "nonessential" improvements like IT services. As the economy started to pick up speed again in 2004, firms focused on expanding business and streamlining operations, turning to IT consultants who came on the scene with core services like software implementation and IT strategy. After the Enron and Worldcom debacles, businesses have also turned their attention to risk management and regulatory compliance, resulting in a heightened demand for IT consulting projects.

Growth in the industry has indeed returned, though not with the same vigor that it once had. The outlook for tech spending is positive, with industry observers predicting a slower, sustainable expansion in the coming years. In 2005, a report from Kennedy Information indicated that the technology consulting market as a whole will expand 8.8 percent annually through 2009. And according to an IDC industry survey in January 2007, spending on tech services will grow at a 5.8 percent compounded annual rate through 2010, with government, banking and manufacturing industries expected to increase spending the most. In the long term, things are looking even better for the IT biz; analysts forecast that globalization, increasing international deregulation and the need to align business processes with IT systems will drive a consistent demand for IT consulting.

Adapt or die

To counterbalance the conservative spending companies have adopted, technology consulting firms have been forced to shift strategies and tweak their service offerings. According to a report by IDC in 2006, as business processes and IT systems become increasingly interconnected, service-oriented architecture (SOA), infrastructure improvements and application services have become hot areas that hold profit-boosting promise for consulting firms in the immediate future. IT consultancies are also focusing on higher profit margin services—like automating business processes—as well as shorter-term engagements, which involve lower upfront costs and provide quicker fee turnaround.

The service convergence

One trend that also continues to play out is the merging of IT consulting and traditional business consulting services. As profit margins for products have declined, spending on services has risen—driving a wider variety of tech firms to try to tap into the consulting market. Traditional software and hardware developers have gradually branched out into IT consulting by buying up management consulting operations, which allows them to provide a wider range of service offerings for clients. While Accenture pioneered the idea of offering both strategy and IT services, EDS was also at the forefront of this trend when it bought out A.T. Kearney in 1995 (which the firm then sold in a management buyout in January 2006). The largest systems integrator, IBM, created its consulting practice when it absorbed PwC in 2002. That same year, Fujitsu formed a consulting arm, purchasing Canadian firm DMR in April, and Atos Origin acquired the consulting division of KPMG in June. These firms were acting on the notion that clients prefer to hire one firm that's capable of doing it all—developing strategy and IT solutions, installing and running those solutions, and even taking over the processes of entire departments such as HR or payroll.

Visit Vault at **www.vault.com** for insider company profiles, expert advice, career message boards, expert resume reviews, the Vault Job Board and more.

VAULT CAREER LIBRARY   235

Moving up the chain

Competition has further heated up as traditionally outsourcing-only firms have begun to vie for higher-end IT consulting engagements. The largest Indian outsourcing firms have long since moved beyond operating call centers toward projects such as enterprise application implementation and process management—areas traditionally dominated by U.S. heavyweights like BearingPoint and Deloitte. Some India-based firms have accommodated this shift in market presence by opening offices closer to target clients. For example, Tata has strengthened its presence in North America, with 50 offices and a New York headquarters, as well as development centers in Minneapolis and Chicago. Wipro opened an office in Boston in 2005 to compete for project management consulting work. Satyam set up a 10-member M&A team at its Indian headquarters in 2006 with the intent to keep an eye out for attractive consulting companies in the U.S. or Europe. Though the firm keeps only 150 consultants in North America, it pulls in about 60 percent of its $400 million consulting business from the region.

When it comes to the more profitable tech strategy engagements, there is no doubt that American firms still have the advantage that comes from long, established relationships with clients. However, industry observers speculate that this could change if Indian outsourcing firms are able to attract competitors' consultants with connections to formidable clients.

The outsourcing buzz

Outsourcing opportunities are still reigning in profits for firms looking to make the most of moderate corporate spending. Companies have outsourced work to low-cost locations for decades, but the practice really gained traction in the early 21st century, when businesses were desperate to find ways to save money. Now, outsourcing is offered by practically every IT consulting firm as a way to increase efficiency and trim costs for clients. IDC research predicts that spending on U.S. outsourcing services will rise 7.1 percent annually between 2005 and 2010. And although there were fewer outsourcing megadeals (contracts worth over $1 billion) in 2006, the market is forecast to grow 7.3 percent from 2004 through 2009, thanks to smaller contracts, according to Gartner Research. With plenty of room left for expansion, consulting firms of all sizes are beefing up their offshoring capabilities. A 2006 *BusinessWeek* article cites research from the McKinsey Global Institute estimating that although $18.4 billion in global IT work has been sent offshore, so far only one-tenth of the potential offshore market has been tapped.

Domestic job decline

But despite its guarantees of profit, outsourcing continues to be a debated issue, especially in the U.S. Some industry observers warn that the escalating outsourcing trend does not bode well for the domestic consulting market in the future. They argue that firms that sell cost savings as opposed to value-added services turn the business into a commodity, rather than a service industry. With U.S. firms expanding their offshore talent and Indian firms deepening their expertise in the U.S., some are bracing for what they feel are the inevitable consequences on the domestic labor market. Analysts anticipate that as long as firms compete on the basis of price, fees will be driven down, ultimately shrinking both job growth and salaries.

The advantage of offshoring

Still, proponents of outsourcing claim that the negative impacts of sending jobs offshore have been minimal in reality. According to a study by the Association for Computing Machinery in 2006, over the next decade, only 2 to 3 percent of tech jobs will be shifted overseas annually. And a 2006 survey conducted by the Society for Information Management found that for 2007, only 3.3 percent of corporate IT budgets were allocated to funding offshore outsourcing programs. Advocates also suggest that the money saved by sending lower-end jobs overseas can be invested into higher-end tech projects on domestic soil that require in-depth skills—which could then drive up demand for expert IT consultants in the U.S.

The world is flatter

For all of its detractors, consulting firms continue to strive for a borderless global delivery model, relocating work anywhere low-cost talent can be found. Gartner Research forecasts that by 2015, 30 percent of all professional IT service jobs will be based in emerging markets such as India and China, rather than in developed countries. Overflowing with engineering grads (many of whom have American degrees) and a large English-speaking population, India dominates the market now, claiming 80 percent of the share of offshore work. U.S. firms have also shifted their strategy to take a larger piece of the offshoring pie, outlining ambitious plans for expansion in India. IBM already has 45,000 staffers in the country, and plans to invest $6 billion there over the next three years. Capgemini counts 12,000 employees in Mumbai, boosted by its acquisition of Indian services firm Kanbay International in February 2007. Accenture has also been bulking up, and expects headcount in India to reach 27,000 by the end of 2007.

As Western firms compete for the best local labor in India, consultants have been able to demand more pay. Salary rates have climbed 15 percent per year over the past five years, and analysts note that India is quickly losing its low-wage advantage. The country is also facing a severe skills shortage. In October 2006, *The New York Times* cited a study conducted by the National Association of Software and Service Companies (NASSCOM), which found that one in four engineering graduates in India had the necessary technical skills, English fluency and oral presentation ability to be employable. According to Gartner Research, these factors could cause India to lose 45 percent of its outsourcing market share by the close of 2007.

The next India

Feeling the effects of mounting salary costs, in 2006, firms ramped up offshoring efforts in other regions. China, the Philippines, Vietnam, Australia and several Eastern European countries, such as Hungary and Poland, are also starting to compete for outsourcing work. Regarded by many as the most promising offshoring market, China produces 400,000 computer science grads per year, compared to 180,000 IT engineering grads in India, according to a 2005 report by Merrill Lynch. Even Indian firms have started to outsource labor to China—Tata Consultancy had 15 percent of its global workforce there in 2005. A cheaper labor market and availability of talent have prompted Kennedy Information to speculate that China's consulting market will grow at a compound annual rate of 32 percent from 2005 to 2008.

Short supply—a good sign

With a revived IT consulting job market, recruiting is a top priority for firms, some of which have had to turn away work due to lack of staff. Moody's Economy.com estimated that 217,000 tech jobs were created in 2006—the most in any year since 2000. Forrester Research claimed that IT jobs will grow at a rate of 3 percent through 2008 and salaries will expand 6 percent. All signs point toward a consistent demand over the next few years, primarily as a result of the economic rebound and regulatory requirements.

In addition, noncompete agreements have ended for three of the Big Four (PwC's noncompete agreement ends in September 2007), meaning that these firms are set to re-enter the IT consulting market. Some observers foresee a tighter talent crunch as these firms rev up recruiting for college grads and experienced hires. With demand close to outpacing the supply of consultants, candidates are in a prime position to negotiate for a better position or more competitive salary and benefits.

Strategists and specialists

The hottest consultants in the market right now are IT strategists and those with a few years of experience in a niche area. The job market strongly favors those with industry-specific consulting skills, and consequently the need for generalist technology consultants has dwindled. Specialized skills, like project management, operations management and SOA, are desirable, and salaries for high-quality consultants have risen. Firms are also after consultants who have some business savvy

Visit Vault at **www.vault.com** for insider company profiles, expert advice, career message boards, expert resume reviews, the Vault Job Board and more.

VAULT CAREER LIBRARY   **237**

along with tech skills. A report published by PwC in 2006 noted that in the IT world, "the battle for talent is about to become even fiercer as companies search for the hybrid employee: workers who excel at collaboration, innovation and managing change." Also among the most valuable are those consultants who can help clients navigate the regulatory maze, especially when it comes to Sarbanes-Oxley compliance.

A Day in the Life: IT Consultant

Kristine is a consultant at a major consulting firm with many IT consulting engagements. Her role is team lead of the design and developer for eight web-based training modules. She has five analysts on her team.

4:30 a.m.: It's Monday morning. Time to wake up. There's time for a shower this Monday morning—such luxury!

5:30 a.m.: I am in a cab on the way to the airport, making a mental list of anything that could have been forgotten. I ask the cabbie to tune the radio to NPR.

6:10 a.m.: At the airport I go up to the self check-in kiosk. I take the boarding pass and head down to the security line, laptop and small carry-on in hand.

6:25 a.m.: At security, I remove my laptop from my bag and place it on the tray. I move through security quickly. No alarms beep.

6:35 a.m.: After a quick stop at Starbucks, I arrive at the gate. I say hello to three other members of my project and check out the other passengers I see every week on this Monday morning flight. I board early along with the other premier fliers—one of the perks of being a frequent traveler.

7:00 a.m.: The flight departs on time. Yay! I relish my window seat close to the front of the airplane.

8:00 a.m.: The beverage cart wakes me up. I ask for coffee and scan *The Wall Street Journal* as I drink.

9:30 a.m.: I arrive at my destination and share a ride with my fellow consultants to the project site.

10:30 a.m.: At the project site. As I crawl underneath my desk to hook my laptop to the client LAN connection, one of my team members informs me that he still hasn't received feedback from his client reviewer. That's not good news.

11:00 a.m.: After checking and responding to e-mail, I call my team member's client reviewer. The reviewer agrees to send me the team member feedback on the training material by noon tomorrow.

11:15 a.m.: I remind the team of the 1 p.m. status meeting. I've got to start it on time—I have a meeting downtown at 3:15 p.m. I start to review the content outlines for the training modules.

12:00 p.m.: I scurry, along with two teammates, to get sandwiches at a nearby eatery. Mine is turkey and cheddar.

12:20 p.m.: Back at my desk, I get a call from the project manager, who is working at a client site in another state. He tells me that clients in the training department are nervous about their job security and asks that the entire team be sensitive to how the training changes may affect the training positions in the organization.

1:00 p.m.: The team holds a status meeting. I pass on the message from the project manager. Each member discusses what has been completed and what he or she expects to complete that week. Two other team members are having difficulty obtaining feedback from their client reviewers. We all brainstorm ideas on how to obtain the feedback.

2:00 p.m.: I finish up the meeting and get directions to my meeting downtown.

2:40 p.m.: Off to the 3:15 p.m. meeting.

3:15 p.m.: I meet the head of the training department to discuss the training courses. He calls in a close associate who has opinions on how the courses should be organized. The associate wants to add several more web-based training modules. I politely suggest that part of the additional subject matter could be covered in the modules that have been agreed to in the scope of the project. We all sketch out the course structure on a white board.

4:45 p.m.: Back at the project site. I check in with my team members via e-mail.

5:45 p.m.: I complete a draft of the course flow in PowerPoint and send it to the client and my manager for review.

7:00 p.m.: I have reviewed 50 percent of the course outlines. It's time to head back to the hotel. I stop by a local diner for a quick dinner.

8:30 p.m.: Time for a workout in the hotel gym.

9:15 p.m.: I'm ready for bed. Clothes for the next day are hanging in the closet. The alarm clock is set to 6:30 a.m.

10:30 p.m.: I go to sleep.

Visit Vault at **www.vault.com** for insider company profiles, expert advice, career message boards, expert resume reviews, the Vault Job Board and more.

V/\ULT CAREER LIBRARY   239

Employer Directory

Accenture
1345 Avenue of the Americas
New York, NY 10105
Phone: (917) 452-4400
Fax: (917) 527-9915
www.accenture.com

Affiliated Computer Services, Inc. (ACS)
2828 North Haskell Avenue
Dallas, TX 75204
Phone: (214) 841-6111
Fax: (214) 821-8315
www.acs-inc.com

Ajilon Consulting
210 West Pennsylvania Avenue
Suite 650
Towson, MD 21204
Phone: (410) 821-0435
Fax: (410) 828-0106
www.ajilonconsulting.com

Alliance Consulting Group
Six Tower Bridge
181 Washington Street
Suite 350
Conshohocken, PA 19428
Phone: (610) 234-4301
Fax: (610) 234-4302
www.allianceconsulting.com

Atos Origin
5599 San Felipe, Suite 300
Houston, TX 77056
Phone: (713) 513-3000
Fax: (713) 403-7204
www.atosorigin.com/en-us

Tour les Miroirs - Bat C
18, avenue d'Alsace
92926 Paris La Défense 3 Cedex
France
Phone: +33-1-55-91-20-00
Fax: +33-1-55-91-20-05

BearingPoint, Inc., Management and Technology Consultants
1676 International Drive
McLean, VA 22102
Phone: (703) 747-3000
Fax: (703) 747-8500
www.bearingpoint.com

Booz Allen Hamilton
8283 Greensboro Drive
McLean, VA 22102
Phone: (703) 902-5000
Fax: (703) 902-3333
www.boozallen.com

BT Global Services
350 Madison Avenue
New York, NY 10017
Phone: (646) 487-7400
Fax: (646) 487-3370
www.btglobalservices.com

Bull
296 Concord Road
Billerica, MA 01821
Phone: (978) 294-6000
Fax: (978) 294-7999
www.bull.com/us

Capgemini
750 Seventh Avenue, Suite 1800
New York, NY 10019
Phone: (212) 314-8000
Fax: (212) 314-8001
www.us.capgemini.com

CGI Group Inc.
1130 Sherbrooke Street West
5th Floor
Montreal, Quebec H3A 2M8
Canada
Phone: (514) 841-3200
Fax: (514) 841-3299
www.cgi.com

CIBER, Inc.
5251 DTC Parkway
Suite 1400
Greenwood Village, CO 80111
Phone: (303) 220-0100
Toll Free: (800) 242-3799
Fax: (303) 220-7100
www.ciber.com

Cisco Systems, Inc.
170 West Tasman Drive
San Jose, CA 95134
Phone: (408) 526-4000
Toll Free: (800) 553-NETS
www.cisco.com

Cognizant Technology Solutions
500 Glenpointe Center West
Teaneck, NJ 07666
Phone: (201) 801-0233
Fax: (201) 801-0243
www.cognizant.com

Computer Sciences Corporation
2100 East Grand Avenue
El Segundo, CA 90245
Phone: (310) 615-0311
www.csc.com

Covansys Corporation
32605 West Twelve Mile Road
Suite 250
Farmington Hills, MI 48334
Phone: (248) 488-2088
Toll Free: (800) 688-2088
Fax: (248) 488-2089
www.covansys.com

CTG
800 Delaware Avenue
Buffalo, NY 14209
Phone: (716) 882-8000
Fax: (716) 887-7464
www.ctg.com

Employer Directory, cont.

Deloitte Consulting LLP
1633 Broadway, 35th Floor
New York, NY 10019
Phone: (212) 489-1600
www.deloitte.com

Detica
Surrey Research Park
Guildford
Surrey, GU2 7YP
United Kingdom
Phone: +44-1483-816000
Fax: +44-1483-816144
www.detica.com

Diamond Management & Technology Consultants, Inc.
John Hancock Center
875 North Michigan Avenue
Suite 3000
Chicago, IL 60611
Phone: (312) 255-5000
Fax: (312) 255-6000
www.diamondconsultants.com

EDS
5400 Legacy Drive
Plano, TX 75024
Phone: (972) 604-6000
Toll Free: (800) 566-9337
www.eds.com

Getronics
290 Concord Road
Billerica, MA 01821
Phone: (978) 625-5000
www.getronics.com

GFI Informatique
199, rue Championnet
75018 Paris
France
Phone: +33-44-85-88-88
Fax: +33-44-85-88-89
www.gfi.fr

Fujitsu Consulting
343 Thornall Street, Suite 630
Edison, NJ 08837
Phone: (732) 549-4100
Fax: (732) 632-1826
www.fujitsu.com/us/services/consulting

HP Services
3000 Hanover Street
Palo Alto, CA 94304
Phone: (650) 857-1501
Fax: (650) 857-5518
www.hp.com/hps

IBM Global Services
New Orchard Road
Armonk, NY 10504
Phone: (914) 499-1900
Fax: (914) 765-7382
www.ibm.com/consulting/services

Infosys Consulting Inc.
6607 Kaiser Drive
Fremont, CA 94555
Phone: (510) 742-3000
Fax: (510) 742-3090
www.infosysconsulting.com

Interactive Business Systems, Inc.
2625 Butterfield Road
Oak Brook, IL 60523
Phone: (630) 571-9100
Fax: (630) 571-9110
www.ibs.com

Keane
100 City Square, 4th Floor
Boston, MA 02129
Phone: (617) 517-2025
Toll Free: (800) 74-KEANE
Fax: (617) 517-2020
www.keane.com

Lockheed Martin Corporation
6801 Rockledge Drive
Bethesda, MD 20817
Phone: (301) 897-6000
Fax: (301) 897-6704
www.lockheedmartin.com

LogicaCMG
10375 Richmond Avenue
Suite 1000
Houston, TX 77042
Phone: (713) 954-7000
Fax: (713) 785-0880
www.logicacmg.com

Stephenson House
75 Hampstead Road
London, NW1 2PL
United Kingdom
Phone: +44-20-7637-9111
Fax: +44-20-7468-7006

Oracle Consulting
500 Oracle Parkway
Redwood Shores, CA 94065
Phone: (650) 506-7000
www.oracle.com/consulting/index.html

PA Consulting Group
4601 North Fairfax Drive
Suite 600
Arlington, VA 22203
Phone: (571) 227-9000
Fax: (571) 227-9001

123 Buckingham Palace Road
London, SW1W 9SR
United Kingdom
Phone: +44-20-7730-9000
Fax: +44-20-7333-5050
www.paconsulting.com

Visit Vault at **www.vault.com** for insider company profiles, expert advice,
career message boards, expert resume reviews, the Vault Job Board and more.

VAULT CAREER LIBRARY   **241**

Employer Directory, cont.

Perot Systems
2300 West Plano Parkway
Plano, TX 75075
Phone: (972) 577-0000
Toll Free: (888) 31-PEROT
Fax: (972) 340-6100
www.perotsystems.com

The Revere Group
325 North LaSalle Street
Suite 325
Chicago, IL 60610
Phone: (312) 873-3400
Fax: (312) 873-3500
www.reveregroup.com

Sapient
25 First Street
Cambridge, MA 02141
Phone: (617) 621-0200
Fax: (617) 621-1300
www.sapient.com

Satyam Computer Services Ltd.
8500 Leesburg Pike, Suite 201
Vienna, VA 22182
Phone: (703) 734-2100
Fax: (703) 734-2110
www.satyam.com

Siemens IT Solutions and Services, Inc.
101 Merritt 7
Norwalk, CT 06851
Phone: (203) 642-2300
Fax: (203) 642-2399
www.usa.siemens.com/it-solutions

Smartronix, Inc.
22685 Three Notch Road
California, MD 20619
Phone: (301) 737-2800
Fax: (301) 866-0528
www.smartronix.com

T-Systems
701 Warrenville Road
Suite 100
Lisle, IL 60532
Phone: (630) 493-6100
Fax: (630) 493-6111
www.t-systems.com

Tata Consultancy Services
101 Park Avenue, 26th Floor
New York, NY 10178
Phone: (212) 557-8038
Fax: (212) 867-8652
www.tcs.com

Technology Solutions Company
55 East Monroe, Suite 2600
Chicago, IL 60603
Phone: (312) 228-4500
Fax: (312) 228-4501
www.techsol.com

Telcordia Technologies
One Telcordia Drive
Piscataway, NJ 08854
Phone: (800) 521-2673
Fax: (732) 336-2559
www.telcordia.com

TIAX LLC
15 Acorn Park
Cambridge, MA 02140
Phone: (617) 498-5000
Fax: (617) 498-7200
www.tiaxllc.com

Unisys
Township Line & Union
Meeting Rds-A
Unisys Way
Blue Bell, PA 19424
Phone: (215) 986-4011
www.unisys.com

Wipro Ltd.
Doddakannelli Sarjapur Road
Bangalore, Karnataka 560 035
India
Phone: +91-80-844-0011
Fax: +91-80-844-0256
www.wipro.com

Xansa
420 Thames Valley Park Drive
Reading, RG6 1PU
United Kingdom
Phone: +44-8702-416181
Fax: +44-8702-426282
www.xansa.com

Telecommunications

Industry Overview

We're all connected

In simpler times, the word "telecommunications" might conjure an image of a telephone—and not much else. These days, though, the telephone is less the shining symbol of telecommunications and more an antiquated relic of the industry's primitive beginnings. Telecom today has gone high tech and mobile, encompassing wireless communication, broadband Internet access, and cable and digital TV while still providing landline phone service to those who have yet to convert to the 21st century. These varying forms of modern communication have bled into each other as well—while your cell phone is busy downloading the latest Weird Al music video, you can call your best friend across the country sans long-distance charges over the Internet. Because of this growing interrelation among telecommunication products, industry biggies like AT&T and Verizon are spreading their reach into Internet and digital television to offer bundled "triple-play" phone, Internet and TV subscription packages to customers.

In the U.S., total telecom spending reached more than $923 billion in 2006, and is expected to surpass the $1 trillion mark by 2009, according to the Telecommunications Industry Association (TIA). In the world at large, the TIA predicts telecom spending, topping $2.6 trillion in 2006, to reach $4.3 trillion by 2010. Much of this growth comes thanks to the ascendancy of the Internet and its junkie-like need for high-speed connections. Telecom holds the trump card with its control of the fiber-optic network that brings broadband connection into millions of homes. In 2007, industry profits are expected to top $72 billion, breaking the industry record set back in the halcyon, pre-bust days of 1998.

The bell tolls for AT&T

Established in 1877 as American Bell, AT&T enjoyed the largest share of the telecom industry pie for nearly a century, thanks to the government's belief that the utility constituted a "natural" monopoly. That monopoly crumbled in 1969, when the Federal Communications Commission (FCC) allowed other companies—such as MCI, which was quick to get in the game—to play in Ma Bell's sandbox. But monopolies don't disappear overnight: to encourage competition in the long-distance market, the Department of Justice (DOJ) followed up with an antitrust suit against AT&T in 1974, resulting in the company's division into a long-distance retailer and seven regional Bell operating companies (RBOCs, or "Baby Bells"), which would compete in the local call market as independent local exchange carriers (LECs). The final breakup of AT&T took place in 1984.

The industry thrived after the breakup, exploding into hundreds of smaller competitors, lowering the cost of long-distance calling dramatically. AT&T, which held about 70 percent of the market in 1984, controlled only a third in 2005, but bounced back following its buyout by SBC to once again become the biggest kid on the playground. Still, it's these so-called "Tier 1" carriers—AT&T, Sprint Nextel and Global Crossing—that make up the bulk of the long-distance market.

Untangling the wires

As the long-distance market diversified, the local exchange market remained relatively homogenous. The Telecommunications Act of 1996 aimed to change that by deregulating entry into local markets and requiring that the Baby Bells, or incumbent local exchange carriers (ILECs), retail their network elements to smaller competitors. The incumbents were required to unbundle their networks for reasonable prices, with the goal of decentralizing the system into a "network of networks." The act also temporarily blocked an RBOC from entering the long-distance market until it could prove sufficient competition in its local territory.

Visit Vault at **www.vault.com** for insider company profiles, expert advice, career message boards, expert resume reviews, the Vault Job Board and more.

VAULT CAREER LIBRARY 243

Another provision of the Telecom Act, allowing RBOCs the right to sell cable television services and phone equipment, proved to be a boon for the strongest RBOCs. Thanks to those services and the entry of the Baby Bells into long distance, the act actually had the opposite of its intended effect, allowing a few RBOCs to solidify their positions and dominate the market through mergers and acquisitions. Today, there are just three RBOCs—Verizon, AT&T and Qwest—that dominate both local phone service and the burgeoning DSL (digital subscriber line) markets. Until recently there were five such companies, but the market contracted in 2005 as SBC took over AT&T (keeping the latter's name), and in March 2006 as the new AT&T announced it would purchase BellSouth.

Not just at home

The dealmaking wasn't limited to America's shores. Telecom became truly global in 1997, when 70 member countries of the World Trade Organization (WTO)—which together control 90 percent of worldwide telecom sales—agreed to open up their telecom markets to each other at the start of the following year. Nearly all telecom companies around the globe had privatized in anticipation of this expanded level of competition. The accord led to a rush of international deals, especially in the world's second-largest telecom market, Japan. In 1999, British Telecommunications and AT&T partnered to acquire a 30 percent stake in LD operator Japan Telecom, combining their Japanese ventures under JT. A few months later, Britain's Cable & Wireless bought Japan's No. 6 carrier, IDC, and in 1999, Global Crossing teamed up with Marubeni to build a brand-new network, called Global Access, to service Japan.

Wall Street highs and lows

As mergers and acquisitions activity heated up, Wall Street took notice: investors poured $1.3 trillion into telecom companies in the five years following passage of the Telecom Act, according to *Forbes* magazine. But with this activity came increased scrutiny and risk. Ultimately, the industry was subject to the same meltdown that hit the rest of the tech sector beginning in late 2000. Again according to *Forbes*, the industry's market value plummeted by $1 trillion after the Dow took its dive. Mergers also fell by the wayside: in July 2000, a proposed merger between Sprint and WorldCom fell through when the Justice Department filed a lawsuit that attempted to block the deal.

Cooking the books

Compounding the gloom, a number of major telecoms had high-profile problems in their accounting departments. The biggest offender was WorldCom, which ran afoul of the feds in 2002. WorldCom filed for the largest bankruptcy in U.S. history in July of that year, racking up $41 billion in debt and an estimated $11 billion in fraudulent expenses—leading to a $100 billion loss to shareholders. Even as the company attempted a rebound, emerging from bankruptcy in April 2004 with a lighter debt load, a moderately healthy outlook and a less tarnished name (the company had reverted to the MCI brand), it had to contend with scores of class-action lawsuits. Former CEO Bernard J. Ebbers also faced a growing list of federal fraud and conspiracy charges. In March 2005 Ebbers was found guilty on all counts, and was sentenced to 25 years in prison. Accounting firm Citigroup, which had conspired with WorldCom, announced in May 2004 that it would pay $2.65 billion to investors for its role in the scandal. Two years later, the beleaguered company was virtually no more, having been gobbled up by Verizon in a deal worth $8.5 billion.

In addition to WorldCom, about a half-dozen other providers of telecom services began Chapter 11 bankruptcy proceedings in 2002, dumping customers and employees as they went. In 2003, Sprint reorganized into separate business and consumer units in an effort to save $1 billion.

Horning in on each other

Competition that got rolling when telecom firms entered the cable game following the Telecommunications Act has only gained momentum since. In recent years, it's gotten downright ugly, with each industry reaching into the others picnic basket of products to get at the goodies—Yogi Bears gone wrong. Because of the onward and upward march of technology, the wires and signals that bring you cable TV can just as easily bring you phone service, and vice versa. Throw Internet access into the mix, and you've got a subscriber feeding frenzy, with phone and cable companies all vying to sell consumers the same services. Verizon and AT&T recently scored a victory in the fight, winning statewide video franchises in California in March 2007. As of May 2007, nine states had passed franchise laws letting phone companies into the TV game, including Texas, Virginia, New Jersey and Michigan. Similar legislation is pending in several other states. In the meantime, AT&T and Verizon continue to lobby the government for a nationwide franchise.

The FCC has stepped in to referee the melee, most recently siding with phone companies in a ruling it handed down in December 2006. The decree limits the amount of time local municipalities can consider if they want to grant phone companies a video franchise in their area to 90 days. Up to now, local governments (heavily lobbied by cable companies, says Verizon) have historically been slow to grant approval of phone companies entering the television game, and often tack on extraneous demands.

Neutral tones

The FCC is also stepping into the ring on the issue of "net neutrality," a term that describes the indiscriminate nature of the Web, where no sites are more readily accessible than others. The crux of the issue is whether or not broadband access providers (namely, telephone companies) can charge higher rates to certain Internet content providers—creating a toll lane on the information superhighway and potentially favoring certain sites over others. The issue is an important one, as demand for broadband has spurred the recovery of telecom companies that started in 2006. The FCC launched an inquiry into the issue in May 2007, specifically looking to see if broadband companies are adhering to the "open Internet" principles laid out by the federal organization in 2005.

Can you hear me now?

It is a truth universally acknowledged that every person in possession of relatively good fortune must have a cell phone, or at least want one. The fact that the $190 billion American wireless market is growing by leaps and bounds and posting double-digit gains backs this up. Wireless revenue increased more than 15 percent in 2006, and the industry plans on its reaching $265 billion by 2009.

The wireless market outpaced long distance for the first time in 2003, according to TIA number crunchers (LD posted $78 billion in spending to wireless' $89 billion), the same year that the number of wireless users was estimated to be above one billion worldwide. By 2007, industry analysts reckoned that three of every four Americans had a wireless phone, and it is projected that 270 million Americans (about 87 percent of the population) will tote a cell phone by 2009.

The wireless boom heralds renewed business activity in telecom. Competition began to sizzle in late 2003, as the first phase of a federal law allowing "portability"—a/k/a letting consumers retain their mobile phone numbers when switching carriers—took effect. One notable event was Cingular's $41 billion purchase of rival AT&T Wireless, announced in February 2004, following a fierce bidding war with Vodafone. Just to show how complicated the industry's family ties are, Cingular was, at the time, owned by rival Baby Bells—though these huge conglomerates can't really be called "baby" anymore—AT&T and BellSouth (which themselves are in the process of becoming one, after AT&T bought BellSouth in 2006); while competitor Verizon Wireless is a joint venture between Verizon and Vodafone.

Visit Vault at **www.vault.com** for insider company profiles, expert advice, career message boards, expert resume reviews, the Vault Job Board and more.

V/\ULT CAREER LIBRARY   **245**

Deals kept perking right along as Sprint merged with Nextel in August 2005, when the companies were, respectively, the No. 3 and 5 wireless carriers. Though the present company is one of the largest telecoms in the world, it's still No. 3 in the U.S. by number of subscribers behind Verizon and Cingular.

Wireless—if not VoIP—is the wave of the future: while landlines were once seen as a source of dependable revenue and a way to spread risk, wireless companies have recently been setting up their landline units on their own and seeing them on their way. Sprint spun off its landlines in May 2006 under the name Embarq, while Alltel, after beefing up its landlines by acquiring Valor Communications, divested the unit under the name Windstream in July 2006.

Off the hook and on the 'Net

Cell phones aren't the only way consumers are making calls these days—Voice over Internet Protocol (VoIP), offered by companies like Vonage and Skype, allows users to turn their personal computers into telephones by sending voice data over a broadband connection in the same way other data is sent online. Growth in the VoIP market has been exponential: in 2005, Internet phone subscribers in the U.S. went from a mere 1.3 million to 4.5 million, according to TeleGeography, an industry research group (they also predict that there will be 19 million VoIP users by 2010).

Bypassing questions of local and long distance networks entirely, VoIP providers allow complete number portability—a subscriber in Iowa, for instance, could have a (212) Manhattan area code. The technology is also advantageous in terms of cost. Thanks to the FCC, VoIP is exempt from some of the taxes and regulations with which regular phone carriers are saddled. But, of course, the major telecoms are busy on Capitol Hill, trying to level the playing field. In June 2005, the FCC ruled that VoIP companies had to contribute, just like any other phone company, to the Universal Service Fund, designed to keep costs down in rural and low-income areas. The contributions to this fund will presumably be passed on to consumers in the form of higher rates.

Verizon cut down an upstart competitor several notches in March 2007, when it won a $58 million suit against VoIP provider Vonage. Found guilty of violating three Verizon patents, Vonage was later ordered to cease using those patents, potentially forcing the company to remove the part of its service that allows Vonage subscribers to talk to non-internet phone users (in other words, most of the world). A judge ruled in April 2007 that Vonage could continue to sign up new users while it appeals the decision.

Working in the Telecom Industry

A job market roller coaster

The numbers are intimidating: telecom seems to thrive on sudden booms and equally rapid readjustments. By some estimates, the industry slashed 300,000 jobs during the troubled period beginning in late 2000. Companies also feel compelled to trim excess fat when they merge—the 2006 MCI-Verizon merger, for example, resulted in the elimination of some 7,000 positions. Even with increased demand for telecom services, the U.S. Department of Labor's Bureau of Labor Statistics (BLS) says that employment in the industry is expected to decline by 7 percent between 2004 and 2014.

But there is still plenty of work out there. According to the BLS, telecom accounted for one million jobs in 2004, the latest year for which statistics are available. Of these employees, three quarters of them work in office and administrative support or sales, while installation, maintenance and repair account for nearly the rest. (This latter portion, however, is expected to decline, due to the increasing prevalence of wireless phones and a trend toward more durable equipment.) The BLS insists that keeping job skills up to date and having a diverse and flexible skill set is crucial in this rapidly changing industry.

Talk the talk

Not surprisingly, communication skills are essential throughout the telecommunications industry. Customer service agents have to field calls from agitated subscribers with grace and good humor. Technicians have face-to-face contact with customers when installing or fixing network equipment in the field. And then there are the sales reps, who pass out smiles and handshakes with aplomb in pursuit of corporate accounts. Communication serves workers well within the office, too, say insiders, because front-line field and call-center workers often serve as an intermediary between subscribers and management.

While rumors of outsourcing jobs rumble throughout the industry—especially with customer service positions that can be handled as easily in New Delhi, India as in Dayton, Ohio—many telecom jobs are here to stay. Because every part of the industry involves on-the-ground networks, be they supported by cell phone towers or fiber-optic cables, telecom companies will always need the people to expand, update and maintain those networks. Accordingly, technical positions abound for those toting undergraduate or associate degrees in electrical engineering and related fields.

Tough sell?

While call-center jobs are ubiquitous and open to those without college degrees (and can offer commission income on top of salary) insiders say there is no upward mobility for people entering the company from this route. Instead, those looking for a sales position in the telecom industry are encouraged to start with an internship after completing their degree. Once your foot is in the company door, our sources stress, networking is crucial to rising through the company ranks. In fact, networking is important throughout the telecom world, regardless of your position. As one consultant in the industry puts it, "networking has to be built into your system because that man in the blue suit at that official gathering could well be your next lead for a $1 million consulting engagement."

Work free

In addition to the obvious perks involved with working in the telecom industry (free TV, anyone? How about free Internet access and cell phone service too?), many workers report flexibile scheduling as a cherished part of their jobs. Salesfolk, marketers and managers alike are allowed to budget their time as they see fit. As long as they're doing their part to push the company forward, no one bats an eye at those extra-long lunches or midday golf sessions. Additionally, telecommuting is becoming more and more acceptable throughout the industry—perhaps because its these companies' products that are facilitating web conferences and work-from-home options for the rest of the business world.

Visit Vault at **www.vault.com** for insider company profiles, expert advice, career message boards, expert resume reviews, the Vault Job Board and more.

VAULT CAREER LIBRARY   247

Employer Directory

Alcatel-Lucent
54, rue La Boétie
75008 Paris
France
Phone: +33-1-40-76-10-10
Fax: +33-1-40-76-14-00
www.alcatel-lucent.com

Alltel Corporation
1 Allied Drive
Little Rock, AR 72202
Phone: (501) 905-8000
Fax: (501) 905-5444
www.alltel.com

AT&T Incorporated
175 East Houston Street
San Antonio, TX 78205-2233
Phone: (210) 821-4105
Fax: (210) 351-2187
www.att.com

BellSouth Corporation
1155 Peachtree Street NE
Atlanta, GA 30309-3610
Phone: (404) 249-2000
Fax: (404) 249-2071
www.bellsouth.com

BT Group plc
BT Centre
81 Newgate Street
London, EC1A 7AJ
United Kingdom
Phone: +44-20-7356-5000
Fax: +44-20-7356-5520
www.btplc.com

Charter Communications Inc.
12405 Powerscourt Drive
Suite 100
St. Louis, MO 63131-3660
Phone: (314) 965-0555
Fax: (314) 965-9745
www.charter.com

Comcast Corporation
1500 Market Street
Philadelphia, PA 19102-2148
Phone: (215) 665-1700
Fax: (215) 981-7790
www.comcast.com

Corning Incorporated
1 Riverfront Plaza
Corning, NY 14831-0001
Phone: (607) 974-9000
Fax: (607) 974-5927
www.corning.com

Cox Communications Incorporated
1400 Lake Hearn Drive
Atlanta, GA 30319
Phone: (404) 843-5000
Fax: (404) 843-5975
www.cox.com

Motorola, Inc.
1303 E. Algonquin Road
Schaumburg, IL 60196
Phone: (847) 576-5000
Toll Free: (800) 262-8509
Fax: (847) 576-5372
www.motorola.com

Nortel
195 The West Mall
Toronto, Ontario M9C 5K1
Canada
Phone: (905) 863-7000
www.nortel.com

Orange PLC
50 George Street
London, W1U 7DZ
United Kingdom
Phone: +44-870-376-8888
Fax: +44-20-7984-1601
www.orange.com

Qwest Communications International
1801 California Street
Denver, CO 80202
Phone: (800) 899-7780
Toll Free: (800) 899-7780
Fax: (303) 992-1724
www.qwest.com

Scientific-Atlanta, Inc.
5030 Sugarloaf Parkway
Lawrenceville, GA 30044-2689
Phone: (770) 236-5000
Toll Free: (800) 433-6222
Fax: (408) 526-4545
www.sciatl.com

Sprint Nextel Corporation
2001 Edmund Halley Drive
Reston, VA 20191
Phone: (703) 443-4000
www.sprint.com

Verizon Business
Verizon Way, 295 N. Maple Avenue
Basking Ridge, NJ 07920-1002
Phone: (908) 559-4000
www.verizonbusiness.com

Verizon Communications
140 West Street
New York, NY 10007
Phone: (212) 395-2121
Fax: (212) 869-3265
www.verizon.com

Viatel
Wick Road
Egham, Surrey, TW20 0HR
United Kingdom
Phone: +44-1784-494-200
Fax: +44-1784-494-201
www.viatel.com

Employer Directory, cont.

Vodafone Group plc
Vodafone House
The Connection
Newbury, Berkshire, RG14 2FN
United Kingdom
Phone: +44-1635-33-251
Fax: +44-1635-45-713

Vonage Holdings Corporation
23 Main Street
Holmdel, NJ 07733
Phone: (732) 365-1328
Fax (732) 231-6783
www.vonage.com

XO Communications
11111 Sunset Hills Road
Reston, VA 20190-5327
Phone: (703) 547-2000

Visit Vault at **www.vault.com** for insider company profiles, expert advice, career message boards, expert resume reviews, the Vault Job Board and more.

VAULT CAREER LIBRARY   249

Transportation and Airlines

Transportation Industry Overview

Planes, trains and automobiles

The vast transportation industry carries people and products (safely and on time, of course) to destinations around the globe—no small feat. That's why it takes hundreds of thousands of workers operating thousands of vehicles—from the high-flying airplanes down to the lowly pushcart—to keep the goods moving. Because the economy is intimately connected to getting things from where they're made to where they're bought, the transportation sector, especially express services like UPS and FedEx Kinko's, are considered a bellwether for the economy's health on both domestic and global levels. As such, it can be said that economy is thriving in the face of high-cost impediments—rising fuel prices have hampered the transportation industry since the dawn of the 21st century, prompting experimentation in alternative energy sources and higher-efficiency vehicles. The industry can be broken into a handful of sectors: airlines, air cargo and express delivery carriers, trucks, railroads and buses.

Up in the clouds

According to the Air Transport Action Group, an airline advocacy organization, more than two billion people fly every year—and boy are their arms tired! But seriously, passenger planes support the business and pleasure travel needs of an increasingly mobile population, with 900 airlines across the planet flying about 22,000 airplanes. However, the events of September 11th, and the attendant drop in air travel, devastated the "Big Six" in the airline industry (United, Delta, US Airways, American, Continental and Northwest). Not helping matters was the subsequent economic recession, skyrocketing cost of fuel and rise in competition from low-cost low-fare carriers like JetBlue and Southwest. The airline industry nosedive has forced job cuts, union wars over wages, executive turnarounds and, in most cases, Chapter 11 filing.

Airport security has continued to be a gnarly issue since the terrorist attacks of 2001. Customers resent the long lines and perceived affronts to their privacy involved in any trip to the airport, and the same security measures are costly to air carriers, who pay fees to the Transportation Security Administration, an agency created by the 2001 Aviation and Transportation Security Act. Along with a tedious ban on carry-on liquids and gels, the quashed August 2006 plot aimed at U.S.-bound flights from London brought with it fears that the rebounding airline industry would again careen into heavy losses. Another foiled plot, this one to strike at New York's John F. Kennedy airport, introduced the possibility that airport workers (of which *U.S.A. Today* reports there are more than one million) could use their access and inside knowledge to attack passengers. A House of Representatives committee on airport security proposed a heightened screening program in June 2007, aimed at weeding out those bad eggs at work in America's airports.

Despite these and other challenges facing air carriers (among them avian flu and trouble making space for a—literally—growing customer base as obesity rates rise), the clouds have a silver lining. The proliferation of e-ticket technology has lowered overhead costs for airlines, which can save on manpower and printing charges as the check-in process becomes more and more automated. Increasing fuel efficiency, achieved partly by introducing lighter plastics into the bodies of new jets, promises to lessen the impact of soaring oil prices, up from $34 per barrel in 2003 to $80 per barrel in 2006. Revenue has steadily grown across the industry, reaching $449 billion in 2006, a 9 percent increase over 2005. In fact, 8 of the 10 largest flight carriers in the U.S. showed a profit in 2006, netting $1.3 billion as a group, a significant improvement over the losses of 2005. Hanging out to dry were Northwest and Delta, who took on restructuring costs due to their bankruptcy status for the year.

Visit Vault at **www.vault.com** for insider company profiles, expert advice, career message boards, expert resume reviews, the Vault Job Board and more.

VAULT CAREER LIBRARY   251

Boy, you gotta carry that weight

Unlike its passenger-toting sister in the sky, the air cargo business remains relatively stable, with major carriers posting profits even during the bleakest years, 2001 and 2002. Still, a few cargo carriers, including Arrow and Atlas, were forced into bankruptcy court alongside their passenger carrier counterparts. UPS, FedEx Kinko's and DHL dominate the express-delivery sector, all three operating their own modes of transportation and leasing space and services on other cargo haulers' vehicles. The Internet boom has had both a positive and negative effect on the industry: while the rise in e-mail has curtailed the shipping of smaller documents, more and more Internet shoppers, online retailers and small businesses are using express delivery companies for direct shipping services and supply chain management.

Many of the challenges the sector faces, including tighter security requirements, high fuel costs and the need to replace an aging fleet of planes, mirror those on the passenger side. Others are specific to the air cargo industry—for instance, the Air Line Pilots Association (ALPA) worries that international shippers may begin routing cargo through Canada and Mexico in response to the new security restrictions, meaning reduced activity in the domestic market. Air cargo services also have to contend with other forms of transport, like ships and trucks. Despite this, the International Air Transport Association (IATA) predicts that worldwide demand for air freight will increase by more than 6 percent annually from 2005 to 2009.

The world delivered (on time)

The package delivery market is a fiercely competitive one, where the industry leaders vie for massive corporate contracts as well as business from individual consumers. FedEx, for one, has strengthened its market position by diversifying, namely through its $2.4 billion buyout in January 2004 of document services provider and copy shop chain Kinko's; there are now more than 1,600 FedEx Kinko's locations worldwide. Dispatching approximately 75,000 ground vehicles and an air fleet of 669 planes, FedEx Kinko's operates separate express, ground and freight units. UPS, on the other hand, has only 282 planes but more than 100,000 ground vehicles. Even if UPS lags in the number of cargo planes, it's still the market leader in the U.S., with revenue of $47 billion in 2006. FedEx is nipping at its heels, though, with revenue of $35 billion in 2006.

Globally, the German logistics and express delivery firm DHL, run by German postal entity Deutsche Post, has the highest revenue, netting more than $80 billion in 2006. The company made aggressive steps in 2003 to solidify its position in the U.S. market, when it acquired Airborne Inc. for $1.1 billion, securing its No. 3 place domestically and further strengthening its dominance in the world market for express delivery services overall. All three companies have set their sights on developing markets overseas: FedEx Kinko's began offering next-day express delivery in China for the first time in May 2007. UPS—which has had operations in the Far East for many years, having bought the Chinese firm Sinotrans Group, for $100 million in December 2004—also invested $20 million in April 2007 to build a new airplane hub in Shanghai.

Greening "Brown"

Both UPS and FedEx have taken steps recently to "green" their ground service fleets, replacing diesel vehicles with more environmentally friendly options like compressed natural gas and electricity. UPS' "green fleet" (about 19,000 vehicles) logged its 100 millionth mile in February 2007, and the company added 50 hybrid electric trucks to its ranks the following May. FedEx is also raising the green stakes by buying a percentage of the power for its retail locations from renewable sources and increasing the amount of recycled content in its packaging. While the companies get PR points for their efforts, what's really driving the green movement is, well, the green-cash, that is. Along with attracting environmentally-sensitive consumers, hybrid electric vehicles use much less fuel than traditional cars, reducing fuel costs by as much as half.

Keep on truckin'

Express-delivery services also share ties—and in some cases overlap—with the trucking sector, which in 2006 alone handled 10 billion tons of fun, or 69 percent of the volume of freight in the U.S. Dominated by bulk truckers like Quality Distribution, JB Hunt and YRC Worldwide (formerly Yellow Roadway, YRC beefed up its business with the May 2005 purchase of supply-chain management firm USF for $1.5 billion), the trucking industry has hit a rough patch of road in the last year, with tonnage (the amount of stuff hauled by trucks) falling through 2006. A possible culprit is America's gifting trends—increasingly ubiquitous gift cards tend to spread the holiday shopping season out over several months, denying truckers their usual October to November spike in business.

The trucking sector also overlaps with the railroad world, with giants like JB Hunt and Schneider International teaming up with old hands on the rails such as Union Pacific, Norfolk Southern, CSX and Burlington Northern Santa Fe. With new technologies allowing real-time cargo tracking and time-specific delivery, this sector of the transportation industry is expected to become increasingly integrated. As the economy grows, both rail and truck transport services will add jobs in order to accommodate the increased quantity of goods in circulation.

Working on the railroad

Unlike its trucker brother, the railroad saw impressive increases in its traffic in 2006. That year freight railroads in the U.S. shipped 1.74 trillion ton-miles (a measure of the volume and distance of the industry's freight output, a ton-mile is one ton shipped one mile), a 2.5 percent increase over 2005 and a record-breaker. The growth over the year was driven by the popularity of coal and ethanol, both energy sources on the rise that, coincidentally, can only be shipped cost-effectively on the rails. And 2006's record may not hold out for long—according to *The Wall Street Journal*, ethanol shipments are expected to increase 33 percent throughout 2007.

Take the A train

While the shipping portion of the rail sector has continued to chug along, the passenger-train sector has contracted dramatically in previous decades. In fact, the railroads have been in decline since the advent of the automobile and the Federal Aid Highway Act of 1956. In the 1960s, the once-mighty railroad was dealt a heavy blow when the U.S. Postal Service turned to trucks and airplanes for its first-class shipping needs. Following 1970s legislation, Amtrak took over the majority of U.S. passenger trains under its National Railroad Passenger Corporation umbrella—though the operator still has trouble turning any sort of profit; the company, after all, cannot compete with the speed offered by airlines or low fares by bus companies. Therefore, with dwindling passenger rolls and increased operating costs, Amtrak has become increasingly subsidized—the organization had taken in $29 billion in government handouts by 2006, and was operating at a loss of over $1 billion per year in 2004 and 2005. Amtrak isn't the only railroad running at a loss: the Long Island Railroad (LIRR), the busiest commuter rail line in the U.S., had posted annual losses of $1 million by July 2006.

It should be noted that almost no form of public transport is self-supporting. All get regular infusions of capital from both states and the federal government, either directly or, in the case of bus companies, in the form of highway maintenance. There is a great deal of carping in the government and the media about the money spent on Amtrak, but, according to the Bureau of Transportation Statistics (BTS), in 2002 (the latest year for which complete data is available) the government gave Amtrak slightly over $1 billion, while giving $7.7 billion in subsidies to maintain highways, airlines and airports.

Get on the bus

For long-haul passenger travel, about the only thing cheaper than riding a bus is sticking out your thumb and hoping for the best. Motorcoaches, as buses prefer to be called these days, transport more than 631 million passengers a year in the U.S.,

Visit Vault at **www.vault.com** for insider company profiles, expert advice, career message boards, expert resume reviews, the Vault Job Board and more.

VAULT CAREER LIBRARY

253

more than half of those passengers being either young (college students) or old (senior citizens), according to the American Bus Association (ABA). The bus sector is unique in its composition: unlike the heavily subsidized rail and airline sectors, motorcoach companies are more likely to go it alone (though the industry received about $25 million in grant funding for security following September 11th).

There are more than 3,500 bus companies on the roads in the U.S., many of which are small, entrepreneurial operators—75 percent operate less than 10 buses. Major operators include Trailways, which has been around for nearly 70 years and operates a group of 65 member companies, and Greyhound, founded in 1914 and acquired in 1999 by Laidlaw Inc. As insurance rates have increased tenfold in recent years, access to affordable coverage is a key challenge faced by the industry, even pricing some operators out of the market.

Airlines Industry Overview

A volatile industry

The airline industry consists of companies that move people and cargo with planes. The International Air Transport Association (IATA) claims that this $470 billion worldwide industry stimulates 8 percent of global GDP through tourism, shipping and business travel. But despite its enormous contribution to world commerce, the industry has historically gone through dizzying booms and alarming busts as it reacts to regulatory changes and economic factors. Airlines are just starting to dig themselves out of the hole caused by September 11th. The IATA says the implementation of security measures has cost the industry $5.6 billion per year. Spats with labor unions, troubles with underfinanced pensions, high jet fuel prices and a string of bankruptcies, from which some carriers are still emerging, have caused further havoc. The July 2007 attack on Glasgow's airport is a reminder that the airline industry is still a target for terrorists. Nevertheless, *The Economist* thinks that once these issues have been resolved (no easy task), the airlines will be in a position to expand.

Cleared for takeoff

The airline industry took to the skies following the Wright brothers' first successful flight in 1905. As with many new technologies, airplanes were first used extensively by the military—namely, during World War I, for reconnaissance, bombing and aerial combat. Following the war, when the U.S. found itself with a surplus of military aircraft and pilots without much to do, the postal service opted in 1918 to start a transcontinental air mail service, which ran from New York to San Francisco. To keep costs down, 12 spur routes were spun off to independent contractors. Thus the familiar scions of the friendly skies— American Airlines, United Airlines, TWA and Northwest—were born.

Passenger flights didn't become a reality until Ford introduced a 12-seat plane in 1925. The Ford Trimotor made carrying people potentially profitable. Pan American Airways, the first airline with international destinations, was founded in 1927. Remarkably, airlines remained generally profitable during the Great Depression. Under the New Deal, the government subsidized airlines to carry mail. In 1934, however, postal reforms reduced the amount of money airlines earned for carrying the mail. By 1938, over a million Americans were flying on airplanes. This industry's rapid growth prompted new government policies. In 1938, Congress enacted the Civil Aeronautics Act. The airlines were happy that an independent agency was in charge of aviation policy. Before 1938 Civil Aeronautics Act passed, numerous government agencies and departments pushed and pulled airlines in many directions.

World War II brought many advances to the civilian air transport sector. Innovations initially intended for bombers made passenger planes larger, faster and able to carry heavier payloads and to fly at higher altitudes. The 1970s saw the introduction of supersonic air travel with the advent of the Concorde. Due to the Concorde's only crash in 2000, as well as world economic effects after the September 11 attacks, the supersonic airliner stopped flying in October 2003.

Big trouble for the Big Six

After September 11th, Congress gave well over $20 billion to the airline industry in the form of reimbursements for losses incurred while planes were grounded following the attacks, monetary help for new passenger and plane security requirements, and pension funding relief. But many of the industry's major players were forced to shoulder massive debt loads to continue their operations; this was on top of debt they had been accumulating since even before the terrorist attacks. Of the "Big Six"—United, US Airways, American, Northwest, Continental and Delta—all but two, Continental and American, have been forced to file for Chapter 11. Smaller airlines including Great Plains, Hawaiian, Midway, National, Sun Country and Vanguard have also shown up in bankruptcy court.

Though passenger confidence continued to grow in the years following the terrorist attacks, the industry's red ink kept on flowing. The SARS scare in Asia, the Iraq war and a slowdown in the economy also hurt airlines. According to a June 2004 Senate report, the industry carried combined debts of more than $100 billion. Accordingly, major carriers continued to lobby the feds for financial support in the form of subsidies and loans.

Looking up?

The industry has struggled with profitability due to a combination of factors. Air carriers have been hit hard by rising fuel costs, with jet fuel prices in 2007 averaging about $80 per barrel. The high cost of oil remains a huge challenge to the airline industry. The IATA projects that in 2007, the industry's fuel bill will grow to $119 billion, an increase of $8 billion from 2005, when fuel costs totaled $111 billion. Labor disputes and underfinanced pensions have also been expensive problems for many carriers. Even JetBlue, which had strong profits for several years, suffered loses recently as it continues to grapple with rapid growth and rising expenses.

Overall, however, costs associated with air travel have dropped significantly over the past five years, as a result of price competition and attempts to keep ticket prices low despite high fuel costs. In early 2007, IATA Director General and CEO Giovanni Bisignani said the industry's distribution costs (the cost of selling tickets, such as ticket processing, credit card processing fees, etc.) are down 13 percent. Bisignani added that nonfuel unit costs, the cost per seat mile excluding the price of fuel, have declined 15 percent. Industry belt-tightening seems to be working. The IATA reports that the industry break-even fuel price went from $22 per barrel in 2003 to $65 per barrel in 2006.

Recently, the airline industry has started to show other signs of recovery. According to the IATA, a stronger world economy saw passenger traffic rise by 7 percent between 2005 and 2006, and air freight experienced a 5 percent gain. In order to accommodate this increased demand for air travel and to lower their fuel expenditures, airlines began snapping up new, more fuel-efficient planes. The airline industry's profitability has improved, and the IATA predicts that the industry will see $5 billion in profits in 2007. However, IATA director general Bisignani pointed out that the airlines still have $200 billion dollars of debt. Moreover, Bisignani warned that an event such as another terrorist attack or a pandemic scare could put many carriers back in the red.

A global network

Around the world, many airlines still are heavily subsidized—or owned outright—by their home nations. While this has been a successful setup for many, others haven't been so lucky. Swissair and Belgium's airline, Sabena, both crumbled when their respective governments couldn't keep up with demands for subsidies. Subsidized international and U.S. carriers have formed global alliances to avoid some regulatory issues and to maximize profits by sharing resources, including routes and marketing strategies. Well-known alliances include Oneworld—an alliance between American Airlines, British Airways and several other carriers—and SkyTeam, a partnership made up of Delta Air Lines, Air France, AeroMexico and other airlines. Such partnerships aren't always successful. An alliance between Dutch carrier KLM and Alitalia fell apart, for instance, after the Italian airline had trouble securing funding from its government patrons.

Visit Vault at **www.vault.com** for insider company profiles, expert advice, career message boards, expert resume reviews, the Vault Job Board and more.

VAULT CAREER LIBRARY   255

Partnerships aside, the airline industry remains remarkably competitive, and in today's tough climate, it's everyone for themselves. Tight regulatory controls in the U.S. make it difficult for major domestic carriers to merge. For example, a plan to join United Airlines and US Airways was shot down due to antitrust regulations. The US Airways name showed up again in merger talks, linked to America West for $1.5 billion, and the two companies made it official in September 2005. Then, in November 2006, US Airways made an offer for Delta. However, in early 2007, Delta's creditors rejected US Airways' $10 billion bid. Even if US Airways had purchased Delta, size (large or small) is no guarantee of profit. Four of the Big Six have gone into bankruptcy since 2001, and smaller budget airlines have also started struggling to make a profit.

Going regional

Regional airlines, which benefit from smaller, newer jets and lower operating costs than the domestic giants, have gained ground in recent years, becoming the fastest-growing segment of the airline market. Approximately 25 to 30 regional, or commuter, carriers operate in the industry today, according to the Bureau of Labor Statistics. Recent statistics from the Regional Airline Association reveal that one in five domestic airline passengers travel on a regional airline, and that planes serving regional markets make up one-third of the U.S. commercial airline fleet on the whole. The big carriers have taken notice, and many now have controlling interests in newer regional airlines—Delta controls Comair, for instance, while American has American Eagle. In April 2006, Compass Airlines became a subsidiary of Northwest. The trend is reflected in Europe, too. Both globally and domestically, alliances with major carriers give the upstart regionals access to major airport hubs. In some cases, however, regional and low-budget airlines have skirted the hub question altogether by choosing to operate out of slightly out-of-the-way airports—Southwest's use of Islip airport, in a suburb of New York, and JetBlue's adoption of Long Beach, near Los Angeles, are two examples. And in other instances, regional airlines have decided to spread their wings and join the burgeoning low-cost boom. Some regional airlines now do longer haul flights. For example, Midwest Airlines (formerly Midwest Express) connects several cities in the Midwest to destinations such as Boston, New York and San Francisco.

The budget boom

The budget airline sector—consisting of top performers like Southwest Airlines and JetBlue, plus a growing number of upstarts—has gotten a good deal of attention lately. But budget flight isn't a new phenomenon in the industry. In fact, Southwest has been around since 1971. The difference is in the branding and public acceptance of these carriers, fueled in part by Southwest's customer-centric approach, and by customers' reduced service expectations post-September 11th. Expanded routes have helped, too. Where once low-budget carriers limited their flights to relatively short hauls in regional markets, today's top discount airlines regularly offer cross-country, and even international, flights.

The budget carrier phenomenon has rocked Europe, too, where about 60 low-cost carriers operated in 2006, compared to just four in 1999. European customers have warmed up to the budget boom as well. British-based easyJet increased its passenger flow more than eight-fold between 1999 and 2004, while low-cost carrier Ryanair, operating out of Ireland, ranked as one of the top performers in the industry worldwide. Some of the larger airlines have decided to take advantage of the low-cost boom, such as United's Ted and Delta's Song, but to not much avail; Song, in fact, was reabsorbed into Delta in 2006, three years after its first plane took off.

The boom in low-budget carriers isn't limited to North America and Europe. There are also low-fare carriers in Asia, where there are now about 45 discount airlines. Examples are Singapore-based Tiger Airways, Pakistani carrier Aero Asia and Jakarta-headquartered Adam Air. In June 2007, South Korea's largest airline, Korean Air Lines, announced plans to start a low-fare unit to compete with discount carriers in Asia. Some budget airlines are also branching out into long-haul flights across the Atlantic and Pacific.

Cutting costs

Above all, cost-savings are seen as key to the success of low-budget carriers. One way air carriers measure their fiscal health is through cost per available seat mile (or CASM), a complex formula involving airplane capacity, operating costs, route lengths and other factors. Whereas American Airlines spends about 9.4 cents for each seat on each mile flown, budget competitors like Southwest and JetBlue lighten their loads with CASMs of 7.6 cents and 6.4 cents, respectively, according to an MSNBC article from December 2003. Those pennies add up over time, and so-called "legacy" carriers are under pressure to pinch them ever harder. But with more liberal work rules and a less-senior workforce overall, low-cost carriers beat their established rivals in terms of labor costs.

Other cost-cutting measures in the airline industry overall include streamlining fleets and retiring older planes; canceling unprofitable routes; greater efficiency in procurement processes involving suppliers; and slashing commissions once paid regularly to middlemen such as travel agencies. Airlines have saved money through online booking, and they encourage customers to book directly through airlines' web sites by offering incentives such online bonus miles. According to a 2006 *International Herald Tribune* article, online booking saves the airline industry $2 billion a year.

These airlines have also realized that consumers prefer to pick and choose their perks. An in-flight cocktail on JetBlue will still set you back $5, but XM radio and DIRECTV are free. Charging for amenities that previously came gratis allows carriers to keep ticket prices low, yet still turn a profit. Many airlines now charge passengers for meals and snacks. On Air Canada, customers now pay $2 for a pillow and a blanket. Moreover, some airlines now charge people for extra legroom. On Northwest, a bigger exit row seat costs an additional $15. United's flyers can sign up for an Economy Plus subscription, which is $299 a year. Subscribers get seats with five inches of extra legroom.

How low can you go?

Low-fare carriers, such as Southwest and JetBlue, were once the darlings of the airline industry. Recently, however, Southwest and JetBlue have had troubles of their own. When an ice storm hit JetBlue's hub at JFK airport in New York in February 2007, passengers were trapped on the tarmac for eight or more hours. It took JetBlue nearly a week to resume normal operations. JetBlue's founder and CEO, David Neeleman, apologized publicly for what happened and also introduced a "passenger's bill of rights." In May 2007, Neeleman stepped down as the airline's CEO.

In June 2007, *The Wall Street Journal* reported on a growing profit squeeze at Southwest. Over the past four years, Southwest's unit costs—the expenses to fly each seat one mile—have risen almost 20 percent due to increased labor costs and higher fuel prices. The airline's hedges to lock in low fuel prices have become less successful, and passengers have resisted increases in fares. Low-cost carriers are also facing greater competition from other airlines, which copied budget airlines' low-cost model during the post-September 11 industry downturn. Southwest has said it will respond to these pressures by reining in its rapid growth.

The lap of luxury

Some new airlines have attempted to attract the super-wealthy and business travelers. Upscale airlines MaxJet, SilverJet and Eos fly between New York and London. On Eos, which was launched in 2005, the airline's "guests" travel in style. They sleep on six-foot, six-inch beds and dine on gourmet meals. L'Avion, a business-class airline that offers service between Paris and New York, boasts that passengers can enjoy comfy seats and French food. In the Middle East, luxury airline Al Khayala aims to attract well-heeled customers by providing service that's somewhere between first class and a private jet. The airline uses specially modified Airbus A319s, which the company has configured to seat just 44 people instead of the usual 170 passengers. The wealthy also have the option of the Eclipse 500. Eclipse Aviation makes this "very light jet," which sells for about $1.5 million. Florida-based company DayJet owns several of the small jets and runs an air taxi service for business travelers.

Visit Vault at **www.vault.com** for insider company profiles, expert advice, career message boards, expert resume reviews, the Vault Job Board and more.

VAULT CAREER LIBRARY　257

Established airlines are also trying to cater to the luxury market. For example, Lufthansa is expanding the airline's first-class lounge in the Munich airport. New additions to the lounge will include day beds, showers, a gourmet restaurant and a bigger bar. Lufthansa is also spending millions of dollars to upgrade luxe lounges in Paris, New York's JFK, Berlin and Düsseldorf. In addition, Singapore Airlines is upgrading its business and first-class cabins on certain flights. The airline announced that, on some flights, it was rolling out 35-inch wide seats in first class. According to Singapore Air, the seats, which fold into beds, are "the largest seat in the sky" and are "exquisitely upholstered in fine-grained leather with mahogany wood trimming."

Investing in a dream(liner)

Major carriers hope to save money in the future by investing in new planes that offer a lower cost of ownership and operation. In late 2003, Boeing's board of directors gave the company the go-ahead to offer the 787 Dreamliner for sale. The following April, Japan's All Nippon was the first airline to order Boeing's new passenger jet, which promises fuel savings of up to 20 percent. By December 2006, Boeing had nearly 450 orders for the new Dreamliner, and the number had soared to more than 580 by June 2007.

Meanwhile, Airbus, the French firm and Boeing's rival for No. 1 aircraft maker in the world, unveiled a brand-new high-scale jumbo jet, the A380, at the start of 2005 at a gala event during the Le Bourget air show in Toulouse, France. Designed to comfortably seat 555, the A380 rocked the airline industry and represented a joint effort with France, Britain, Germany and Spain, all of whom contributed to the 10-year, $13 billion program that designed the plane. The double-decker leviathan, the largest plane ever built, boasts a 262-foot wingspan and extra space companies can use to install bedrooms, gyms, bars and lounges.

The conservation end, though, is where the A380 packs its biggest punch: its carbon fiber components and fuel-efficient technology are estimated to match or exceed Boeing's 20 percent fuel savings, and slash cost per passenger. However, in October 2006, Airbus announced that the delivery of the new jet would be delayed until the second half of 2007, with the industrial ramp-up finished in 2010. As of June 2007, Airbus had 13 signed contracts from two airlines for the A350, and another five customers had agreed to purchase 148 A350s.

It's not easy being green

Global warming is a hot topic, and airplanes are one of the biggest contributors to carbon emissions. Environmentalists have also criticized the airline industry for planes' air pollution in general. In 2006, Al Gore's documentary *An Inconvenient Truth* was a surprise hit, and a number of businesses have started going "carbon-neutral." Members of the airline and aviation industries are finally starting to address concerns about airplanes' emissions. In June 2007, the IATA has asked the aerospace industry to build zero-emissions airplanes within the next 50 years. Later that month, Louis Gallois, the CEO of Airbus, called on aircraft makers to work together to invent more environmentally friendly technology. In addition, the European Commission proposed a $2.13 billion public-private plan, dubbed the Clean Sky program. The program, which would start in 2008, would help Europe's air-transportation sector develop technologies to reduce planes' pollution.

Labor pains

According to the Bureau of Labor Statistics (BLS), labor costs make up roughly 38 percent of many airlines' operating costs—that's around 40 cents for every dollar spent by an air carrier. Passenger safety regulations and a workforce made up of highly specialized and rarely cross-trained professionals, half of whom are unionized, make it tough for airlines to trim costs from their labor budgets. One way they've done this is by cutting staffs to the bare bones. Following September 11th, Continental Airlines and US Airways were the first to make dramatic cuts, laying off about 20 percent of their respective workforces and paring flight schedules. Most other carriers followed suit.

Cuts in salaries and benefits

At many airlines, employees agreed to salary and benefit cuts to help keep airlines from going bankrupt. For example, in June 2006, Delta's pilots union agreed to a 14 percent pay cut. Other employees at Delta also agreed to pay cuts, including CEO Gerald Grinstein, whose pay was chopped by 25 percent. In May 2007, Northwest Airlines departed bankruptcy protection following a 20-month reorganization. The restructuring attempted to make the airline competitive for future years. Among other things, Northwest's new labor contracts pay employees less. Flight attendants for the airline used to make as much as $44,190, but now their pay tops out at $35,400.

Although American Airlines posted an annual profit for the first time in six years, employees were angry during the airline's annual stockholder meeting in May 2007. The employees, who agreed to salary cuts in recent years to keep the airline flying, were unhappy because top executives got bonuses worth millions of dollars. At Northwest, the airline cut pilots' wages by 40 percent and increased their hours. Pilots have been calling in sick, which has resulted in more cancelled flights.

Visit Vault at **www.vault.com** for insider company profiles, expert advice, career message boards, expert resume reviews, the Vault Job Board and more.

V/\ULT CAREER LIBRARY 259

Employer Directory

ACE Aviation Holdings Inc.

(Air Canada)

5100 de Maisonneuve Boulevard West

Montreal, Quebec H4A 3T2

Canada

Phone: (514) 422-5000

Fax: (514) 422-5909

www.aceaviation.com

Air France-KLM Group (Air France and KLM)

45, rue de Paris

95747 Roissy

France

Phone: +33-1-41-56-78-00

Fax: +33-1-41-56-56-00

www.airfrance.com

Alaska Air Group

19300 International Boulevard

Seattle, WA 98188

Phone: (206) 392-5040

Toll Free: (800) 252-7522

Fax: (206) 433-3379

www.alaskaair.com

Alitalia - Linee Aeree Italiane S.p.A. (Alitalia)

Viale A. Marchetti 111

00148 Rome

Italy

Phone: +39-06-6562-2151

Fax: +39-06-6562-4733

www.alitalia.it

AMR Corporation (American Airlines)

4333 Amon Carter Boulevard

Fort Worth, TX 76155

Phone: (817) 963-1234

Fax: (817) 967-9641

www.aa.com

AMERCO

(U-Haul International, Inc.)

1325 Airmotive Way, Suite 100

Reno, NV 89502

Phone: (775) 688-6300

Fax: (775) 688-6338

www.amerco.com

Amtrak

60 Massachusetts Avenue NE

Washington, DC 20002

Phone: (202) 906-3000

Fax: (202) 906-3306

www.amtrak.com

British Airways Plc

Waterside, Harmondsworth

London, UB7 0GB

United Kingdom

Phone: +44-087-0850-9850

Fax: +44-20-8759-4314

www.british-airways.com

C.H. Robinson Worldwide, Inc.

8100 Mitchell Road

Eden Prairie, MN 55344-2248

Phone: (952) 937-8500

Fax: (952) 937-6714

www.chrobinson.com

Continental Airlines, Inc

1600 Smith Street, Dept. HQSEO

Houston, TX 77002

Phone: (713) 324-2950

Fax: (713) 324-2637

www.continental.com

Con-way Inc.

2855 Campus Drive

Suite 300

San Mateo, CA 94403

Phone: (650) 378-5200

www.con-way.com

CSX Corporation

500 Water Street, 15th Floor

Jacksonville, FL 32202

Phone: (904) 359-3200

www.csx.com

Delta Air Lines, Inc

Hartsfield Atlanta International Airport

1030 Delta Boulevard

Atlanta, GA 30320-6001

Phone: (404) 715-2600

Fax: (404) 715-5042

www.delta.com

Deutsche Lufthansa AG (Lufthansa)

Von-Gablenz-Strasse 2-6

D-50679 Cologne, 21

Germany

Phone: +49-69-696-0

Fax: +49-69-696-6818

www.lufthansa.com

DHL Holdings (USA)

1200 South Pine Island Road

Plantation, FL 33324

Phone: (954) 888-7000

Fax: (954) 888-7310

www.dhl.com

Enterprise Rent-A-Car Company

600 Corporate Park Drive

St. Louis, MO 63105

Phone: (314) 512-5000

Fax: (314) 512-4706

www.enterprise.com

Expeditors International of Washington, Inc.

1015 3rd Avenue, 12th Floor

Seattle, WA 98104

Phone: (206) 674-3400

Fax: (206) 674-3459

www.expeditors.com

FedEx Corporation

942 S. Shady Grove Road

Memphis, TN 38120

Phone: (901) 818-7500

Fax: (901) 395-2000

www.fedex.com

FirstGroup PLC

395 King Street

Aberdeen, AB24 5RP

Scotland

Phone: +44-1224-650-100

Fax: +44-1224-650-140

www.firstgroup.com

Employer Directory, cont.

Hertz Global Holdings, Inc.
225 Brae Boulevard
Park Ridge, NJ 07656-0713
Phone: (201) 307-2000
Fax: (201) 307-2644
www.hertz.com

Houston Airport System
16930 JFK Boulevard
Houston, TX 77032
Phone: (281) 233-1800
Fax: (281) 233-1859
www.fly2houston.com

Kansas City Southern
427 W. 12th Street
Kansas City, MO 64105
Phone: (816) 983-1303
Fax: (816) 983-1108
www.kcsi.com

Japan Airlines Corporation (JAL)
4-11, Higashi-shinagawa 2-chome,
Shinagawa-ku
Tokyo, 140-8605
Japan
Phone: +81-3-5769-6097
Fax: +81-3-5460-5929
www.jal.co.jp

JetBlue Airways Corporation
118-29 Queens Boulevard
Forest Hills, NY 11375
Phone: (718) 286-7900
Toll Free: (800) 538-2583
Fax: (718) 709-3621
www.jetblue.com

Massachusetts Port Authority
One Harborside Drive, Suite 200S
East Boston, MA 02128
Phone: (617) 428-2800
www.massport.com

Norfolk Southern Corporation
3 Commercial Place
Norfolk, VA 23510-2191
Phone: (757) 629-2600
Fax: (757) 664-5069
www.nscorp.com

Northwest Airlines Corporation
2700 Lone Oak Parkway
Eagan, MN 55121
Phone: (612) 726-2111
Fax: (612) 726-7123
www.nwa.com

Qantas Airways
Qantas Centre, Level 9, Building A
203 Coward Street
Mascot, New South Wales 2020
Australia
Phone: +61-2-9691-3636
Fax: +61-2-9691-3339
www.qantas.com.au

Pacer International
2300 Clayton Road, Suite 1200
Concord, CA 94520
Phone: (925) 887-1400
Toll Free: (877) 917-2237
Fax: (925) 887-1503
www.pacer-international.com

Port Authority of New York and New Jersey
225 Park Avenue South
New York, NY 10003
Phone: (212) 435-7000
Fax: (212) 435-6670
www.panynj.gov

Ryder
11690 NW 105th Street
Miami, FL 33178
Phone: (305) 500-3726
Fax: (305) 500-3203
www.ryder.com

Sabre Holdings Corporation
3150 Sabre Drive
Southlake, TX 76092
Phone: (682) 605-1000
Fax: (682) 605-8267
www.sabre-holdings.com

Southwest Airlines Co.
2702 Love Field Drive
Dallas, TX 75235
Phone: (214) 792-4000
Fax: (214) 792-5015
www.southwest.com

Swiss International Air Lines Ltd.
Aeschenvorstadt 4
CH-4051 Basel
Switzerland
Phone: +41-61-582-00-00
Fax: +41-61-582-33-33
www.swiss.com

UAL Corporation (United Airlines)
77 W. Wacker Drive
Chicago, IL 60601
Phone: (312) 997-8000
www.united.com

UniGroup, Inc.
1 Premier Drive
Fenton, MO 63026
Phone: (636) 305-5000
Fax: (636) 326-1106
www.unigroupinc.com

Union Pacific Corporation
1400 Douglas Street
Omaha, NE 68179
Phone: (402) 544-5000
Fax: (402) 271-6408
www.up.com

United Parcel Service, Inc.
55 Glenlake Parkway NE
Atlanta, GA 30328
Phone: (404) 828-6000
Fax: (404) 828-6562
www.ups.com

United States Postal Service
475 L'Enfant Plaza SW
Washington, DC 20260-3100
Phone: (202) 268-2500
Fax: (202) 268-4860
www.usps.com

Visit Vault at **www.vault.com** for insider company profiles, expert advice, career message boards, expert resume reviews, the Vault Job Board and more.

VAULT CAREER LIBRARY   261

Employer Directory, cont.

US Airways Group, Inc.
111 W. Rio Salado Parkway
Tempe, AZ 85281
Phone: (480) 693-0800
Fax: (480) 693-5546
www.usairways.com

Virgin Atlantic Airways Limited
The Office, Crawley Business Quarter
Manor Royal, Crawley
West Sussex, RH10 9NU
United Kingdom
Phone: +44-1293-747-747
Fax: +44-1293-538-337
www.virgin-atlantic.com

Wabash National Corp.
1000 Sagamore Parkway South
Lafayette, IN 47905
Phone: (765) 771-5300
Fax: (765) 771-5474
www.wabashnational.com

Werner Enterprises, Inc.
14507 Frontier Road
Omaha, NE 68145
Phone: (402) 895-6640
Fax: (402) 895-6640
www.werner.com

YRC Worldwide Inc.
10990 Roe Avenue
Overland Park, KS 66211
Phone: (913) 696-6100
Toll Free: (800) 846-4300
Fax: (913) 696-6116
www.yrcw.com

Venture Capital

The Financial Industry and Venture Capital

Where does VC fit into the world of finance? The financial industry can be divided into two general segments: the buy-side and the sell-side. Sell-side refers to those financial firms that have services to sell, such as investment banks, brokerages and commercial banks.

For instance, when a large company wants to sell stock on the public stock exchanges, an investment bank's corporate finance department handles the legal, tax and accounting affairs of the transaction as well as the sale of those securities to institutional or individual investors. For providing these services, the investment bank receives a fee (between 2 percent and 10 percent of the money raised by selling stock). An investment banking firm's primary motivation is to sell such services, characterizing them as sell-siders.

Brokerages are paid a fee for the service they provide of buying and selling stocks. Commercial banks are paid for managing deposit accounts, making and then managing loans, etc. Again, they sell these services, so they are sell-side firms.

Venture capital firms, on the other hand, are on the buy-side because they control a fund or pool of money to spend on buying an equity interest in, or assets of, operating companies.

For the sake of this discussion, most buy-side venture capital firms have only one way to realize a return on their investment: selling their ownership stake to another private investor, a corporation (trade sale) or to the public markets for more money than they paid (often termed to be "in the money"). While some later-stage private equity shops invest in or acquire companies for their cash flow potential, venture capital is about building young companies and finding an exit (liquidity event) on the back side for "x" times their original investment. Descriptions of each segment of the buy-side are included below. Keep in mind that these definitions are intended to be very general in nature and that many buy-side organizations cross organizational boundaries.

Friends and family

Sometimes referred to as "friends, family and fools," this is usually the first source of funding for startups at the idea stage of development. The amounts invested per individual are quite small, averaging $5,000 to $10,000. These people may not have an in-depth understanding of the business, product, technology or market, and are simply making an investment in someone they know. While this is probably the easiest money for an entrepreneur to find, it can also be bittersweet. If a startup fails, telling Aunt Edna that she's lost her nest egg could be the low point of one's career.

Angels

These are high-net-worth individuals who normally invest between $15,000 and $1 million in exchange for equity in a young company throughout the seed and early stage rounds, averaging $50,000 to $500,000. Angels prefer to invest within their immediate geographic area, and on average within one day of travel. According to businessfinance.com, angels fund an estimated one-seventh of the 300,000 startup/early growth firms in the U.S. They are often the first investor segment who have the opportunity to sit on the board of directors and contribute experience and contacts, guiding young companies through the difficult initial stages of growth. That said, most of the value added by angel investors occurs in the pre-institutional (or Series A) rounds of funding. As the professional investors come into play, venture capitalists take over board seats previously held by angels.

Angels can be doctors, lawyers, former investors, though increasingly they are former entrepreneurs who have had a lucrative exit in their chosen professional field. Microsoft co-founder and multibillionaire Paul Allen has made headlines for his angel investing as well as his investments through his VC firm, Vulcan Ventures. Intel co-founder Andy Grove has made angel

Visit Vault at **www.vault.com** for insider company profiles, expert advice, career message boards, expert resume reviews, the Vault Job Board and more.

VAULT CAREER LIBRARY 263

investments in numerous companies, including Oncology.com. Given the large number of new companies seeking funding as well as the rise in the number of wealthy individuals, in recent years the industry has seen the emergence of angel groups. These investor alliances create more structure for angel investors, and a more efficient conduit for moving startups along from seed funding to professional venture investors. Perhaps the best-known group of angels is Silicon Valley's "Band of Angels," a formal group of about 150 former and current high-tech entrepreneurs and executives who meet monthly to consider pleas from three startups for venture financing. This group has injected nearly $100 million across some 150 startups. Angels are often involved with hiring, strategy, the raising of additional capital and fundamental operating decisions. These alliances also allow for better coordination of due diligence in "vetting" new deals. Angels are not without their own issues, however. Collectively, angel investors have been accused of being fair weather friends; one of the first sources of private equity to dry up when public markets fall or macroeconomic conditions deteriorate. With less money to invest across fewer deals than their VC brethren, many of these individuals have a lower tolerance for losses. This risk aversion is compounded by their generally lower position in the capital structure. While angel groups may be able to negotiate preferred stock instead of common, their equity rarely has the same level of preferences or security demanded by later stage investors. Though angels, of course, expect a significant return on their investment, they are also thrill-seekers of a sort—motivated by getting close to the excitement of a new venture.

High-net-worth private placements

Sell-side companies, such as investment banks, may organize a group of very wealthy individuals, corporations, asset management firms and/or pension funds to make a direct investment into a private company. The amount raised from these sources is typically between $5 million and $50 million. In essence, the sell-side company enables investors to invest in the venture capital asset class.

While these transactions may include a traditional venture fund as part of the round, in many cases they do not. As a whole, investment banks have historically been seen as having less perceived value in the early stages of the venture process. Since early-stage investing is not Wall Street's core competency, the downside is that (1) the startup company may not benefit from the domain expertise, operational savvy and rolodex of the venture capital firm, and (2) the sell-side company takes a fee for its services, typically between 2 and 10 percent of capital raised. While there is a credible value proposition to using private placements and participation by investment banks in funding some types of deals, this is expensive money on several fronts.

Asset management firms and pension funds

These groups include a diverse collection of limited partnerships and corporations that manage between $5 million to $100 billion plus. Most focus on diversified investment strategies, typically with public instruments including stocks, bonds, commodities, currencies, etc. They rarely invest in private companies, due to the large amount of time required to find and execute a private transaction, as well as the ongoing commitment of time to monitor such an investment. Instead of directly participating in individual startup fundings, many will allocate 5 percent to 7 percent of total funds to higher-risk alternative investments like VC partnerships, hedge funds, and distressed turnaround situations. The California Public Employees' Retirement System (CalPERS) is one of the largest players in this space.

Leveraged buyout firms

These are limited partnerships or corporations that take over private or public firms using their own capital as equity, combined with debt (leverage) financing from third-party banks. After acquiring a company, the LBO firm normally changes management and strategic direction, or may divide and sell its assets. The size of LBOs ranges from a few million to many billions of dollars. These firms look and behave very much like venture capital firms, but their investments differ in size and purpose. Both LBOs and VCs fall under the umbrella descriptor "private equity."

Hedge funds

These are limited partnerships or corporations that buy and sell public market instruments including stocks, bonds, commodities, currencies, etc. These firms take bets on market fluctuations and are often considered high risk/high return investors. The size of these funds ranges from a few million to several billion dollars.

Trading

Sell-side companies such as merchant banks, commercial banks and investment banks have trading departments that control and invest huge sums of money into public markets. These groups also take relatively risky bets on market fluctuations.

A Day in the Life: Venture Capitalist

7:00 a.m.: Arrive at the office.

7:01 a.m.: Read *The Wall Street Journal*, paying careful attention to the Marketplace section covering your industry focus.

7:20 a.m.: Read trade press and notice four companies you haven't seen before. Check your firm's internal database to see if someone else on your team has contacted the companies. Search the Internet to find out more. Of the four companies you find, only one holds your interest. Send yourself an e-mail as a reminder to call them during business hours.

7:45 a.m.: Clip out some interesting articles and put them in the inboxes of other associates or partners with a note explaining why you found the information interesting. The other members of your firm have more expertise in the areas covered by the articles. You stay and talk for a few minutes with each of the people in their offices, exchanging the latest word about the people and technology you follow.

8:00 a.m.: Respond to e-mails or voicemails from the day before. People you are communicating with are primarily entrepreneurs, other VCs and personal acquaintances.

9:00 a.m.: You attend a meeting with a group of entrepreneurs who want to make their pitch. You read the business plan for five minutes. One general partner (GP) sits in with you. The other GP, who planned to be there, cannot make it because he has a conference call with a portfolio company facing some challenges. The computer projecting the entrepreneur's presentation crashes, so you have to take their paper version of their presentation and work with your assistant to make four photocopies before the meeting can proceed.

During the 10-minute delay, the partner talks with the team informally, and learns more about the opportunity than he or she would in any one-hour presentation. You sit politely through the presentation, and identify the three critical issues facing the company. During the question and answer phase, you think of how to politely extract more information about those three issues, all the while evaluating whether you would want to work with this team or not.

In the end, you decide to make some calls to gather more information about the market, but you feel that there's a very low probability you would ever invest. You wish you could just kill the deal, but the management team is reasonable (though not great), the customer need they have identified may actually exist (you don't know firsthand, so you will need to call around), and you may learn something by taking it to the next step. Plus, in the back of your mind, you know the market for good deals is very competitive, and you don't want to reject a deal too quickly.

11:00 a.m.: Phone the people who called during your meeting. These people include entrepreneurs, analysts, other VCs and your lunch appointment. You find out from another VC that the company you almost invested in two months ago was just funded by a competing firm. You wonder if you made a mistake. You find out from an entrepreneur you were hoping to back that he wants his son to be a co-founder and owner of the firm. You abandon all hope. You learn from an analyst that AT&T has decided to stop its trial of a new technology because it doesn't work, which creates an opportunity for companies with an

Visit Vault at **www.vault.com** for insider company profiles, expert advice, career message boards, expert resume reviews, the Vault Job Board and more.

VAULT CAREER LIBRARY   265

alternative solution. You happen to know about two small companies, one in Boston, one in Denver, that have alternative solutions. You make a note to yourself to call them back to get a status report.

12:30 p.m.: Lunch with an executive recruiter. This person is very experienced in finding management talent in your area of expertise. You have kept in touch with her over the years, and try to see her every quarter to hear the latest buzz and to make sure she will be available when you need her services quickly. It's a fun lunch, freely mixing personal and professional information.

2:00 p.m.: Call new companies you have heard about over the last few days. Ideally, you could do this task a little bit every day, but you find you need to be in a friendly and upbeat mood to make these calls, so you batch them. Also, if you actually get in touch with the CEO, you may be on the phone for 90 minutes, so you need to have an open block of time. You leave the standard pitch about your firm on the voicemail of the CEOs of four other companies. You get through to one CEO, and although you can tell in the first five minutes that you won't be interested in investing, you talk for 30 minutes. You spend most of the 30 minutes probing about competitors who might be better than the company you're talking to and finding out more about his market space.

3:00 p.m.: You and a partner meet with a portfolio company on a conference call. The company is facing some challenges and you offer to screen executive recruiters to help find a new CFO for it. The GP offers to talk to two M&A firms to get a first opinion about what might be done to sell the company over the next six months. At the end of the call, the GP gives you three names and numbers of recruiters, which you add to your own two contacts.

3:30 p.m.: You call the recruiters, explaining the situation and asking about their recent experiences in similar searches. The critical element is whether the recruiters actually have time and interest in doing the search. You talk to two recruiters and leave voicemails for the other three.

4:30 p.m.: You make due diligence calls for a potential investment you have been following for two months. Last week you called the company's customers, and they seemed happy for the most part. Today, you are calling the personal references of the management team. The idea is to get as much negative information as possible. You need to discover any potential character or personality flaws any member of the team may have. VC firms are "due diligence machines," doing the hard work of making sure a company is what it says it is.

5:30 p.m.: You make calls to the West Coast. You also check your stocks and confirm dinner plans. You do some miscellaneous surfing on the Web to gather some articles about the technology areas you cover.

6:30 p.m.: You stand around the halls talking with other members of your firm, brainstorming and filling each other in about what's happening in your area.

7:00 p.m.: Dinner with two other young VCs downtown. You talk mostly about life, sports, travel and relationships, but also about the latest deals, cool business ideas and recent successes. You find out that a competing firm just made 30 times their money on a deal you never saw. You also find out that a company you turned down, which was invested in by someone else, is about to go bankrupt. A train missed; a bullet dodged.

VC Uppers and Downers

Uppers

- There is a reason that very few people ever willingly leave their VC careers. Where else can you have so much fun investing other people's money (plus some of your own), while being "in the middle of it all?"

- You often get to be the one making decisions because you have money.

- Over the long term, financial security will cease to be an issue, because the job is well paying and you should eventually get "carry" or equity in the firm.

- You have access to the best minds—the people you work with are typically some of the smartest and most interesting. Successful venture capitalists have interests and hobbies as diverse as mountain climbing to playing jazz in nightclubs.

- Your job is to absorb and enjoy the positive creative energy of entrepreneurs and direct it toward successful execution.

- You could suddenly become rich if one of your companies does extremely well and you were able to co-invest or you have carry.

- You have access to the best information systems.

Downers

Because so many think of the venture capital industry as "the hot job to have," people often forget to question whether it is the right job for them. Here is a list of some of the negatives we hear from those who have worked in the industry for a while.

- Unless you work with a hands-on, early-stage VC firm known for taking an active role in building successful companies, you don't have pride of ownership in anything. You're just an investor, not a builder.

- VC is a slow path to wealth compared with the immediate cash income you get in investment banking, hedge funds or even management consulting.

- It can be argued that venture capital is fundamentally a negative process. Because you reject 99 of every 100 plans, year after year, over time you focus on figuring out what is wrong with a company. You can then reject it and get on to the next deal. What is wrong with the management? The technology? The deal terms? The strategy? If you tend to have a contrarian disposition, after just a few years, that mentality may bleed into your life. What is wrong with my partners? What is wrong with my spouse? What is wrong with me? Oh, the angst! If this reaction hits too close to home, venture capital might not be for you. What fun is it to search through hundreds and thousands of business plans and ideas for that one rare gem, if you aren't an eternal optimist?

- Because you reject 99 of every 100 entrepreneurs, you can make some enemies, no matter how nice and helpful you try to be. No one likes rejection, and passionate entrepreneurs have long memories.

Visit Vault at **www.vault.com** for insider company profiles, expert advice, career message boards, expert resume reviews, the Vault Job Board and more.

V/\ULT CAREER LIBRARY   267

Employer Directory

Accel Partners
428 University Avenue
Palo Alto, CA 94301
Phone: (650) 614-4800
Fax: (650) 614-488
www.accel.com

Apax Partners
495 Park Avenue, 11th Floor
New York, NY 10022
Phone: (212) 753-6300
Fax: (212) 319-6155
www.apax.com

ARCH Venture Partners
8725 W. Higgins Road
Suite 290
Chicago, IL 60631
Phone: (773) 380-6600
Fax: (773) 380-6606
www.archventure.com

Austin Ventures
300 West 6th Street
Suite 2300
Austin, TX 78701
Phone: (512) 485-1900
Fax: (512) 476-3952
www.austinventures.com

Benchmark Capital
2480 Sand Hill Road
Suite 200
Menlo Park, CA 94025
Phone: (650) 854-8180
Fax: (650) 854-8183
www.benchmark.com

Charles River Ventures
1000 Winter Street #3300
Waltham, MA 02451
Phone: (781) 487-7060
Fax: (781) 487-7065

Draper Fisher Jurvetson
2882 Sand Hill Road, Suite 150
Menlo Park, CA 94025
Phone: (650) 233-9000
Fax: (650) 233-9233
www.drapervc.com

Hummer Winblad Venture Partners
2 South Park, 2nd Floor
San Francisco, CA 94107
Phone: (415) 979-9600
Fax: (415) 979-9601
www.humwin.com

JAFCO America Ventures
505 Hamilton Avenue
Suite 310
Palo Alto, CA 94301
Phone: (650) 463-8800
Fax: (650) 463-8801
www.jafco.com

Kleiner Perkins Caufield & Byers
2750 Sand Hill Road
Menlo Park, CA 94025
Phone: (650) 233-2750
Fax: (650) 233-0300
www.kpcb.com

Mayfield Fund
2800 Sand Hill Road
Suite 250
Menlo Park, CA 94025
Phone: (650) 854-5560
Fax: (650) 854-5712
www.mayfield.com

Menlo Ventures
3000 Sand Hill Road, Building 4
Suite 100
Menlo Park, CA 94025
Phone: (650) 854-8540
Fax: (650) 854-7059
www.menloventures.com

New Enterprise Associates
1119 St. Paul Street
Baltimore, MD 21202
Phone: (410) 244-0115
Fax: (410) 752-7721
www.nea.com

Norwest Venture Capital
525 University Avenue, Suite 800
Palo Alto, CA 94301
Phone: (650) 321-8000
Fax: (650) 321-8010
www.norwestvc.com

Sequoia Capital
3000 Sand Hill Road
Building 4, Suite 180
Menlo Park, CA 94025
Phone: (650) 854-3927
Fax: (650) 854-2977
www.sequoiacap.com

Split Rock Partners
10400 Viking Drive
Suite 550
Minneapolis, MN 55344
Phone: (952) 995-7474
Fax: (952) 995-7475
www.splitrock.com

TL Ventures
435 Devon Park Drive
700 Building
Wayne, PA 19087
Phone: (610) 971-1515
Fax: (610) 975-9330
www.tlventures.com

U.S. Venture Partners
2735 Sand Hill Road
Menlo Park, CA 94025
Phone: (650) 854-9080
Fax: (650) 854-3018
www.usvp.com

Venrock Associates
30 Rockefeller Plaza
Room 5508
New York, NY 10112
Phone: (212) 649-5600
Fax: (212) 649-5788
www.venrock.com

APPENDIX

About the Editor

Vault Editors

Vault is the leading media company for career information. Our team of industry-focused editors takes a journalistic approach in covering news, employment trends and specific employers in their industries. We annually survey 10,000s of employees to bring readers the inside scoop on industries and specific employers.

Much of the material in *The MBA Career Bible* is excerpted from Vault titles for specific industries or career titles. Vault publishes more than 120 titles for job seekers and professionals. To see a complete list of Vault titles, go to www.vault.com.

Visit Vault at **www.vault.com** for insider company profiles, expert advice, career message boards, expert resume reviews, the Vault Job Board and more.

VAULT CAREER LIBRARY 271

V/ULT
THE MOST TRUSTED NAME IN CAREER INFORMATION

Vault guides and employer profiles have been published since 1997 and are the premier source of insider information on careers.

Each year, Vault surveys and interviews thousands of employees to give readers the inside scoop on industries and specific employers to help them get the jobs they want.